D1260630

Outperform with
Expectations-Based Management™

Outperform with Expectations-Based Management™

A State-of-the-Art Approach to Creating and Enhancing Shareholder Value

Tom Copeland

and

Aaron Dolgoff

WILEY

John Wiley & Sons, Inc.

Published by John Wiley & Sons, Inc., Hoboken, New Jersey.
Published simultaneously in Canada.

Designations used by companies to distinguish their products are often claimed as trademarks.
In all instances where John Wiley & Sons, Inc. is aware of a claim, the product names appear
in initial capital or all capital letters. Readers, however, should contact the appropriate
companies for more complete information regarding trademarks and registration.

EVA is a registered trademark of Stern Stewart & Co.

Expectations-Based Management (EBM) is a registered trademark of the Monitor Group.

For general information on our other products and services or for technical support,
please contact our Customer Care Department within the United States at (800) 762-2974,
outside the United States at (317) 572-3993 or fax (317) 572-4002.

Wiley also publishes its books in a variety of electronic formats. Some content that appears
in print may not be available in electronic books. For more information about Wiley products, visit our web site at www.wiley.com.

ISBN-13 978-0-471-73875-6
ISBN-10 0-471-73875-1

Printed in the United States of America.

10   9   8   7   6   5   4   3   2   1

Contents

Preface

Why should you read this book? Because it will improve your company's performance by focusing your management team on what counts, namely beating your (i.e., management's) and the market's (i.e., investors') expectations. We show that the correlation between the return to shareholders and changes in expectations is about ten times stronger than it is with earnings, earnings growth, economic value added (EVA®), and the growth in EVA.[1] We show how Expectations-Based Management (EBM™) helps you to understand communications with potential investors, helps you to set internal performance standards, and how it can refocus your strategy.[2] We believe you will find EBM to be simple, direct, and common sense. You will wonder, as we have, why it has not been part of every manager's toolkit for a long time. Indeed, many will recognize EBM principles and practices in their own current behavior—behavior that often seems at odds with existing systems but that managers instinctively know to be correct.

One day in the early 1980s an entrepreneur by the name of David Murdock, owner of Pacific Holding Corporation, was invited to speak to a corporate finance class at UCLA's Graduate School of Management about why he had paid $200 million—a one hundred percent premium—to buy Cannon Mills and take it private. The marketplace thought it was worth only $100 million.

---

[1]EVA is a registered trademark of Stern Stewart & Co.

[2]Expectations-Based Management (EBM) is a registered trademark of the Monitor Group.

Cannon Mills is a textile producer of high-quality white goods such as sheets and bath towels. Located in the town of Cannonapolis, North Carolina, it was closely held by various members of the Cannon family. Not long before, another tender offer for the company had been refused.

Listen to this story and identify the various expectations that led to the transaction and subsequent events. Certainly the market as a whole had expectations that caused it to value Cannon Mills at roughly $100 million. The members of the Cannon family had expectations that led them to turn down a substantially higher offer than the $100 million. And David Murdock had expectations that led him to believe the company was worth over $200 million.

What Murdock said in the classroom that day made the class realize that he understood very well that his own expectations had to be better founded in fact than those of the other parties. Simply put, Murdock had to have better judgment and better ideas.

He told the class that day that his first step was to buy more than five percent of the outstanding shares. According to the Williams Act this made him an insider and required him to announce the fact to the public. It also gave Murdock the right to visit the company and look over its records. After having done so, he quickly tendered for the remainder of the outstanding stock.

"How did I recover the $100 million premium?" he asked rhetorically. "Let's review the facts. First, the company had a defined benefit pension plan that was overfunded by $80 million. Second, it had a $60 million LIFO inventory reserve.[3] Third, it owned most of the housing in Cannonapolis, and carried it on the books at original purchase price. Finally, it owned 100,000 acres of prime timber land that was also undervalued on the books." These numbers alone easily added up to more than the $100 million premium.

But then he said, "These facts are not why I bought the company. They were already publicly available information and were baked into the stock price." The class could hardly believe what they were hearing. Murdock was right. Efficient markets do actually reflect relevant economic information in the stock price. It contains all public information about expectations of future performance—the so-called market expectations.

Murdock then continued, "Now let me tell you why I bought the company. First, I learned during my visit that the top 120 managers were all family relatives—brothers, sisters, aunts, uncles, cousins, nephews, nieces, and

[3]A last-in-first-out (LIFO) inventory reserve refers to potentially higher profits that may result in the future if the company should accelerate sales and begin to expense older layers of inventory that are carried at lower cost.

the like. I replaced them all with 12 carefully selected managers. Second, the plant was operating during six day shifts per week. I cut prices, gained market share, and now operate 12 shifts per week." It is not difficult to interpret what Murdock had said. His two ideas earned him over $100 million by cutting corporate overhead by 80 to 90 percent, and nearly doubling the return on invested capital (*ROIC*) by dramatically increasing the ratio of sales per dollar of capital employed. Neither the family owners nor the other takeover firm had similar expectations. David Murdock created value by understanding what information was already included in the stock price and not paying for it twice. He understood the market expectations. He also understood management expectations. There was a huge disconnect between his own expectations and those of management. Murdock arbitraged the difference.

Expectations-Based Management

Expectations-Based Management is about the link between performance standards, performance measurement, and the achievement of performance. It says that stock price goes up if performance exceeds the market's expectations. David Murdock's takeover of Cannon Mills dramatically changed its expected performance and he eventually sold the company for a sizeable gain. We will talk about how to set and revise expectations later in the book. For now let's stick with the challenge of defining EBM.

When a CEO defines performance measurement right, then performance improvement follows. But what are the attributes of the "right" measure of performance? Which measure comes closest to being the "ideal," and how do you use it to improve performance? These three themes are what this book is all about.

We want the measure of performance that has the strongest link to the creation of wealth for the owners of the company—its shareholders— whether they are private or public. Chapter 1 discusses the details, but the final word is that in order to create wealth for shareholders by raising the stock price, companies must exceed expectations both short-term and long-term, expectations of both income statement and balance sheet performance, and expectations about daily operating value drivers.

In 1890 Sir Alfred Marshall explained in *Principles of Economics* (Vol. 1, p. 142) a concept called economic profit. It is "What remains of his [the owner's or manager's] profits after deducting interest on his capital at the current rate..." Marshall's economic profit is the accounting definition of profit minus a charge for the use of capital. It requires that the rate of return on capital invested be greater than the cost of capital. It extends the definition of profitability from sole focus on the income statement to also include the balance sheet. It predicts that if two companies have the same profit, the one that uses less capital to generate said profit will have greater value for shareholders.

We agree that economic profit is an important and useful concept (especially for making capital investment decisions), but it falls short of the complete reality because it fails to include the rate of changing expectations as it affects the stock price. Consider two companies with the same economic profit. Suppose that they both earned 20 percent on $1,000 of invested capital, and that their cost of capital was 10 percent. They would both report economic profit of (20% − 10%)$1,000 = $100 to their boards of directors. Yet suppose the first company was expected to earn a 30 percent return on invested capital while the second was expected to earn 15 percent. The stock price of the first company will fall as the market revises its expectations downward, while the stock price of the second company will rise because it exceeded expectations. This example exposes the major shortcoming of economic profit—it does not compare actual with expected performance and is therefore decoupled from stock price movements.

Because EBM is based on changes in expectations of economic profit, it is more complete than other measures. Its correlation to (market-adjusted) total return to shareholders is an order of magnitude higher than traditional measures such as earnings per share and earnings growth (that do not include balance sheet information and ignore expectations), and economic profit and the growth in economic profit (that both ignore expectations.)

All measures of performance other than EBM fail to use expectations. As an example, take economic value added (EVA), which is defined as the amount of capital employed multiplied by the spread between the return on capital and its cost—the same definition as economic profit. Positive EVA results from good income statement and balance sheet management, and growth in EVA requires a multiperiod point of view. But EVA does not measure performance against expectations. It is positive when a business earns more than the cost of capital employed—an objective standard. For example, suppose your cost of capital is 10 percent and you earned 15 percent last year and 18 percent this year on $1 billion of capital employed (both years). Last year your EVA was $50 million and this year it is $80 million. Proponents of EVA argue that this performance surely implies that your stock price will increase. What if we told you that your owners expected you to earn a 20 percent return on invested capital both years and in the long run? If so, you would have failed to meet or exceed their expectations and when they revise those expectations downward, your stock price will fall.

Chapter 2 presents documentary evidence that compares earnings, earnings growth, EVA, and EVA growth to EBM in a horse race to see which of these performance measures actually provides the best link to the (market-adjusted) total return to shareholders. The results were refereed and published in *The Review of Accounting Studies*, a top academic journal, and indicate that EBM is roughly 10 times better at explaining the total return to shareholders (TRS) than the other performance metrics with which it was compared.

Three other results emerge as well. First, the market reaction to changes in expectations of long-term earnings growth is eight to ten times larger than its reaction to changes in expectations about next year's earnings. Second, changes in expectations this year about this year's earnings are not significantly related to the return to shareholders in the presence of changes in expectations about next year's earnings and in long-term earnings growth. Third, increases in noise are associated with lower return to shareholders.

How to Use EBM

Over our 25 years as consultants, we have spent hundreds of hours with CEOs ruminating over the topic of which measure of performance is best and how to use it to run a company. EBM is not a new fad. It is common sense. We define it as a system of three mutually consistent and linked ways of measuring and managing performance. We have proved that changes in expectations have a stronger logical and statistical link to the actual total returns to shareholders than any of the alternative measures.

A simple numerical example illustrates the fundamental difference between EBM and EVA when measuring business unit performance. Suppose that we are valuing a company with two business units, each with perpetual, level cash flows. The entity value is simply the expected cash flow divided by the cost of capital, assumed to be 10 percent per year. Data for the example is given in Table P.1. Relative to the cost of capital, both divisions did well, and so did the company.

But the value of the company is defined as its expected after-tax operating income divided by the cost of capital. Expectations at the beginning of the period are given in the "$E_0(ROIC)$" column (column 2) of Table P.1. Therefore, the beginning-of-period value of the company is 17.5 percent

TABLE P.1 Numerical Example Comparing EVA and EBM

Business Unit	$E_0(ROIC)$	$A_1(ROIC)$	WACC	I_0	EVA	EBM
A	20%	15%	10%	$1,000	$50	−$50
B	15%	20%	10%	$1,000	$100	$50
Total Company	17.5%	17.5%	10%	$2,000	$150	0

(the expected *ROIC*) times the $2,000 of capital invested (i.e $350) divided by the cost of capital of 10 percent—resulting in a current entity value of $3,500.

To determine the change in the value of the company from the beginning to the end of the time period, we need to know what the end-of-period expectations are. To keep the example simple, let's assume that investors believe the actual period-one results, $A_1(ROIC)$, will continue unchanged forever. For example, they revise their expectations for business unit A downward from 20 percent to 15 percent. Consequently, column 3, the actual period-one results, becomes the new forward-looking expectations, $E_1(ROIC)$. The end-of-year value, based on the revised expectations, becomes 17.5 percent times $2,000 of capital, divided by the unchanged 10 percent cost of capital. The beginning-of-period value is $3,500 and so is the end-of-period value. There is no change in shareholders' wealth.

If we compare EVA to EBM, we see that EBM for the company as a whole is $0 and that this is consistent with the change in value that we just calculated. On the other hand, EVA is positive $150, and presumably we should see an increase in value to accompany it. But we do not. Why? Because the market rewards management for performance that *exceeds* expectations and the company has failed to do so.

In review, both EVA and EBM include income and balance sheet information combined in the form of free cash flows. Both can be extended to a multiperiod context, but EVA does not include any information about the changes in expectations that drive stock prices. Therefore it is not surprising that EVA is not highly correlated with the (market-adjusted) total return to shares. EBM is highly correlated because it is based on changes in expectations.

Change in Mindset

The tone and character of companies that measure their performance relative to expectations is very different than those that measure their performance vis-à-vis the cost of capital. When the management team realizes just how important expectations are, they try to become better informed in order to better establish internal expected performance standards. They also become more investor-oriented because they believe that successful performance means understanding and exceeding investor expectations rather than earning more than the cost of capital. If we were to characterize the difference in corporate personality between companies that use EBM and those that do not, we would say that EBM companies are more extroverted and communicate better. Their standards are set by what others think of them—and they know it.

What Will I Do Differently
and How Will My Company Use EBM?

A chapter in a book called *The Europeans*, strangely enough, is dedicated to the idiosyncracies of the Americans. They are, the book claims, incredibly enamored with what is new. In fact, to be worthwhile at all, a fashion, an idea, or a strategy must be new and distinctive. This fetish is strange to Europeans, who live in a world where thousands of years of history lead one to believe that things may be better or worse, but are rarely new. Whether the reader judges what we have to say as new or better is a matter of opinion—but you will do things differently. You will:

Understand the cause-and-effect relationship between performance and your stock price. Business unit performance should not be measured relative to the cost of capital, but rather whether actual performance is better than expected. Your stock price is handicapped like a horse race. The investor who bets on your company makes good returns when your company beats the odds. A horse that is favored to win but finishes second doesn't earn much, while a horse that was supposed only to show but ends up winning the race earns handsome returns.

Use two hurdle rates (if investment is to increase your stock price)—not one. The market has baked its expectations for the return on existing invested capital into your share price. Maintenance investments are made to keep this existing capital performing at expected levels and therefore must earn the expected return on invested capital in order to lift your share price—at successful companies, this is usually a percentage that is greater than the cost of capital. Maintenance investments that earn less than expected but more than the cost of capital are better than no investments at all, but your stock price will not grow enough to return the cost of equity.

New investments, such as acquisitions, are unexpected and, if they are competitive, will create value as long as they earn more than the cost of capital.

Thus, to increase your stock price it is necessary to earn an ROIC greater than what the market expects on maintenance investment—one hurdle rate. And for new (unexpected) investments it is necessary to earn more than the cost of capital—a second hurdle rate.

Communicate better with potential investors. Management sets expectations, if it chooses to do so, because it is better informed about the destiny of the company. EBM provides strong empirical evidence that information about the long-run growth of the firm is much more important than information about this quarter's earnings, and that more noise in communication with the market is associated with lower share prices.

Have stronger budgeting and planning. The budgeting process has been described as being as painful as a root canal, and less useful. EBM, however, requires that you beat expectations when you want to manage business unit performance, and they are established via the budgeting and planning process. It is a subjective process to be sure, and therefore requires active and knowledgable participation of all levels of management.

Have incentives better aligned with performance. We recast compensation. Instead of thinking about salary and bonus, we parse total compensaton into expected and unexpected components—and then define the unexpected component as pay at risk. It turns out that the median amount of pay at risk for the CEO of a U.S.–based firm is only 17 percent of total compensation. We also suggest that the pay-for-performance relationship be made more linear with skin in the game.

Be able to reverse engineer your stock price to understand what the market expects. There is a lot of information in your stock price. By reverse engineering it and working back to the set of market expectations about revenue growth, operating profit, the return on invested capital, capital turnover, and financial leverage, you will build insight about differences between what the market expects and what you can deliver.

The Three Parts of EBM

Figure P.1 shows EBM as a three-part system, but all three are tied together logically so that they form an integrated managerial perspective. There is a "golden thread" that extends from daily performance on operating value drivers to annual performance as measured by EBM, to the value of the firm that is driven by the changes in expectations over the indefinite future. An improvement in performance on a value driver, such as the number of sales calls per sales person, can, in principle, be traced through to its effect on EBM for the relevant business unit, and to the value of the firm as a whole.

What is different is that performance must exceed expectations to create shareholder value. This is a subjective criterion and to get it right you will have to put more time into getting your planning and budgeting process retuned, changing your firm's incentive system, listening to what the market is telling you about its expectations for your company, and stressing value creation as the search for ways to exceed expectations.

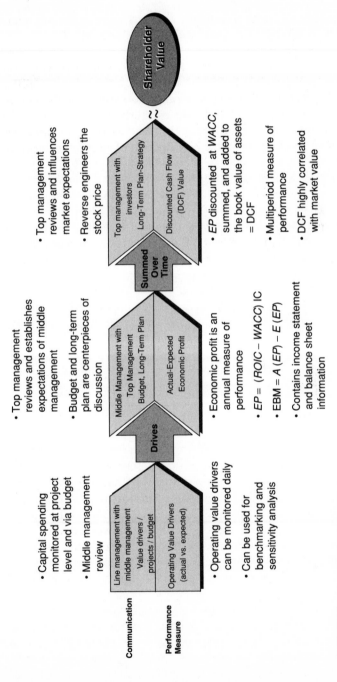

Communication

Performance Measure

Line management with middle management
Value drivers / projects / budget

Operating Value Drivers
(actual vs. expected)

- Operating value drivers can be monitored daily
- Can be used for benchmarking and sensitivity analysis

- Capital spending monitored at project level and via budget
- Middle management review

Drives

Middle Management with Top Management
Budget, Long-Term Plan

Actual-Expected Economic Profit

- Economic profit is an annual measure of performance
- $EP = (ROIC - WACC)\ IC$
- $EBM = A\ (EP) - E\ (EP)$
- Contains income statement and balance sheet information

- Top management reviews and establishes expectations of middle management
- Budget and long-term plan are centerpieces of discussion

Summed Over Time

Top management with investors
Long-Term Plan-Strategy

Discounted Cash Flow (DCF) Value

- EP discounted at $WACC$, summed, and added to the book value of assets = DCF
- Multiperiod measure of performance
- DCF highly correlated with market value

- Top management reviews and influences market expectations
- Reverse engineers the stock price

Shareholder Value

FIGURE P.1   Tripartite EBM system.

Guidelines for Reading this Book

"The devil is in the details," as they say. But the details can be thorny and tedious. If you want the top line, read Chapter 1—it compares various measures of performance and discusses their shortcomings. Your current performance standard is undoubtedly there. Read only the first four parts of Chapter 2. They summarize the rest of it. Skip to Chapters 3, 4, and 6, which discuss how to make capital expenditures wisely, then to Chapter 8 (external communications) and Chapter 9 (incentive design).

If your philosophy is "In for a pound, in for a ton," then the whole book is a good read. Chapter 2 presents irrefutable empirical evidence that confirms the strong link between EBM and the return to shareholders. Chapter 5 discusses the weighted average cost of capital. Chapter 10 discusses training and implementation. Chapter 11 takes the investor's perspective. Chapter 12 compares competing value-based management systems. Chapter 13 discusses public policy implications

Dedication and Acknowledgments*

The intellectual foundations of our work go back centuries but emerged in modern times with the valuation work of Miller and Modigliani [1962], Malkiel [1963], and Gordon [1959]. These were all formula-based mathematical models, and have since been replaced by spreadsheet modeling—an approach pioneered by Al Rappaport and his partner Carl Nobel, and refined by others including Bennett Stewart and Joel Stern. The idea that expectations are important we trace back to John Maynard Keynes [1936] and Paul Samuelson [1965] and Robert Lucas [1975] in economic theory and to Al Rappaport [1986, 2001], more recently for good advice to investors. The theme of managing for value has also been around a long time and is traceable all the way back to Alfred Marshall [1890] and his notion of economic profit. In modern times Al Rappaport (ALCAR), Joel Stern (Stern Stewart), Jim McTaggert (Marakon) Bart McFadden (HOLT and BCG), and Tom Copeland, Tim Koller, and Jack Murrin (McKinsey and Monitor) are among the larger list of advocates.

We wish to thank the many people who helped make this book possible. First, our loved ones who supported us throughout—Maggie, Timothy, and Michael Copeland; and Jennifer and Maya Dolgoff. Then our colleagues: J. Fred Weston, Al Rappaport, Rob McLean, Hardy Tey, Alberto Moel, Alan Kantrow, Betsy Seybolt.

And finally the hard-working people at John Wiley & Sons: Bill Falloon, Todd Tedesco, and Jennifer MacDonald.

---

*See the back of the book for details of bibliographic citations.

Measuring Performance

This section sets the stage. Chapter 1 discusses the major flaws in traditional measures of performance and points out the salient fact that they are not correlated with the total return to shareholders (TRS) because they have no information about expected outcomes. Expectations-Based Management™ (EBM™) does have high correlation with TRS because it looks at performance relative to expectations. Chapter 2 provides irrefutable empirical evidence that EBM is highly correlated with market-adjusted total return to shareholders while other measures are not.

CHAPTER 1

The Right Objective, Strategy, and Metric

We are writing about one of the most important CEO top-of-mind issues—performance measurement. The way people behave in the workplace and the value that they create depends on it. The challenge is to align performance measurement and the resulting behavior with shareholder wealth creation. There are many gurus who claim to have found the secret link, but they all fail to account for the effect of changes in expectations. Consequently, none of their own measures of performance is highly correlated with the total return to shareholders (TRS). This book introduces, for the first time, an Expectations-Based Management (EBM) system, which measures performance in a way that is highly correlated with TRS.

But this book is not just for management, although they play a fundamental role in setting expectations. It is also written for investors who believe in using fundamental information to set their expectations of company performance, and analysts who forecast financial results and make investment recommendations. It is also, incidentally, for legislators who regulate the rules that determine the cost and flow of information that affect all securities prices.

To create a TRS higher than the normal return, a company has to exceed expectations. Why? Because expectations are already baked into its stock price. In October of 1998, Intel, a company that was regularly earning a return on invested capital 30 to 40 percent more than its cost of capital, announced that its earnings were up 19 percent over the year before. Immediately thereafter, its stock price fell six percent—because analysts had been expecting a 24 percent earnings increase. Intel's price corrected downward because it failed to meet expectations. Expectations count!

Any human endeavor involving teamwork requires three things: a common objective, a way of measuring progress toward that objective, and

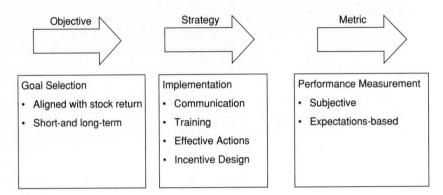

FIGURE 1.1   Goal selection, Performance Measurement, and Implementation.

methods for achieving the desired performance. Figure 1.1 illustrates these three interrelated issues.

We often take them for granted. But if any of the three is wrong, the team is likely to fail. Even agreement about what the objective should be is sometimes hard to achieve—some would say impossible. This book is about management's choice of an objective—maximization of owners' wealth, the choice of a measure of performance that is aligned with it, and the management implementation method that best achieves the desired performance.

For the objective function, or goal, of a company we use the expression "owners' wealth" as a synonym for TRS to call attention to the fact that this objective applies equally well to privately as to publicly owned firms. When a company has publicly traded stock, the objective by corporate charter is to maximize the total return to shareholders.

Sometimes a team chooses the wrong objective. For example, we knew of a college soccer team where the coach stressed defense, and rewarded the team because it led the league for having the lowest average number of goals scored against them. No one can deny that the goal of having a good defense is laudable. But what if we tell you that the team won only 2 of 14 games that season and finished dead last? It lost many games 1 to 0 or 2 to 1. Good defense is fine, but not as good as scoring more goals than your opponent before the last whistle sounds. The team was pulling together and working hard—achieving an "A" for effort—but it had the wrong objective.

Sometimes an organization has the right objective. However, mistakes about the appropriate measure of performance have resulted in classic failures—the stuff that Barbara Tuchman wrote about in *The March of Folly.* For example, she writes of Britain's loss of America (1763–1765):

> *Britain's self-interest as regards her empire on the American continent in the 18th century was clearly to maintain her sovereignty, and for every reason of trade, peace, and profit, to maintain it with goodwill and by the voluntary desire of the colonies.*[1]

Britain's goal was clear, yet her ministries repeatedly took measures that injured the relationship, and in the end she made rebels where there had been none. Tuchman goes on to analyze the folly: "...while the colonies were considered of vital importance to the prosperity and world status of Britain, very little thought or attention was paid to them."[2] This myopic behavior was caused by failure to give proper weight to the value (in investment terms, the net present value) of the colonies to England. Instead, Britain placed greater weight on immediate concerns, such as raising taxes to provide reimbursement for the standing army in the Americas to defend against Native Americans and resurgence of the French. This short-term behavior caused England to lose sight of the larger goal of keeping the Americas. As we shall see, the analogy extends to companies and their managements—namely, the misapplication of myopic performance measures, such as maximizing short-term earnings at the expense of long-term earnings growth.

If the team's objective is appropriate, and if it chooses measures of performance that are appropriately aligned with the objective, there is still the problem of implementation. This third part of the management system is at the grass roots of everyday management and is discussed later in the book as training, identification of value drivers, and incentive design.

This book is about a management system that we call Expectations-Based Management. It accepts the maximization of owners' wealth as the objective of companies, shows that performance measurement must be based on changes in expectations in order to link the performance measurement to the stated objective, and then discusses implementation. All three parts of an EBM system should work together to achieve the best possible performance toward achievement of the goal.

Why Is Performance Measurement Top-of-Mind?

The team that has the right goal and the right resources usually wins—regardless of the competitive activity. In the United States at the beginning of the third millennium, one can confidently argue that the economic, legal, and socially desirable objective of corporations is to maximize owners' wealth. Yet this tautology is discussed endlessly, because management does

---

[1]Tuchman, Barbara, *The March of Folly*, New York: Ballantine Books, 1985, p. 128.
[2]Ibid., p. 129.

not have direct control over a firm's stock price. Rather, management influences the share price by achieving and communicating past, present, and future performance. The trick is to find a strong link between the measure of performance and actually winning in the stock market, thereby creating wealth. It may surprise you to learn that Economic Value Added (EVA®) (also called economic profit) and commonly used performance measures, such as earnings per share and the growth in earnings per share, are definitely *not related* to the total return to shareholders. (See Chapter 2, which reviews the preponderance of empirical evidence that confirms this fact.)

Like a team of horses, a high-performance management team has to pull together to win in competition, but it also must steer in the right direction. That is why performance measurement is always a top-of-mind topic for CEOs. This book not only suggests a common-sense performance measure; it also provides concrete evidence (taken from real market data) that this measure is closely linked to your firm's stock price.

Commonly Used Performance Measures and Their Shortcomings

Every top manager becomes a believer in a causal linkage between the company's performance objectives and its stock price. The only problem is that there are a lot of choices. A partial (but not exhaustive) list, based on our experience, is broken down here. Every performance measure has its problems.

Top-Line Growth

Top-line growth is simply the growth in sales revenues (or sales turnover). Its link to shareholder returns is weak at best, for several reasons. First, sales growth is a double-edged sword when it comes to value creation. It increases value when sales are profitable, but destroys value when each unit sold is unprofitable. Table 1.1 shows what we mean. On one axis is the five-year average sales growth rate for companies, broken down into five categories ranging from very high sales growth rates (greater than 12 percent per year) to very low or negative growth rates. Along the other axis is the spread between the company's return on invested capital and its cost of capital (a decent measure of economic profitability). Within each of the 30 cells is the ratio of the market price per share divided by the book value per share—its market-to-book ratio. Higher market-to-book ratios are representative of strong economic growth. The table clearly indicates that revenue growth is related to higher stock prices only if it is profitable growth.

For example, if the company's return on invested capital is less than the cost of capital, the market-to-book ratio stays flat or goes down (except in a few cells). If you look at the last column, however, where companies earned more than four percent above their cost of capital, the market-to-

TABLE 1.1   Unprofitable Top Line Growth Means Lower Value

| | Return on Invested Capital Minus Cost of Capital | | | | |
| | (5-Year Average) | | | | |
5-Year Average Revenue Growth	<−2%	−2% to 0	0 to 2%	2 to 4%	> 4%
< 0%	3.13	N/A	N/A	N/A	3.37
0–3%	3.37	2.63	N/A	2.32	5.89
3–6%	2.67	4.69	3.28	4.20	7.16
6–9%	N/A	2.71	2.91	N/A	8.11
9–12 %	N/A	2.92	2.84	2.82	7.70
> 12%	3.35	3.15	3.37	3.19	6.59

Note: Cells contain five-year average (1993–1997) market-to-book equity multiples.
      "N/A" means there were fewer than five companies in a cell.

Source: Valuation: Measuring and Managing the Value of Companies, 3rd Edition, by McKinsey & Company Inc., Tom Copeland, Tim Koller, Jack Murrin, Copyright © 2000, McKinsey & Company, Inc. Reprinted by permission of John Wiley & Sons, Inc.

book ratio increases dramatically with higher growth. Also, as you move across any row (holding revenue growth constant), you see that higher multiples are associated with higher spreads. The take-away lesson is that growth alone is not enough—it must be profitable growth.

A second problem with revenue growth as a performance measure is that it includes neither balance sheet information nor any information about expectations. It should. A company that generates one dollar of revenue with one dollar of invested capital is worth more than a company that needs two dollars of invested capital to produce the same dollar of revenue.

Earnings-Based Measures (Bottom-Line Growth)

Earnings-based measures, such as earnings per share and the growth in earnings per share, are also too limited to be useful. To illustrate, take a thorough look at Table 1.2. The pro-forma income statements for two firms are illustrated for the next six years. Big Plant Inc. is worth much less than Small Plant Inc., assuming that the firms are like projects that end in the seventh year and that they both have a 10 percent cost of capital. Can you figure out why Small Plant Inc. is worth more?

Since every number over the next six years is exactly the same, it is impossible to say which company has greater value. If earnings were all that mattered, the two companies would have the same value. But managers need to manage efficiently the balance sheet as well as the income statement. If two companies in the same industry have the same earnings per share—let's say five dollars per share—it makes a difference how much

TABLE 1.2 Pro-Forma Income Statements (Six Years)

Big Plant Inc.	Year 1	Year 2	Year 3	Year 4	Year 5	Year 6	Sum
Revenue	$1,000	$1,000	$1,000	$1,000	$1,000	$1,000	$6,000
– Cost of goods sold	–600	–600	–600	–600	–600	–600	–3,600
– Sales, general & admin	–100	–100	–100	–100	–100	–100	–600
– Depreciation	–100	–100	–100	–100	–100	–100	–600
= *EBIT*	200	200	200	200	200	200	1,200
– Taxes	–80	–80	–80	–80	–80	–80	–480
= Net income	120	120	120	120	120	120	720

Small Plant Inc.							
Revenue	$1,000	$1,000	$1,000	$1,000	$1,000	$1,000	$6,000
– Cost of goods sold	–600	–600	–600	–600	–600	–600	–3,600
– Sales, general & admin	–100	–100	–100	–100	–100	–100	–600
– Depreciation	–100	–100	–100	–100	–100	–100	–600
= *EBIT*	200	200	200	200	200	200	1,200
– Taxes	–80	–80	–80	–80	–80	–80	–480
= Net income	120	120	120	120	120	120	720

capital was required to generate the earnings. The company that uses five dollars of capital to generate five dollars of earnings will be worth much more than a competitor that uses $10 of capital to generate the same earnings.

Instead of earnings information alone, suppose that we also add (or subtract) information about how management is using or generating resources on the balance sheet. Taken together, the two types of information are called free cash flows, and it is the free cash flow of the firm that ultimately determines the value of each company.

Table 1.3 shows that the free cash flows of the two companies are different. We define free cash flow as the operating cash from the income statement (net income plus depreciation, a non-cash charge) minus cash used to grow the balance sheet, namely capital expenditures and increases in working capital (e.g., inventories). It is common to think of free cash flow as the funds available from operations to pay to investors after all reinvestments are made to sustain the business. Notice in Table 1.4 that the main difference in our example is the timing of investments. Big Plant Inc. invests $300 every three years, and depreciates $100 per year. Small Plant Inc. invests $100 each year and since the plants have one-year lives, depreciation is $100 per year also. Big Plant Inc. also requires earlier investments in working capital than Small Plant Inc.; however, the total working capital requirements are the same. If the time value of money (often called the discount rate) is 10 percent, then the values of the two companies are $13 and $127 million, respectively, even though they have the same earnings every year.

In our example, although earnings and earnings growth were identical for the two firms, there was a dramatic difference in value that was attributable to just timing differences in free cash flow. Had Small Plant Inc. used less total capital to generate the same earnings, its value advantage would have been even higher.

The take-away from this discussion is simple and dramatic. *In order for a performance measure to be complete, it must include balance sheet as well as income statement information—summarized as free cash flows.*

Combined Objective of Top- and Bottom-Line Growth

The combination of top- and bottom-line growth is also a bad measure of performance, although many chief executive officers use it zealously. We have often heard the assertion that if a firm grows both revenue (the top line) and earnings per share (the bottom line), then it follows that the firm must be achieving profitable growth. Unfortunately, this theory does not hold true if the company's return on invested capital is falling at the same time. This can easily happen if debt is used to finance new investments that are returning less than the weighted average cost of capital but more than the after-tax cost of debt.

Take a look at the example in Table 1.5. Revenue, the top line, grows every year and averages 10.0 percent per year. Net income, the bottom line,

TABLE 1.3 Pro-Forma Cash Flow Statements

Big Plant Inc.	Year 1	Year 2	Year 3	Year 4	Year 5	Year 6	Sum
Net Income	$120	$120	$120	$120	$120	$120	$720
+ Depreciation	100	100	100	100	100	100	600
− Capital expenditures	−300	0	0	−300	0	0	−600
− Increase in working capital	−350	−100	−50	−20	−10	−10	−540
= Entity free cash flow	−430	120	170	−100	210	210	180

Small Plant Inc.	Year 1	Year 2	Year 3	Year 4	Year 5	Year 6	Sum
Net Income	$120	$120	$120	$120	$120	$120	$720
+ Depreciation	100	100	100	100	100	100	600
− Capital expenditures	−100	−100	−100	−100	−100	−100	−600
− Increase in working capital	−150	−70	−50	−50	−110	−110	−540
= Entity free cash flow	−30	50	70	70	10	10	180

TABLE 1.4 Discounted Cash Flow Values of Big Plant Inc. and Small Plant Inc. (10% Discount Rate)

Year	Free Cash Flow Big	Free Cash Flow Small	Discount Factor	Present Value Big	Present Value Small
1	−430	−30	0.909	−391	−27
2	120	50	0.826	99	41
3	170	70	0.751	128	53
4	−100	70	0.683	−70	48
5	210	10	0.621	128	6
6	210	10	0.565	119	6
Present Value				13	127

grows at 4.2 percent, so the firm has achieved its objective of top- and bottom-line growth. However, if its weighted average cost of capital is 10 percent, it will destroy value with its new investments. As we can see from the next to last line in the exhibit, the rate of return (after tax) on new capital invested never exceeds 7.6 percent. Shareholders can earn 10 percent after taxes if the capital is paid out to them as dividends or share repurchases. Every dollar spent on new investment destroys value and the company's return on invested capital (*ROIC*) deteriorates over time. Consequently, its stock price will fall even though revenue and net income are both growing. As long as the capital is financed with debt that has an after-tax cost less than the after-tax return on invested capital, it is possible to achieve both top- and bottom-line growth even when the *ROIC* is less than the cost of capital. One way of saying the same thing is that it is always possible to grow the top- and the bottom-line by finding (marginally) bad projects and taking a lot of them.

Return on Invested Capital

The return on invested capital has problems of its own. It is defined (on a pre-tax basis) as the earnings before interest and taxes (*EBIT*) divided by the book value of invested capital. The definition of invested capital includes net property plant and equipment, net operating working capital, and goodwill.

The good thing about *ROIC* is that it contains information from both the income statement, namely *EBIT*, as well as from the balance sheet (i.e., invested capital). Therefore, it is an improvement over revenue growth and earnings growth (both ignore all balance sheet management issues).

For now, let's focus on the major managerial problem, which is that if a company uses *ROIC* as its measure of performance, the most likely managerial response will be to harvest the business by underinvesting and allowing the book value of capital to decline as it depreciates. This is

TABLE 1.5 Return on Invested Capital (*ROIC*) Falls While the Top and Bottom Lines Both Grow

	Year 1	Year 2	Year 3	Year 4	Year 5	Year 6	CAGR*
Revenue	$1,000	$1,100	$1,210	$1,331	$1,464	$1,611	10%
− Operating costs	−600	−675	−755	−839	−951	−1,063	
= *EBIT*	400	425	455	492	513	548	
− Interest on debt (5%)	−10	−20	−31	−43	−56	−71	
= Earnings before tax	390	405	425	449	457	477	4%
− Taxes (50%)	−195	−202	−212	−224	−228	−238	
= Net Income	195	203	213	225	229	239	4%
Invested capital	2,000	2,200	2,420	2,662	2,928	3,221	
Return on invested capital**	10.0%	9.7%	9.4%	9.2%	8.8%	8.5%	
Return on new capital**	N/A	6.3%	6.8%	7.6%	3.9%	6.0%	
Debt	200	400	620	862	1,128	1,421	4%

*Cumulative Average (annual) Growth Rate

**Return on invested capital (*ROIC*) and return on new capital are after-tax

because it is simply easier to shrink the denominator of the *ROIC* equation than to grow the numerator. At the building products division of an integrated forest products company, we attended a planning meeting that was being held three years after *ROIC* had become the main performance measurement standard. Everyone bragged about how they had achieved increases in *ROIC,* but in the next breath, complained that aging equipment was beginning to eat into productivity. They were harvesting the business.

Coca-Cola provides an example of a company that is *ROIC*-focused and not necessarily, in spite of management announcements to the contrary, maximizing value. We are certain that any of the company's managers who read this paragraph will adamantly deny our assertion, but let's examine the facts. Coca-Cola (ticker symbol KO) owns minority interests in its many bottling affiliates. Once upon a time they were part of KO, but they are capital-intensive and so the parent company shed them off into minority interest affiliates in order to take their assets off the balance sheet. By shedding them, KO was able to rid itself of capital without losing much margin and its *ROIC* rose significantly. For example, according to our calculations, KO averaged 47 percent *ROIC* (after taxes) during the five-year period 1998–2002. So what is wrong with that, you say? Nothing is wrong, except that the bottlers have correspondingly low *ROIC*—they have more capital on the balance sheets, but earn low margins due to the high cost of paying for KO's ingredients to put into sodas. Bottlers are often reluctant to make the new investments (e.g., in coolers and in better distribution) that are needed to grow market share faster. Faster growth of Coca-Cola beverage sales creates enormous value at KO, which has high *ROIC*—but this growth is a marginal or even negative value creator at the bottlers, who have low *ROIC.* When KO shed the invested capital resident in bottling it created an agency problem for itself. When bottlers invest, they cannot capture the profit from additional syrup sales. Before their separation from KO, the returns were all under the same roof. Now KO has to try to control investment decisions at the bottlers from its minority ownership position. Because of the agency problem that was created along with the independent bottlers, it seems to us that worldwide sales are lower than they otherwise might have been.

Spread Between *ROIC* and *WACC*

The spread between the return on invested capital (*ROIC*) and the weighted average cost of capital (*WACC*) is not any better than *ROIC* by itself. Management tends to treat the *WACC* as something that is provided by the rocket scientists at headquarters—something over which there is no managerial control. Consequently, the major reason given for using the spread is that one can objectively stipulate that value is created when a company earns an after-tax *ROIC* that is greater than its weighted average cost of capital. Managers are told that their business unit must earn more than the cost of capital in order to create value. The spread target simply takes the *ROIC* objective and adds a hurdle rate. As we shall see, positive spread business units, even those that increase their spread, may drag down the company stock price if their spread is less than expected.

Balanced Scorecards

Balanced scorecards are the mud pie of finance. They may or may not be actually logically tied to wealth creation. Usually they are not expectations-based, often their components are self-contradictory, and even when appropriate, their components are redundant. For a while in the early 1990s, AT&T used a balanced scorecard that had three parts: total return to shareholders, employee satisfaction, and customer satisfaction. It is not at all clear whether these three parts work together to create shareholder wealth. Can employee satisfaction and shareholder wealth conflict? Yes, it is possible. Rather than being clear, balanced scorecards muddy the waters in a misguided attempt to mollify multiple constituencies. Chapter 12 goes into balanced scorecards at greater length.

Summary of one-period performance measures

Table 1.6 summarizes the discussion up to this point. The commonly used one-year performance measures fail for two reasons. First, they do not contain all the information that managers need to make good decisions. Even more important, as we shall explain in the next section, none of the performance measures except for Expectations-Based Management is closely linked to the actual total return to shareholders. Chapter 2 provides strong empirical evidence that changes in expectations about the key value drivers provide the best ties to stock prices.

TABLE 1.6   Comparison of Commonly Used Performance Metrics

	Income statement info?	Balance sheet info?	Avoids tendency to harvest?	Contains expectations linked to stock price?	Multiperiod tradeoffs acknowledged?
Revenue growth	Yes	No	N/A	No	No
Earnings or earnings growth	Yes	No	N/A	No	No
ROIC	Yes	Yes	No	No	No
ROIC – WACC	Yes	Yes	No	No	No
EVA	Yes	Yes	Yes	No	No

Expectations-Based Management

As we mentioned earlier in the Preface, in October of 1998, Intel announced that its earnings were up 19 percent over the year before. Its return on invested capital was roughly 50 percent—much higher than its cost of capital. On the day of the announcement Intel's stock price fell 6 percent. The explanation was simple. The analyst community was expecting an earnings increase of 24 percent. The market was disappointed by the news and consequently Intel's stock price fell.

Expectations are everything. Stock prices reflect investor expectations of the future cash flows that a firm can deliver. If expectations are revised downward, as in the Intel example, then the stock price will fall. Although Intel's earnings grew, it grew less than expected.

The stock market is like a horse race. To make money, your bet should not be on the favorite—the fastest horse. Rather, it should be on the horse that runs faster than expected and finishes in the money. Often the fastest horse is also the favorite due to high expectations but pays little even if it wins because heavy betting drives down the odds and therefore the payoff.

Like betting on horses, the stock market handicaps companies by paying more for those that have high *expected* levels of performance. To earn high rates of return companies must exceed expectations. Take Chevron in the 1990s for example. Figure 1.2 plots Chevron's earnings per share (designated by each box), its total return to shareholders relative to the market return (right vertical axis as the dotted line), and analyst expectations about the earnings per share starting two years before the earnings announcement (the thin lines that end in each earnings box). For example, take 1994 to 1995. Earnings per share increased from roughly $2.50 to $3.00—a 20 percent growth rate. Yet, relative to the market, the total return to shareholders declined the entire year (about 22 percent). If management is using traditional performance measures that do not look at expectations, then the market stock price behavior seems to be nonsense. Earnings went up but the (market-adjusted) return to shareholders was negative. However, if we take expectations into account, we notice that in 1993 analysts were expecting that two years later, at the end of 1994, Chevron would earn about $3.50 per share. Throughout 1993 and 1994 they had to revise their expectations downward and as a result, Chevron's stock price fell. It fell because it earned only about $3.00 per share when earlier, people had expected it to earn around $3.50.

Any performance measure that focuses on revisions in expectations would be an improvement, but as we said earlier, it is best if the measure also contains both income statement and balance sheet information. We now add to the list changes in the cost of capital, and soon will add multiperiod aspects. We define annual EBM as the difference between actual and expected economic profit (*EP*), or EVA. Economic profit contains information

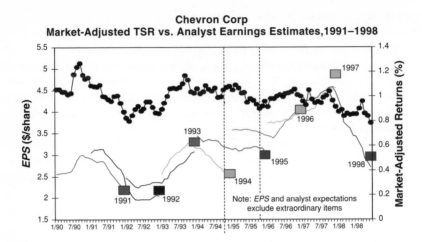

FIGURE 1.2   Changes in analyst earnings estimates match TSR.

from the income statement as well as the balance sheet, as well as the cost of capital. It is the spread between *ROIC* and *WACC*, multiplied by the amount of invested capital, *I*, and can be written as follows:

$$EP = (ROIC - WACC)(I) \qquad (1.1)$$

But *EP* does not include any expectations. It is actual *ROIC* minus actual *WACC* times actual invested capital.

$$EP = [\text{Actual } ROIC - \text{Actual } WACC] \times \text{Actual } WACC$$

Next, we add expectations into the picture by breaking down the definition into the differences between actual and expected performance of the three generic value drivers, namely *ROIC*, *WACC*, and invested capital. Our Expectations-Based Management measure of one-period performance is:

$$EBM = \text{Actual } EP - \text{Expected } EP$$

or,

$$\begin{aligned} EBM = &[\text{Actual } ROIC - \text{Expected } ROIC\, (I) \\ &- [\text{Actual } WACC - \text{Expected } WACC](I) \\ &+ [ROIC - WACC][\text{Actual } I - \text{Expected } I] \end{aligned} \qquad (1.2)$$

We can interpret the first term as creating value by earning more than expected on existing invested capital. In other words, earn more on core assets. The second term says we can create value by reducing the cost of capital more than expected. The third term says that growth via new (unexpected) investment adds value only if the new investment earns more than its cost of capital.

EBM *is different from other performance measures primarily because it measures business performance relative to expectations and they do not.* Some measures (e.g., EVA) attempt to be objective because the hurdle rate becomes the cost of capital—an objective criterion. EBM *is subjective in nature* because the hurdle rate is the expected return—a number that is based on judgment.

To illustrate our point, consider the following example. Suppose business units A and B have the same cost of capital, 10 percent, and have the same size, with invested capital of $100,000. Neither business unit makes new investments during the year and unit A achieves a 30 percent return on invested capital, while unit B achieves only a 15 percent return. If we use economic profit (*EP* as defined in Equation 1.1) as our measure of performance, we would conclude that value was created by both units because they both earned more than the cost of capital, and that unit A created more value than B.

What if you were told that at the beginning of the period unit A was expected to earn a return on invested capital of 40 percent while B was expected to earn 10 percent? Now we have more information—the beginning of period expectations—and can calculate the EBM. Unit A earned 10 percent less than expected and consequently the market value of the firm went down $10,000 in value. Unit B earned 5 percent more than expected and created $5,000 of value. In total, the value destruction for the company was $5,000. It was expected to earn $50,000 and it actually earned $45,000—less than expected. Hence, its stock price would fall. This simple example illustrates the failure of *EP* as a measure of business unit performance.

So far, we have the result that the stock price will fall if the return on invested capital is greater than the cost of capital but less than expected. Should management refuse to reinvest in the company given this set of circumstances? In economics the answer always depends on the next best alternative, which is choosing not to invest. If management were to return to shareholders the funds for investment, then shareholders could earn only the cost of capital (assuming they reinvest the money at the same level of risk). Hence shareholders are better off if management makes the investment. If it does the share price will fall, but it will fall even more if it does not. This subtle issue is covered in detail in Chapter 3.

Another way to conceptualize the distinction we are making is to distinguish between economic value and shareholder value, and realize that the two need not be correlated in the short run. Shareholder value is created at the time that investors recognize the potential for excess risk-adjusted cash flow returns in the future. Shareholder value, therefore, is realized at the time investor expectations change. Economic value is confirmed at the actual time at which such cash flows are realized. Over the long run, shareholder value must be related to economic value creation—

but only because in the long run investors will adjust their expectations to the reality of the level of cash flows being realized. Especially in industries with particularly long investment horizons, shareholder value creation driven by changes in expectations may not be correlated at all with the realization of economic value over the life of investment projects.

How does EBM work when management is contemplating new investment, rather than evaluating business unit performance? Try out the following problem. You have told the market that you are going to take two new projects and that each is expected to return 40 percent. Your cost of capital is 10 percent. Suddenly, you learn that the second project will earn 20 percent instead of the predicted 40 percent. Should you cancel it? If you don't your stock price will fall because the project will fail to meet the market's expectations. Even so, the correct answer is to take it, because if you don't the shareholders will be able to earn only 10 percent, which is what they can earn elsewhere at equivalent risk. Consequently, if you don't take the project at a 20 percent rate of return, your stock price will fall even more than if you do take it. The decision rule that this exemplifies is contained in the third term of our EBM equation, namely that management should take all new investment that earns more than the cost of capital. Chapter 4 goes into greater depth.

Next, let's return to Table 1.1, which demonstrated that higher revenue growth improved market-to-book multiples only if the company also earned a healthy spread over its cost of capital. Table 1.7 revises the same table by

TABLE 1.7   No Relationship Between *TRS*, Revenue Growth, and Spread (1999–2003)

Average Revenue Growth	Average Spread (*ROIC − WACC*)				
	< −3%	−3%–0%	0%–3%	3%–6%	> 6%
< 0%	−5.8%	−1.8%	2.9%	0.8%	−4.2%
	N = 18	N = 16	N = 26	N = 7	N = 11
0%–5%	−4.9%	9.3%	4.5%	4.9%	3.0%
	N = 6	N = 20	N = 44	N = 9	N = 15
5%–10%	7.8%	7.1%	5.3%	3.6%	5.6%
	N = 7	N = 14	N = 39	N = 7	N = 11
10%–15%	NA	14.5%	9.9%	9.9%	1.2%
		N = 7	N = 25	N = 9	N = 3
> 15%	11.0%	16.3%	10.3%	7.4%	13.4%
	N = 21	N = 22	N = 49	N = 15	N = 4

Note: Each cell consists of the five-year average market adjusted Total Share-holder Returns and its respective sample size.

Source: Thomson Financials, CRSP Monitor Analysis

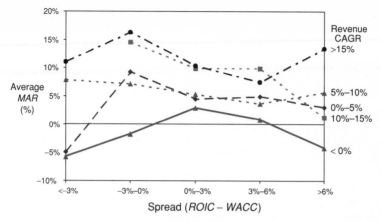

FIGURE 1.3   No relationship between TRS and (*ROIC* – *WACC*) spread.

replacing the market-to-book ratios with the five-year geometric average market-adjusted return to shareholders (*MAR*).[3] Now there is no recognizable relationship between the average spread between *ROIC* and *WACC* and the *MAR*. If a company has a high market-to-book because it has a high spread (*ROIC* – *WACC*), then the market is likely to expect high performance. This implies that the company's market capitalization is high at present because high performance expectations are baked into the multiple. If it performs as expected, the multiple will remain unchanged and shareholders earn the expected rate, i.e., the cost of equity. Figure 1.3 charts these data to highlight the lack of relationship between spread and *MAR*. We should not be surprised that there is virtually no relationship between economic spreads and shareholder returns. We are reminded that the firm should maximize the return to shareholders, not its market-to-book ratio.

The Puzzle Explained

The empirical research indicates unambiguously that there is little or no relationship between earnings, EVA, earnings growth, or the growth in EVA and the return to shareholders. This body of evidence has been replicated in numerous studies and is a fact (see Chapter 2). Figure 1.4 shows why these traditional measures fail and why EBM is highly correlated with shareholder returns.

---

[3]The market-adjusted return to shareholders, *MAR*, is defined as (one plus) the return on the *i*th stock dividend by (one-plus) the market return during the *t*th time period. It expresses the stock return relative to the market.

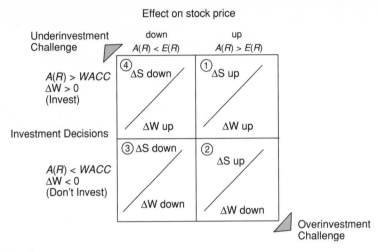

FIGURE 1.4   The puzzle solved.

In each cell are the effects of management decisions on shareholders' wealth (lower right) and on the stock price (upper left). Start with a company whose actual performance is greater than expected (cells 1 and 2). Its stock price will go up, $\Delta S > 0$. This is regardless of its weighted average cost of capital (*WACC*).

Whether the result puts the firm in cell 1 or cell 2 depends on whether it earns an actual return on invested capital, $A(R)$, that is greater than the cost of capital (*WACC*). If $A(R) < WACC$ but is greater than expected, then $A(R) > E(R)$, and the firm will experience an increasing stock price. Investment with $A(R) > WACC$ increases shareholder wealth (cell 1). But if it is in cell 2, where it earns less than the cost of capital (i.e. $A(R) < WACC$), it should return the cash to shareholders instead of investing, because they can earn the cost of capital—a rate greater than $A(R)$. We call cell 2 the *overinvestment challenge* because when $E(R) < A(R) < WACC$ the stock price will go up when the company invests because $A(R) > E(R)$, but shareholders will be worse off because the company invested when $A(R) < WACC$.

Cells 3 and 4 are the opposite. In cell 3, expectations are not met, $A(R) < E(R)$, and investment earns less than the cost of capital $A(R) < WACC$; consequently, the stock price goes down and shareholders are better off if the firm does not invest. Cell 4 we call the *underinvestment challenge*. The firm is expected to earn more than it actually does—i.e., $A(R) < E(R)$— therefore the share price will fall. Yet it should still invest because shareholders can earn $A(R) > WACC$, which is better than the *WACC* (what they can earn on their own). Yes, the share price will fall, but shareholders are better off than the next best alternative, which is not investing and returning the cash to them.

EBM has the following important managerial implications:

1. It is highly correlated with the market-adjusted return to shareholders.
2. It ranks corporate and business unit performance differently and in line with TRS.
3. It helps management understand and overcome the over- and under-investment challenges.
4. It helps management understand and improve both external and internal communications.
5. It helps improve incentive design.

In the next chapter we will provide empirical evidence that has been published in a top-flight refereed academic journal (*Review of Accounting Studies*, June 2004). It shows that traditional measures of performance that do not contain expectations are essentially uncorrelated with the total return to shareholders. In sharp contrast, when changes in expectations about earnings, the cost of capital, and capital expenditures are regressed against TRS, they explain up to 50 percent of the variation in TRS—a highly significant result.

Now that we have defined EBM in a one-period setting, we can extrapolate it into a more general system that extends deeper into the company to performance measures called value drivers, and across time to include the valuation of your company and its businesses.

An EBM System

As defined in Equation 1.2, EBM is limited to one time period and (implicitly) to business activities that have an income statement and balance sheet (companies and their business units). Figure 1.5 illustrates a more complete view of what we call an EBM *system*. At its center is the one-period definition of EBM. This definition extends downward from the corporate and business unit levels into the daily operations of the company by using an *ROIC*-tree as shown in Figure 1.6. The *ROIC* is, of course, part of the annual EBM definition. In turn, *ROIC* (defined as *EBIT*/Invested Capital) is the product of operating margin (*EBIT*/Sales) and capital turns (Sales/Invested Capital). Thus, operating margin and capital turns are generic value drivers common to all businesses. They can be linked to business unit–specific value drivers, such as customer mix, and to sales force productivity. These value-drivers can be linked one level further down to provide performance measures at the daily operating level—for example, sales force productivity might be driven not by the number of visits made by sales representatives, but by the expected profit margins on the products being sold.

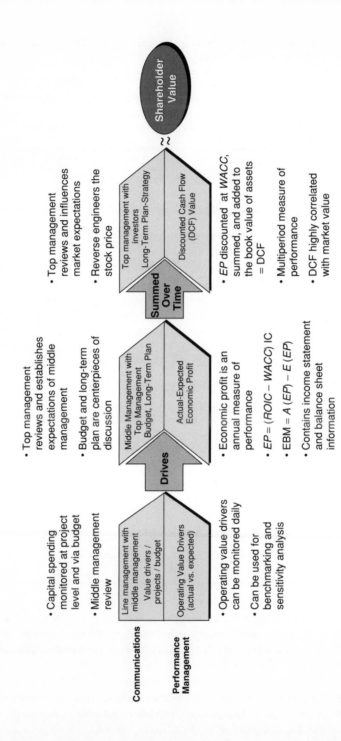

Communications

- Capital spending monitored at project level and via budget
- Middle management review

- Top management reviews and establishes expectations of middle management
- Budget and long-term plan are centerpieces of discussion

- Top management reviews and influences market expectations
- Reverse engineers the stock price

Performance Management

Line management with middle management
Value drivers / projects / budget

Operating Value Drivers (actual vs. expected)

Middle Management with Top Management
Budget, Long-Term Plan

Actual-Expected Economic Profit

Top management with investors
Long-Term Plan-Strategy

Discounted Cash Flow (DCF) Value

Shareholder Value

Drives

Summed Over Time

- Operating value drivers can be monitored daily
- Can be used for benchmarking and sensitivity analysis

- Economic profit is an annual measure of performance
- $EP = (ROIC - WACC)\,IC$
- $EBM = A\,(EP) - E\,(EP)$
- Contains income statement and balance sheet information

- EP discounted at $WACC$, summed, and added to the book value of assets $= DCF$
- Multiperiod measure of performance
- DCF highly correlated with market value

FIGURE 1.5 Integrated EBM system.

By pushing its understanding of value drivers deep into the organization while maintaining the "golden thread" back to value, management can develop focus.*

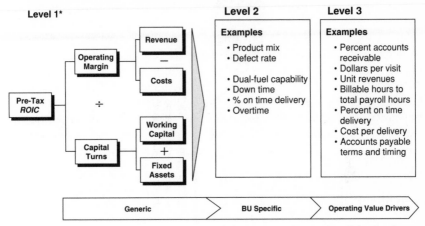

*The value drivers will address *only* economic factors for management's attention; obviously, other issues such as employee and customer satisfaction also need to be accounted for.

FIGURE 1.6 Various levels of value driver identification.

If we return to Figure 1.4 and move to the total value of common stock as a performance measure, we shall prove later in the book that the discounted value of forecasted economic profits when added to the book value of assets in place is equal to the discounted cash flow value of the company. Furthermore, the DCF value is highly correlated with the actual market value. In this way, Figure 1.5 illustrates an integrated EBM system that starts with daily operating value drivers, links directly to annual EBM, and annual EBM links to a multiperiod valuation of the company. This integrated EBM system provides a "golden thread" all the way from daily operations to the total return to shareholders.

Alphabet Soup

Value-Based Management (VBM) has been touted for at least two decades. Virtually every consulting firm is happy to provide expensive advice on how to create value for shareholders. One hears of EVA (economic value added) by Stern Stewart, CFROI® by Holt (now with Credit Suisse First Boston and formerly with the Boston Consulting Group), and more traditional approaches used by Marakon, McKinsey, Booz Allen, and Bain. Every advisor claims to have the best approach. Many have published their own books on the subject. Later on in the book, in Chapter 12, we do our best to describe the approaches to VBM used by each of these advisors, and to give a frank opinion of their pros and cons.

Many value-based management systems have failed—some spectacu-larly so. There are more explanations for causes of failure than there are systems. Sometimes management changes and the new management team has its own favorite way of measuring performance. More often, however, failure is the result of the fact that most measures of company performance are simply not correlated with movements in the stock price relative to the market (recall the Chevron example in Figure 1.2). Sometimes the per-formance measures are a "black box" to management with the result being that management becomes dependent on its advisors to set performance standards. And occasionally, the measures of performance are so intricate that management does not really understand how they are calculated, nor can they explain it to the board of directors or investors.

Something Old, Something New

When EBM is described for the first time to management, we've been struck by two seemingly inconsistent reactions. Some react as though EBM were nothing new at all because we are advocating what many in our field advo-cate, namely that managers need to pay more attention to valuation in how they plan and run their businesses. Others believe EBM is too radical a change as it abandons fixed benchmarks and other objective standards—and in so doing, leaves the door open to managerial abuses and confusion. Our response to comments of both types is that they are both right and wrong. EBM builds on a theory of value that has been common both among academics and practitioners for decades—i.e., that value is the (dis-counted) value of expected future cash flows. In this regard, EBM is not new. There have been many previous efforts to translate financial theory into a management system that relates measures of value to managerial decisions. While we agree that metric choice is important, we believe an effective management system needs to understand not only how to meas-ure value, but how to measure and manage returns (changes in value). This is both a new and subtle change in perspective, one that can change such fundamental decisions as how best to set performance targets, evaluate per-formance, and motivate performance.

Perhaps a more thoughtful response is to note that EBM builds on the old value-based frameworks to create something new. EBM is something old and something new.

Something Old

Subjectivity / Judgment
The most senior executives and board members tell us that their jobs are inherently subjective. The business context is changing and they find them-

selves constantly struggling to make the right decisions and motivate managers to deliver. They tell us that they approach budgeting and planning as a subjective exercise requiring their judgment. But they are frustrated because they find themselves fighting against their own systems—systems that require X percent return on capital or who reward managers who were lucky enough to be in a high-growth product niche.

EBM *is actually very old* in one sense. Rather than forcing managers to adapt to a rigid system, EBM recognizes the dynamic nature of target setting, performance measurement, and managerial evaluation. Expectations from the glue that holds it all together, as they provide a way for managers to ground their subjective instincts in quantitative terms that can be discussed, tested, and tracked.

Metrics

Though we have our complaints with some of the metrics in use today (see chapter 12), EBM does not propose a radically different metric. Economic profit, discounted cash flow, real options value—these are the basic ways to measure value. Metrics should incorporate both income statement and balance sheet information and adjust for risk and the time value of money. EBM builds on these basics by asking managers to measure these metrics in terms of forward-looking, long-term expectations. Note that EBM does introduce some new metrics—for example, the measurement of market noise or the tailoring of performance metrics to incorporate both actual performance and changes in expectations.

Acting on Expectations Gaps

It is well established that when expectations gaps develop—say, between what managers believe a company is worth and what the market believes it is worth—that managers and/or investors take actions to close that gap. Mergers and acquisitions (M&A), divestitures, capital structure decisions, dividend policy, and similar choices are all used to deal with under- or overvalued stock prices. EBM builds on this long-standing practice first by formalizing the measurement of expectations for different constituencies (investors, analysts, executives, business unit management, and line management). EBM also more formally requires managers to address explicitly expectations gaps in their regular planning cycles rather than waiting for gaps to grow into problems.

Focus on the Long-Term

We've heard time and again that managers are tired of the earnings game—of chasing quarterly *EPS* targets supposedly set by the market and "imposed" on managers who have no choice but to deliver on market targets. EBM sets the "game" back the way it was originally, where managers truly did focus on long-term decisions and communicated what they could to the market so that investors could value the firm correctly. EBM does not ignore the market's expectations, but does recognize that managers often have better information about the firm's potential, and therefore should not blindly chase quarterly numbers. Short-term performance is useful as a guide—it helps managers understand how they are performing against the long-term plan, but it is not the end-all and be-all.

Something New

Rigor / Quantification of Subjective Factors / Expectations
While forming budgets and strategic plans around expectations is nothing new, it is quite rare to see companies that have in-depth tracking systems to understand and manage around expectations. At best there may be some variance analysis conducted to compare budgeted with actual results. Infrequently there are full balance sheet and income statement forecasts tracked—for example, for capital project post-mortems. But never have we seen companies systematically tracking long-term expectations, except by way of periodic planning sessions whose forecasts play little role in actually operating the business.

EBM is a methodical approach, one that tracks expectations across a range of dimensions. Systems should be able to track and compare expectations for different constituencies—investors, analysts, senior management, business unit management, and even line management. Expectations should also be clearly monitored to understand short-term versus long-term expectations. Last, systems need to be created to monitor and thereby help management influence market noise.

Understanding and Managing Noise
We've mentioned noise a few times now, but not defined it. Noise is the uncertainty in the market about the firm's future prospects. One can think of noise in a shorthand way as disagreement between different investors and/or analysts as to what the firm's future financial performance will be. Given the uncertain nature of the future it is impossible to eliminate noise. But poor management communications can worsen the uncertainty and in so doing negatively affect share price. In later chapters we provide more detail about noise as well as implications for improving investor relations.

Flexibility / Real Options Approach to Failing to Meet Expectations
What happens when you miss expectations? Under a traditional approach to planning, managers seek to understand why performance fell short and then go back to try to improve—better operational implementation of strategy, additional cost reductions, or other actions. If the negative earnings surprises continue, the firm eventually goes back to the drawing board to revisit its strategy. EBM asks for a more flexible, adaptive approach. Understanding

expectations is the first step toward mapping a view of the future that allows management to also understand what uncertainties are faced, how those uncertainties may play out under different scenarios, and what actions can be taken contingent on how these uncertainties unfold. Integrating this "real options" approach to strategy can help firms capture more value. Expectations are the foundation around which such planning revolves.

Summary—For Whom Is This Book Written?

This book is written for managers, investors, and legislators who want to understand how corporate performance translates into the total return to shareholders. Managers can better set performance standards, can provide better incentive systems, make better resource allocation decisions, and can communicate better with analysts and potential and existing investors. Investors can make better informed choices about the securities in their portfolios. Legislators can better understand that there is an equilibrium market for information and that laws and regulations affect that equilibrium.

Value is all about expectations. Companies that exceed expectations create new wealth for the economy. This idea is fundamental. The expectations about company performance are baked into the market price of every security (stocks, bonds, and options). If the company meets expectations, every security holder will receive their expected returns and the wealth of all parties will be preserved. But failure to meet expectations will cause them and the security prices to be adjusted downward and that wealth will be destroyed. This can cause some surprising results. Two companies in the same industry can have stock returns that are the opposite of the level of performance. A company with a 30 percent return on invested capital can do worse in the stock market than a competitor that has 15 percent *ROIC*; because the first company was expected to earn 40 percent and failed to meet expectations, while the second company was expected to earn only 10 percent and exceeded expectations.

Investors do not rely exclusively on corporate communiqués for information. At their own cost, they seek out and process information from other sources as they form their own expectations. Some of them pay higher costs while others pay low costs or none at all. But the expectations of potential investors are reflected in stock prices. Management needs to understand what those expectations are and take the appropriate action when they differ from management's own expectations.

Legislators affect the way expectations are formed. Laws and regulations that create greater costs and noisier conduits for the delivery of information destroy wealth. Legislators set the rules and those determine who bears the cost of generating information and what the timing of its release should be.

CHAPTER 2

Expectations Count

The Evidence

This chapter builds a body of empirical evidence that proves beyond a shadow of doubt that there is little or no factual relationship between the total return to shareholders (TRS) and earnings, earnings growth, economic value added (EVA), and EVA growth. It also proves a strong and statistically significant relationship between changes in expectations (about earnings, primarily) and TRS. This work has been published in a refereed academic journal, the *Review of Accounting Studies*, one of the top journals in the field.[1]

What follows in this chapter is tough sledding for most readers. If you could not care less about the details, we advise you to read the first four sections. They describe the intuition behind Expectations-Based Management (and the results of other researchers), summarize our empirical results (which have been several years in the making), and discuss the managerial implications of EBM. If you are interested in the finer details, then roll up your sleeves and dig in. It is worth the effort.

Why Does EBM Provide a Better Tie to Shareholder Returns?

In the first chapter we compared an extensive list of financial performance measures that management has traditionally used to guide their companies. The list included revenue growth (the top line), earnings and earnings

---

[1]Reprinted from Kluwer Academic Publishers, *The Review of Accounting Studies*, Vol. 9, 2004, pp. 149–188, "The Role of Expectations in the Cross-Section of Returns," Copeland, T. A. Dolgoff and A. Moel, [original copyright notice as given to the publication in which material was originally published]. With kind permission of Springer Science and Business Media.

growth (the bottom line), the return on invested capital (*ROIC*), the spread between *ROIC* and the weighted average cost of capital (*WACC*), and economic profit (*EP*). We argued that all were deficient for one reason or another. For example, revenue growth is inadequate because it does not capture profitability; and earnings is deficient because it fails to include any information about balance sheet management—about the amount of capital investment that was used to generate each dollar of earnings. The common problem among all of the measures that were discussed is that stock prices are driven by changes in expectations, yet none of these performance measures captures expectations about anything. EBM is based on expectations.

Figure 2.1 (left panel) explains why there is a weak correlation between the total return to shareholders and EVA, i.e., a company's actual economic profit (*A(EP)*). We start with the premise that the stock price is set so that if expectations are met, then shareholders will earn their cost of equity (K_s). It does not matter whether the company's expected return on invested capital is high or low—if the firm's actual *ROIC* turns out to be as expected, the TRS will equal K_s. The lightly shaded upper half of the left panel of Figure 2.1 shows that TRS will be greater than the cost of equity whenever EBM is positive, i.e., actual economic profit exceeds expected economic profit.

Note that the correlation between EVA and TRS breaks down in the left panel of Figure 2.1. When *ROIC* exceeds the cost of capital (*WACC)* and exceeds expectations, then TRS will be greater than K_s. But if *ROIC* exceeds the *WACC* but is less than expectations, then TRS will be lower than K_s—not what is predicted by EVA. The prediction made by EVA is also wrong for the upper right-hand box where a company earns less than its cost of capital but more than expected. The stock price will go up, but EVA-based measures predict it will go down.

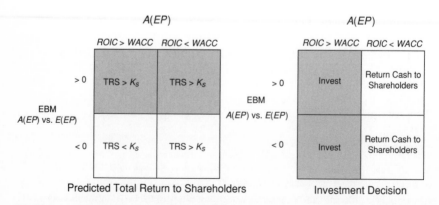

FIGURE 2.1   Predicted TRS and investment decisions.

While the left panel is a prediction that the return to shareholders will be correlated with the change in expectations (and not with EVA)—a prediction whose validity is supported by the research results in the remainder of this chapter—it is not a prescription for investment.

The right-hand panel of Figure 2.1 says that the company should invest whenever the *ROIC* is greater than the *WACC*, otherwise the capital should be returned to shareholders who can reinvest to earn the cost of capital. Chapters 3 and 4 discuss the investment decision in detail. Here we return to the correlation between TRS and various measures of performance.

There now exist good databases that have collected analyst expectations, especially about earnings. For example, IBES and Zacks both collect and report updated analyst forecasts of company earnings for the current fiscal year, the next year, and three- to five-year earnings growth. Value Line reports forecasts by their own analysts of revenue growth, operating margins (earnings before interest and taxes divided by revenue), and capital expenditures. Over time these data sets have become more comprehensive and contain fewer errors. We use data about analyst expectations for our empirical research because we believe it is a good proxy for the expectations of investors and of management. Later on, we discuss what happens when the expectations of these various parties differ.

Summary of Our Findings

We studied the empirical relationship between the total return to shareholders (with the effect of general market movements removed) and various measures of company performance at the company level, i.e. we did not group companies. Our sample included 2,318 company-years for companies from the S&P 500 between 1992 and 1998. The results indicated that:

- There is at best a very weak relationship at the company level (i.e. ungrouped data) between the return to shareholders and the level of earnings per share (scaled by dividing by the previous year's share price), growth in earnings per share, the level of EVA, and growth in EVA. The higher correlations (five to six percent) are with earnings and earnings growth.
- There is a very strong relationship, with a correlation of 47 percent, between the return to shareholders and changes in expectations about earnings.
- By itself, the change in expectations this year (from January to December) about this year's earnings has a 31 percent correlation with the return to shareholders, but any measurable relationship becomes statistically insignificant when changes in longer-term expectations are also included as explanatory variables.

■ There is a persistent strong relationship between the return to shareholders and changes in expectations about next year's earnings and
about long-term earnings growth.

■ The impact of changes in expectations this year about long-term earnings growth is 8 to 10 times more important than any other explanatory variable.

■ Unexpected increases in the cost of capital are associated with lower
returns to shareholders.

■ Unexpected increases in capital expenditures seem to have no effect
on the return to shareholders.

■ Increases in noise, measured as the dispersion of analyst forecasts, are
significantly associated with negative returns to shareholders.

Our first result merely confirms the work of other researchers, but all
of the other results are new and are surprisingly consistent with a discounted cash flow view of the world—that changes in the stock price are
the result of changes in expectations about the long-run earnings perspective for the firm.

What Related Research Has Been Reported?

We are not the first to discover that traditional measures of performance are
not correlated with the total returns of shareholders. The impact of information arrival on stock returns has been studied extensively in the accounting and finance literature. Early research by Ball and Brown (1968) on the
relationship between earnings and stock prices led to a series of papers that
develop the link between earnings announcements, expectations, and share
prices. Jones, Latane, and Rendleman (1982), and Foster, Olsen, and Shevlin
(1984) investigate daily stock price movements around quarterly earnings
announcements, while Bernard and Thomas (1990) investigate 100,000 quarterly earnings announcements and their effect on share prices. Easton and
Harris (1991) analyze earnings as an explanatory variable for stock returns.

Research by Biddle, Bowen, and Wallace (1997) and Biddle and Seow
(1991) shows that reported earnings are more highly associated with the
total return to shareholders (TRS) and firm values than economic profit [as
proxied by Stern Stewart's measure, economic value added, or EVA (1991)],
residual income (defined as operating profit minus a capital charge), or
cash flow from operations.

However, this literature concentrates predominantly on the impact on
stock returns of *short-term* information. A subset of the accounting literature is concerned with the value relevance or information content of *long-
term* expectations. For example, Collins, Kothari, Shanken, and Sloan
(1994) add the future year's earnings into the regression of current annual

returns on current annual earnings. They note that this addition increases the explanatory power of the regression three to six times as compared to a regression of returns on current earnings alone. Lundholm and Myers (2004) characterize current stock returns as a function of unexpected earnings for the current period and the change in expectations about the sum of the next three years' earnings. Their analysis is carried out in the context of how voluntary disclosure affects the explanatory power of future earnings in the returns-earnings regression. Liu and Thomas (2000) test a model that has unexpected returns as its dependent variable and the present value of unexpected earnings as independent variables. They find that this specification dramatically improves the explanatory power, and that the elasticity of changes in unexpected returns to changes in the present value of unexpected earnings converges to unity, as predicted by the residual income model.

A paper by Amir, Lev, and Sougiannis (1999), based on cross-sectional data from 1982–1997, finds that analyst expectations explain roughly 40 percent of the variation of the total return to shareholders, but when causality is investigated, only 12 percent of the variation of TRS seems to be causally attributable to analysts. Furthermore, the influence of analysts appears to be asymmetric, with 11 percent of the TRS of "good news" firms explained by analyst-generated expectations and 40 percent of the TRS of "bad news" firms attributable to changes in analyst expectations.

The central distinction that separates EBM from more traditional measures of performance is that information about changes in analyst expectations, both short-term and long-term, is immediately relevant for stock returns. Although the literature on biases in analyst earnings forecasts is related to our work, it is not central to it.[2] Even though the level of expectations may be biased, changes in the level of expectations are not necessarily biased (particularly if the bias is constant and known) and most certainly contain information.

Our research also is relevant to an extensive literature that tests for systematic factors that are observed at the beginning of each time period and that can explain the cross-section of equity returns. Over a decade ago, Fama and French (1992), using monthly returns data for stocks listed on the NYSE, AMEX, and NASDAQ during the 1963–1990 period, concluded that the book-to-market value of equity ratio and market capitalization (size) were significant factors and that beta added no additional explanatory power. Kothari, Shanken, and Sloan (1995) commented that, among other things, it is better to use annual data to avoid the January effect [see Keim (1983)] and to avoid a sample selection bias introduced when book-to-

---

[2]For example, see Ackert and Athanassakos (1997), Easterwood and Nutt (1999), and Lim (2000).

market data is taken from Compustat. In this spirit, our analysis also deliberately uses annual data for large companies (S&P 500). Furthermore, we
introduce changes in expectations (about earnings, earnings growth, the
cost of equity, and capital investment) as logical drivers of TRS relative to
the market. The aforementioned papers on systematic factors do not measure company-specific changes in expectations, thereby relegating all of
this information to the error term. Indeed, it is the error term, the unexpected component of TRS generated by the arrival of information, that we
seek to explain, not the systematic factors of equilibrium pricing.

Managerial Implications of EBM

Our research establishes that there is a strong link between market-adjusted
returns to shareholders and changes in expectations about future earnings
along with the beneficial impact of reduced noise. A reasonable question
at this point is: *So what?* What exactly would top management do differently? Although there will be much more to say about this later in the book,
the highlights can be summarized here.

How to Measure Business Unit Performance

First, it is inadvisable to judge performance of business units by measuring
their realized return on invested capital vis-à-vis the weighted average cost
of capital (WACC)—an objective criterion. It is not necessarily true that the
firm's stock price will go up if a business unit earns more than its cost of capital. To understand how the stock price will move, we must use a subjective
criterion—namely, did the business unit earn more or less than expected? If
it earned more than expected, the stock price will adjust upward, and vice
versa. Other so-called objective measures of performance that do not measure performance versus expectations—for example, earnings per share,
earnings growth, the return on invested capital, and sales revenue growth—
all have unacceptably low correlation with the total returns to shareholders.

Expectations are subjectively determined via communications channels
from top management to the external world of analysts and shareholders,
and via channels internally between top and middle levels of management
(see Figure 2.2).

How to Communicate with Analysts and Investors

The most often asked question regarding external communication is: "What
prevents management from misleading the analysts by manipulation of the
reported performance?"

As we shall see later on, what counts is the signal-to-noise ratio. That
is, the change in expectations—the signal, divided by noise, measured as

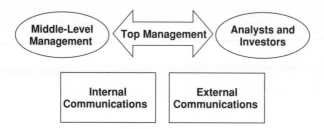

FIGURE 2.2   Importance of internal and external communication.

the dispersion of various estimates of the signal. If management has a constant bias in the signal that it sends to the market—for example, being overly optimistic or pessimistic—the market will learn what the bias is and correct for it when interpreting the message. If the bias is constantly changing, then noise is greater and the stock price will decline. If then, top management is compensated in stock they may, for a short time, be able to manipulate the stock price upward; however, when their deceit is discovered, the stock price will decline to a price lower than the starting price because more noise has been introduced into the communications channel.

How to Communicate with Middle Management

The big question about internal communications is: *How can top management set reasonable expectations for middle (and even lower levels) of management?* This is a function that is supposed to be implemented via a budgeting process. Every company has one, but implementation—namely, the debate necessary to set appropriate expected targets—is often worse than useless. One executive commented that doing the budget was more painful than having a root canal and a lot less useful. Yet there are plenty of examples of chief executive officers who use the budgeting and planning system as their primary management tool. At Emerson Electric, CEO Chuck Knight is alleged to have spent about 55 percent of his time conducting business unit reviews that established expected performance. He was very well informed about the economics that drove his businesses and could not be sandbagged by executives who tried to set expectations too low. Later on in the book there will be much more on how to budget and plan by setting expectations well.

How to Decide on an Investment Strategy

Aside from the aspect of understanding just how management should best go about the setting of expectations, there are important implications for operational decisions. Two of the major choices are what mix of businesses should a company have in its portfolio and which of the portfolio of busi-

TABLE 2.1   A Strategic Framework for Resource Allocation

Can we exceed expected Business Unit performance?		Can we earn *ROIC* > *WACC* on new investment?	
		Yes	No
	Yes	Grow	Harvest
	No	Transform	Sell or Abandon

nesses should receive allocations of fresh capital (and other resources) to accomplish their mission.

Both new investment and core assets (i.e., existing businesses) should earn the cost of capital. A high-*ROIC* business that can earn more than its cost of capital on new investment and can exceed expectations on existing invested capital should receive fresh capital and grow. If, however, it cannot earn more than the cost of capital on new investment, but can still exceed expectations, then it should be harvested. Next, if it cannot exceed expectations with existing capital, but can earn more than the cost of capital on new investment, then it should transform itself by making the new investment. Finally, if it can neither earn more than expected nor earn its cost of capital, then it should be sold or abandoned.

Together, the four policies described can be used to provide a framework for assessing the strategy of a company (see Table 2.1). A more in-depth discussion of this framework is provided in Chapter 4. Its main value is to force one to find those activities that have the greatest likelihood of bettering expected performance that is already built into the stock price.

What Are We Trying to Explain?[3]

Our research begins with more than passing curiosity about what it is that we are trying to explain. Of course, it is the total return to shareholders (TRS). Yet, we want a company-specific measure. For this we started with the total return to shareholders defined as the capital gains and reinvested dividends during the year divided by the stock price at the beginning of the year. But because we want to study company-specific performance, we remove the effect of general market movements.

To show why this is important, take a look at Table 2.2, where we provide an example of returns for two hypothetical companies. As seen in

---

[3]If you do not wish to be mired in details, and are willing to accept our conclusions, skip to the summary of this chapter. Otherwise, read on.

Figure 2.3(a), both are positively correlated with the market. They move up and down with the market. Figure 2.3(b) graphs the returns of Company X against Company Y and because they are both driven by what happens in the market, their unadjusted total returns are positively correlated. But we are especially interested in looking at the unexpected company performance relative to the market. When we do, we should see that the two companies are actually negatively correlated with each other. Unexpected company performance is one of the components of the total return to shareholders:

$$\begin{aligned} \text{Total Return to} \\ \text{Shareholders} = &\text{ Cost of equity} \\ &+ \text{unexpected market movements} \\ &+ \text{unexpected company-specific} \\ &\quad\text{return relative to the market} \end{aligned} \quad (2.1)$$

Unexpected market returns are not of interest to us because management performance should be measured by changes in things that it can control. Note that the expected total return to shareholders is the same as the cost of equity at the start of each day. However, at the end of each day (ex post), the actual TRS can even be negative—if, for example, the unexpected market movement is negative and unexpected company performance is zero.

Consequently, we remove the effect of the market from company returns in order to see how the company did relative to the market. This is done by dividing the total return to shareholders by the market return as follows:

$$MAR = (1 + \text{TRS})/(1 + \text{Market return})$$

The last two columns of Table 2.2 show the calculation of market-adjusted returns (*MAR*) and in Figure 2.3(c), the *MAR* for Company X is

TABLE 2.2 Hypothetical Returns of the Market and for Shares of Companies X and Y

Market Index	Price of Stock X	Price of Stock Y	Unadjusted Returns			Market-Adjusted Returns	
			Market	Stock X	Stock Y	Stock X	Stock Y
100	$10.00	$10.00	—	—	—	—	—
110	10.50	12.00	10%	5%	20%	−5%	9%
150	12.00	20.00	36%	14%	67%	−16%	23%
105	10.00	10.00	−30%	−17%	−50%	19%	−29%
90	10.00	7.00	−14%	0%	−30%	16%	−19%

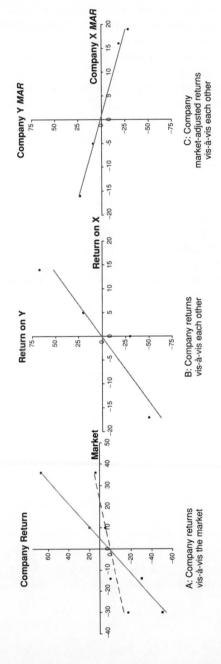

FIGURE 2.3   Rate-of-return regressions.

plotted against the *MAR* for Company Y. Now their company-specific performance: having removed the market effect, is seen to be negatively correlated relative to each other. In Figure 2.3(b), when the market effect was driving their returns their unadjusted returns were positively correlated. This result is called spurious correlation and it is caused when a missing variable that is affecting both companies (e.g., the market return) masks the company-specific performance.

This is a long way of saying that we have chosen to remove the effect of general market movements from the total returns to shareholders. Most companies are positively correlated with the market. By removing the market effect, we get a clearer look at the relationship between company-specific performance and company-specific unexpected returns to shareholders.

Test of Traditional (but Incomplete) Performance Measures

We collected data for the S&P 500 firms for a seven year period, 1992–1998. Of 3,500 observations, about 13.7 percent were missing. Using the market-adjusted returns for each company in each year as the variable we were trying to explain, we tried four traditional measures of performance as drivers of *MAR* in a simple regression. The four measures are, respectively, earnings per share, the growth in earnings per share, EVA, and the growth in EVA. This second variable, EVA, is called economic value added, and is defined as the spread between *ROIC* and the cost of capital multiplied by the amount of capital invested. We purchased our EVA data from Stern Stewart, the company that has registered the mnemonic. Because market-adjusted returns are expressed as percentages, and *EPS* and EVA in dollars, we divided each of the four explanatory variables by the beginning-of-period price per share so that all variables were percentages.

The results shown in Table 2.3 confirm the published work of others (e.g., Biddle et al). There is an extremely weak relationship between the traditional performance measures and shareholder returns, but the highest *r*-squared is only six percent. Furthermore, the *r*-squared statistics for EVA are worse than those for *EPS*.

The failure of these variables to explain the return to shareholders should not be surprising because neither contains revisions in expectations.[4] The next section gives the empirical results when changes in analyst expectations enter the picture.

---

[4]Note that the regressions are individual company observations and are not grouped. See Chapter 12 for a discussion of grouping.

TABLE 2.3   Very Low Correlation

| | MAR versus EPS, EPS growth, EVA, or EVA growth (t-statistics in parentheses) | | | |
	A	B	C	D
Intercept	−0.099	−0.0441	−0.003	−0.004
	(14.02)	(−8.33)	(−5.59)	(−6.87)
EPS_t / S_{t-1}	1.086			
	(12.89)			
$\Delta EPS_t / S_{t-1}$		0.669		
		(11.10)		
EVA / S_{t-1}			0.001	
			(6.786)	
$\Delta EVA / S_{t-1}$				0.003
				(10.02)
Number of observations	2,582	2,579	2,194	2,185
Adjusted R-squared	0.06	0.05	0.02	0.04
F-statistic	166.1	123.3	46.1	100.4

Source: Copeland, Dolgoff and Moel, Review of Accounting Studies, 2004.

What Are the Results Regarding Changes in Expectations of Earnings?

Two data bases, IBES and Zacks, provide weekly updates of sell-side analyst expectations of earnings—one year ahead (i.e., the current fiscal year), two years ahead (next year), and long-term earnings growth (three to five years).

Before showing the results, let us describe the model that we believe in. First, the total return to shareholders is defined as capital gains plus free cash flows (usually paid out as dividends):

$$\text{TRS} = \frac{S_1 - S_0 + FCF_1}{S_0} \tag{2.2}$$

Next, we assume that the current stock price is the present value of cash flows (available to shareholders) expected in the future based on information available at the current time. We use E_0 to designate current expectations, and k is the cost of (equity) capital in the following equation:

$$S_0 = \frac{E_0(FCF_1)}{1+k} + \frac{E_0(FCF_2)}{(1+k)^2} + \ldots + \frac{E_0(FCF_t)}{(1+k)^t} \tag{2.3}$$

During the period new information arrives and new expectations, E_1, are formed. Thus, the stock price at the end of the period can be written as the present value of cash flows from that period on, and are based on a new set of expectations.

$$S_1 = \frac{E_1(FCF_2)}{1+k} + \frac{E_1(FCF_3)}{(1+k)^2} + \ldots + \frac{E_1(FCF_t)}{(1+k)^t} \qquad (2.4)$$

By substituting the definitions of the beginning and end-of-period stock price into the equation for the total return to shareholders, we get the following expression:

$$\text{TRS} = \frac{1}{S_0}\left\{ FCF_1 - \left[\frac{E_0(FCF_1)}{1+k}\right] + \left[\frac{E_1(FCF_2)}{(1+k)} - \frac{E_0(FCF_2)}{(1+k)^2}\right] \right.$$
$$\left. + \ldots + \left[\frac{E_1(FCF_t)}{(1+k)^{t+1}} - \frac{E_0(FCF_t)}{(1+k)^{t+1}}\right]\right\}$$

Notice that the total return to shareholders is a function of the change in expectations this time period about every time period in the future, except for the difference between actual and expected cash flows in the first year. Note also that (one over) the beginning-of-period stock price plays an important role because it contains information.

From our earlier discussion we want to focus on company-specific stock market performance and by so doing, prevent the spurious correlation that would result if market return information inadvertently were to be included in both sides of our regression. Undoubtedly, there is market information imbedded in changes in expectations of company earnings—the explanatory variables in our regression. But by using market-adjusted returns instead of TRS, we have removed market information from the dependent variable that we wish to explain and thus avoid spurious correlation.

The multiple regression equation that we actually tested was

$$MAR_{it} = a + b\ln\left[\frac{E(1,1)}{E(1,0)}\right] + c\ln\left[\frac{E(2,1)}{E(2,0)}\right] + d[E(L,1) - E(L,0)] + e\ln\left[\frac{1}{S_{t-1}}\right]$$
$$(2.5)$$

The left-hand side is the variable that we wish to explain, namely the market-adjusted returns for the ith company in the tth year. The first term on the right-hand side is a constant. The second term, $b\ln[E(1,1)/E(1,0)]$, is the percent change in the expectation of the current year's earnings estimated as the natural logarithm of analyst expectations of this year's earnings at the end of the year, $E(1,1)$, divided by analyst expectations of earnings at the beginning of the current year, $E(1,0)$.[5] The third term is the percent change in the expectation of earnings for next year by the average analyst during the current year. The fourth term is the change in expectations about three- to five-year earnings growth made by the average analyst this year. Finally, the fifth term is the natural logarithm of the inverse of the beginning-of-period stock price,

Results are given in Table 2.4, and are highly significant. In column A the r-squared is 47 percent, roughly 10 times higher than those in Table 2.3. Changes in expectations explain close to half of the company-specific returns to shareholders. This result is hardly surprising given that it is necessary for company earnings performance to exceed what was expected in order for market-adjusted returns to be positive.

Even more interesting are the results for the individual earnings expectations variables. A measure of statistical significance called the t-test is given in parentheses. If it is greater in absolute value than 1.96, the coefficient that it tests is said to be statistically significant at the 95 percent confidence level. Note that the change in expectations this year about this year's earnings in column B are statistically significant when the other changes in expectations are left out. But in column A, where changes in expectations about next year's and long-term earnings expectations are included, it washes out and is not significant.

When information about this year's earnings is all that we have, its correlation with information about second-year earnings and earnings even more distant in time is high enough to make it significant as a stand-alone variable that can explain the current year's return to shareholders. However, when information about the long-term performance of the company is also used to explain current returns, then the current year's earnings loses its explanatory power.

The significant variables in the full multiple regression (column A of Table 2.4) are changes in expectations this year about next year's earnings and about long-term earnings growth. In both cases the probability of get-

---

[5]Note that if r is the percentage growth in earnings then

$$E(1,1) = E(1,0)e^{rt}$$
$$e^{rt} = \frac{E(1,1)}{E(1,0)}$$
$$r = \ln\left(\frac{E(1.1)}{E(1,0)}\right)$$

since $t = 1$.

TABLE 2.4   Market-Adjusted Stock Returns Are Highly Correlated with Changes in Expectations

	A	B	C	D
Intercept	0.360	0.430	0.420	0.461
	(18.108)	(19.81)	(18.88)	(20.74)
$\ln[E(1,1)/E(1,0)]$	0.018	0.324		
	(0.94)	(22.25)		
$\ln[E(2,1)/E(2,0)]$	0.389		0.280	
	(18.22)		(23.25)	
$E(L,1) - E(L,0)$	3.269			4.105
	(16.08)			(19.79)
$\ln(1/S_{t-1})$	0.117	0.142	0.139	0.159
Number of observations	2,318	2,491	2,365	2,560
Adjusted R-squared	0.47	0.31	0.32	0.28
F-statistic	512.9	567.7	562.1	489.3

ting these results by chance is less than one-thousandth of one percent. Both variables are highly significant. Their impact on market-adjusted returns (*MAR*) is measured by the regression coefficients found in Table 2.4. The coefficient of the change in the expectation of this year's earnings from the beginning of the year to its end has a value of 0.018 in column A. This means that 1 percent higher expectations about this year's earnings is associated with 0.018 percent higher *MAR* for the year—a trivial and insignificant result. In contrast, a 1 percent increase this year about the expectation of next year's earnings growth increases *MAR* by 0.389 percent. Most interesting of all is the coefficient of long-term earnings growth. It says that a 1 percent increase in expectations results in a 3.269 percent increase in *MAR*.

The form of the variables makes interpretation a necessity. Remember that the first two variables are changes in earnings expectations, which are dollar numbers expressed as a ratio in logarithmic form. For example, if expected earnings per share was $2.00 at the beginning of the year and rose to $2.30 per share at the end of the year, the measure that we use is $\ln(\$2.30/\$2.00) = \ln(1.15) = 14\%$. Note that the natural logarithm, $\ln(1.15)$, is the continuous compounding rate of return. The third variable, the change in the expectation of three- to five-year earnings growth is already expressed as a percentage—therefore no logarithmic transformation is necessary.

If you believe in a discounted cash flow valuation model of the market value of equity that we used in our derivation of the regression equation, then the empirical results are very consistent with such a model.

TABLE 2.5   Median Values of the Independent Variables in Table 2.4

Year	ln(E(1,1)/E(1,0))	ln(E(2,1)/E(2,0))	E(L,1) − E(L,0)
1992	−0.0159	−0.0336	0.0670
1993	−0.0202	−0.0413	−0.1790
1994	0.0013	0.0012	−0.0290
1995	0.0097	0.0042	0.0000
1996	0.0038	0.0001	0.1790
1997	−0.0016	−0.0094	0.1490
1998	−0.0358	−0.0466	−0.1085

Changes in expectations about current earnings add very little to the discounted cash flow valuation of the firm, therefore it is not surprising that expectations about this year's earnings have an insignificant effect on this year's market-adjusted return. Next year's earnings are more uncertain to begin with; consequently, a change in expectations about them is statistically significant. But the coefficient of changes of expectations about long-term earnings growth is 8 to 10 times larger—and its effect on market-adjusted returns is larger—than changes in expectations about second-year earnings.

Table 2.5 shows the median values of the three independent variables that were used in the multiple regression of Table 2.4. First, note that the values are all of the same order of magnitude, which means that we have made a reasonable interpretation of the relative impact of each variable as measured by the size of its coefficient. Second, note that the signs of the median changes in expectations about the first and second year's earnings are the same in seven out of seven years, indicating that they tend to be signals of similar information. The sign of changes in expectations about long-term earnings growth is the same in three years, the opposite in three years, and zero in one year. This indicates that long-term earnings tend to contain different information, a fact that helps to explain why they have a much larger impact on current MAR. Over the entire sample we found that expected earnings for this year and next year are highly correlated (roughly 80 percent), but that both have relatively low correlation with three- to five-year earnings growth expectations (roughly 30 percent correlation).

What are the conclusions that we can draw from the empirical evidence that has been presented and published by others as well as ourselves?

1. Measures of performance that do not contain changes in expectations have low correlation with company-specific performance (as measured by MAR).

2. A multiple regression that uses changes in expectations this year about this year's earnings, next year's earnings, and about three- to five-year earnings growth has a highly significant correlation with company-specific performance (as measured by *MAR*).
3. In the presence of the other two expectation variables, changes in expectations about the current year's earnings are not significantly different from zero.
4. In the multiple regression, the expectations variable with the greatest impact on current *MAR* is changes in expectations about long-term earnings growth.

The emerging story is that expectations matter. But there is more. First, we provide evidence that expectations about three- to five-year earnings growth is a proxy for long-term earnings growth. Then we look to see if changes in expectations about the cost of capital and about capital expenditures matter (they don't). Then we establish that noisy signals have less effect on *MAR* than clear signals (noise is bad.)

Three- to Five-Year Earnings Growth Is a Proxy for the Value of Long-Term Earnings

We believe that analyst expectations of three- to five-year earnings growth serve as a proxy for long-term earnings growth. If so, those firms with a higher percentage of their current market value represented by the value of growth should also have greater sensitivity to changes in analyst expectations about the growth in earnings. To test this intuition we measured the value of growth, G_{it}, as the current market value of the entity, V_{it}, minus the perpetuity value $EBIT(1-T)/WACC$.[6]

$$G_{it} = \frac{V_{it} - [EBIT(1-T)/WACC]}{V_{it}} \qquad (2.6)$$

For each company across the seven years of data, we averaged this estimate of the percentage of the value of the firm attributable to growth. We then rank-ordered the resulting sample into growth deciles and reran the regression equation to obtain estimates of the coefficients of the three

---

[6]*EBIT* is earnings before interest and taxes, *T* is the tax rate, and *WACC* is the weighted average cost of capital.

TABLE 2.6   Regression Results

The relative impact of changes in expectations about three- to five-year growth, F_{it}, regressed as the percentage of market value represented by growth, G, with t-statistics in parentheses.

Intercept	0.655
	(11.53)
Percent of Entity Value attributable to Growth (G)	0.214
	(2.35)
Number of observations	10
Adjusted R-squared	0.335
F-statistic	5.54

Source: Copeland, Dolgoff and Moel, *Review of Accounting Studies*, 2004.

change in expectation variables. Next, we measured the relative strength of the coefficient of three- to five-year earnings growth as follows:[7]

$$F = \frac{d}{b+c+d} \tag{2.7}$$

The final step was to run a simple regression to see if F is related to G:

$$F_j = a + bG_{avg} + \varepsilon_j \tag{2.8}$$

The result is shown in Table 2.5. There is indeed a statistically significant positive relationship between the sensitivity of *MAR* to changes in analyst three- to five-year expectations (measured by F) and the percentage of the total value of the firm attributable to growth (measured by G). Table 2.6 shows the relationship, which is also plotted in Figure 2.4.

What Are the Additional Effects of Changes in Expectations of *WACC* and CAPEX?

If we go back to the previous chapter where the one-period definition of EBM was developed (see Equation 1.2), we recall that it had three terms. The first was the difference between actual and expected return on invested capital multiplied by the amount of capital in place and could be inter-

---

[7]The coefficients b, c, and d are defined in Equation 2.5.

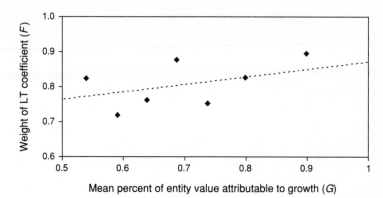

FIGURE 2.4   The relationship between *F* and *G*.

Note: *F* is the relative impact of revisions in analyst expectatons about long-term growth on *MAR*; *G* is the percentage of market capitalization attributed to growth. Thus, the vertical axis, *F*, is the change in *MAR* per unit of change in analyst expectations of long-term growth in earnings (relative to the changes in all expectations). The horizontal axis, *G*, is a measure of the percent of market value attributable to growth (i.e., the entity market cap minus the perpetuity value).

Source: Copeland, Dolgoff, and Moel, *Review of Accounting Studies*, 2004.

preted as "work core assets harder." The second was the difference between the actual and expected cost of capital multiplied by the amount of capital in place and implied that unexpected declines in the cost of capital pushed value up. And third, unexpected new investment, if profitable (i.e., if *ROIC* > *WACC*), would create value. The algebraic expression is repeated below.

$$
\begin{aligned}
\text{EBM} &= \text{Actual } EP - \text{Expected } EP \\
\text{EBM} &= [\text{Actual } ROIC - \text{Expected } ROIC]\,(I) \\
&\quad - [\text{Actual } WACC - \text{Expected } WACC]\,(I) \\
&\quad + [ROIC - WACC][\text{Actual } I - \text{Expected } I]
\end{aligned}
\tag{2.9}
$$

Note that the regression results used analyst expectations of earnings as input data, but the one-period definition provided in Equation 2.9 tells us that unexpected changes in the cost of capital and in the amount of profitable investment should also be important. This section of the chapter reports the results.

To test the effect of unexpected changes in the cost of equity, we use the capital asset pricing model to estimate the beginning- and end-of-year cost of equity, and assume that the difference between the two is unexpected. The beginning-of-year cost of equity is calculated as:

$$
k_t = r_{jt} + \left[E(r_m) - r_{jt} \right] \beta_{ft}
\tag{2.10}
$$

where the risk-free rate r_{ft} at the beginning of the year was given by
the expected one-year forward 10-year Treasury spot rate implied by the
Treasury yield curve. The market risk premium $[E(r_m) - r_f]$ is assumed
to be constant, and equal to 5.5 percent. The BARRA predicted beta is
used for both the beginning-of-year and end-of-year calculations.[8] At the
end of the year, we calculate the cost of equity in a similar way, using
end-of-period values for the risk-free rate (i.e., the actual 10-year Treasury
spot rate) and beta. Unexpected changes in the cost of equity are highly
significant with a negative sign, indicating that when there are unexpected
increases in the required return on equity, total return to shareholders is
reduced.

Although the theoretical model of total return to shareholders predicts
a relationship between unexpected increases in capital expenditures and
TRS, we do not find a statistically significant relationship for any of the
models of unexpected capital expenditures. We believe this to be more a
result of our incomplete modeling of expected capital expenditures than
a problem with the theory. Perhaps as analyst data tracking services
become more sophisticated and complete, future tests of expected capital
expenditures will be more fruitful.

What Is the Effect of Noise?

Thus far we have been speaking of signals (primarily about changes in
expected earnings) between management and the analyst/investor community. Now we focus on the signal-to-noise ratio. To explain why the
signal-to-noise ratio is important let's use a simple example. Suppose that
two companies are expected to earn $5.00 per share, and that both
announce that they unexpectedly have earned $1.00 per share more than
expected. However, prior to the announcement, the lowest analyst expectation for company A was $4.90 per share and the highest analyst expecta-
tion was $5.10 per share—a fairly narrow range, indicating a low level of
noise about expectations. Consequently, given the announcement that earnings per share will be $6.00, every analyst will upgrade company A. For
company B, suppose that the range of forecasted earnings extended from
a low of $2.00 to a high of $8.00, reflecting much greater uncertainty in the
minds of analysts—uncertainty that we measure by the standard deviation
of analyst forecasts and refer to as "noise". For company B, an announcement of $6.00 per share will not be greeted unanimously with upgrades.

[8]BARRA is a firm that provides estimates of forward-looking betas, in contrast to
the historical betas normally derived through regression analysis by practitioners.

Those analysts who held expectations of earnings greater than $6.00 may actually downgrade company B.

We define the signal-to-noise ratio as

$$\text{SNR} = \frac{\text{change in analyst expectations}}{\text{standard deviation of analyst expectation}} \qquad (2.11)$$

and we expect two effects of noise on the market-adjusted returns. First, companies with greater variability in returns also have greater dispersion of analyst forecasts, i.e. greater noise. Second, we expect that an increase in noise during a given period of time will imply more uncertainty and therefore a lower stock price—with the implication that increases in noise will be associated with lower market-adjusted returns.

The results are shown in Table 2.7. Table 2.7(a) indicates that there is a statistically significant positive relationship between the standard deviation of total return to shareholders and the level of noise. This is a fact of life, it seems. Companies that are in riskier businesses are more difficult to forecast and, consequently, there is greater disagreement among the analysts that follow them. Likewise, companies in industries going through sig-

TABLE 2.7   Noise and Total Return to Shareholders

Table 2.7(a) shows a regression where the standard deviation of TRS (calculated from monthly return data) is the dependent variable and where the three independent variables are the standard deviation of analyst expectations at the beginning of the period, scaled by the beginning-of-period *EPS* (for each of the three intervals—the current year, next year, and long-term).

	Panel A
Intercept	(0.217) (50.13)
$\frac{SD[E(1,0)]}{EPS(0)}$	−0.0036 (−0.53)
$\frac{SD[E(2,0)]}{EPS(0)}$	−0.0001 (−0.02)
$SD[E(L,0)]$	0.0169 (14.87)
N	2,331
Adjusted R-squared	0.086
F-statistic	73.834

TABLE 2.7   Noise and Total Return to Shareholders

Table 2.7(b) shows regression results where *MAR* is the dependent variable and where there are two sets of three independent variables. The first set of variables uses the same measures of changes in expectations from Table 2.4. The second set measures the change in noise about each of the three expectations (this year, next year, and long-term) measured by the natural logarithm of the ratio of the standard deviation (*SD*) of the end-of-year analyst forecasts to the standard deviation of the beginning-of-year analyst forecasts (*t*-statistics in parentheses).

	A	B	C	D
	Panel B			
Intercept	0.009 (2.23)	−0.006 (−1.08)	0.360 (18.11)	0.340 (15.92)
$\ln[E(1,1)/E(1,0)]$	−0.006 (−0.34)	−0.016 (−0.89)	0.018 (0.94)	−0.0059 (0.31)
$\ln[E(2,1)/E(2,0)]$	0.465 (22.30)	0.471 (21.73)	0.389 (18.22)	0.401 (18.09)
$E(L,1)-E(L,0)$	3.492 (17.73)	3.888 (16.40)	3.269 (16.08)	3.552 (14.66)
$\ln(1/S_{t-1})$			0.117 (18.82)	0.114 (17.41)
$\ln\left(SD[E(1,1)]/SD[E(1,0)]\right)$		−0.016 (−2.74)		0.011 (−1.83)
$\ln\left(SD[E(2,1)]/SD[E(2,0)]\right)$		−0.016 (−2.64)		−0.019 (−3.28)
$SD[E(L,1)]-SD[E(L,0)]$		−0.655 (−2.35)		−0.364 (−.26)
N	2,699	2,318	2,318	1,981
Adj. *R*-squared	0.38	0.41	0.47	0.50
F-statistic	558.7	270.6	512.9	280.1

Source: Copeland, Dolgoff and Moel, *Review of Accounting Studies*, 2004.

nificant changes (e.g., due to regulatory changes) may have higher levels of noise associated with their expected earnings.

Table 2.7(b) finds that increases in the level of noise are associated with lower market-adjusted returns, in a multiple regression that (in effect) holds all other variables constant. In column D, three variables measure changes in expectations, one measures the inverse of the historic stock price, and the last three measure the percent changes in the level of noise. Overall, the multiple regression explains 50 percent of the cross-sectional variation of market-adjusted returns (an *r*-squared that is 10 times the *r*-squared of traditional performance measures such as eps, the growth in EPS, EVA, or the growth in EVA). Furthermore, all three variables that measure the change in noise have the predicted sign—there is a negative relationship between noise and *MAR*. Two of the three terms that measure the change in noise are "marginally significant" and the third (the change in noise this year about forecasts of next year's earnings) is strongly significant.

Summary and Conclusions

Evidence that was presented in this chapter and was published in the *Review of Accounting Studies* concludes that

1. Measures of performance that do not capture changes in expectations (e.g., earnings growth, EVA, and EVA growth are, for any practical purposes, unrelated to the total return to shareholders.
2. Expectations-based measures of performance are highly correlated with market-adjusted TRS. In particular,
   - Changes this year in expectations about this year's earnings are not statistically significant.
   - Changes this year about expectations of next year's earnings and about three- to five-year earnings growth are both highly significant, but the latter variable has 10 times the impact on TRS as the former.
   - High-growth firms are more sensitive to changes in three- to five-year growth expectations than lower-growth firms.
   - Increases in noise, as measured by changes in the variance of analyst expectations, are associated with lower return to shareholders.

These simple facts have profound implications for management. Most of them are chapters in this book. One can summarize them all by observing that EBM is subjective in nature. You create value by exceeding expectations rather than setting an objective hurdle such as cost of capital.

Managerial Implications

This section is written with management in mind. It reviews the specific implications of Expectations-Based Management for managing existing businesses, for making wise capital expenditure decisions, for understanding the role of the weighted average cost of capital, for creating value via capital efficiency, for understanding the market's expectations for your company by reverse engineering your stock price, and for thinking about incentive design. Chapter 10 is a capstone that talks about how to implement EBM for impact.

CHAPTER 3

Management of Existing Businesses

In the first two chapters we saw why our understanding of the return to shareholders focuses on changes in expectations. Chapter 1 set up EBM as it contrasts with common metrics used to manage corporations. Chapter 2 showed the evidence proving that shareholder returns are driven by changes in expectations about firm performance. To many this conclusion seems self-evident, since they frequently see share prices reacting to earnings surprises. Chapter 2 also showed the evidence for a more complex view of the world—that the market really does discount short-term surprises and focuses on changes in expectations about the long term. A manager or an investor must understand how different factors affect short-term and long-term expectations differently—those effects that are temporary and those that are permanent.

We have demonstrated that the market does not really react to short-term earnings, but instead it reacts primarily to news about long-term earnings growth. It just so happens that a good deal of the time news about short-term trends coincides with news about the long-term. When they differ, however, the current stock price changes along with changes in long-term expectations.

In this and the following chapters of Part II we focus on the managerial implications of EBM. It is not just the conventional wisdom about the way that the marketplace reacts to short-term earnings that's wrong—it's also the conventional wisdom about how to manage a business for value creation. When we apply EBM thinking to basic managerial decisions about investment and business performance measurement, we get some results that point toward two common categories of management error. We introduced them in Chapter 1 where we called them investment traps.

This chapter focuses on EBM implications for running an existing business. Specifically, we discuss such questions as how to measure business unit performance, make decisions related to reinvestment of capital, and how EBM intersects with business unit planning and budgeting. In the next chapter we extend EBM toward new investment decision-making, portfolio management, and related decisions.

Measuring Business Unit Performance

There are two ways that business unit performance is typically evaluated—against seemingly objective standards and against relative standards. Objective standards include those we discussed in earlier chapters such as EVA, which sets the *WACC* as the hurdle rate for value-creating performance. Most companies make adjustments to these metrics to focus on business unit operating performance—for example, looking at operating profit or cash flow (EBITDA) rather than EVA or earnings per share (*EPS*). More sophisticated approaches tend to include some measure of balance sheet costs attributed to divisional performance, either through the use of direct measurement of balance sheet assets or through charges for the use of capital "allocated" from the corporate parent.

Objective standards are those that are most frequently used for evaluating managerial performance, creating and managing divisional budgets, and sometimes making investment and divestment decisions. In managing the business mix, the corporate center more frequently compares the performance of business units relative to each other rather than each relative to its own expectations. Later, in Chapter 4, we explore this issue in depth.

We've already mentioned the problems with some of the most common benchmarks used to evaluate corporate performance, such as *EPS* and *ROIC*. For example, a focus on *EPS* can encourage value destruction through "purchases" of earnings using capital expenditures—ignoring the balance sheet while focusing on the income statement. Similarly, an *ROIC*-focus can encourage harvesting as short-term performance becomes favored over the alternative, namely meeting or exceeding long-term expectations. As many corporations take corporate objectives down to the business unit level, these metrics-driven issues frequently cause issues for line management as well.

Moreover, the way in which these metrics are typically implemented at the business unit level may create even more problems for value management. For example, as most companies implement EVA systems, they set business unit targets that require either positive or increasing EVA. Table 3.1 provides a simple numerical example of a company that has four business units all with the same weighted average cost of capital, but different performance depending on the way it is measured.

TABLE 3.1 Performance Measured Two Ways

	Capital	EBIT/ Actual ROIC = R	Capital Charge/ WACC = W	EVA/ (R − W)	EBIT Expected/ R	EBM/ A(R) − E(R)
Large stable unit	$5,000	$1,200	$500	$700	$1,500	$−300
		24%	10%	14%	30%	−6%
Start-up unit	1,000	100	100	0	200	−100
		10%	10%	0%	20%	−10%
Harvest unit	2,000	200	200	0	−100	300
		10%	10%	0%	−5%	15%
Medium unit	2,000	300	200	100	400	−100
		15%	10%	5%	20%	−5%
Company	10,000	1,800	1,000	800	2,000	−200
		18%	10%	8%	20%	−2%

The company overall is expected to earn a 20 percent return on its invested capital, i.e., $2,000. It has failed to accomplished this objective, falling short by $200; therefore the total return to shareholders will be less than the 10 percent they expected. The capital market will establish a beginning-of-year value for the company that reflects their expected 20 percent after-tax return on invested capital. EBM measures the performance of the business units as shown in the last column of Table 3.1. Expected, i.e., forecasted, *ROIC* is subtracted from actual *ROIC* to determine the amount by which the business unit exceeded expectations, and the spread is multiplied by the amount of capital invested to get an EBM measure of value creation. Note that the large, stable unit was expected to earn $1,500 but actually earned only $1,200; therefore it failed to meet expectations (forecast) and destroyed $300 of value. The harvest unit was expected to lose five percent, but earned 15 percent instead, thereby contributing $300 of value for the firm.

There are two equivalent ways of valuing the firm at the beginning of the year, assuming that cash flows are constant over time. The first capitalizes expected operating cash flow by dividing it by the cost of capital; therefore the value is:

$$V = E[EBIT(1 − T)]/ WACC = 20\%(\$10,000)/.1 = \$20,000$$

The second, which is called the residual income approach, capitalizes expected EVA or economic profit, by dividing it by the cost of capital and then adding the book value of invested capital, *I*, as shown next:

$$V = \{E[EBIT(1 - T)] - WACC\}/WACC + I$$
$$= [20\%(\$10,000) - 10\%(\$10,000)]/.1 + \$10,000 = \$20,000$$

It is not difficult to see that both approaches estimate the same present value of the firm. Now let's see how the value changes when expectations are revised downward when the actual results become known. EBM predicts that the value of the firm will increase less than expected. Had the firm earned its cost of capital, it would have gone up in value by 10 percent, i.e., by \$2,000. EBM tells us that it will increase by only \$200 capitalized at 10 percent, i.e., \$2,000, because actual performance fell \$200 short of expectations. The net outcome predicted by EBM is that the value of the firm will fall from \$20,000 to \$18,000 because it failed to meet expectations.

EVA interprets the same outcome with very different language. For the firm as a whole, EVA predicts that the value of the firm will go up by 18 percent—to exactly the same value (\$18,000). This number has two parts. First is the return on capital, 10 percent, that must be achieved to earn the opportunity cost of capital for shareholders. Ten percent of \$10,000 is \$1,000 of earnings, which becomes \$10,000 when capitalized at the 10 percent cost of capital, and is, of course, equal to the book value of capital employed. Second is the economic value added because the firm earned eight percent more than the cost of capital. This adds an additional \$8000 to the value, bringing the total to \$18,000.

The new value of the firm is the same regardless of approach, after expectations have been reset to conform with the actual results. However, the rhetoric and the managerial decisions are quite different. EVA interprets the result as value creation because the firm earned more than its cost of capital, resulting in a market value greater than book. EBM interprets the result as value destruction because the firm failed to meet expectations and the share price fell. This key difference in the interpretation of what it means to create value explains why EBM is correlated with the total return to shareholders and EVA is not—especially at the company level where grouping of the data does not obscure the basic relationship. Furthermore, the rank ordering of the business unit's performance according to EBM is completely different from that according to EVA, as illustrated in Table 3.1. The right ranking is necessary for appropriate resource allocation within multibusiness firms.

Decision Rules for Allocating Capital to Investments

While the previous section dealt with an entire company that earned less than expected, we turn now to capital expenditure decisions. We note that net present value (NPV) is almost universally applied by today's CFOs, yet there are still holdouts where payback, IRR (internal rate of return), and earnings accretion are used by managers to make large investment decisions. NPV has taken hold in almost all companies where there are large-scale capital budgeting decisions.[1]

NPV is a decision rule for making investments. For any project with cash inflows and outflows, NPV is equal to the discounted value of expected future cash inflows, net of the discounted value of expected future cash outflows. Because discounting adjusts for the expected return on investor's capital, any value above zero is "extra" return that can be distributed to shareholders. Thus, the NPV rule is simply to invest in any project with a positive NPV. In some cases companies might set the bar higher due to perceived capital constraints or a desire to pursue only those projects they are most confident will create value.

Three problems come to mind as we consider the effectiveness of this "tried-and-true" NPV decision rule. First, companies rarely implement it with consistency and rigor.[2] Many projects are never evaluated on an NPV basis, while others don't receive the scrutiny they should. Thus, with the NPV rule we find some businesses overspending in their capital budgets, while others underinvest. We address this shortfall in firms' capital budgeting systems in Chapter 6.

Second, the NPV methodology assumes no flexibility to change decisions in the future. As a result, projects with significant "option value" may be passed up in favor of projects with more certain future cash flows. Analyzing only NPV can misallocate capital by rejecting projects with significant total value potential, though NPV might be negative. In Chapter 4 we will address "real options"—the application of option pricing concepts to making corporate investment decisions in a way that measures both NPV value and the value of flexibility.

Third, from an EBM perspective we will show that what has to be understood is whether the investment is already expected. It makes a difference whether capital spending is expected baseline capital expenditures or new (unexpected) investments.

Shareholder Value Creation and Investment

What we are about to suggest is that there are two hurdle rates that determine the outcome of capital expenditure decisions—not one. More specifically, there are two hurdle rates that determine whether investment

---

[1]Campbell, C. and J. Wansley, "Stock Price-Based Incentive Contracts and Managerial Performance: The Case of Ralston-Purina Company," *Journal of Financial Economics*, February 1999, Vol. 51, pp. 195–217.

[2]Copeland, T., "Cutting Costs Without Drawing Blood," *Harvard Business Review*, October 2000, pp. 155–164.

decisions result in shareholder returns greater or less than the cost of equity and, simultaneously, whether shareholder wealth increases. Here we explain in more detail the issue raised by Figure 2.1 in the prior chapter, that optimal investment decision-making does not necessarily correlate with positive shareholder returns. One hurdle rate is the expected return, while the other is the weighted average cost of capital.

It is worthwhile at this point to recall Equation 1.2, that indicated three ways value is created:

$$\text{EBM} = \text{Actual } EP - \text{Expected } EP \qquad (1.2)$$

$$\begin{aligned} \text{EBM} = &[\text{Actual } ROIC - \text{Expected } ROIC]\,(I) \\ &- [\text{Actual } WACC - \text{Expected } WACC]\,(I) \\ &+ [ROIC - WACC][\text{Actual } I - \text{Expected } I] \end{aligned}$$

Recall that EP stands for economic profit, or EVA, and is defined as the difference between the return on invested capital, $ROIC$, and the weighted average cost of capital, $WACC$, multiplied by the amount of capital invested, I. The EBM measure of performance is the difference between actual and expected economic profit.

From Equation 1.2 we can see the three ways to create value by raising the stock price: Earn a return greater than expected on existing investments, lower the cost of capital below expectations, or make profitable unexpected investments.

Like it or not, the bulk of capital investment is *not* unexpected, consisting as it does of what we would call baseline capital expenditures. This might include true "baseline" capital intended to extend the life of capital equipment. It may also include replacement capital expenditures as well as purchases of new equipment previously planned to meet expected growth. *The necessary hurdle rate for deciding whether to make expected (i.e., baseline) capital expenditures is the weighted average cost of capital. But the necessary hurdle rate for baseline capital to increase the stock price (further than the cost of capital) is the expected rate.* Projects that earn more than the cost of capital but less than expected should be accepted, but doing so will cause the total return to shareholders to be less than the cost of equity. The stock price will either fall (relative to the market) or increase less than expected, but it will fall less than the alternative, namely not making the investment and returning the cash to shareholders who would earn less on it.

It is important to note that our notion of "baseline" capital expenditures includes purchases of new equipment as long as investors anticipate such purchases. Such expectations may have been formed through an explicit dialog—e.g., management had previously announced the level and type of capital expenditures they intended to pursue. These expectations may have been formed implicitly as investors evaluated the business' expected growth rate and estimated a reasonable level of capital expenditures needed to support that growth. Investors do not evaluate expected growth in isolation of investment rates to sustain that growth. Likewise, managers must look holistically at the amount of investment required to meet their growth targets.

This chapter focuses on running an existing business, and so the next section discusses the baseline capital expenditure decision in more detail. *The hurdle rate necessary for new (unexpected) capital expenditures to create value for shareholders is the WACC.* This is the single hurdle rate that, if exceeded, will increase both the share price and shareholder's wealth. Not only should new capital expenditures be approved if they earn more than the cost of capital, but also they will create value for shareholders. In the next chapter we discuss decision-making for new (unexpected) investments.

Baseline Capex

We define any capital expenditure that is expected as a "baseline capital expenditure." For most companies these investments are needed to stay in business. For example, a steel company spends money to maintain its existing capital base, to make additions to capacity to accommodate expected growth in production, and investments in its operating working capital. Chapter 4 discusses investments that are unexpected—new investments such as acquisitions or the addition of new business lines.

What follows is controversial, so we build it up with a series of examples that show the unambiguous value changes that occur when a company decides to make an investment or not. Table 3.2 illustrates a company with perpetual (constant) free cash flows.

There is no working capital, and the amount of invested capital is constant at $1,000. We assume that the firm has no debt, therefore the cost of

TABLE 3.2   Perpetual Constant Free Cash Flows

Revenue	$1,000
Variable operating costs	−400
Depreciation	−100
EBIT	500
Tax at 40%	−200
Earnings after taxes	300
Depreciation	+100
After-tax cash flow from operations	400
Baseline investment (Capex)	−100
Free cash flow	300

equity equals the cost of capital, namely 20 percent. The expected return on invested capital is 30 percent. The market expects that these results will be maintained perpetually. The value of the company is therefore:

$$V = \$300/.20 = \$1,500$$

The annual return on the market value, k, is free cash flow (dividends) divided by initial value:

$$k = (EBIT - \text{tax})/\$1,500 = \$300/\$1,500 = 20\%$$

The return on invested capital, $ROIC$, is

$$ROIC = (EBIT - \text{tax})/\$1,000 = 30\%$$

If all baseline investment earns 30 percent, as expected, the value of the all-equity firm will grow at 20 percent per year.

Next, let us consider several decisions. Suppose the firm suddenly learns that next year, that the baseline investment of $100 will earn only 25 percent. Based on the discussion in Chapter 2, it is tempting to argue that the firm should not make the investment because it will earn less than expected and therefore the stock price will fall. Let's take a closer look and see what happens. Table 3.3 shows the first 10 years of cash flows and the present value of the base case—a perpetual return on invested capital of 30 percent after taxes and a firm value of $1,500.

If the annual investment of $100 returns only 25 percent instead of 30 percent, the firm can decide either to invest or to cease further investment. Either way the value of the firm will decline. But if baseline investment stops, the value of the firm will fall more, because shareholders can earn only 20 percent on the uninvested capital, while the firm can earn 25 percent. Let's see what happens to the value of the firm if baseline investment continues, but earns only 25 percent. This is illustrated in Table 3.4.

In this case the value of the firm declines from $1,500 to $1,374. Expectations-Based Management predicts this result, but recommends that the firm invest anyway, because the alternative of not investing at all results in even lower value.

What happens if the firm decides not to invest? This outcome is illustrated in Table 3.5 where the firm terminates after year 10 because its pool of invested capital becomes exhausted. Note, however, that the return on invested capital remains unchanged at 30 percent, until all capital is exhausted. The value of this alternative is lowest of all, namely $1,165. The firm could do worse, of course—but not much worse.

Next, what should a company do if it is expected to earn less than its cost of capital? If our example company were expected to earn 15 percent perpetually, it would sell for less than book. As shown in Table 3.6, if it is

TABLE 3.3 The Base Case, Expected *ROIC* = 30%, *WACC* = 20%, Value = $1,500

	1	2	3	4	5	6	7	8	9	10	11
Revenue	1,000	1,000	1,000	1,000	1,000	1,000	1,000	1,000	1,000	1,000	1,000
Variable cost	400	400	400	400	400	400	400	400	400	400	400
Depreciation	100	100	100	100	100	100	100	100	100	100	100
EBIT	500	500	500	500	500	500	500	500	500	500	500
40% tax	–200	–200	–200	–200	–200	–200	–200	–200	–200	–200	–200
Net Income	300	300	300	300	300	300	300	300	300	300	300
Maint. Investmt.	100	100	100	100	100	100	100	100	100	100	100
Total capital	1,000	1,000	1,000	1,000	1,000	1,000	1,000	1,000	1,000	1,000	1,000
Cash flow	300	300	300	300	300	300	300	300	300	300	300
ROIC	0.3	0.3	0.3	0.3	0.3	0.3	0.3	0.3	0.3	0.3	0.3
Discount factor	0.833	0.694	0.579	0.482	0.402	0.335	0.279	0.233	0.194	0.162	0.162
PV of *FCF*	250	208	174	145	121	100	84	70	58	48	48
PV of firm	1,500										

TABLE 3.4 Expected *ROIC* Declines to 25%, Value = $1,374

	1	2	3	4	5	6	7	8	9	10	11
Revenue	1,000	1,000	1,000	1,000	1,000	1,000	1,000	1,000	1,000	1,000	1,000
Variable cost	408	417	425	433	442	450	458	467	475	483	483
Depreciation	100	100	100	100	100	100	100	100	100	100	100
EBIT	492	483	475	467	458	450	442	433	425	417	417
40% tax	-197	-193	-190	-187	-183	-180	-177	-173	-170	-167	-167
Net Income	295	290	285	280	275	270	265	260	255	250	250
Maint. Investmt.	100	100	100	100	100	100	100	100	100	100	100
Total capital	1,000	1,000	1,000	1,000	1,000	1,000	1,000	1,000	1,000	1,000	1,000
Cash flow	295	290	285	280	275	270	265	260	255	250	250
ROIC	0.295	0.29	0.285	0.28	0.275	0.27	0.265	0.26	0.255	0.25	0.25
Discount factor	0.833	0.694	0.579	0.482	0.402	0.335	0.279	0.233	0.194	0.162	
PV of *FCF*	246	201	165	135	111	90	74	60	49	40	
PV of firm	1,374										

TABLE 3.5 No Investment, *ROIC* = 30%, Value Falls to $1,164

	1	2	3	4	5	6	7	8	9	10
Revenue	1,000	1,000	1,000	1,000	1,000	1,000	1,000	1,000	1,000	1,000
Variable cost	450	500	550	600	650	700	750	800	850	900
Depreciation	100	100	100	100	100	100	100	100	100	100
EBIT	450	400	350	300	250	200	150	100	50	0
40% tax	−180	−160	−140	−120	−100	−80	−60	−40	−20	0
Net Income	270	240	210	180	150	120	90	60	30	0
Maint. Investmt.	0	0	0	0	0	0	0	0	0	0
Total capital	900	800	700	600	500	400	300	200	100	0
Cash flow	370	340	310	280	250	220	190	160	130	100
ROIC	0.3	0.3	0.3	0.3	0.3	0.3	0.3	0.3	0.3	NA
Discount factor	0.833	0.694	0.579	0.482	0.402	0.335	0.279	0.233	0.194	0.162
PV of *FCF*	308	236	179	135	100	74	53	37	25	16
PV of firm	1,165									

TABLE 3.6   Expected *ROIC* = 15%, *WACC* = 20%, Value = $750

	1	2	3	4	5	6	7	8	9	10	11
Revenue	1,000	1,000	1,000	1,000	1,000	1,000	1,000	1,000	1,000	1,000	1,000
Variable cost	650	650	650	650	650	650	650	650	650	650	650
Depreciation	100	100	100	100	100	100	100	100	100	100	100
EBIT	250	250	250	250	250	250	250	250	250	250	250
40% tax	-100	-100	-100	-100	-100	-100	-100	-100	-100	-100	-100
Net Income	150	150	150	150	150	150	150	150	150	150	150
Maint. Investmt.	100	100	100	100	100	100	100	100	100	100	100
Total capital	1,000	1,000	1,000	1,000	1,000	1,000	1,000	1,000	1,000	1,000	1,000
Cash flow	150	150	150	150	150	150	150	150	150	150	150
ROIC	0.15	0.15	0.15	0.15	0.15	0.15	0.15	0.15	0.15	0.15	0.15
Discount factor	0.833	0.694	0.579	0.482	0.402	0.335	0.279	0.233	0.194	0.162	0.162
PV of *FCF*	125	104	87	72	60	50	42	35	29	24	24
PV of firm	750										

TABLE 3.7 *ROIC* Goes Up from 15% to 18%, *WACC* = 20%, Value = $900

	1	2	3	4	5	6	7	8	9	10	11
Revenue	1,000	1,000	1,000	1,000	1,000	1,000	1,000	1,000	1,000	1,000	1,000
Variable cost	600	600	600	600	600	600	600	600	600	600	600
Depreciation	100	100	100	100	100	100	100	100	100	100	100
EBIT	300	300	300	300	300	300	300	300	300	300	300
40% tax	−120	−120	−120	−120	−120	−120	−120	−120	−120	−120	−120
Net Income	180	180	180	180	180	180	180	180	180	180	180
Maint. Investmt.	100	100	100	100	100	100	100	100	100	100	100
Total capital	1,000	1,000	1,000	1,000	1,000	1,000	1,000	1,000	1,000	1,000	1,000
Cash flow	180	180	180	180	180	180	180	180	180	180	180
ROIC	0.18	0.18	0.18	0.18	0.18	0.18	0.18	0.18	0.18	0.18	0.18
Discount factor	0.833	0.694	0.579	0.482	0.402	0.335	0.279	0.233	0.194	0.162	0.162
PV of *FCF*	150	125	104	87	72	60	50	42	35	29	29
PV of firm	900										

expected to earn 15 percent when its cost of capital is 20 percent, its market value will be $750, less than its $1,000 book value.

Suppose the company cannot sell or liquidate the company for anything more than $600, but it finds a way to make baseline investments that bring the return on invested capital up to 18 percent—still less than the cost of capital, 20 percent. Should it make the investment? EBM *would argue that even though the stock price will increase if it does, it should not invest at less than the cost of capital because shareholders can invest the money elsewhere at the cost of capital and attain even greater value.*

In other words, an investment that earns less than the cost of capital but greater than expected will result in a total return to shareholders that is greater than the cost of equity. Table 3.7 shows the results. When the *ROIC* increases from 15 percent to 18 percent, the value increases from $750 to $900. However, if the capital is not invested and is returned to shareholders instead, their wealth will increase even more, because they can earn 20 percent on it instead of 18 percent. In this case the value of the stream of cash flows is $1,000.

Note that if the firm can be sold or liquidated for an after-tax value that exceeds $1,000, it is better to do the transaction. However, it would not be unusual for the liquidation value and the potential sale price to be less than the going concern value, which is $900 in this case.

The General Rule for Baseline Investment

Given an amount of invested capital, earn the highest return possible. The total return to shareholders (TRS) will be greater than the cost of equity (K_s) when the actual return on invested capital, $A(R)$ exceeds what the market expected, $E(R)$. TRS will equal the cost of equity (K_s), when actual *ROIC* equals the expected *ROIC*, and TRS will be less than the cost of equity (K_s) when actual *ROIC* falls short of expectations. Figure 3.1 summarizes these rules. Note the two shaded boxes because they depart from conventional wisdom. They are easy traps for management.

The first shaded box represents opportunities where baseline investment earns less than is expected $(E(R) > A(R))$ yet more than the cost of capital $(A(R) > WACC)$. In this case the firm should make the investment even though the observed total return to shareholders will be negative, because their expectations will not be met. Investing is the right decision because the alternative—i.e., not investing at a rate of return greater than the cost of capital—yields even lower value. While the decision to invest is consistent with managers' intuition to invest whenever returns are greater than the cost of capital, managers need to understand how this situation can result in share price dropping, even though they made the right decision. Always remember that the alternative (not investing) could result in share price dropping even further, but would not be an observed outcome

Conventional wisdom predicts the same optimal action, but the opposite effect on the total return to shareholders in the two shaded boxes.

Outcome (1)	If we do Invest (2)	If we do not invest (3)	Optimal action (4)	Sell at book? (5)	
$A(R)>E(R)>WACC$	TRS>k	TRS<(2)	Invest	No	
$E(R)>A(R)>WACC$	TRS<k	TRS<(2)	Invest	No	←Underinvestment Trap
$A(R)=E(R)=WACC$	TRS=k	TRS=(2)	Indifferent	Indifferent	
$WACC>A(R)>E(R)$	TRS>k	TRS>(2)	No investment	Yes	←Overinvestment Trap
$WACC=A(R)>E(R)$	TRS>k	TRS=(2)	Invest	Indifferent	
$WACC>E(R)>A(R)$	TRS<<k	TRS	No investment	Yes	

FIGURE 3.1   What is new about EBM and maintenance investment?

if it does not happen. Investor communications, addressed in Chapter 8, need to take into account this divergence between the optimal investment decision and shareholder returns.

The second shaded box covers those situations where the expected return is less than the cost of capital, but baseline investment will have an *ROIC* that is higher than expected. Furthermore, there is no transaction to sell or liquidate the business. First note that if this investment is made, shareholder returns will be greater than the cost of equity (*k*). This may seem counterintuitive because investments that earn less than the cost of capital are presumed to be as inherently value-destroying. But note that given this set of circumstances, the investment should not be made even though the total return to shareholders will be greater than the cost of equity. If the capital is returned to shareholders instead, they can earn the *WACC* and therefore have higher value than if the same amount of money is reinvested in the firm at less than *WACC*. Therefore, the firm should not invest even though the stock price will go up, because shareholder wealth is higher if they invest at the *WACC* instead. Again, investor communications need to be clear about management's decision to pay cash dividends rather than make investments.

Shareholder Wealth Can Be Maximized Even When the Stock Price Falls— The Underinvestment Trap

The first shaded box in Figure 3.1 is an example of a situation that is often faced by a company that has a high rate of return (e.g., 50 percent) on invested capital, and a low cost of capital (e.g., 10 percent). What will management do if a large expected investment under evaluation is predicted to earn 15 percent?

We know that if the project earns 15 percent (which we assume causes the market to lower its expected return for the firm), the stock price will fall. However, the stock price will fall even more if the investment is not taken. This result will never be observed because management actually makes the investment. Thus shareholder's wealth is maximized, even though the stock price falls.

EBM therefore does not fundamentally change investment criteria—one should always accept the set of projects with the highest NPV—i.e, the one that produces the highest combination of expected *ROIC* investment. EBM does, however, explain why share prices can decline even as the company makes positive NPV project decisions. As long as these projects collectively earn less in expected economic profits than those already baked into share price, the share price will fall.

A Rising Stock Price May Not Maximize Shareholder Returns— The Overinvestment Trap

The opposite temptation to do the wrong thing happens when a company is expected to earn less than its cost of capital, but finds an opportunity to earn a rate of return greater than expected but still less than its cost of capital. If it invests, the stock price will go up because it exceeds the market's expectations—but shareholders would be even better off were the cash to be put into marketable securities that earn the cost of capital. There is the temptation to overinvest because the stock price will go up.

Figure 3.2 shows the TRS to shareholders of Bethlehem Steel Company between January of 1997 and mid-April of 1998—a 17-month interval where their total return was roughly 80 percent.[3] During that entire period, Bethlehem's actual after-tax return on invested capital was less than its after-tax weighted average cost of capital. However, as shown by the thin lines in Figure 3.2, it exceeded analyst expectations by achieving net income of $281 million (roughly $1.10 per share). A year earlier analysts were forecasting $0.45 earnings per share in 1998. Their expectations were revised upward throughout 1998 and early 1999. This explains why the stock price went up, even though Bethlehem earned less than its cost of capital. Later, in 2001, it entered Chapter 11 bankruptcy.

---

[3]Bethlehem Steel's market-adjusted return from January 1997 to mid-April of 1998 was roughly 28 percent.

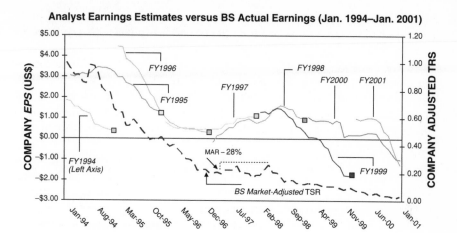

FIGURE 3.2   Bethlehem Steel and the overinvestment trap.

Note: Boxes denote actual *EPS* before extra and nonrecurring items; lines that terminate in boxes ldenote consensus analyst estimates for the current and next fiscal year.

Source: IBES, CRSP, Monitor analysis

With 20-20 hindsight, Bethlehem shareholders would have been better off if the company had not invested, earning less than its cost of capital.

The Timing or Pattern of *ROIC*

ROIC is rarely as well-behaved as the simple examples that we discussed earlier. This is a matter that has attracted much discussion and heated debate. Many authors have pointed out that the return on invested capital is often less than the cost of capital during the project gestation period, then goes positive as the project hits full stride, and increases dramatically as the capital base depreciates. This is not unusual and it is not a problem if one is using Expectations-Based Management. For every project, it is possible to map out the expected *ROIC* year-by-year over its life.

A problem with many business unit value metric programs is the failure to customize targets for business life cycles. From an EBM perspective it is clear that value can be created even if year-on-year economic profits are positive but declining. Consider a business unit in a mature industry facing an imminent decline in profitability as substitute products erode demand. Expectations would already be set so that the business unit's value reflects the anticipated decline in profits. But, if management were to develop a unique marketing campaign capable of slowing (but not stopping) the decline in sales volumes, value would increase, even as the business continued to decline. Figure 3.3 illustrates this concept.

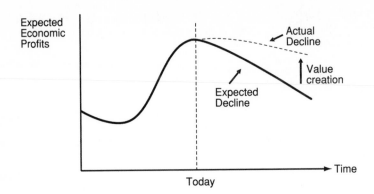

FIGURE 3.3 Value creation with declining profits.

Similarly, there are cases where negative economic profits are *not* indicative of value destruction at the business unit level. The obvious example is a business unit in the midst of investment with a long-term investment payback. Such a business might be forgiven for negative profits on "strategic" grounds, but other business units with negative profits may not be so lucky. Take, for example, a mature, cyclical business at the trough of its cycle. One would expect economic profits to be negative in the short term, but to recover as economic conditions improve. Should a cyclical business be penalized for following the industry cycle? We do not think so; however, myopic business unit performance management systems do just that. We illustrate in Figure 3.4 a situation where value is created even as a cyclical business is earning less than its current cost of capital. We conclude

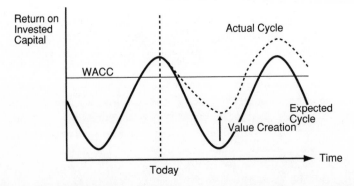

FIGURE 3.4 Value creation at cyclical business earning less than cost of capital.

from this discussion that we need a system that encourages performance better than the industry, even if profitability is (as expected) low in cyclical downturns.

Some advocates of value-based management systems advocate the creation of "capital suspense" accounts in order to smooth calculations of economic profit over the life of a capital-intensive investment. If one uses EBM, this is not necessary because success is measured by beating the expected return each year—and not by beating the cost of capital. If anything, use of such "capital suspense" accounts can confuse matters even more as managers will not have a clear picture of profitability as it actually is in order to compare with competitors, expected business life cycle profitability, and other benchmarks.

A Capital Budgeting Process Tied to Expectations

Because investors already have expectations of baseline capital expenditures incorporated into their estimates of share prices, managers need to evaluate their capital allocations to their core businesses with these expectations in mind. We recommend the sequenced approach to the problem shown in Figure 3.5:

Identify the universe of available capital investment projects. While this sounds like a straightforward step already included in most capital budgeting exercises, we caution that significant amounts of capital spending happen "under the radar." Managers may hide expenditures on small capital items in operating budgets, or the budgeting process itself may only require formal project proposals for capital spending in excess of some threshold. While it is natural to lump the remaining plans for capital

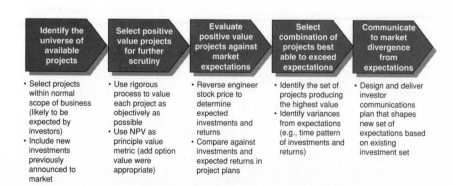

FIGURE 3.5   Capital budgeting process for baseline capital.

spending into a single bucket (e.g., "all spending <$1mm"), that grouping does not help later in the process as we decide between alternative capital spending patterns. For example, a pharmaceutical R&D group may designate a significant amount of capital for spending on small pieces of equipment, say, in increments of no more than $100,000 per scientist. Accumulating such spending either into a single bucket—or, more commonly, by department, misses the critical division between expected and new investments. Effort should be made to divide these investments into spending on existing or previously announced R&D efforts and spending on new lines of research.

The universe of capital spending for review should also include previously announced, but not executed, projects. This may include, for example, plans to pursue a stream of acquisitions to drive industry consolidation. Such plans are often incorporated by investors into the current share price and cannot be ignored when assessing other capital investment opportunities. We have found time and again that managers treat mergers and acquisitions (M&A) as a special event, sometimes with its own distinct group, with limited coordination with the capital budgeting process. But in the end, M&A is simply another form of capital spending—purchasing other firms' existing assets rather than developing such assets internally. Chapter 4 discusses in more detail M&A as it relates to investor expectations.

Select projects with positive value for further scrutiny.[4] Notice that we said positive value rather than positive NPV. The difference may be driven by option value, discussed in more detail later. At this stage care must be taken to ensure objectivity in project cash flow estimates. We've rarely encountered a project proposal with a negative NPV—after all, why would any manager propose something that clearly doesn't meet the company's existing investment thresholds? The hockey-stick phenomenon is all too real and pervades not only operating budgets but also capital budgets.

We've come across several mechanisms for injecting more objectivity to capital project forecasts. One such mechanism is the use of disinterested administrative staff to create and/or assess project plans in conjunction with input from line managers. These staff need to be trained in both financial analysis and the general economic aspects of the line businesses. For example, at one pharmaceutical R&D group with which we've worked, business plans and forecasts are the responsibility of administrative managers reporting directly to the finance function, with dotted lines to scientific staff. We found the most effective of these planners to be ex-scientists who also

---

[4]Note: Later in the chapter we discuss exceptions to the rule for scrutinizing only positive-value projects.

knew the basics of accounting. Accounting knowledge was required to properly put spending into financial statement formats, while scientific knowledge was required to understand the true equipment and expense needs for various projects. Departments with admin staff without a science background typically had budgets dictated by those doing the spending.

Another mechanism to increase capital spending objectivity is to force project plans to include objective criteria for creating forecasts—e.g., price quotes from equipment manufacturers, and construction contractors. We have also seen feedback mechanisms used to good effect. Over time, effective project variance tracking allows managers to learn how to forecast better by understanding past mistakes. None of this is to say that managers should be punished for these variances—that is a question requiring knowledge of what caused the variance.

Evaluate positive value projects against market expectations. The trick here is to understand what the market's expectations are. Unfortunately, there is not (yet) any single resource that surveys market participants for their expectations about a company's prospects except with respect to *EPS*. While Zacks, IBES, and other data providers survey sell-side analysts to determine their expected *EPS* forecasts, no similar service compiles forecasts of capital expenditures. The best way then to figure out the market's expectations is to reverse engineer share price. This is discussed in Chapter 7. Management would be advised then to look critically at any such analysis as bias can creep into the calculations. Where possible, specific sell-side analyst reports can be referenced to test the reasonableness of a reverse-engineered share price model. Where management has an open line of communication to investors and buy-side analysts, these sources should also be used to understand baseline capital expenditure expectations.

Assuming you have done the hard work to identify the market's capital expenditure expectations, you need to compare internal capital expenditure forecasts to those expectations. Answering the following questions provides a solid understanding of how internal capital expenditure plans stack up against investor forecasts:

- For the short-term forecast horizon:
  - What is the total amount of capital expenditures expected by the market (e.g., in dollars)? How does this compare to the amount currently in internal plans?
  - What is the market's anticipated level of depreciation? How does that compare with internal forecasts?
  - What is the reinvestment rate expected by the market (capital expenditures as a percent of after-tax operating profits)? How does that reinvestment rate compare internally?

- o What is the expected return on new investments forecasted by the market?
- o Does the market anticipate external investments (M&A) as a component of capital expenditures? If so, how much?
- For the long-term horizon:
  - o What is the market's assumption about the firm's long-term or steady-state reinvestment rate?
  - o What is the market's assumption about long-run return on capital and growth rate?

Select the value-maximizing set of capital projects and *compare the investment plan with market expectations.* Selection of projects is straightforward to the extent management has already been using cash flow–based project valuation metrics like NPV or real options value. The set of projects that should be selected—either at the business unit or corporate level—is the set that maximizes firm value. Where there are constraints such as those on capital availability or management time and attention, a linear programming exercise can be used to maximize value subject to these constraints. In the interest of space we will not review these techniques as they are well documented in the corporate finance literature.[5]

While traditional capital budgeting techniques can help select the optimal set of projects, it does not prepare management for how the market will react. This is where a thorough comparison of planned and market-expected investments is critical. The following dimensions need to be considered as you make such comparisons:

- Is the firm planning to make more or fewer investments than the market expects?
  - o What is the reason for any variance in the level of investments: lack of profitable investment opportunities, capital or time constraints, desire for slow growth and focus on margins?
- What is the expected return on capital for these investments? How does it compare with the market's expected return?
  - o Will the investments raise or lower the firm's overall profitability?
  - o Will the investments raise or lower the firm's overall growth rate?
- What is the composition of investments across the firm's portfolio of businesses, and how does that compare with the market's expectations?
  - o Is the firm planning investments in the same markets that investors are expecting it to pursue?

[5]For example, see Copeland, Weston, and Shastri, *Financial Theory and Corporate Policy,* 4th edition, Addison-Wesley, 2005, or Brealey and Myers, *Principles of Corporate Finance,* 7th edition, McGraw-Hill, 2002.

- o What are the reasons for any shifts in the pattern of investments?
- ■ How does the time pattern of investments stack up against market expectations? Is there an acceleration or deceleration of investments? If so, why?

Communicate to the market divergences in capital investment plans. Here the goal is to manage shareholder expectations toward the economic circumstances management believes most closely describes the firm's investment opportunities. Of course, share price will react—either positively or negatively—if the description of the capital plan varies significantly from the market's prior expectations. But that is, of course, the point—to get share price more closely to reflect the underlying fundamentals of the business. We address market communications in much more detail in Chapter 8. For now we note that market communications is a byproduct of understanding internal plans and market expectations. Thus, in an EBM-driven system market communications will be a logical extension of internal planning (rather than an intrusion on internal planning seeking to force arbitrary goals on line managers who are closest to their product markets). We return to the problem of shareholder communications in Chapter 8.

Comingling of Capital Project Expectations

Once a set of baseline and new capital projects is approved, the firm's capital plan will reflect the combined planned spending on all projects. Except in industries characterized by large, lumpy investments (e.g., petrochemicals, mining, aerospace), most investors do not distinguish between specific capital projects as they form their expectations of the firm's capital spending.

Because investors often treat capital spending as one large pool of projects, it is tempting to believe a single hurdle rate would suffice. For example, if only projects with a positive net present value are pursued, isn't that enough? This simple decision rule is correct, but as was shown earlier in the chapter it does not necessarily predict the effect on the stock price:

- ■ If baseline investment is made in uses that are positive NPV, but have expected returns that disappoint the market, then the stock price will fall even though shareholders are better off if the investment is made than if it is not.
- ■ New or unexpected investment should also always be positive NPV, but since it is unexpected your share price will go up, unambiguously.
- ■ If you do not know whether an investment is considered to be baseline or new, or if investment expectations are comingled, don't worry—the correct decision is always to accept all positive NPV projects. Unfortunately, you may not be able to predict whether your stock price will go up or down.

■ Managers frequently face both capital and managerial talent constraints on the amount of capital spending and projects that can be pursued. If managers believe the hurdle rate is higher than the one suggested by expectations, then they will ration off value-creating projects at the margin.

Can You Beat Expectations?

It just so happens that the Boston Red Sox won the World Series of baseball in 2004. In the pennant playoffs, a best-out-of-seven series against the New York Yankees, they were down three games to zip, and Kurt Schilling, their 20+ game–winning pitcher was suffering from a disabling ankle injury. The Red Sox won the next four games against the Yankees and swept the World Series by winning four straight. It is the understatement of the century to say that they exceeded expectations. In fact, it had been almost a century—86 years—since the Red Sox had won a World Series. It was nothing short of a miracle. However, the individual team members worked hard and played smart. Jason Veritek, a catcher, organized the pitching staff around detailed observations of the hitting habits of opposition sluggers. Star pitcher Schilling refused to give up, even after a serious tendon injury threatened to end his pitching career.

Sports analogies are apt for management problems because both endeavors are based on the performance of teams. One thing is sure. If your team does not believe that it can exceed its own expectations, there is no point in trying. The Red Sox never stopped trying, even when the odds seemed impossible.

This is not a book about behavioral finance, but it is not a book about giving up either. Follow these six common-sense rules:

1. Your expectations must be reasonable. Set your hopes high—not your expectations. Stretch targets are often self-defeating. The Red Sox hoped to win the World Series of baseball, not to build a space shuttle. Baseball players are compensated with a base salary supplemented with additional incentives based on actual versus expected performance.
2. Remember that your competitors are human, too. Research the plans, skills, and capabilities of your competition. Understand their strengths and weaknesses as well as their strategy.
3. Work hard, work smart, and be willing to sacrifice. Nobel prize–winners are smart, but are distinguished by their passion for their work and their commitment to it.
4. Have skin in the game. Feel the agony of defeat as well as the thrill of victory. Chapter 9 discusses the details of appropriate incentive design.

5. It takes a team at the top. Individual efforts must be coordinated around an appropriate performance standard such as maximizing the value of the company.
6. In business, remember that long-term performance counts the most. If you do not meet short-term earnings expectations, and it is viewed as an anomaly, there will be little or no effect on your stock price. But if it is viewed as the beginning of a trend, it will be taken as a permanent effect, and that will cause a major drop in returns.

The top management team of a company, like a sports team, competes to win. Since expected performance is baked into the firm's stock price, the company must do better than expected—which is not an easy task. But if the team at the top does not understand what performance is expected of them, how can they hope to do better? And if they do not understand any differences between the expectations of investors (owners of the firm) and expectations that they themselves have—how can they close the gap.

It may be difficult to infer what is expected of a firm, but it is necessary. To win for shareholders, the management team must beat the expected long-term growth in expected cash flows.

Forecasting Guidelines

Though we have focused thus far on the decision to reinvest in an ongoing business, capital spending is only one part of the puzzle of managing an existing business for value creation. Management needs a reasonable picture of whether value can be created in these businesses, not only for capital spending decisions, but also in setting its operating budgets and line management performance targets for the year.

It is easy enough to formulate a forecast—but difficult to evaluate its achievability. Achievability, though, is the underlying factor driving our understanding of whether there is any room for value creation in an existing business.

Some guiding questions are appropriate as line managers create their forecasts and senior managers evaluate them for achievability:

■ Does the forecast represent a serious departure from past results?
■ How do critical elements of the forecast stack up against industry benchmarks?
■ What are the assumptions underlying the expected results? What are the probabilities of such assumptions being true?
■ Is the forecast grounded in underlying factual data, or built on a series of assumptions about market size or growth rate?

■ Is the forecast internally consistent? Does it incorporate known relationships and/or tradeoffs between:
  o prices and volume?
  o capital investment and returns on capital?
  o margins and volumes (via competitive responses)?
  o time pattern of cash flows from investment to return?
  o investment and asset depreciation?
  o profitability, investment, and cash taxes?

Value Drivers

One of the best ways to evaluate and track forecasts is to drive the analysis down to the lowest level possible—what we call value drivers. Managing a business is not simply managing some generic financial metrics.
Ultimately, value is created at the front line, at the intersection of customers
and suppliers with the business' internal functions (production, marketing,
distribution, etc.). Business units create value by managing value drivers on
a daily basis.

"Value driver" is a loaded term these days, as many different things
have been labeled a value driver. The most common approach is to label
a "value driver" any financial ratio that has a significant leverage effect on
firm value. For example, if a 1 percent change in the sales growth rate
results in a 10 percent change in company value, then the sales growth rate
might be termed a "value driver." While understanding the sensitivity of
value to various factors like sales growth, margins, and capital investments
is important, these are not factors that business unit managers actually manage. (See Figure 3.6.) They are outputs, not inputs. Unfortunately, there is
no lack of consultants telling clients to "get the growth rate up" because
that's their key value driver. Savvy (or frustrated) managers reply, "Of
course growth rate is important—tell me something I don't know. Tell me
how to grow faster without overextending myself, cutting into margins, or
using too much capital."

Expectations can be extended right down to the shop floor level. While
there is an inevitable degree of subjectivity in such a process, the value of
conducting such an exercise is immense, as it provides management with
a much more granular view of what actually drives value. Ultimately, we
see a linked system of metrics at the business unit level extending from
company value straight down the line.

How does one identify operating value drivers? First, one can conduct
rigorous financial modeling exercises, where each input of a valuation
model is decomposed into its component parts. This modeling effort
should be supported by quantitative research into the relationship between
firm performance and economic/industry conditions. Such research may

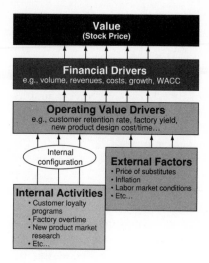

FIGURE 3.6   Financial versus operating value drivers.

include using regression analysis or other modeling techniques to find the relationship between hypothesized value drivers and financial results. Of course, a significant cross-section or time series of data is required to be able to do this.

Because quantitative data is always inadequate to identify operating value drivers with confidence, a second approach would be to use the strategic planning process to identify value drivers. Most strategy processes today decide on strategic courses of action by articulating a strategic rationale or logic. It is this underlying logic behind a chosen business strategy that can highlight key value drivers. Specifically, if there are key variables whose values determined the specific choices made, those variables are important value drivers. For example, suppose the management of a business unit decided it would pursue an organic growth strategy through an expanded product line offering. Moreover, this choice was made with the belief that customers valued the brand image more than the brand image of competitors. In this case, the strategic logic depended on relative brand positioning. Going forward, this brand positioning becomes a critical value driver—particularly because any drastic change in the value driver will either reinforce or undercut the chosen strategy, and ultimately be manifest in financial results. At one client of ours, a major change in strategy depended critically on the ability to shape a new brand image in consumers' minds—in this case, the key value drivers were found to be specific consumer sentiment survey results as well as how those survey results translated into retail store traffic, sales volume, and product mix.

Another approach toward identifying operating value drivers is to survey experts. Industry analysts, market research firms, and even major investors (particularly buy-side) will each have considered the dynamics of the market sufficiently to provide insight into what metrics matter most to a particular business. The particular metrics that investor analysts track are particularly relevant as they help management understand how the market values a particular business unit—and may also highlight areas where investors need to be educated more about business dynamics.

A last value driver identification approach is to survey key line managers. While not the most robust process, this method usually yields reliable results. Of course, managers need to be asked the right questions so that they understand what a value driver means. The survey should be open to the fact that some value drivers are in management's control, while others are not. To the extent value drivers are later to be used in compensation and performance evaluation, it is important to distinguish between controllable and uncontrollable drivers. Managers will of course focus on the controllable factors—but it is the entire economic system that is important for senior management to understand.

Once expectations are driven down to the value-driver level, analysis and planning can have much more meaning. There will be no end in sight for senior and line management to argue about what is to be expected in terms of financial results—e.g., is it three percent growth at 10 percent margins or four percent growth at eight percent margins? This argument (to call it that) needs to be brought down a few levels to where work actually gets done. Benchmarking, historical experience, and real-world technical factors can be used to forecast value drivers more objectively. Aggregating these forecasts up to the business unit level is what a good forecast does.

Note that starting with value drivers as the key input to line management expectations does not make forecasts accurate. The goal is to ground the discussion of expectations in hard data, data that can be discussed internally until a consensus emerges as to what a business unit is both capable of doing and expected to achieve.

Planning and Budgeting

While investment and portfolio management decisions are important elements to managing value, it is important that EBM principles be applied also to more routine business planning activities. Every company has some form of budgeting process in which line and corporate managers analyze and forecast performance, allocate scarce resources, and set performance goals. We turn now to how this critical activity can be improved through the application of EBM principles.

In any firm there are tensions among investors/analysts, senior management, and line management, all of whom may have different expectations of what the company is capable of doing in the future. In Chapter 8 we discuss the intersection of externally determined expectations (investors and analysts) and management's expectations. Here we discuss the budgeting process precisely because it is the primary vehicle by which most firms develop their internal expectations.

A useful starting point is to note some common ways in which budgeting processes fail. Of course, the most commonly known of these is the infamous "hockey stick" budget. Hockey-stick forecasts, where historical negative trends are somehow transformed into forecasts of ever-improving performance, are a natural response to the demands placed on line managers by senior management. Senior management "demands" plans that will produce a certain level of earnings growth (or related goal), and each individual manager delivers a budget that meets this goal. Budgets that do not fit senior management's goals are sent back to the line for revisions—asking for expense cuts or other changes that will help the corporation as a whole meet its targets.

This dynamic puts the cart before the horse. Targets are set before any thorough review of budgets is completed. Targets are somehow derived without a bottom-up understanding of what is a reasonable set of performance targets given industry conditions, the company's competitive position, and line management's tactical and strategic plans to optimize performance in that context.

A second common budgeting problem is expense padding. Line managers know there is a finite amount of resources available, and usually only one time per planning cycle at which to secure those resources. Expenses are padded for different reasons by different managers—as contingency money in case top-line revenues fall short of expectations, as a way to accumulate "power" in corporate cultures dominated by those commanding the greatest number of resources, and as a way to ensure bonuses at the end of year (by under-forecasting expected profitability it is easier for the manager to hit a budget-based target by year-end).

Overall we agree with the observation made by a colleague of ours that "budgets are an excuse to lie."[6] Because budgets are the result of subjective analysis and they are an integral part of most management incentive compensation systems, it is no wonder that many professionals we en-

---

[6]Michael C. Jensen, "Paying People to Lie: The Truth About the Budgeting Process," Harvard NOM Research Paper No. 01-01, and HBS Working Paper No. 01-072 (April 2001).

counter have little faith in budget numbers. Whenever someone has control over their own targets he or she will do their best to set low targets. There are three important elements to fixing these budgeting problems: realigning compensation, improving the internal dialog, and changing the scheduling of the budget cycle.

Realigning Compensation

The primary motivator for budgets that fail to tell senior management the true capability of the organization is compensation. But there are ways to break the link between line management's compensation and hitting budget targets. A more complete EBM-based incentive compensation system that focuses on long-term expectations will remove much of the motivation for management to try to set lowball targets through the current-year budgets. Managers must see it in their best interest to achieve improvement of long-term expectations regardless of performance relative to a short-term budget.

There may be cases, though, where hitting short-term expectations is important—for example, in a turnaround situation or in a low-growth business with limited opportunities for long-term investments. In such cases, mechanisms must be set up to check management's budget requests for reasonableness in light of historical and comparable company performance.

One can also break the link between budgets and compensation by more rigorously basing compensation on controllable versus uncontrollable factors. Managers may be more objective in their budget requests if they know they will not lose compensation due to factors outside their control. Later, in our chapter on management compensation, we discuss this issue in more depth, as it is not always straightforward to decide what should be excluded from consideration in management compensation.

A last technique for controlling for managerial bias in budget formulation is to use quantitative analysis of past budget variances to look for systematic biases. For example, managers of business units that systematically under-forecast sales may have their forecasts automatically revised upward. It is important, though, to do this using a transparent quantitative methodology; otherwise, managers will feel they are being unfairly penalized.

Improving the Budgeting Dialog

A problem with budgeting processes is a lack of fact-based discussion. Most of the dialog between senior and line management focuses on outputs—expected revenues and margins. But an effective, more objective, budget derives from a shared understanding of inputs, forecast assumptions, and how they fit together to determine expected financial performance. This understanding is often lacking simply because too little information is passed back and forth between line and senior management.

There are four primary obstacles to a quality planning and budgeting dialog: mindset, information systems, incentives, and organizational structure. By mindset we mean that people often take a blinkered view toward the world. Thus, a manager with a background in operations may be more focused on the supply capacity of a business while a marketing-oriented person may assume supply will adjust to meet demand. It is possible that each will come to the same conclusions about a business's prospects (say, that sales revenue will grow five percent), but each arrives at that conclusion in vastly different ways. Only by surfacing these mindsets can an informed dialog about expectations take place.

Understanding how different managers form expectations is only a part of the puzzle. The available information set also plays a critical role. This information set can include both internal and external data. As with all managerial problems, the available data are usually quite noisy—and so developing a shared understanding of what causes data to be more or less reliable is helpful for reconciling different sets of expectations. The next step after building a shared understanding is to start building more robust information systems that both senior and line management can use in forming their expectations. Particular emphasis should be given to external data—competitor benchmarks, consumer surveys, industry analyses—for these are often more "objective" in that they are removed from internal managerial biases.

Last, it is important to put the budget and expectations dialog firmly in the context of incentives and organizational structure. It is difficult for managers not to introduce biases into their forecasts that result from their place in the organization and their career objectives. It is rare indeed to see a capital project proposal that recommends a negative NPV project. Likewise, the phenomenon of hockey sticks in budgets is pervasive. Removing the incentives to create these biased forecasts is one part of the equation. The other is to create structures that help control these biases—for example, through independent third-party reviewers (internal strategy auditors and external consultants).

Given these obstacles to a quality dialog about forecasts, only wholesale structural and cultural changes will bring the necessary objectivity required. On the structural front firms need to invest in information systems that track operating value drivers for each business and its competitor benchmarks in addition to financial metrics that are normally tracked for all businesses. Compensation incentives need to be revamped to remove line managers' motivation to bias their forecasts. Last, new organizational forms must be pursued that reinforce the desired outcomes through appropriate monitoring systems, work processes, and decision-making systems, all aimed toward reducing the bias in forecasts.

Toward that end, an important process that needs to take place in any budgeting and planning exercise is the reconciliation of expectations at the corporate and business unit level (see Figure 3.7). This reconciliation process actually begins a step back, when the corporate center and line managers form their expectations. Ideally, the former takes a top-down approach so that expectations for each of the business units are consistent with expectations for the corporate total (ensure that the total equals the sum of the parts). The latter requires a bottom-up planning exercise that forms business expectations from forecasts of operating value drivers.

Whereas many planning processes begin and end with the target setting, we think targets should be evaluated last. The first step should always be an honest evaluation of each business's baseline potential. What will happen to the business if its existing plans are left in place, as if on autopilot? Scenarios can be constructed around this baseline that reflect major new investment initiatives, opportunities for cost-cutting or restructuring, or other fundamental changes to the business plan. Each scenario should be self-contained and internally consistent. Scenarios should be constructed both by line managers knowledgeable about the underlying economics of the business and senior managers with a more global perspective (aided, perhaps by input from analysts, investors, etc.). Both the baseline and various scenarios need to be reconciled between line and senior management's expectations.

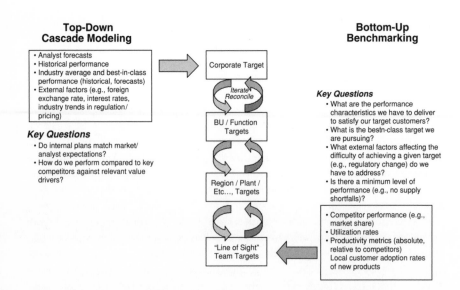

FIGURE 3.7   Reconciling expectations between corporate and operating.

The reconciliation process should be iterative and continuous. Iterations are needed to let each side understand the other's perspective. Line managers need to understand why investors, for example, may be skeptical that the business might achieve an organic growth rate well in excess of industry norms. Corporate managers need to understand the micro-level details of the business to understand what specific value drivers are behind anticipated results. As iterations progress, the two forecasts need to come together. It may be the case that senior management needs to revise its own expectations—with implications for outward communications to investors. Also, line managers need to adjust their expectations (usually to more realistic levels).

This reconciliation process should also be continuous—i.e., it should not start and end with the annual budgeting process. In fact, as we argue below, the budget process itself should not be fixed to an annual process. Maintaining the dialog about expectations on a regular basis—say, monthly or quarterly, allows both senior managers and line managers to move their expectations in tandem, and thereby create a shared understanding of what value has been created, and what value potential remains to be pursued.

Budgeting Need Not Be a Regularly Scheduled Event

Planning around an annual cycle is an arbitrary relic, passed down from years ago when seasonal cycles drove much of an agricultural economy. But in today's economy, driven by technology and information, and spanning multiple geographies, there is no necessity for most companies to follow an annual cycle (except, perhaps to plan for taxes).

A frequent complaint from line managers is their frustration for having to plan budgets up to 18 months in advance. This isn't to say they don't understand the value of forecasting that far out, but instead their complaint is that they are asked to commit to a certain level of resource need far in advance of the time at which they know what they need. Providing directional guidance to senior management as to what resources may be required 12 to 18 months down the road is one thing, but locking in those decisions is quite another. Although budget allocations are never "locked in," it is often a cumbersome and political process to go back to management asking for more resources, especially when no one gives back resources they don't need.

The end result is that companies are slow to adapt their resource allocations to changing market conditions. If line management sees an opportunity to capture value through an investment not previously anticipated, it can take weeks or months to get the resources approved. In the meantime, value is being lost, either through opportunity costs or direct losses to competitors.

While some companies have experimented with rolling budgets to solve this problem, we go a step further and suggest several complementary changes to the budgeting cycle:

1. Customize the planning horizon to the individual business unit in question.
2. Experiment with different planning horizons for different elements of the budget, even within a business.
3. Create corporate-level procedures for handling changing conditions (for example, fund a continual pool of contingency-based resources to allocate as new opportunities arise).
4. Create positive incentives for line managers to "return" unused resources mid-cycle.

Summary

This chapter is careful to point out that your stock price and your wealth if you own shares is always maximized by taking the action that gives you the best outcome relative to all other possibilities. In this chapter, we have limited our attention to what we call "baseline investment," i.e., capital spending that is expected. Chapter 4 discusses new (i.e., unexpected) investments made by the firm.

Going back to Equation 1.2, and remembering that "I" designates the amount of capital in place, then the stock price will go up if

$$[\text{Actual } ROIC - \text{Expected } ROIC]\ (I) > 0$$

This is the first of three ways to increase your stock price that are found in the definition of EBM. It says literally that if you can earn more than is expected (by the market), on assets in place, I, then your stock price will go up—in other words, "work your core assets harder."

Figure 3.8 shows two traps that are familiar to the top management of the many companies that have fallen into them. The first, the underinvestment trap, applies to companies that are assessed by the market as having very high expected return on invested capital, $E(ROIC_H)$. The trap occurs when management is confronted with an investment opportunity that it believes will earn less than $E(ROIC_H)$, but more than the cost of capital. In this case, there is the temptation not to invest for fear that the stock price will fall when the company's actual $ROIC$ turns out to be less than expected. This is the Underinvestment Trap. The stock price will fall because, in fact, the market's expected $ROIC$ on the company's existing assets will be revised down. Nevertheless, the investment should be made as long as it

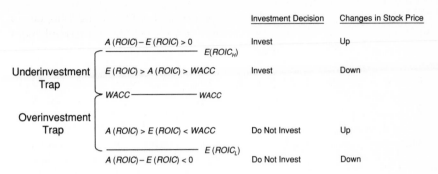

FIGURE 3.8   Traps for management.

earns the cost of capital, because if the capital is returned to shareholders, the best they can do with it is earn the cost of capital, *WACC*.

The second trap results in overinvestment, and applies to companies that are expected to earn less than their cost of capital on core assets. Management decides to invest in restructuring core assets. The investment will earn more than expected but still less than the cost of capital. Sure enough, the stock price will go up, but nevertheless, the company should not invest. Instead, it should return the cash to shareholders who can earn the cost of capital on it—a better result than reinvesting in the company at a rate less than the *WACC*.

Of course, getting the right level of baseline capital expenditures is only one of the challenges of managing existing businesses. This chapter also addressed the need for robust planning processes that provide management with the information it needs to form realistic expectations. An iterative, continuous planning process that reconciles both bottom-up and top-down approaches can help. Changes to the firm's planning organization, management incentives, and information systems can also improve the objectivity of forecasts.

CHAPTER 4

New Investment and Business Mix Decisions

The difference between maintenance capital (the subject of Chapter 3) and new investment is that the former refers to capital spent on an existing, and therefore, an expected, business activity. By way of contrast, new investment is unexpected from the market's point of view. It is the third term of Equation 1.2:

$$\begin{aligned} EBM = &[A(ROIC) - E(ROIC)]\ I \\ &- [A(WACC) - E(WACC)]\ I \\ &+ [ROIC - WACC]\ [A(I) - E(I)] \end{aligned} \qquad (1.2)$$

New investment can be a greenfield capital expense to start up a new line of business, or it may be an acquisition or joint venture.

The commonly accepted decision rule for capital projects is to invest if the net present value of a project is positive. A project with zero NPV is expected to return sufficient funds to pay back investors their opportunity cost of capital. All value above zero NPV accrues to shareholders, as residual claimants on the firm. Implementation of NPV is straightforward, as it only requires a forecast of cash flows over the life of the project and an estimate of the weighted average cost of capital. In this chapter, we argue that the hurdle for new investments is the weighted average cost of capital. Positive NPV projects are thought to meet this criteria. In merger and acquisition (M&A) situations, however, management may be confronted with a situation where the best alternative can have a negative NPV, if the second best alternative's NPV is even more negative.

In practice, discounted cash flow analysis—where it is conducted at all[1]—often runs into difficulties, both real and artificially imposed by management. Some of the former include the difficulty in accurately estimating a project-specific discount rate and obtaining from management unbiased forecasts of future cash flows. Some of the latter constraints include artificially increasing the discount rate (e.g., to counteract inflated project estimates) or imposing capital constraints without testing the ability to raise funds externally.

This chapter goes deeper than did Chapter 3 into the equivalence of the classical discounted cash flow method of estimating value and the residual income method. It then tackles the top management issue of the mix of businesses that the company should hold in its portfolio. This is followed by a discussion of merger and acquisition, and divestiture decisions in an EBM™ framework. Finally, we cover the relationship between real options thinking (that is replacing NPV) and EBM.

Formal Comparison of DCF and Residual Income Valuation

A popular modification of the NPV calculation is to measure the discounted value of expected economic profits. This is called the residual income method of valuation and is equivalent to calculating NPV, as it is simply a rearranging of the same terms that go into a discounted cash flow calculation.[2] In Chapter 3 we discussed this issue with a simple numerical example. We address it more formally here.

Mathematically, the present value of a perpetuity (i.e., a nongrowing annual cash flow that continues indefinitely) is equal to Equation 3.1 with $g = 0$, and is written as

$$V_0 = \frac{NOPLAT}{WACC} = \frac{E(EBIT)(1-T)}{WACC} \qquad (4.1)$$

Equation 4.1 is the discounted cash flow value, DCF. *EBIT* is earnings before interest and taxes, T is the cash tax rate on *EBIT*, before financing,

---

[1]Our discussion here is focused on decision-making analytics. It should be noted, however, that problems with most companies' capital budgeting exercises (for new projects) is not which metric they use, but the failure of internal processes to use those metrics (e.g., by failing to calculate any NPV at all for small projects).

[2]The equivalence between discounted cash flow NPV and the discounted value of expected economic profits is most straightforward with projects of finite lives; with infinite-lived projects and businesses, care must be taken so that "terminal value" calculations are consistent between the two methods. See Copeland et al, *Valuation*, 3rd Edition, Chapter 8.

and *WACC* is the cost of capital. If instead, we were to discount economic profit, i.e.,

$$EP = [E(ROIC) - WACC]I_0 \qquad (4.2)$$

and add the book value of capital, I_0, we would have what is called the economic profit (or residual income) version of the value of the firm.

$$V_0 = \frac{E(EP)}{WACC} + I_0 \qquad (4.3)$$

By substituting the definition of economic profit, Equation 4.2, into the definition of present value, Equation 4.3, we can prove that the definitions of value are the same.

$$V_0 = \frac{[E(EBIT)(1-T)/I_0 - WACC]I_0}{WACC} + I_0$$

$$= \frac{E(EBIT)(1-T)}{WACC}$$

We illustrate the two methods in Figure 4.1. The sum of the discounted cash flows equals the book value of the capital that was invested plus the discounted economic profit, defined as the spread between after-tax return on invested capital and the weighted average cost of capital, multiplied by the amount of invested capital.

For those using economic profit (or residual income), the advantage of this method is to facilitate better understanding among managers as to the

Initial investment (end of year 0)	1,000 IC
Annual after-tax operating profit	250 *EBIT* (1 –*T*) = *NOPLAT*
Annual depreciation	100
Cost of capital	10% = *WACC*

	DCF Analysis				EP Analysis			
Year	*NOPLAT*	Depreciation	Free Cash Flow	PV	Ending PP&E	Capital Charge	Annual *EP*	PV
0	(1,000)	—	(1,000)	(1,000.00)	1,000	—	0	—
1	250	100	350	318.18	900	100.0	150	136.36
2	250	100	350	289.26	800	90.0	160	132.23
3	250	100	350	262.96	700	80.0	170	127.72
4	250	100	350	239.05	600	70.0	180	122.94
5	250	100	350	217.32	500	60.0	190	117.98
6	250	100	350	197.57	400	50.0	200	112.89
7	250	100	350	179.61	300	40.0	210	107.76
8	250	100	350	163.28	200	30.0	220	102.63
9	250	100	350	148.43	100	20.0	230	97.54
10	250	100	350	134.94	—	10.0	240	92.53
				1,150.60				1,150.60

FIGURE 4.1 Equivalence of DCF and economic profit.

economic pattern of returns between new projects and existing businesses. But in terms of improvement to the underlying decision, the switch from discounted cash flows to discounted economic profits does not improve decision-making at all for new capital projects (some might argue it has made it potentially vulnerable to management manipulation, given the frequent number of adjustments that are sometimes made to accounting statements to derive economic profit calculations).

No matter what method is used, DCF or discounted economic profits, the new investment decision is ultimately what economists call an "ex ante" decision. It is made given the set of information available at the time and looking forward at expected cash flows. Selecting a positive NPV positive does not necessarily mean that the project will actually create value once it is implemented. After all, a wide range of factors can cause the project to deviate from expectations. Such deviations may be due to managerial failures such as poor project management leading to cost overruns, or to external factors such as unanticipated changes in the cost of capital, product market demand, or competitor responses.

If expectations are met exactly, the value of the firm goes up by the weighted average cost of capital and, consequently, shareholders get the cost of equity, k_s. To prove this (still assuming perpetuities and defining D as debt and S as equity) we solve for (one plus) the rate of return, k_s, on equity:

$$1 + k_s = \frac{S_1 + Div_1}{S_0} = \frac{V_1 - D_1 + Div_1}{V_0 - D_0}$$

$$= \frac{[E_1(ROIC)(1-T)I_0 / WACC] - D_1 + E_1(ROIC)(1-T)I_0 - rD(1-T)}{[E_0(ROIC)(1-T)I_0 / WACC] - D_0}$$

and if $E_0(ROIC) = E_1(ROIC)$, and $D_1 = D_0$ then k_s equals

$$1 + k_s = 1 + \frac{E_1(ROIC)(1-T)(I_0) - rD(1-T)}{[E_0(ROIC)(1-T)I_0 / WACC] - D}$$

$$1 + k_s = \frac{E(NI)}{S}, \quad \text{where } NI \text{ is net income after taxes}$$

Thus, shareholders' wealth increases at a rate just equal to the cost of equity if expected $ROIC$ equals actual $ROIC$, regardless of the level of $ROIC$. If, for example, the expected and actual $ROIC$ is 50 percent and the cost of equity is 15 percent, the total return to shareholders will be 15 percent.

When properly implemented, NPV is consistent with an EBM perspective since both are forward-looking metrics focusing on investor expectations. As far as EBM principles are concerned, there are two questions management needs to ask when evaluating new capital projects.

First, is the investment expected or unexpected? If it is expected, as was the maintenance investment covered in Chapter 3, one should invest as long as the project will earn at least the cost of capital, but if its *ROIC* is less than the expected *ROIC*, even though greater than the *WACC*, the stock price will go down. If it is an unexpected investment, and therefore a new investment, the stock price will go up as long as it earns an *ROIC* greater than the *WACC*. Why is there a difference? Because an investor pays the market value for the right to make expected investments at the expected *ROIC*. If the actual *ROIC* turns out to be less than expected, the market value is repriced downward. However, for unexpected investments, the investor pays an amount whose book value equals its market value, and gains value whenever *ROIC* is greater than the *WACC*.

Second, management is responsible for assessing the reasonableness of its expectations vis-à-vis those of the market.

New Investment

How can one say when a project is truly new, i.e., when is it unexpected? At first glance this question seems easy because any "new" project could be defined as unexpected. The flaw in this approach is that the market (investors and analysts) is not kept up-to-date on every single capital project in a company or its businesses. Given this lack of detailed information, market analysts tend to make high-level assumptions about the nature of a firm's capital investment. They may focus on such topics as capital devoted to an M&A program versus internally developed projects. Or, they simply make assumptions about the level of investment—either in absolute dollars, or relative to some benchmark such as sales or operating earnings. Thus, the market does not "expect" specific projects, but does expect a set of projects. Embedded in this expectation are both the amount of investment and the expected return on that investment.

We believe the following EBM guidelines are the starting point for segregating "new" (unexpected) from baseline expected capital investments.

- Is the product/service, market segment, or way of delivering the product/service significantly different from existing operations? In other words, would investors be surprised to learn about this project?
- Does the project materially change the expected volume growth, pricing power, or cost structure of the business beyond that already expected by investors?
- Is/are the project(s) part of a deliberate effort to significantly change the rate of capital investment?
- Is the project of sufficient scale to warrant discussion with investors as a unique investment opportunity?

■ Is the project a material change in the way in which the business makes its investments—for example, a switch from greenfield development to acquisition-driven investments?

The second set of questions management must ask involve assessing the reasonableness of cash flow forecasts in new project plans. While the reasonableness of forecasts is not a new problem for senior managers evaluating proposals put forth by line managers, EBM suggests a new standard. The right benchmark for evaluating forecasts is whether an investor would come to the same forecast conclusion, given the information management has at its disposal as well as other third-party information available to investors.

How to evaluate forecasts against this benchmark is more of an organizational problem than it is a financial one. An unbiased observer—not an advocate—must act to represent shareholder interests. This is often the CFO who is charged with providing a perspective on how investors would react to particular capital projects if they were to be informed with the same information management has at its disposal. Project proposals should incorporate not only financial forecasts, but also information used by line managers to derive the forecasts. The CFO is free to seek out additional third party information to validate or contradict management's information. At the end of the day, senior management should not have any concerns about sharing their forecasts with investors, should they be called on to do so.

Analyzing the Mix of Businesses

Senior management not only concerns itself with individual investment decisions related to specific lines of business, but also with evaluation of the portfolio as a whole, including how the various lines of business fit together. Before we apply EBM to portfolio analysis, it is worthwhile critiquing some analytical techniques we've encountered in practice. These techniques are the bread-and-butter of many consultants (we should know).

Price-to-Book Analysis

Some portfolio analysts compare businesses in the portfolio on the basis of market value multiples. One such analysis compares the price-to-book (P/B) values of different businesses, where 'price' is estimated using either market-value benchmarks or discounted cash flow analysis and 'book' is the book value of capital invested in the business. Businesses with P/B greater than one are sometimes described as "value creators" and those with P/B less than one are sometimes described as "value destroyers" (or diluters) (see Figure 4.2). Policy recommendations are thought to flow naturally from this taxonomy—capital investment should be diverted toward value-creating businesses, while value-destroying businesses should be restructured or divested.

Figure 4.2 illustrates P/B analysis scaled for the size of various business units. The amount of value created by a given business unit is the dollar difference between its estimated market value and the amount historically invested in the business. Because of scale differences, a large business with a P/B ratio slightly higher than 1.0 could have created more value (in total dollars) than a smaller business unit with a higher P/B ratio.

There are multiple problems with this kind of analysis. First, this look across the portfolio makes no allowance for synergies and cross-portfolio risk reduction. It is not necessarily true that divesting one of the "value-destroying" units will necessarily increase the total value of the corporation. Second, and more importantly from an EBM perspective, the analysis mixes up historical and forward-looking information. While value is forward-looking, book value reflects the historical amount of money invested in a business (including retained profits not distributed as dividends). Thus, the only thing we can conclude from looking at P/B is whether a business has created value relative to historical investments—not whether it is expected to create or destroy value in the future.

To understand this point in more detail, let's consider the cash flows, value, and price-to-book multiple of a single business from initial growth and investment phase through the business's maturity. We assume for simplicity that cash flows are completely paid out in dividends. The business starts in an investment phase with negative cash flows requiring outside capital. As the business grows it gradually needs less outside capital and eventually starts throwing off significant cash. After more time passes, cash

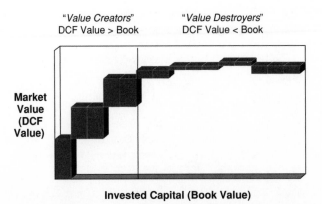

FIGURE 4.2 Illustration of typical corporate portfolio analysis.

flow begins to drop off as competition in the industry reaches a more mature phase. At any point in time, investors are assumed able to reinvest dividends in alternative investments of the same risk/return profile.

As can be seen from Figure 4.3, shareholder wealth starts out as a positive value—we've assumed the investment is positive NPV. Thus, right from the start the price-to-book ratio is greater than one, even though cash flows are negative. As time passes, shareholder wealth increases at a steady rate—in fact, it rises at exactly the cost of capital. As time passes, the NPV of the remaining cash flows rises because the negative cash flow years drop off from the NPV calculation. While this is happening, the total invested capital does not increase at the same rate. Thus, the price-to-book ratio rises. What value has been created? Investors earned exactly their expected cost of capital—though positive value was created when the original positive NPV business was created. Last, note what happens as cash flows begin to tail off. The NPV of future years declines through time, and the price-to-book ratio falls commensurately.

The point of this exercise is to show that price-to-book ratios (or any other value multiple such as P/E) change naturally through the evolution of a business's lifecycle. Moreover, a price-to-book greater than one does not indicate potential *future* value creation. The important question for management is not what the market multiple is today—nor even how it is *expected* to rise or fall in the future, given current performance expectations—but instead, what the potential market multiple can be through improved performance. EBM tells us to focus on potential *changes* in expectations, while P/B examines only the level of value in relation to amounts invested. P/B analysis can certainly help assess which businesses

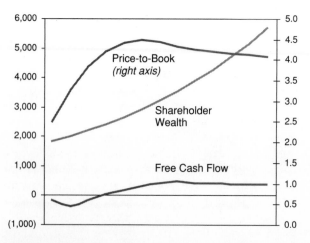

FIGURE 4.3   Price-to-book ratio changes of business matures.

or managers have historically made value-creating investments, but further analysis is required to know whether any particular business is capable of increasing expectations in the future.

Of course, the price-to-book analysis is not the only method used in portfolio analysis. Others focus on such factors as business unit returns on capital, operating margins, revenue growth rates, industry attractiveness, or position relative to competitors. In Chapter 1 we presented problems with looking strictly at financial metrics such as *ROIC*, earnings, or even revenue growth—namely, none of these metrics presents a comprehensive picture of value. And as we know from EBM, these metrics often are implemented or analyzed in a way that ignores expectations.

Strategic factors such as industry attractiveness or competitive position can help the analyst conceptualize the differences between businesses in a portfolio—but they do little to tell us about value creation. A company with a dominant market share in a growing market may not necessarily create value if share price already reflects this information. While we think it critical to understand these factors in forming and understanding expectations, using them as the basis to assess businesses within a portfolio simply takes the analyst one step further away from measuring value.

These critiques go to the heart of an EBM approach to evaluating the corporate portfolio. Businesses need to be evaluated against the *potential* for value creation, not simply their current value (based on expectations) or their historical performance. Yes, historical performance is an important element of understanding current and potential performance—but it is only one input of many toward understanding how the portfolio can be improved.

Portfolio analysis can be taken to one of two extremes, neither of which we feel is helpful to senior management. On the one hand is the analysis that focuses almost entirely on "strategic" considerations, such as competitive positioning, the capabilities of various business units, or the underlying market growth in each business segment. This analysis typically falls short for making the simple assumption that qualitative analysis of individual business units will suffice to fully capture the potential for value creation. Unfortunately, we have seen examples where good strategic logic fails under the light of financial analysis. At a minimum, this type of analysis may fail adequately to identify and measure cross-portfolio synergies and risk management opportunities.

On the other hand financial analysis often occurs in isolation of any deep understanding of strategy. Value creation is ultimately a function of strategic advantage and the ability of the company to capture more value from a business than any other potential owner might capture. Finance-focused analysis risks making broad assumptions that fail to hold up in practice. One such assumption is that capital expenditures should be directed to the high-return business units. That may or may not be the case, but a bottom-up strategic review that measures potential value creation from incremental investment is much more compelling than simply directing capital to those units already earning a high return. After all, past returns are no guarantee of future returns.

Low-Return Businesses

Another example of faulty thinking is that there is limited potential for value creation in low-return businesses. All too often the finance-focused portfolio review focuses on returns instead of scale. But even a small increase in profitability *above expectations* on a large, low-return business will likely create more value than growing, a small startup business with high margins slightly more than expected.

Any evaluation of portfolio composition should start with understanding strategic advantage and its link to financial performance. As finance practitioners we note that all good strategies in the end must provide acceptable returns in the context of industry competition. Thus, even analyses of portfolios that measure the "strategic positioning" of individual units must be judged financially. EBM presents portfolio analysts with new ways to view this old problem.

Note that EBM highlights that there are only two ways a business unit can create value (assuming that the cost of capital is beyond line management's control). The first is to find new investment opportunities that are expected to earn a return in excess of the business's cost of capital. This is the old NPV story we've explored above. The second is to exceed or raise expectations for ongoing operations. This is the expectations story that has been the common thread this book.

Value Realization

While there are only two ways to *create* value, there are a variety of ways to "realize" it. By realize value, we mean to say that once a set of expectations about an investment or business has been formed, there is still the problem of execution. In the long run, the business cannot keep going on mere promises of future returns—at some point it needs to actually generate returns. Those that excel at execution will be better suited to taking a business with a set level of expectations and delivering against that. Those that are not adept at execution may "realize" value by monetizing it—i.e., by selling it to a buyer willing to recognize and fulfill its expectations. When small firms go public or are acquired—and hand over control to professional managers—they are essentially taking the value created and turning it into real cash today.

It follows that a healthy corporate portfolio will have a mixture of opportunities for value creation and value realization. Value creation opportunities may be derived from investments in the traditional sense—R&D,

product launches, new technologies, etc. Alternatively, value creation opportunities may derive simply from the chance to turnaround failing businesses. It is worth noting that many investors in so-called "distressed" securities earn a substantial return on their investment (on average). Though some of this return is compensation for the illiquidity involved, much of it reflects the fact that there is often much value potential in taking an existing business with its existing systems and employees and raising its expected performance to even that of its peers. Turnaround value potential need not strictly be through internal turn around—value creation through sale to a more appropriate owner is a legitimate way to "create" such value (as long as the sale price allows the seller to capture the value creation).

A healthy portfolio may also have various business units devoted to value realization. This can include businesses whose valuations management believes are near their peak—and therefore should be sold to willing buyers where possible. Other business units may have steady and/or strong cash flows that can be a source of cash flows to investors or an internal source of funds for investment opportunities.

A mistake we often see in portfolio analyses conducted by consultants and managers alike is to assume the same type of mix of business is appropriate to all companies. Thus, all high–cash flow businesses are "attractive" while low–cash flow businesses are either candidates for investment or divestiture. We think this approach is too generic and therefore misses out on the point of portfolio decisions. In the end, the portfolio mix must reflect both corporate objectives and management's capabilities.

By corporate objectives we mean such basic goals as the choice between delivering steady, growing dividends or going after capital gains through internal growth and investment. In the extreme, it is the difference between treating the business like a bond or a growth stock. A bond-like business will require a portfolio disproportionately comprised of cash flow–generating businesses. It will also have some small number of (relatively) low-risk investments to grow businesses that will deliver cash flow in the future. Management at such a company will be most adept at "execution"—it will be able to deliver investors their expected return, and do so in a way that does not compromise the future. Firms with an objective of capital accumulation will, of course, have a portfolio weighted toward new investment opportunities or turnaround opportunities.

An EBM Approach to Portfolio Management

An EBM perspective on the corporate portfolio combines analysis of the potential for existing businesses with the potential value creation from new investment opportunities (Figure 4.4). For any business in the portfolio there are four possible responses to this opportunity set. Business units

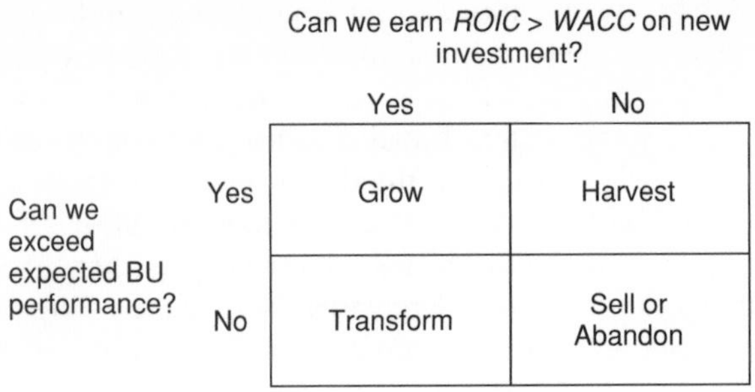

Can we earn *ROIC* > *WACC* on new
investment?

		Yes	No
Can we exceed expected BU performance?	Yes	Grow	Harvest
	No	Transform	Sell or Abandon

FIGURE 4.4   A strategic framework for resource allocation.

with opportunity to improve the existing business while also making new value-creating investments should pursue growth aggressively. Units that have limited opportunities for new investment opportunities should either be harvested to release untapped value potential or exited through value-maximizing sale, spin-off, or liquidation options. Last, units whose core business faces limited potential for improved value but with new investment opportunities, say, to new product or market segments, should transform the business through reallocation of capital from old to new uses.

The above grid is only one part of the story of a line of business as it shows value potential, but does not tell us anything about risk or achievability. It may be the case that management identified the *potential* to improve performance above market expectations, but, after considering implementation risks, believes the probability of realizing that potential is quite low. Next-best alternatives can suddenly seem that much more appealing when value potential is filtered by achievability.

EBM and M&A Planning

Mergers, acquisitions, and joint ventures are usually considered to be new investment. Many companies use mergers and acquisitions (M&A) as a critical tool toward achieving earnings growth. As far as making M&A decisions goes, EBM does not invalidate much of what has been written elsewhere, both in practitioner and academic texts. M&A decisions must still be based on a robust, forward-looking assessment of cash flows. Ideally the price paid for an acquisition will be less than the after-synergies discounted cash flow value of the target. While this is not often the case—the target often captures much of the value created in a deal—acquisitions do create value by lowering combined costs or increasing revenue potential between two firms. Fundamental considerations about the amount of synergies available, the likelihood of attaining them, and cultural/merger integration issues should still be first and foremost for M&A planners in an EBM-driven organization

Sometimes it is possible that it makes sense to overpay for an acquisition so that the net present value of the deal is negative. Once upon a time, in a country far, far away, the government owned the fifth-largest bank and decided to privatize it via a sale to the highest bidder. Let's think through the bidding strategy of the fourth-largest bank. Being a very efficient operator, it knew that upon consolidation many synergies could be achieved by restructuring the operations of the government bank, as well as capturing economies of scale from the combined operations post-merger. These value creation opportunities implied that Bank 4 could pay a high price indeed for Bank 5. But, Bank 4 also realized that Banks 1 through 3 were doing similar calculations and that they too could afford to pay high prices. It was at this point in the logic that Bank 4 asked itself this question:

What will our market price be if one of the three larger banks wins the bidding and we are relegated to being a second-tier bank for the foreseeable future? It was not a pretty picture, and one that that produced a value estimate much lower than the current market value of Bank 4. After due deliberation the management of Bank 4 realized that they could (and should) bid a price higher than the combined value of Banks 4 and 5, including synergies. When they did overbid, and won the bidding, their stock price fell. But it fell less than it would have had they lost the bidding. Their plan of action had a negative NPV, but it was higher than the next-best alternative (i.e., losing the bid). By the way, as the combination of Banks 4 and 5 positioned the merged company as the new #1 bank, the market values of Banks 1 to 3 fell even more than did the value of Bank 4.

Another circumstance where EBM changes the M&A picture is how to consider communication of M&A strategy with investors. Consider the case of a company built as a roll-up of many small, privately held companies. Management identified a universe of 50 additional potential targets and believes this is a critical factor to communicate to investors. Investors will take such an announcement into consideration when forecasting the value of the business. Market expectations will thereafter include expectations for the capital costs of making these acquisitions (cash or stock deals) as well as the anticipated synergies from these acquisitions. Since synergies are difficult to estimate, investors will most likely extrapolate from synergies realized in past deals. If the potential for 50 additional acquisitions was not previously expected by investors, we would expect share price to change by the net value of synergies from 50 deals less the present value of anticipated deal costs.

Now, is anything wrong with this picture? If the 50 targets are "true" targets—i.e., management will be able to acquire them at reasonable prices and realize synergies in line with historical experience—then is it worthwhile to pre-announce the acquisitions? If the acquisitions are deemed value-creating, the increase in share price could actually help fund the deals by provided stock as more valuable deal currency.

But what if the 50 targets are less sure deals? Any number of considerations might make anticipated value creation from 50 additional acquisitions less than management believes. The owners of these firms might be more cognizant of management's strategy and demand higher deal prices to sell out. Economic conditions might change such that deal financing becomes more expensive. Synergies might be less than anticipated (which may be the particular case here if we assume that management targeted the "easy" acquisitions in the past and is now moving on to the more difficult ones). If any of these downside risks to the M&A strategy becomes true, the share price will react negatively as new information comes to light. In this context, the original announcement has served only to add volatility to share price—running up share price in light of an anticipated M&A program, but then dropping share price as the truth comes out.

What does all this mean? In the prior chapter we discussed how business unit plans need to be rigorously tested for achievability. This same goes for M&A programs. Broad-brush communications to the market about an M&A plan that has not been thoroughly tested is likely to only bring greater uncertainty to the market's expectations. It would be better in that sense to announce deals on a case-by-case basis, letting the market infer from the pattern the extent of additional deal opportunities. Management may even go a step further and discuss with analysts (e.g., in conference calls) the uncertainties surrounding anticipated future acquisitions, thereby setting more realistic market expectations.

Divestiture

There is an old saying that the opposite of love is not hate—it is indifference—just ask any child. At corporations one could say that the opposite of acquisition is not divestiture—it is doing nothing—just ask the market. Like acquisition, divestiture is intended to create value. Ambivalence too often destroys value. At Royal Dutch Shell, the job is no longer EVP of M&A—rather, it is EVP of A&D, i.e. acquisitions and divestitures.

Criteria for Divesting a Business

Deciding to divest a business is often agonizing. Were purely financial considerations to prevail, we suspect divestitures would take place more often than they currently do. Management often feels they can improve the economic performance of even the worst of businesses. Or, if they get around to shopping the business, they may come to the conclusion that it is worth more than what outsiders are willing to pay.

Putting aside the frequent intrusion of nonfinancial considerations into the divestment decision, EBM can at least further refine the financial criteria involved. Simply put, a business should be divested if the corporation as a whole is more valuable having sold it (or, at the least, if divestiture is expected to prevent the future loss of value).

We've often seen the wrong criteria applied to the divestiture decision. The most common criterion cited by management is a return on capital less than the cost of capital (the economic spread). This spread is usually assessed on a historical basis for the businesses in a portfolio, and those earning negative spreads are slated for divestiture.

We saw in Chapter 3 that businesses that continue to earn a negative spread "destroy value" if they reinvest at rates less than expected, but can create value even if the return on invested capital is less than the *WACC*, given that the *ROIC* is greater than expected. But we have to remember what benchmark we are using when that judgment is made. The next-best alternative may be a transaction that sells the business for more than it is worth. If this is possible, the maintenance investment should not be made because selling it provides higher value.

To understand this point in more detail, consider the following stylized example, based in part on a true story. A change in regulation opened up an entire new industry. Due to high capital costs and regulatory controls, few companies entered this new industry and the average return on capital was at 10 percent, compared with an average cost of capital of 10 percent. Company Q was the first entrant to this market, having invested $100 million back when regulations were uncertain and the expected return on capital equaled the cost of capital. Its original market value, then, was $100 million since the company was effectively a project with an NPV = 0 (i.e., it delivered exactly the 10 percent expected of it). Since the company pays out all free cash flows as dividends, the stock's value does not change over time.

Once regulations changed, though, the market value of the firm halved. After some years, lobbying by competitors opened up a whole new set of competitors. In fact, these new competitors had a substantial cost and capacity advantage over the incumbents. Overnight the expected return on capital fell from 10 percent to 5 percent. Value fell commensurately, from $100mm to $50mm.

Now, let's fast-forward several years. The business earned 5 percent return on capital for these years, with no change in expectations for the future. Should management divest the business? The simple spread rule (*ROIC* > *WACC*?) suggests that they should—why continue running a business expected to earn a negative economic profit indefinitely? Before we rush out to sell, let's explore management's options in more detail.

First, management can retain the business as is without making any strategic or operational changes to it. The business produces an annual cash flow equal to 5 percent of their existing investment—$5mm in this case. Assuming the business still pays out 100 percent of free cash flows as dividends, the share price will stay constant. Thus, market value remains constant at $50mm. Shareholders earn their steady, risk-adjusted 10 percent = $5mm annually on $50mm market capitalization. While it is unfortunate that shareholders in the past lost value when the competitive landscape changed, there is nothing inherent in the existing business outlook that says there will be more value lost in the future.

Second, management can pursue an industry-consolidating acquisition. Perhaps this would allow it to realize significant cost-saving synergies in the short run, and through elimination of industry capacity raise the long-run expected return on capital from 5 percent back to 10 percent. In this case, expected cash flows will rise from $5mm to $10mm annually—but, depending on the price paid for the acquisition, the capital investment may or may not outweigh these additional cash flows. The worst case would be for management to overpay for this acquisition, thus having a market value less than $100mm after acquisitions. The best case would be to pay less than the value of the anticipated synergies, and thus allow existing shareholders to capture some of the value that is created. But again, as in the prior case, no matter what management does, after the acquisitions are complete and the synergies realized, share price will adjust so that investors again earn their 10 percent cost of capital. This option should be pursued if and only if management believes it can capture more value through appropriate acquisition pricing and execution than can be captured through alternative strategies.

Third, management can sell to a financial buyer—i.e., divest immediately. In this case, the value implications are easy to define—they are simply the selling price (after capital gains taxes, if any) less the existing value of the business ($50mm). This value may be higher or lower than other strategy alternatives, but also may entail less risk than pursuing a turnaround or consolidation play strategy.

Fourth, management can sell to a strategic buyer, acting as the target in the same type of industry-consolidating combination described above. As in the prior case, the price received is the critical factor. The only difference is that with a strategic buyer, the probable size of the premium earned on the sale is higher.

Fifth, management can liquidate the business, receiving nothing for it. Assuming liquidation costs are minimal, this is actually a value destroying move. Why? Because the business had positive value even on an as-is basis equal to $50mm. Liquidation would lose that value. We saw that although the return on capital was less than the cost of capital, cash flows were still positive, and because share price reflected this expected level of cash flows, shareholders would earn the appropriate return on their investment.

Sixth, management can pursue a turnaround plan. For example, a serious cost restructuring may make the business competitive with the recent industry entrants. Any turnaround plan that successfully raises expectations from a five percent return on capital to any level higher will have created value. The salient issues to understand, though, are whether this option creates more value than selling the business, as well as what the risks are involved with pursuing a turnaround plan. There may be significant value potential, but realization of that potential is another thing, as that requires convincing investors that the revised expectations are achievable and likely.

One of the lessons of this example is that divestiture may not always be the optimal choice even for negative spread businesses. The critical decision rule always should be what the impact is for shareholders. Keeping this in mind, the following outlines the elements of the divestment decision consistent with EBM:

- Divest only if the shareholder wealth is the same or higher without the business than with it.
- Explore all possible restructuring opportunities—set as the relevant baseline benchmark value.
- Value should be measured as total value, including real options (see below).
- Search for expectations gaps to find ways to maximize sell-off price (e.g., by selling to financial or strategic investors who may have higher expectations than current management, whether due to perceptual differences or expected synergies).
- Close business (rather than sell) only if liquidation value is greater than the after-tax, post-transaction cost value of all alternatives.
- Carefully consider the likelihood that the divestment decision would remain unchanged if new information were to come to light. What is the value of deferring the exit decisions? Is reentry feasible? What are the costs involved? What is the uncertainty behind expected future cash flows?

The above discussion of divestitures focused on criteria and process used to make the divestiture decision. We should add that these criteria should *not* be the same as those used to evaluate the performance of managers running the business in question. The question of pay for performance must be separated from the decision to exit a business.

Why is this the case? In a consistent EBM framework, managers must be motivated to deliver results that increase the value of the corporation. In the context of paying for performance, the relevant criterion is not whether the business will be retained, but instead whether the manager in question increased value. This view simplifies to one that rewards managers for maximizing the selling price of any business being divested (whether it be by sale, spin-off, or partial IPO).

When Does New Investment Become Expected?

In early 2000 an energy company called AES sold for a market-to-book multiple of 1.25 while at the same time most other energy companies were selling for much lower multiples, e.g., 0.50. A careful look at the mix of businesses would have indicated no significant differences between AES and its bretheren. They all had the same mix of power generation and distribution assets. There were no material differences in technology. Capital structure and the cost of capital were also similar.

There were two main differences—its operating margins and its growth rates. As shown in Figure 4.5, AES had made a number of successful acquisitions, particularly in South America, where as circumstance would have it, there were almost no competing bidders, and where operating skills could be transferred to improve operating margins. Furthermore, AES was able to achieve an *ROIC* in the 9–12 percent range—while its *WACC* was about eight percent. As AES began to repeat this success in acquisition after acquisition, the market began to anticipate—to expect—more growth via the same methods.

Figure 4.6 shows that AES beat analyst expectations every year from 1992 to 1998. Between January 1992 and September 1999 its stock outpaced the market by over 60 percent while other power companies were flat.

A DCF analysis that uses analyst estimates from late 1999 is shown in Figure 4.7. At that time there was only a $1 per share difference between

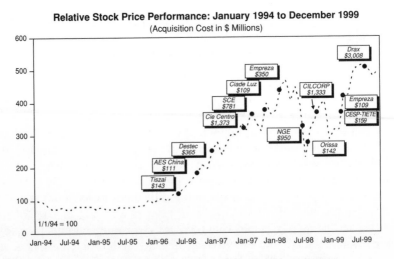

FIGURE 4.5   AES had an aggressive and successful acquisition strategy.

Source: CRSP, Center for Research in Security Prices. Graduate School of Business, The University of Chicago [2005]. Used with permission. All rights reserved. www.crsp.uchicago.edu. Monitor analysis

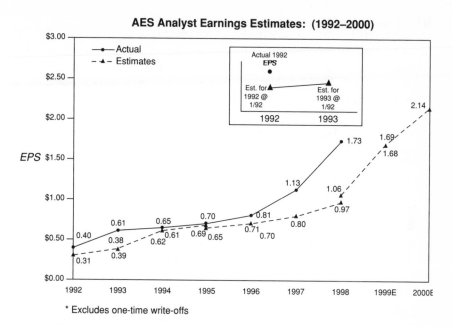

FIGURE 4.6   AES consistently beat analyst estimates.

Source: AES financials, Zack's

the model price per share of AES ($61) and the market price ($62). Note, however, that analysts were expecting 39 percent revenue growth in 2000, 58 percent in 2001, and 40 percent in 2002. This implied revenue of $3,253 million in 1999, $4,522 in 2000, $7,144 in 2001, and $10,002 in 2002. In addition, *ROIC* was expected to remain high.

If you are beginning to get the impression that sometimes the market builds unreasonable expectations into the current stock price—you are right. Figure 4.8 shows what happened in 2001–2003. In January 2001 analysts were forecasting $2.50 of earnings per share for AES in January 2003. By December 2002 this expectation had dropped to roughly $0.90 per share. Not only did the revenue growth projections prove wildly optimistic, but also the company ran into operating difficulties in its South American operations.

The playing field is littered with the wrecks of companies that were willing to allow the market to think whatever it wanted, or even to encourage market misperceptions. High levels of growth are difficult to sustain and are impossible in the long run, especially if growth if supposed to originate from a single industry. Bank One made dozens of acquisitions a month for several years; so did Waste Management and others, such as Sunglass Hut.

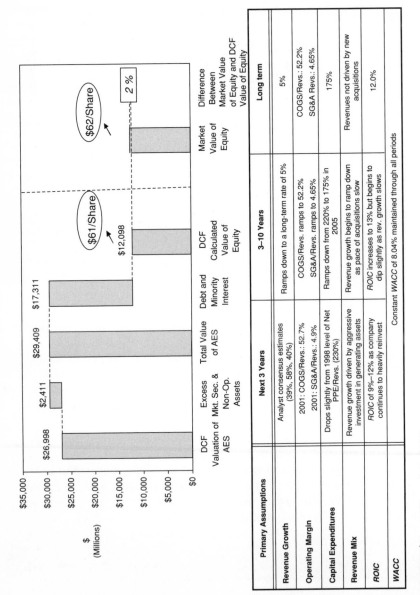

FIGURE 4.7 DCF model of AES.

Source: Monitor analysis

The chart shows ($ Millions):

- DCF Valuation of AES: $26,998
- Excess Mkt. Sec. & Non-Op. Assets: $2,411
- Total Value of AES: $29,409
- Debt and Minority Interest: $17,311
- DCF Calculated Value of Equity: $12,098 — $61/Share
- Market Value of Equity — $62/Share
- Difference Between Market Value of Equity and DCF Value of Equity: 2%

Primary Assumptions	Next 3 Years	3–10 Years	Long term
Revenue Growth	Analyst consensus estimates (39%, 58%, 40%)	Ramps down to a long-term rate of 5%	5%
Operating Margin	2001: COGS/Revs.: 52.7% 2001: SG&A/Revs.: 4.9%	COGS/Revs. ramps to 52.2% SG&A/Revs. ramps to 4.65%	COGS/Revs.: 52.2% SG&A Revs.: 4.65%
Capital Expenditures	Drops slightly from 1998 level of Net PPE/Revs. (230%)	Ramps down from 220% to 175% in 2005	175%
Revenue Mix	Revenue growth driven by aggressive investment in generating assets	Revenue growth begins to ramp down as pace of acquisitions slow	Revenues not driven by new acquisitions
ROIC	ROIC of 9%–12% as company continues to heavily reinvest	ROIC increases to 13% but begins to dip slightly as rev. growth slows	12.0%
WACC	Constant WACC of 8.04% maintained through all periods		

110

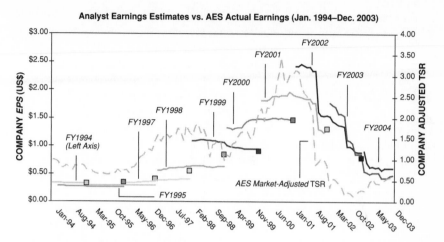

FIGURE 4.8 AES earnings expectations could not be met.

Note: Boxes denote Actual EPS before extraordinary items; Solid lines denote consensus analyst estimates for the current and next fiscal year.

Source: IBES, CRSP, Monitor analysis

At first, the market treats each new investment as unexpected, and value is created when the return on capital invested in the acquisition exceeds the cost of capital. But before long the growth in capital invested becomes expected. The third term in the EBM equation becomes a nightmare as new investment is converted by optimistic market expectations into expected investment. When high rates of growth in invested capital become expected, and when management does not have either the opportunity or capacity to meet expectations, then there will inevitably be a crash in the stock price.

Management should not be motivated to encourage market misperceptions. Not only is it unethical and illegal to intentionally do so, but it also results in greatly increased noise that produces a resulting decline in the total return to shareholders. Therefore, responsible management should provide good information about the limits to growth in order to prevent information mirages in the market place.

Real Options and EBM

Thus far we have discussed investment decision rules in terms of net present value, the metric used by most firms in their capital budgeting process. As a reminder, net present value is simply the discounted value of expected future cash flows associated with a project. These expectations are only point estimates of future cash flows, arrived at by taking management's best guess as to the future, taking a probability-weighted average of different future cash flow scenarios, or running various simulations of possible future cash flows (e.g., Monte Carlo simulations).

Our point is that expectations are not rock solid—there is a considerable amount of judgment in them. In fact, the further out a forecast is, the greater the guesswork becomes. Small deviations from forecasts in the short-term can compound through time, thus widening the spread of potential outcomes, as shown in Figure 4.9.

In addition to this embedded uncertainty in DCF cash flow expectations, there is also an implicit assumption behind NPV calculations that management has no discretion to change course through time. NPV assumes that management will continue a project to completion, no matter how events turn out. For example, NPV assumes an R&D project will continue even after scientists determine that a technology is not as feasible to use as originally believed. Management would be foolish to continue spending money on an irrelevant technology, but NPV makes no adjustments for this possibility.

Management has options to change course as it receives new information. An option is the right, but not the obligation, to take a course of action upon the receipt of information in the future. These options that management has are called "real options" because they are related to the "real" investments in tangible or intangible assets rather than strictly financial options such as an option to buy a share of stock.

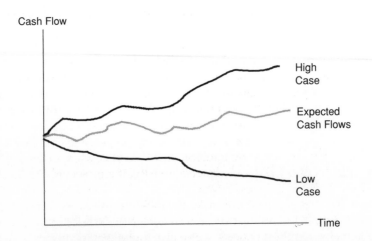

FIGURE 4.9   Cash flows for NPV.

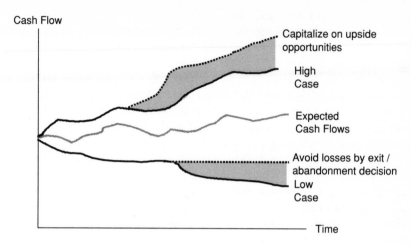

FIGURE 4.10 NPV cash flows modified by real options.

Figure 4.10 illustrates how options add value over and above that measured by NPV. We start with expected cash flows expressed as a range of possible outcomes—this is the basis for standard NPV calculations. Now, what if management has the right to abandon a project if financial results are too low? In many of the "down" states of the world, management would exit rather than continue to run the project to completion. By exercising this abandonment option management avoids the downside risk inherent in the expected cash flows. This essentially cuts off the negative tail of the distribution at some floor.

Furthermore, suppose that the project does better than expected—for example, prices were 20 percent higher than anticipated. Higher pricing allows management to enter additional markets not included in the original project plans (e.g., more distant geographies previously excluded from consideration due to transportation costs). This option to expand the project is not cost-free; management must make an additional investment to reach this new market. But this follow-on investment is only made if there is already enough new information available to suggest it is a positive value move. This expansion option raises the ceiling on possible cash flows, over and above that suggested by traditional NPV cash flow expectations.

Option value is always incremental to NPV. If a project is NPV-positive, one does not need to assess option value in order to make the investment decision. But option value can make the difference between accepting and rejecting projects with negative or near-zero NPVs. Based on our experience implementing real options, we've also found that incorporating option values into project valuations can change the rank ordering of projects—

relevant for cases where senior management believes a capital or managerial talent constraint prevents pursuit of all value-enhancing projects.

Real options do not always matter in the sense that sometimes their contribution to value is so small that traditional discounted cash flow analysis suffices. There are two factors that together can be used as a rough gauge of whether real options are important to a particular business or investment opportunity. First is whether there is uncertainty—e.g., uncertainty about market demand, input costs, technology, and so on. The second factor is whether management has flexibility to respond as new information comes to light. Where management has no flexibility to respond and there is substantial uncertainty, it is basically a bet. Where flexibility is high but uncertainty is low, option value will be small (i.e., because management's flexibility will not materially change cash flows). Figure 4.11 illustrates the combined impact of managerial flexibility and uncertainty on option value.

The highest valued real options, relative to the NPV of the underlying inflexible project, are found when the NPV is close to zero. In these situations, exercise of the real options is likely, but far from certain. If the present NPV is very high, any options (calls) will be certain to be exercised and therefore provide little extra value relative to a base case that would assume their exercise. If the project is way-out-of-the-money, exercise is so unlikely that optionality adds little value. Therefore, near-the-money real options add the greatest percentage value.

There are several ways in which real options modify EBM-based investment decision-making and performance evaluation.

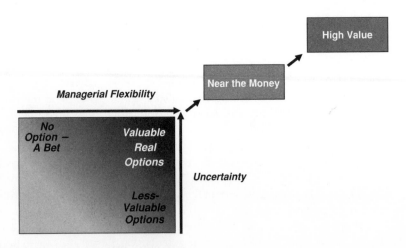

FIGURE 4.11   When do real options matter?

Source: Monitor analysis

Real Options and New (Unexpected) Projects

Where real options are valuable and consequential to value, NPV will not necessarily provide the correct answer as to whether or not a project should be pursued. Measuring total project value will give a better picture of the value of new investment opportunities. Conducting the real options analysis will also give more insight into what the optimal timing is to pursue various projects. For example, a project may be valuable, but deferring it until a later date when new information is available may be the optimal course of action.

Real Options and Baseline (Expected) Projects/Managerial Performance

No project ever goes exactly to plan. We discussed in Chapter 3 that management should evaluate maintenance/core business projects against expectations for the business. How do we reconcile this with the observation that expectations are only a probabilistic view of the future? How do we judge managerial performance when no matter what happens, variances from expectations are inevitable?

There are two factors that need to be separated when evaluating management performance in project implementation. The first factor is the sources of variance from expectations. In this regard it is important to measure and judge the following:

- Did management have control over the factors driving variances from expectations?
- Were these variances—and the underlying factors driving them—within the original range of uncertainty outlined by management?

The second factor is how management responded to the variances. Using the terminology of real options, did management exercise its options appropriately given the arrival of new information? Here it is worth asking the following:

- What options did management have at its disposal?
- What trigger points (timing and market or technical conditions) had been previously identified for exercising these options?
- Did management exercise these options in a timely manner?

This latter point is particularly important. Though it is increasingly commonplace among finance practitioners to understand the sources of option value, it is still unclear to many the value loss from suboptimal exercise of options. It is not enough to simply identify the options; if management is habitually slow to respond to new information, much of this option value evaporates.

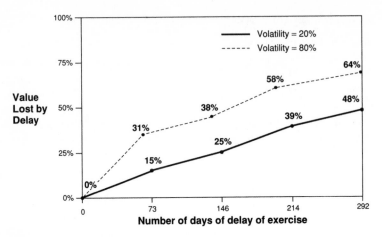

FIGURE 4.12   Cost of being asleep at the wheel.

Source: Reprinted by permission of Harvard Business Review, an exhibit from "A Real-World Way to Manage Real Options," by Tom Copeland and Peter Tufano, March 2004, Copyright © 2004 by the President and Fellows of Harvard College, all rights reserved.

In a *Harvard Business Review* article, Copeland and Tufano (2004) report that a major problem with real options is that managers don't always exercise them at the right time. Given an American put, such as the right to abandon a failed line of research, where the option is out-the-money and the underlying value has a 20 percent volatility, the cost of being asleep at the switch is 15 percent after only a few months, as shown in Figure 4.12.[3] Early exercise also destroys value. The temptation is to exercise as soon as the option is in-the-money. Figure 4.13 shows the cost of exercising a one-year American call on a new dividend-paying stock too early. Clearly, management can lose substantial value by exercising either too early or too late.

In order to capture as much option value as possible, management needs systems that encourage optimal exercise of these options. This requires real options analysis embedded in the original project or business planning effort. Such analysis would identify the most critical options, the key drivers of uncertainty, and the specific market or technical outcomes for exercising various decisions. Ongoing project or business information systems must be set up to focus on the critical information needed to exercise these options, providing frequent updates on the state of the world management faces.

---

[3]A put is the right to sell (or abandon) an asset for a predetermined price (e.g., the money that is saved by abandoning a line of research).

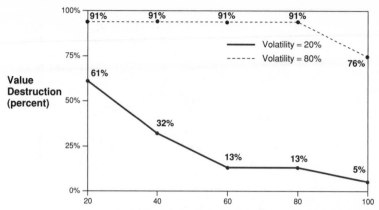

Early exercise: Percentage by which market price exceeds exercise price.

FIGURE 4.13   Cost of an itchy trigger finger.

Source: Reprinted by permission of Harvard Business Review, an exhibit from
"A Real-World Way to Manage Real Options," by Tom Copeland and Peter Tufano, March
2004, Copyright © 2004 by the President and Fellows of Harvard College, all rights reserved.

As an example, we evaluated the optimal exit decision for a high-tech conglomerate with a business that had substantial negative NPV. Our analysis determined that in spite of this negative NPV, there was sufficient uncertainty and managerial flexibility to justify deferring the exit decision for some time. In fact, together with management we determined that the earliest optimal exit decision was not for another year, and was contingent on the technical success of our client and its main competitor in their respective new product launches. The analysis provided senior management with clear signals and timing for making an exit decision. Without this analysis, it is certain that the whole financial analysis of the business would be repeated every few months as board members continued to question the need to stay in a negative cash flow business.

Real Options and Strategic Planning

As finance-oriented practitioners who work with strategy-focused managers, we're often struck by how traditional approaches to strategic planning are biased against option value. In fact, we know many who fall into this trap, imposed, it seems, by the historical approach to investment decision-making. This approach sought to identify a set of mutually exclusive strategies that could then be evaluated for their potential to create value. Although there are many approaches as to how particular strategies are derived or formulated, in the end they are almost always measured against

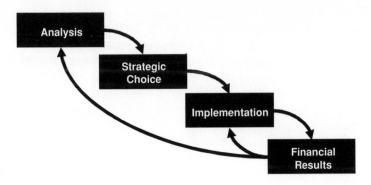

FIGURE 4.14   Traditional strategic planning feedback loop.

NPV or, more commonly, a set of metrics that tend to correlate with NPV, such as expected future return on capital.

This traditional evaluation process, rooted as it is in thinking similar to the logic used in NPV analysis, forces managers to make a single, non-contingent strategic choice as to which plan is better for the business going forward. Significant improvements have been made in strategic planning by doing this supposedly simple task better—for example, by using more rigorous methods to ensure strategies are truly mutually exclusive. Another improvement has been the replacement of "boil the ocean" analysis with targeted research that identifies the critical information needed to select among these mutually exclusive choices.[4]

A consequence of the traditional approach is a long timeframe between analysis, action planning, implementation, feedback, and course correction. This feedback loop is illustrated in Figure 4.14. One of the defining characteristics of this loop is the delay between deterioration of financial performance and the selection/implementation of an alternative strategy. The sequence thus usually goes like this: select a strategy → take time to implement → wait for financial results to validate strategy → if financial results are inadequate, revisit implementation or go back to strategy drawing board.

Another defining characteristic is the emphasis on financial results—revenues, income, or similar metrics—as indicators of potential problems. This emphasis on outputs (results) rather than inputs forces an additional layer of analysis to determine why results are inadequate. Was it due to poor implementation, poor strategic choice, or a changed external environment?

---

[4]See, for example, Roger Martin, "Changing the Mind of the Corporation," *Harvard Business Review*, November–December 1993.

The traditional approach fails to adequately incorporate uncertainty as well as management's ability to respond to new information. Simply put, the strategy that may be most appropriate today may not be the most appropriate strategy in the future once new information comes to light. A real options approach to strategy allows management not only to capture flexibility value, but to incorporate such value capture into their entire approach to strategy. Among the changes a real options mindset brings to strategy are:

■ Strategies are not mutually exclusive, but instead are contingent. Under one set of conditions strategy A may be optimal, while under a different set of conditions strategy B may be optimal.

■ More rapid switch from a failing strategy to a more optimal choice given current market conditions. This derives from an emphasis on inputs, not outputs. Real options analysis forces managers to understand the underlying drivers of uncertainty and value in a way that allows them to monitor these inputs on a constant basis, searching for signals to change course. There is no need to revisit the original strategy analysis unless significant changes to industry economics are evident.

■ Greater confidence from investors and/or senior management by pre-committing to optimal courses of action. We know many a board member, for example, who would be greatly relieved to hear specific timing and conditions for making strategic choices in the future—no need to keep revisiting the same questions each time a new set of disappointing results arise.

So how would a real options approach to strategy be implemented? As with any decisions about strategy, the firm's value proposition to customers must be our starting point. As with traditional strategy analysis, managers should investigate which value proposition is most appropriate to winning in today's competitive environment. The real options analysis must then assess what key uncertainties are affecting the competitive and economic landscape. More specifically, a map should be drawn based on the key uncertainties driving the choice of one value proposition over another.

As an example, suppose a designer clothing retailer determines that its optimal value proposition today is to provide men with a narrow, premium-priced line of clothing aimed at high-income young professionals based on the unique styling approach of an elite set of designers. This retailer's value proposition, though, is premised on several factors that, although true today, could change in the future: the size and growth of the premium clothing segment, the availability of low-cost/high-quality manufacturing, and the fashion relevance of the firm's design team.

A typical approach to strategy would end there. The flexible approach would determine contingent strategies for both upside and downside scenarios. If competitive conditions are favorable, for example, the firm might

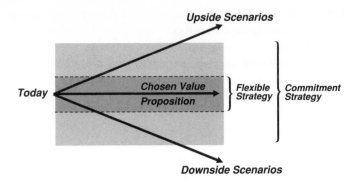

FIGURE 4.15   Real options approach to strategy.

expand its product offering (e.g., offer home furnishings) or offer clothing to new target customers (women or children). On the downside, the contingent strategy might be to drop the high-cost design team in favor of product design capable of rapidly adopting in-fashion styles at low cost.

The real options strategist would take the above strategic choices and determine specific signals for switching from today's value proposition to one of the contingent strategies. One such signal might be the growth rate in incomes for 25- to 35-year-old men. If the growth rate exceeds six percent the firm might offer its expanded product line for men. If the growth rate drops below three percent the firm might abandon its high-cost, premium-priced strategy in favor of the strategy of rapid adoption of in-fashion styles. If either signal is seen in the market data, the firm would switch strategies immediately instead of reanalyzing the market.

There might be cases where the firm chooses a strategy that requires commitment even in the face of changing market conditions. Another retailer might choose to be the low-cost provider, sourcing its clothing through long-term fixed rate contracts with overseas manufacturers. By locking in low-cost supplies, the retailer might secure itself a dominant position as the low-priced provider (at "good enough" quality levels).

Figure 4.15 illustrates how one might approach strategic choices with a real options mindset. The flexible strategy would select a value proposition that could succeed across a narrow base case of industry conditions. The commitment strategy would select a value proposition that could succeed across a wide range of industry outcomes.

Real Options and Budgets

The budgeting process that most companies follow tends to be quite rigid—they result from following the typical annual budgeting process. Most managers are smart enough to know that there is considerable uncertainty in their forecasts and so they try to build in some "padding" in their budgets.

We can think of such padding as an option—if competitive conditions present opportunities, having funds available immediately is preferable to having to continually go back to corporate for permission. At the end of the year, if these excess funds are not used managers then look all the more productive for having exceeded their budget targets. In some firms this padding is made explicit in the form of slush funds or pools of capital that line managers have discretion to spend as they see fit.

These approaches—budget padding and discretionary pools of funds—are partially effective as stop-gap measures, but they fail to inform senior management of critical information. As an example, by padding budgets senior management is deprived of an accurate picture of what the businesses truly expect. Moreover, senior managers lack any information as to what might change that would cause a business to spend more (or less) than originally budgeted.

There are alternatives to these approaches. One way to get around the problem is to move away from annual budget cycles. Some firms have experimented with rolling 12-month budgets, for example. It makes more sense to us to go a step further and integrate the strategic and operating planning processes in a way that produces a single, longer-range "budget" for each business. Each business is able to update that plan at any point, as new information comes to light or new decisions are made by management. Some revisions would require the approval of corporate management, while others might be at the discretion of line management. The budget then becomes a tool for communicating upwards line management's revised expectations and resource needs.

Another alternative is to create conditional budgets. A conditional budget would first use real options analysis to identify the uncertainties the business faces and the flexibilities management has at its disposal. In order to be manageable analytically, these uncertainties and flexibilities could be restricted to those deemed most important to business valuation. Management would create a set of budgets, one of which would be a baseline, but others would be conditional on certain real options triggers being hit. For example, management may have the flexibility to expand its marketing presence into a new geography but would only do so if industry demand in that area exceeded some baseline volume level. With this real option, a conditional budget would include the necessary expenditures to enter the new market, the expected revenues from doing so, and would also highlight the trigger factor for switching from the baseline to that conditional budget.

Conditional budgets would allow corporate management to have a better handle on its baseline set of expectations—as well as the range of possible outcomes across all the various businesses. For example, corporate could create an integrated picture of all the budgets that might be conditional on a single factor (e.g., the price of key commodity input used by multiple businesses) to stress test the corporate-wide budget against this factor.

Summary

This chapter focused on one of three general ways that EBM creates value—namely, make profitable, new [unexpected] investments:

$$[ROIC - WACC] \times [\text{Actual } (I) - \text{Expected } (I)].$$

Profitable investments are those in which $ROIC > WACC$.

From this simple principle we elaborated several key points related to new investments:

- While the "old" net present value decision rule still applies to new investments, it is important to determine whether a particular investment qualifies as "new" or unexpected.
- The divestiture decision, typically thought of as the reverse of an investment decision, should not be decided solely on the basis of the spread between $ROIC$ and $WACC$. Divestiture decisions must be considered relative to all available options including internal restructuring, reinvestment, harvesting, or running the business as is. For low-return businesses, wealth was destroyed back when expectations fell. Divestitures are forward-looking decisions that should not be clouded by past losses in value. Note, however, that when the spread is negative, value can be created if actual investment is less than expected.
- The businesses in the corporate portfolio need to be evaluated for their potential value creation, not their historical performance. Value creation may derive from either earning more than expected on existing projects, or making new, unexpected investments. After evaluating potential value creation, businesses can then be assessed for growth, transformation, harvesting, or divestiture.
- While the NPV decision for investments is well established, real options analysis can provide a more complete picture of value that reflects uncertainty in expectations as well as management's flexibility to respond to new information. Real options analysis suggests not only new ways to think about investment decisions, but also ways to think about strategies, budgets, and planning decisions in a more flexible, adaptive way.
- M&A strategy and its related investment decisions also need to be evaluated in an expectations framework that delineates between expected acquisitions versus unexpected acquisitions. This has implications both for M&A decisions themselves as well as how management communicates to the market its overall acquisition versus organic growth strategies.

CHAPTER 5

What About the *WACC*?

Introduction

Prior chapters have shown why the weighted average cost of capital (*WACC*) is an inappropriate guideline for understanding the link between performance measurement and changes in the stock price. Businesses earning returns well above the *WACC* may cause a decline in stock value if they fail to live up to expectations or do so only at the expense of future performance. Businesses earning returns below the *WACC* may experience increases in their stock price if they perform better than expectations or raise expectations about the future.

In this chapter we discuss how the *WACC* fits into an EBM framework. Specifically, we make a case that the *WACC* should not be discarded because all investments must earn more than *WACC* in order to create shareholder wealth. We also discuss how one might estimate the *expected* cost of capital in the future, as this is relevant for businesses undergoing a significant restructuring or when macroeconomic conditions are changing rapidly. We also discuss measuring the *WACC* at the business unit level—something we have found all too often neglected by many of our clients. Finally, we end the chapter with a discussion of capital structure—an important decision tied not only to the firm's cost of capital, but also expectations of operating and investing results.

The *WACC* Doesn't Matter—Or Does It?

In Chapters 3 and 4 we showed clear cases where the *WACC* is relevant—the evaluation of capital projects. As a key input to standard capital budgeting techniques, every business needs to know its *WACC* in order to calculate net present values (NPVs).[1] But how does the *WACC* intersect with value creation at existing businesses? Recall the equation showing the three paths to value creation.

$$\text{EBM} = \text{Actual } EP - \text{Expected } EP \qquad (1.2)$$
$$\text{EBM} = [\text{Actual } ROIC - \text{Expected } ROIC]\ (I) \qquad (a)$$
$$\quad - [\text{Actual } WACC - \text{Expected } WACC]\ (I) \qquad (b)$$
$$\quad + [ROIC - WACC][\text{Actual } I - \text{Expected } I] \qquad (c)$$

As a reminder, term (a) indicates that value is created by earning a return on capital greater than the expected return on capital for existing investments—by working core assets harder. Term (b) indicates that unexpected decreases in the cost of capital can lead to value creation (proportional to the amount of capital previously invested in the business). The final term (c) represents value creation through pursuit of NPV-positive projects (i.e., projects that earn on a discounted cash flow basis a return on invested capital greater than the cost of capital).

Thus far we have not focused on the second term in this equation for several reasons. First, managing the cost of capital is typically seen as the domain of the CFO, who has primary responsibility for making capital structure decisions. However, we note that the primary determinant of the company's cost of capital will be the business risk of its portfolio. This leads to the second point—that the business risk is largely something beyond the control of line management, even though managers can choose how much of this risk to hedge, how to do so, and which lines of business to pursue. Third, much of the unexpected changes in the cost of capital derive from macroeconomic factors that affect unexpected changes in interest rates or capital market changes in expected risk premia on stocks and bonds. Although senior management at a high level may control the cost of capital through investment and financing decisions, unexpected changes in the cost of capital will frequently derive from factors outside even senior management's control.

We argue, though, that management should pay careful attention to *WACC*—and not just because of its use in making investment decisions. The *WACC* can also be a critical factor in making harvest versus investment decisions, or in deciding the weightings to place in evaluating short-term and long-term expectations. Later in the chapter we explain these issues in more detail. We turn now to explaining how managers can form a view on how the *WACC* is expected to evolve through time.

---

[1]Note that where real options methods are used to value new projects, the analysis starts with the traditional NPV of the project (without flexibility). This, of course, discounts cash flows at the *WACC*.

Expectations and the Calculation of the *WACC*

Before we discuss the *expected* cost of capital, it is worthwhile reviewing what the weighted average cost of capital is. The *WACC* is a weighted average of the firm's marginal costs of capital—the average of the expected rates of return that investors require to compensate them for their risk. The *WACC* is defined by the following equation:

$$WACC = k_b\left(1-T\right)\frac{\text{Debt}}{\text{Capital}} + k_p\frac{\text{Preferred}}{\text{Capital}} + k_s\frac{\text{Equity}}{\text{Capital}} \qquad (5.1)$$

In this equation, k_b, the cost of debt (bonds), is measured as the *expected* yield on the firm's debt. This may be directly observed if the firm has publicly traded debt whose prices can be used to calculate yield-to-maturity. Where publicly traded prices are not available, the yield on comparable bonds of similar credit risk can be used instead (taking care to distinguish between the yield differences between secured and unsecured securities). T is the marginal statutory tax rate, k_p is the cost of preferred stock, measured simply as the expected yield on this stock (equity), and k_s is the cost equity, which is typically estimated using the capital asset pricing model (CAPM).

In practice, firms often calculate a single *WACC*—usually using interest rate maturities that roughly match either an arbitrary maturity length (say, 10 years) or the duration implied by valuation models.[2] For example, the free cash flow pattern of a large, established company may have a duration of about 10 years—in which case a single *WACC* is estimated using 10-year maturities for the components, and that single 10-year *WACC* is applied to all cash flows. In reality, this single point estimate of the *WACC* may encompass a cost of capital that varies through time.

For most purposes, the added precision of knowing the year-by-year *WACC* estimate is not worth the added estimation complexity. We do recommend estimating yearly costs of capital for analyzing leveraged buyouts, distressed company turnarounds, or other situations where capital structure may be expected to change rapidly through time. For now, our focus is not so much on having year-by-year *WACC* estimates, but instead presenting some basic mechanics for how one would estimate the expected *WACC*—and therefore whether to expect the *WACC* to increase or decrease through time.

---

[2]Duration may be defined as the percent change in the present value of a financial instrument with respect to a percentage change in interest rates, roughly equivalent to the weighted average timing of expected cash flows measured in present value terms.

The Expected Cost of Debt

Some companies still think of the cost of debt as the coupon rate they agreed to pay when they borrowed. This is just like a homeowner believing that the eight percent mortgage rate on his home when he borrowed 15 years ago is the appropriate rate for today's decision making. It isn't. New mortgage rates at which he could refinance are forward-looking and might be as low as four or five percent. They are his opportunity cost of debt. This section reviews the methodology for determining what your expected *WACC* is today.

Expected Risk-Free Rate

There are two primary drivers for the cost of corporate debt—the default-free rate (e.g., the yield on U.S. Treasury securities) and the credit spread. Let's explore the default-free rate first. "Risk-free" is something of a misnomer because even a default-free bond will change in value when interest rates change. U.S. government debt is commonly believed to be default-free. In order to understand the market's expectations for yields on government securities, we have to understand the yield curve. The yield curve (as illustrated in Figure 5.1 at four different points in time) is simply a plot of the yield by bond maturity. For theoretical reasons, we plot the yield on "stripped" U.S. Treasuries as being the closest indicators of the yield at various maturities.[3]

There are several theories as to what causes a yield curve to be shaped the way it is—upward-sloping, flat, downward-sloping, and so on. We subscribe to the expectations hypothesis that the yield curve reflects the market's expectations for interest rates in the future (after all, the central theme of this book is that, on average, security prices reflect expectations). The following equation helps us to do so:

$$(1 + {_0}R_t)^t = (1 + {_0}R_1)(1 + {_1}f_2)...(1 + {_{t-1}}f_t)$$ (5.2)

where ${_0}R_t$ = geometric average annual yield to maturity (cost to borrow from today to time *t*)

${_{t-1}}f_t$ = expected spot rate from time *t* −1 to time *t*, also called the forward rate

Rearranging terms, we can infer the expected one-year interest rate for any particular year as:

---

[3]A U.S. Treasury strip is a security created by "stripping" the coupon payments out from principal repayment on U.S. Treasury securities. By stripping out coupon payments and repackaging the interest and principal by payment date, investors can create the equivalent of zero-coupon bonds.

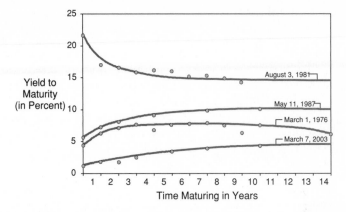

FIGURE 5.1 Yield to maturity on U.S. Treasuries.

Source: Financial Theory and Corporate Policy, 4th ed., by Thomas E. Copeland, J. Fred Weston, and Kuldeep Shastri, ISBN: 0321127218, December 2003 pp.260. Reprinted by permission of Pearson Education, Inc., Upper Saddle River, NJ.

$$_{t-1}f_t = \frac{\left(1+ {_0R_t}\right)^t}{\left(1+ {_0R_{t-1}}\right)^{t-1}} - 1 \qquad (5.3)$$

where $_0R_t$ = spot rate yield for t maturity (cost to borrow from today to time t)

$_{t-1}f_t$ = expected one year borrowing from time $t-1$ to time t

Thus, using the yield curve above, the expected one-year interest rates for the 10 years from today (June, 2004) are given as the dashed line in Figure 5.2.

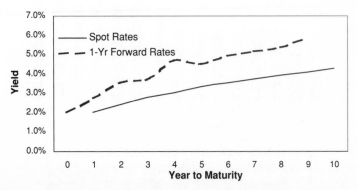

FIGURE 5.2 Estimated one-year forward rates (as of June 2004).

So, based on the yield curve today, we know that short-term risk-free borrowing rates are low and are expected to rise significantly in the next few years. Along with the increases in the risk-free borrowing rate, we would expect the yearly cost of debt for any company to increase as well.

Expected Credit Risk Spread

The second input to the cost of corporate debt is the credit risk premium above the default-free rate. There are two determinants to this risk premium—company-specific credit risk and the economy-wide spread for comparable credit risks.

Economy-wide credit risk spreads are difficult to forecast—if they weren't, we'd certainly be richer. We suggest a simple approach that assumes the credit risk spread either remains unchanged from current levels or returns to historical averages. Figure 5.3 illustrates the 10-year yields for different credit rating qualities relative to U.S. treasuries. They are called "promised yields" because they assume that all payments and their timing occur exactly as promised. In Figure 5.4 we show the historical credit risk spread for A-rated industrial bonds at both the 1- and the 10-year maturities. Based on this data, we could forecast that the 10-year spread either continue at the current 50–basis point spread, or return to the historical average of 65 basis points. Figure 5.5 is also presented to illustrate how spreads over Treasuries have changed for different credit ratings—and in particular, how

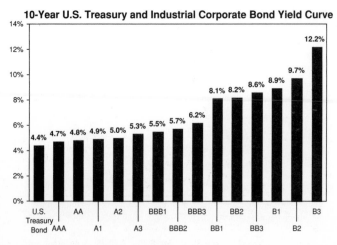

FIGURE 5.3   Promised yields to maturity, U.S. corporate bonds.

Source: Financial Theory and Corporate Policy, 4th ed., by Thomas E. Copeland, J. Fred Weston, and Kuldeep Shastri, ISBN: 0321127218, December 2003. Reprinted by permission of Pearson Education, Inc., Upper Saddle River, NJ.

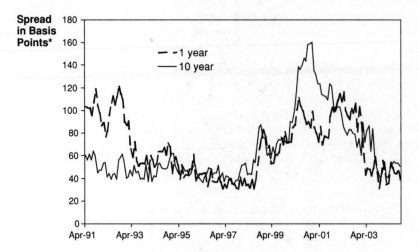

FIGURE 5.4 A-rated bond yield spreads over U.S. Treasuries (1991–2004).

*A basis point is one-hundredth of one percentage point.

Source: Bloomberg

the spread for lower credit qualities such as BBB-rated firms can vary with overall economic conditions.

Forecasting company-specific credit risk requires understanding how the firm's capital structure and other financial characteristics will change and how those changes interact with credit rating. We need to forecast

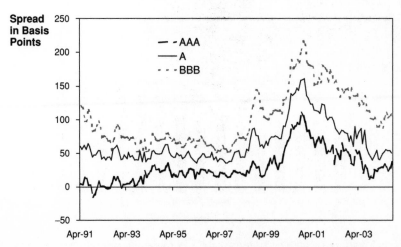

FIGURE 5.5 10-year bond yield spreads over U.S. Treasuries by credit rating, 1991–2004.

Source: Bloomberg

credit rating in order to have a reasonable basis for forecasting company-specific credit risk. While there is no single best model for estimating a credit rating, cross-sectional analyses we have conducted suggest the following factors are critical components to a firm's credit rating: size, industry, liquidity, solvency, and volatility.[4]

It is unlikely that a firm will materially change its size or industry in a short time frame. Likewise, we would not expect volatility to change quickly as it is often the result of operating leverage combined with the underlying business risk of the firm's industry. Liquidity is itself a result of the firm's capitalization choices. And so, the primary driver of credit rating in the near term is the expected capital structure for the firm determining its overall solvency.

By capital structure we mean the ratio of total debt (including preferred stock) to the market value of equity. Where possible, the market value of debt should be used, but that is not often available and for normal firms operating at investment grade credit ratings, book values will approximate market values for many debt instruments. For any given industry, plotting the credit ratings translated onto a numeric scale against debt-to-market-equity ratios will show the relationship between credit rating and capital structure (see Figure 5.6).

To pull all this together to forecast the cost of debt for a firm, we need to forecast its target capital structure. The market value of equity can be forecasted using an efficient markets approach that assumes that stock price is correctly valued today—and does not forecast any specific new information that would cause the stock price to change. Assuming such new information does not arrive within our forecast horizon, the stock price should increase at an annual rate equal to the cost of equity, less any dividend yield earned by investors (see the next section for discussion of cost-of-equity forecasting). Assuming no change in shares outstanding, market capitalization will adjust at the same rate. Where the analyst has specific information regarding warrants or convertible securities that will change the number of shares, such effects should be included in the forecast for market capitalization. Likewise after a merger or stock buyback program is announced, there may be known changes in shares outstanding

---

[4]In order to measure these variables in building bond-rating models, we have used proxies as follows: natural log of total revenues (size), two-digit SIC code (industry), ratio of short-term to long-term debt (liquidity), ratio of total debt to market value of equity (solvency), and the volatility of operating earnings as a percent of sales (volatility). These same variables may not always produce the best fit with available data—readers are encouraged to supplement these factors with others of their own.

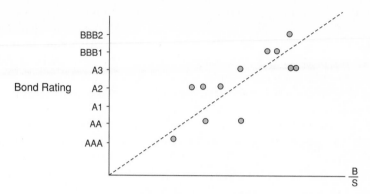

FIGURE 5.6   Debt to equity regressed against credit rating.

Source: Financial Theory and Corporate Policy, 4th ed., by Thomas E. Copeland, J. Fred Weston, and Kuldeep Shastri, ISBN: 0321127218, December 2003. Reprinted by permission of Pearson Education, Inc., Upper Saddle River, NJ.

that should be taken into account. Equation 5.4 shows the efficient markets approach to forecasting your expected stock price, *S*, in the future.

$$E\left(S_{t+n}\right) = S_t * \left(1 + k_s - \frac{d}{P}\right)^n \tag{5.4}$$

where $E(S_{t+n})$ = expected market value of equity *n* years from today (*t*)
S_t = current market value of equity
k_s = cost of equity
d/P = dividend yield (ideally, expected yield; current or historical average may be used)

We can turn this into a forecast for equity market capitalization by multiplying by the expected number of shares outstanding. Next, we need a forecast for the amount of debt on hand. We assume first that there is a target capital structure that the firm is striving to meet. In absence of a robust model that allows us to know the firm's optimal capital structure, we often default to using long-term industry median debt-to-equity ratios. Now, if a firm is below its target debt-to-equity ratio, we assume it can quickly remedy that by borrowing. In such a situation, we would forecast a fairly quick change in debt levels—say, within a year or two.

If a firm is above its target debt ratio, it must find ways to reduce its debt load. While it is not unreasonable for firms to use financing transactions (e.g., issuance of new securities) to pay down their debt loads, a reluctance to dilute equity leads many to pursue internal sources of funds as the preferred route to debt reduction. A cash flow forecast model comes in handy as it allows us to predict the availability of funds for repaying debt principal. Remember, though, that the market value of equity is changing through time as well, and so the debt-equity ratio may return to normal without any debt repayment as long as equity values are increasing. Where a cash flow forecast is unavailable, historical data for the firm and its industry peers will likely be able to indicate the usual time required for a firm with excess debt to return to industry norms.

Now that we have a forecasted credit rating, we can tie it all together to have forecasts for the cost of debt. We use the following steps to do so:

1. Use the yield curve to forecast year-by-year risk-free interest rate.
2. Use historical data or other analysis to forecast the year-by-year credit risk spread for a given credit rating.
3. Use our understanding of the firm's current position and anticipated future economics to forecast credit rating on a year-by-year basis.
4. The firm's expected cost of debt is the forecasted risk-free rate (step 1) plus the forecasted credit risk spread (step 2) applicable to the firm's year-by-year credit rating (step 3).

The Expected Cost of Equity

Forecasting the cost of equity can be difficult—especially in light of the lack of any consensus on what, exactly, is the best way to measure the cost of equity. There are no lack of texts available discussing the relevant issues. For a good review of some of the issues involved we refer you to *Valuation*.[5] For now, we assume the cost of equity is estimated using the Capital Asset Pricing Model, or CAPM.

The CAPM estimates the cost of equity as the return required by investors to compensate them for undiversifiable risk (so-called "systematic risk"). The standard calculation for the CAPM cost of equity is:

$$k_s = R_f + \beta_s(R_m - R_f) \tag{5.5}$$

where
k_s = Cost of equity
R_f = Default-free interest rate
R_m = Expected return on the market portfolio
β_s = Sensitivity of the firm's stock returns to return on the market portfolio
$(R_m - R_f)$ = Market risk premium

---

[5]Copeland, T.E., J. Murrin, and T. Koller, *Valuation: Measuring and Managing the Value of Companies*, 3rd Edition, John Wiley & Sons, 2000.

It is common to estimate a single cost of equity for all time periods, though as we saw earlier for debt, it is possible that the year-by-year expectations of investors differ from the average rate calculated to apply for all years.

If we were to estimate the expected future cost of equity, we would want to know the following:

- How will the default-free rate change through time?
- How will beta change?
- Will the expected market risk premium change?

With respect the default-free rate, we discussed in the last section how to use the yield curve to forecast changes in the one-year Treasury rate. The same default-free rate used as the basis for cost-of-debt forecasts should be used in the CAPM as well.

Will the market risk premium change? Here we are on dangerous ground, theoretically speaking. While it is possible for the market risk premium to change through time, there are no standard techniques for forecasting such changes and no market data that can be used to infer expected changes. Our advice is to leave the market risk premium unchanged over the forecast horizon.

Figure 5.7 shows a set of estimated U.S. market risk premia from 1963 to 2002. If we were to use this data our estimate of the market risk premium would be 11.1 percent (the arithmetic average return on the S&P index) minus 6 percent (the arithmetic return on intermediate U.S. government bonds). Thus the estimated market risk premium would be roughly 5 percent in nominal terms.

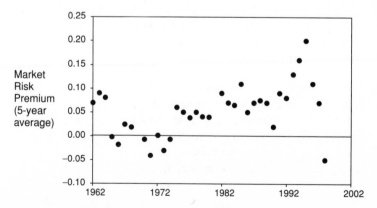

FIGURE 5.7 The U.S. market risk premium 1963–2002.

Source: Financial Theory and Corporate Policy, 4th ed., by Thomas E. Copeland, J. Fred Weston, and Kuldeep Shastri, ISBN: 0321127218, December 2003. Reprinted by permission of Pearson Education, Inc., Upper Saddle River, NJ.

A time series regression of the market risk premium (40 observations) was:

$$\text{MRP} = \quad .041 + \quad .0002 \text{ (year)}$$
$$\qquad\qquad (0.33) \qquad (.044)$$

The t-statistics are given in parentheses and show that neither the slope nor the intercept are different from zero. Consequently, we find no evidence for a trend in the market risk premium. We would forecast the premium to remain unchanged. Were the data to include the years 1926 to 2002, the answer would not change.[6]

As for beta, we start with a recommendation to use some form of forward-looking beta rather than a beta based solely off historical returns. BARRA provides betas that have done a reasonably good job of predicting future realized betas. Other sources include Ibbotson's and Bloomberg's "adjusted betas." Ibbotson follows multiple-regression procedures similar to BARRA's method. Bloomberg's method is much simpler—it uses a straight-line weighted average technique that brings all betas back toward the market average of 1.0 (based on academic evidence that indicates that betas are in fact mean-reverting).

Now, once you have a single estimate of beta today, the question is whether that beta is likely to change through time. Here, the best rule of thumb is simply to see if the beta is significantly higher or lower than industry peers. Forecasted betas should use this comparison as the basis for moving the beta up or down gradually toward industry norms (say, within three to four years).

Now, once we have a forecasted cost of debt and cost of equity, estimating the expected future *WACC* is a trivial exercise of weighting each of these forecasts by the anticipated capital structure through the forecast horizon (recall that we made these forecasts as part of our cost-of-debt forecast).

Expected Returns and the Cost of Capital for Small Companies

Our discussion of the cost of equity and debt can be applied to just about any large firm. Some in our field advocate inclusion of at least one or more

---

[6]Note that the academic research on whether and how the market risk premium varies through time is not settled due to difficulty estimating what is, by definition, a forward-looking measure. There are some who have argued that the market risk premium has changed through time—in particular, that it has declined in the post–World War II era. While we might argue that the risk premium should not be expected to change, different forecasts may rely on different assumptions and data suggesting the risk premium may rise or fall in the future. For one of the more thorough discussions of the salient issues in measuring the market risk premium, see Cornell (1999).

additional risk factors other than systematic market risk in estimating the cost of capital—that is, use a model other than the standard capital asset pricing model (CAPM). The most common factor added is a small company risk premium. The academic basis for this derives from studies showing that small-company stocks earn returns in excess of that predicted by the capital asset pricing model.[7] Ibbotson's annual yearbook, for example, calculates the return differentials between firms of different sizes as organized into portfolios grouped by market capitalization.

At this point, however, nonmarket factors such as size and style have only empirical work behind them without any solid, agreed-upon theory to justify the premium. In other words, the observed higher returns for smaller firms appear to be an anomaly for which academics have yet to find a consensus explanation.

We believe smaller firms should not go through the extra effort to include a small firm premium into their cost of capital. It is possible that the observed higher returns earned by smaller firms is a function of survivor bias—i.e., if we were to also include the returns of firms that fail we would observe returns more in line with CAPM predictions. One could think of it the same way one can distinguish between the promised and expected return on debt of different credit quality. At very low credit ratings we observe promised yields on debts much higher than is justified by extrapolating from investment-grade debt yields. The higher promised yields are simply compensation for the probability of default being so much higher. Smaller firms have a higher probability of default—and so their promised returns to capital investors will have to be higher than investors' expected returns.

Invest or Harvest—Importance of *WACC* and Range of Uncertainty

At the start of this chapter we noted that the *WACC* may impact decision-making for managing existing business units. An example demonstrates why this is the case. Consider an underperforming business unit in a mature industry earning a steady five percent return on capital. Expectations are that investors do not believe that the five percent will materially change in the future considering the unlikelihood of competitors exiting the business and a belief that demand will not recover to previous highs.

Assume that management brings in two advisors that suggest different possible paths to value creation. The first involves investing in new production technologies that will allow the business to considerably alter its cost curve so that it is more competitive. This investment would take some

---

[7]See, for example, Fama and French, "The Cross-Section of Stock Returns," *Journal of Finance*, 1992.

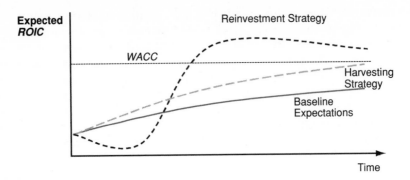

FIGURE 5.8   Harvest or invest decision.

years to implement, but afterwards the return on capital is projected to rise significantly. The second option effectively amounts to a harvest strategy with little or no investment. Specific costs are targeted for cuts, with immediate improvement in cash flows and profitability. However, the overall impact on *ROIC* is less than what could be expected by investing in the new technology. Figure 5.8 illustrates the choices facing management.

Which turnaround plan should be pursued? EBM principles state that one should pursue the option that raises long-term expectations the most. Does that mean the investment option should be pursued because it raises the perpetuity level of *ROIC?* Not necessarily. Table 5.1 converts *ROIC* forecasts into economic profit forecasts and shows the present value of future

TABLE 5.1   How *WACC* Affects the Harvest versus Invest Decisions

Year	PV of Future Economic Profits Discounted at 10%			PV of Future Economic Profits Discounted at 14%		
	Baseline	Harvest	Invest	Baseline	Harvest	Invest
1	(182)	(159)	(1,045)	(175)	(154)	(1,009)
2	(145)	(103)	(496)	(135)	(96)	(462)
3	(113)	(56)	—	(101)	(51)	—
4	(85)	(34)	17	(74)	(30)	15
5	(62)	(16)	31	(52)	(13)	26
6	(42)	(14)	71	(34)	(11)	57
7	(26)	13	103	(20)	10	80
8	(23)	23	128	(18)	18	96
9	(21)	32	138	(15)	23	100
CV	(212)	424	1,484	(154)	308	1,076
Value	(911)	110	430	(778)	4	(20)

Source: Monitor analysis

economic profits using two alternative *WACC*s. In both cases, the baseline value of the business is negative. However, at a 10 percent *WACC,* the "invest" decision has the greater value, while the answer is reversed in favor of the "harvest" decision when *WACC* increases to 14 percent.

As is clear from the discounted *EP* calculations, the restructuring choice is dependent both on the timing of economic profits and on what the *WACC* is (and may even depend on whether we use a single *WACC* estimate or a year-by-year forecast). While both options created value relative to baseline expectations, in a low-*WACC* setting, the investment strategy is most valuable, while a harvest strategy is preferred in a high-*WACC* setting.

We have seen that changes in expectations are not the only factor to consider when running a business. The time pattern to those changes is important as well—with more weight given to the near-term (long-term) future when the *WACC* is high (low).

Fast or Slow Growth—Importance of *WACC* and How to Calibrate Performance Evaluation Models

The harvest/invest decision is just one situation where the time pattern of expectations makes a difference. Another consideration is whether the business is growing quickly or not—and how that growth intersects with performance evaluation. In the end, performance evaluation of a business or its managers should be based on changes in value derived from changes in expectations. But when everything is said and done, EBM requires translating these changes in expectations into metrics we can use. Ultimately, we need more than a discounted cash flow value for each business—we need a multiperiod forecast for cash flows and their value-driver determinants.

If we have a set of expectations-based (forward-looking) performance metrics to track and evaluate, how do we know what weight to place on different forecast time horizons? For example, if management raises expected sales revenues for the current and next year with a modest reduction in long-term revenue growth, is that value creating or destroying? The answer always goes back to a valuation model.

Figure 5.9 illustrates the relative weight in a typical DCF valuation model for medium-term expectations (the next five years' cash flow, assuming a 10 percent *WACC*). Notice that as the growth rate increases (assuming the growth rate for all years move together), the weight given to short-term expectations declines. This is because of compounding—as the growth rate increases, the out-years' cash flows become that much higher, thus driving down the importance of the next few years.

We can do a similar sensitivity analysis using the *WACC* (this time, holding growth rate constant at four percent). As Figure 5.10 illustrates, the higher the *WACC*, the more important short-term expected cash flows are

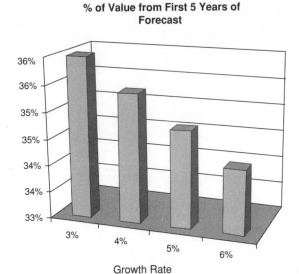

% of Value from First 5 Years of
Forecast

Growth Rate

FIGURE 5.9   Impact of growth rate on value derived from short term.

Source: Monitor analysis

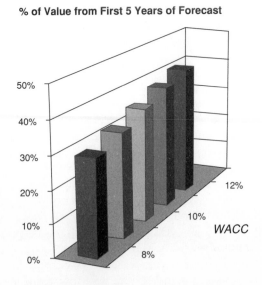

% of Value from First 5 Years of Forecast

WACC

FIGURE 5.10   Impact of *WACC* on value derived from short term.

Source: Monitor analysis

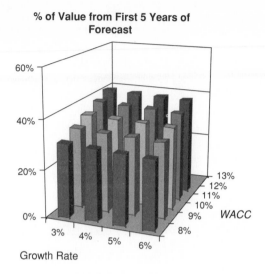

% of Value from First 5 Years of Forecast

FIGURE 5.11   Combined impact of growth rates and *WACC*.

Source: Monitor analysis

as a percent of the valuation model. Intuitively, a higher *WACC* means we discount what happens in the future more.

When we put these pieces together, we can derive sensitivity factors that tell us how much weight to place on near-term and long-term changes in expectations (see Figure 5.11). For example, a slow-growth mature business that is managed to produce stable cash flows will require a much higher weight be placed on management maintaining short-term expectations than building long-term growth potential. New start-up businesses should compensate managers for building the long-term profitability and growth potential of the business, with modest emphasis on maintaining short-term control over cash flows.

As you can see from this discussion, the *WACC* is certainly not irrelevant for management decisions. Expectations are still the hurdle for performance evaluation. The *WACC*, however, is not a hurdle rate for per-for-mance but instead is a calibration tool that places the appropriate weights on expectations of various time horizons for each business unit. Note that while we've consistently said in this book that it is long-term expectations that count, it is worth remembering that the short-term outlook is not irrelevant—and in some cases is more important than others. The *WACC* is a critical tool for making such distinctions between business units. Thus, even if expected *EP* is used as a business unit evaluation metric, the *WACC* can tell us much more about whether to focus on this year's, next year's, or long-term expected *EP*.

Business Unit–Level WACCs

Of course, applying the WACC toward understanding business unit decisions and performance requires actually knowing the WACC at a business unit level. While there is no lack of both academic and practitioner texts on how to estimate the cost of capital for a business unit, we have frequently seen these techniques ignored as companies impose a single WACC on all business units. At best, we have seen multibusiness firms assign businesses to various categories each with its own WACC.

In the interest of brevity we will not discuss all the details of calculating a business unit WACC. Instead, we present below some simple rules to follow in doing the calculations:

1. *Capital structure.* Use comparable companies to find industry average capital structures for each business. Be careful to examine the capital structures for comparables over a long enough time horizon to see normal fluctuations around a business cycle.

2. *Cost of debt.* Use the parent's cost of debt as the business unit is able to draw on the corporation's overall borrowing capacity. When evaluating a business unit for possible spin-off or sale, estimate cost of debt using the likely debt rating that would prevail were it a stand-alone business (usually a lower rating because size is a major factor in credit rating models).

3. *Cost of equity—beta.* Use the median unlevered beta of comparable companies as a reference point, and then apply the business unit's own leverage ratio to determine the levered equity beta. Many corporate finance texts can provide formulas for estimating unlevered betas from levered betas.

Putting It All Together—WACC, Growth and Performance Targets

Note that once all the analysis is complete, you may find some surprising results when setting up a performance evaluation system. The table below illustrates some of the major factors we've discussed above and how they combine to influence EBM at the business unit level. For comparison's sake, we show the hypothetical weighting on long-term performance for each business unit and the company overall if a single WACC is applied to all units.

As can be seen in Table 5.2, variations in the cost of capital across business units can significantly affect how they should be treated in an EBM performance evaluation system.[8] In this example, Business Unit B has

---

[8]Table 5.2 assumes all business units start with equal levels of cash flows that grow at different rates. Business unit values are calculated using a discounted cash

TABLE 5.2   Business Unit (BU) versus Corporate Cost of Capital

BU	Corporate WACC	BU WACC	Long-run Growth Rate	Performance Weightings (%)			LT Weight % Assuming Corporate WACC
				Current Year	Next 3 Years	Long-Term	
A	10%	14%	8%	5	14	81	93
B	10%	15%	3%	10	25	65	77
C	10%	8%	7%	1	3	97	90
D	10%	7%	3%	3	8	89	80
							Overall 88

a higher-than-average *WACC.* Due to the greater amount of discounting of future results, expectations for B's short-term performance should be weighted relatively more than other units. We would also expect that in an analytical exercise to select B's optimal strategic direction, a harvesting strategy designed to optimize near-term results may dominate over a longer-term investment plan. While these observations about unit B are true simply because it has a higher cost of capital, the fact that it is expected to grow slower than other units increases even further the importance of exceeding near-term expectations. B's managers would do best to focus on short-term execution through concerns for such things as optimizing its marketing mix, stripping out unnecessary costs, winnowing out unprofitable customers, speeding up the working capital cash cycle, or eliminating underutilized fixed assets.

Business Unit C presents the opposite situation—it has a relatively low cost of capital and a high expected long-run growth rate. In this setting, management needs to stay focused almost entirely on factors affecting long-term growth. While such factors will differ across industries, it is no stretch of the imagination to realize that C's management must stay focused on innovation in developing new products, improving distribution and access to demand, or developing a lasting brand image. One could even see C's managers being given some slack to miss short-term targets so long as they develop the business for long-term growth—and do so in a credible, even quantifiable way (by measuring, for example, changes in customer brand image ratings, new product introduction rates, or number and quality of distribution outlets).

---

flow model with the relevant *WACC* (corporate or BU-specific). Performance weightings are determined by the percent of total value represented by the present value of cash flows in each time horizon (for example, the present value of the next three years' cash flows as a percent of business unit total value).

Expectations and Capital Structure

Does understanding expectations help senior management with its capital structure decision? We think it does. Without going into too much technical detail, we discuss here how expectations may shape the level of debt and equity used to fund the business.

Ever since Miller and Modigliani published their famous proposition,[9] academics have been divided on the question of what should determine the firm's optimal mix of debt and equity. Miller and Modigliani prove that under certain assumptions, total firm value is independent of capital structure. They allow that taxes (that give advantages to the use of debt) lead to greater use of debt than otherwise—in fact, their model implies that the capital structure should be almost all debt when such tax advantages are present.

Empiricists, however, note that capital structures not only vary across industries, but tend to stay relatively stable over the long-term, suggesting that there are capital structure targets—and that managers, at least, perceive some optimum level of debt. Thus we see pharmaceutical firms with very low levels of debt, while utilities and financial services tend to have much more leverage on their balance sheets.

More recent academic research has identified two factors as likely explanations for the capital structure decisions firms make. The first of these factors is business disruption costs, which can affect the firm's expected cash flows. When a firm is under bankruptcy protection (but still operating) there are both direct and indirect costs incurred by the firm. Direct costs include such factors as litigation and turnaround consulting fees. Indirect costs result when the firm's operating cash flows are affected by its bankruptcy status. One example of an indirect cost is decreases in revenue due to customers avoiding purchases from a firm operating in Chapter 11. How many people would buy a car, for example, from a company in trouble, given the uncertainty of whether the warranty would be honored? Bankrupt firms may need to lower prices just to get customers to stay with them through the restructuring. Similar effects happen on the cost side—employees quit for more stable firms or demand higher salaries for staying around. Suppliers may likewise demand payment on delivery or not supply materials at all.

Of course, a firm need not go into Chapter 11 to incur the indirect costs of bankruptcy—the higher the probability of bankruptcy, the lower revenues will be and the higher costs will be. Customers, employees, and suppliers are generally aware of the financial health of a firm. If you consider

---

[9]"The Cost of Capital, Corporation Finance, and the Theory of Investment," Franco Modigliani and Merton M. Miller, *American Economic Review*, 48: 261–97, 1958.

that firms with greater levels of debt have higher probabilities of going bankrupt, then it follows that bankruptcy costs can affect the firm's chosen debt level. The higher the costs or probability of bankruptcy, the less likely the firm will take on high levels of debt. Thus, firms with volatile cash flows (e.g., capital equipment manufacturers) may choose lower amounts of debt than those with more predictable cash flows (e.g., utilities).

Notice the role of expectations in a capital structure decision guided by bankruptcy costs. Management needs to have some expectation of the level and probability of bankruptcy. Such expectations will be a natural consequence of their own forecasts. But they will also be a function of the uncertainty surrounding those forecasts. If there is significant uncertainty about the future, one action that management can take is to choose lower levels of debt than otherwise, ensuring that the firm is unlikely to enter (or approach) bankruptcy even if results disappoint. Alternatively, the firm can use hedging or other risk-management practices to manage known risks.

What if there is an expectations gap between what management forecasts and what outsiders such as customers, suppliers, or investors believe? In that case it is possible for management to choose a suboptimal debt-equity mix. If management is more bullish on the future than investors it may choose too much debt relative to what the market thinks is appropriate to prevent incurring excessive bankruptcy costs. These sorts of gaps, though, are unlikely to persist for long periods of time, as management will see signals from investors—sometimes implicit signals such as changes in equity or debt prices, and sometimes explicit signals such as credit ratings or pricing of newly issued debt or equity securities.

If there is an expectations gap, however, between management and suppliers or customers, management can use financial signals to adjust its financial strategy. But noise intervenes. Are suppliers demanding more stringent payment terms because they perceive the firm as a greater default risk or because they are having their own cash flow problems? Are customers not purchasing as much volume because they are concerned with the firm's financial viability or because they simply find its products or services less valuable relative to those of competitors? Given the ambiguity in these signals, management needs to test actively what factors are motivating supplier, customer, and even employee decisions.

The second possible explanation for how firms choose capital structure is the need for operating/investing flexibility.[10] Firms with very little flexibility in how they operate or how much they invest would choose lower levels of debt. Why? Because more debt gives management less financial

---

[10]For example, Graham and Harvey (2002) report that financial flexibility is managers' number one concern when deciding on capital structure.

flexibility: The firm must make coupon and principal repayments on time or else risk defaulting on debt agreements. Pharmaceutical companies, for example, have little flexibility in how much is spent on their R&D programs. If a pharma company cuts back on R&D, it will only delay product development needed to keep the revenue pipeline full (otherwise, as drugs go off patent the firm's revenue drops off precipitously). On the other end of the spectrum are banks whose assets are highly liquid, allowing the bank to reallocate its investments as conditions change. Banks are not tied to any specific expenses or assets and so can easily manage with much higher levels of debt.

Under the flexibility view of capital structure, management's decisions regarding the firm's underlying investment strategy directly affect the optimum level of debt. To the extent management pursues a flexible investment strategy—a strategy reliant on value from real options, as described in the last chapter—it will have more flexibility to rely on debt financing. Management that has a good understanding of expectations for the business can craft strategies that are more flexible. As a result, we see increased scope for connections between the financing and strategic planning processes than has historically been the case. Although capital structure decisions will remain the primary responsibility of the CFO, a thorough understanding of the firm's investment strategy, including detailed knowledge of key uncertainties, real options, and decision trigger signals, is required to manage capital structure through changing conditions.

One last point to keep in mind about capital structure decisions is that they are tied to hedging and risk-management strategies. Management can substitute risk management for decreases in leverage, depending on the relative transactions cost of each. Moreover, risk management itself may be an integral part of strategic planning, tied as it must be to operating and investment uncertainties. In fact, operating and investment decisions themselves may serve as the functional equivalent of financial hedges—for example, investing in local overseas production can substitute for the hedging costs of managing currency fluctuations affecting an export-driven strategy. Once again we see that expectations are the glue that binds the company—not only with regard to the "left hand" side of the balance where operating and real asset investment decisions have an impact, but also the "right side," where financing and risk management decisions are important.

Summary

This chapter focused on *WACC*—the cost of capital. In prior chapters we showed why a comparison of the return on investment capital to *WACC* is not a true measure of value creation for maintenance investment. To know about value creation, we need to know about returns relative to expectations. In this chapter we are reminded that even in an EBM-driven organization the cost of capital is still relevant. Specifically, we've noted three ways in which knowing the expected cost of capital affects an EBM performance evaluation system:

- First, the cost of capital may be expected to decline [or increase] in the future. Expectations for the future cost of capital can impact the pattern of expected future economic profits.
- Second, the cost of capital can affect the relative attractiveness of different courses of action, even if all choices can increase expected future performance. When the *WACC* is high, near-term results become more important to value, and therefore there is a *relatively* greater bias toward harvesting decisions. Lower *WACC*s encourage a *relatively* longer-term outlook, biasing toward making investment decisions regardless of short-term impact.
- Third, we noted that the cost of capital is linked to expected future growth—and that management's degree of emphasis on short-term versus long-term expectations and performance will vary with different combinations of growth and discount rates. All else equal, a faster growth firm will require greater emphasis on long-term expectations.

The chapter continued with a reminder that the cost of capital is really a business-specific factor that may vary across various lines of business within a company. We have seen dozens of firms treat all businesses the same by using a corporate *WACC*, but such an approach risks obscuring important drivers of value that can differ by business. Knowing each business's *WACC*—or at least its *WACC* relative to other businesses in the corporation—is an essential part of a properly structured EBM system. Finally, we noted that expectations play a role in managers' financing decisions, given the close connection between operating and investment risks and the factors driving debt and risk-management decisions.

CHAPTER 6

Capital Efficiency

$\mathbf{M}$ost managers are not used to thinking about balance sheet management. They do not know how to look for sources of capital efficiency, do not know how to make tradeoffs between capital spending and profits, and are poor at tradeoffs between spending this period versus next period. Savings from expected capital spending can result either from working core assets harder (Chapter 3) or from making new investment better (Chapter 4).

One of the easiest ways to exceed expectations (even your own) is to take a hard look at capital efficiency—focusing on the first term of EBM Equation 1.2—work your core assets harder. Cuts in wasteful capital spending usually require that you challenge accepted assumptions and in so doing, cut expected capital spending without changing the quantity or quality of goods and services supplied to customers. To do so you must examine and improve your capital spending process.

This chapter begins with a premise that most companies spend capital inefficiently, therefore providing an opportunity to create value by reducing expected capital spending. A series of warning flags (symptoms) are presented that help identify inefficient capital spending. Next, suggested cures are discussed that can help reduce capital spending immediately. We end the chapter with thoughts on changing the capital planning process to permanently improve the firm's ability to limit capital spending without negatively affecting profits.

Permanently Cut Capital Spending by 10 to 25 Percent

We start off with an assertion—namely, that at most companies it is possible to permanently reduce planned capital spending by 10 to 25 percent

147

without changing the quantity or quality of goods and services provided to customers. You will find this assertion in an article published in the *Harvard Business Review* in September 2000, and entitled "Cutting Costs without Drawing Blood." Table 6.1 is taken from that article.

A *permanent* cut in planned capital spending has a current effect on value that is a multiple of the dollars cut in any one year. Also, there is no severance pay for capital cuts—only for cuts in headcount. Table 6.1 clearly points out that companies that seek value improvements should look to the balance sheet as well as the income statement. Kodak, for example, could have cut planned capital spending by 14.5 percent in order to have the same value impact as the layoff of 10,000 employees that was announced in September of 1997.

The Typical Capital Spending Program Is Out of Control

The idea of focusing on capital efficiency arose out of a meeting in the early 1990s with the CFO of one of England's largest public utilities. He wanted to talk about his "capital constraint problem." He had more positive net present value projects than he had capital to spend on them. With only a slight hesitation, we responded that he should issue new debt and new equity in the same proportion as the company's optimal capital structure, so that there would be no alteration in the firm's financial risk, and that the funds should be used to take all of the positive NPV projects because each would create new value. He smiled and gave a classic practitioner's answer for why he would not follow our advice. "The equity market is not good right now," he said, "and come to think of it, the debt market is not right either—so I won't do it."

TABLE 6.1 Job Dollars versus Cuts in Capital Spending (Dollars in Millions)

Date	Kodak Sept. '97	Nike Jul. '98	Goodyear April '99	DuPont June '99	Hasbro Dec '97	Motorola June '98
Layoffs (people)	10,000	1,600	2,600	1,400	2,500	14,000
Annual savings from layoffs	$400	$300	$100	$90	$50	$840
Value-equivalent Capex cut	$280	$68	$72	$69	$30	$538
Capex cut as a % of total	14.5	15.1	10.3	3.1	20.6	22.5

Source: Copeland, T., Reprinted by permission of *Harvard Business Review*, an exhibit from "Cutting Costs without Drawing Blood," by Thomas E. Copeland, September 2000, Copyright © 2000 by the President and Fellows of Harvard College, all rights reserved.

It was our turn, so we asked what, exactly, he planned to do. "I will raise the hurdle rate from 10 to 25 percent," he exclaimed. Now we smiled and asked, "What will the engineers do in response?" He admitted that, "They will cook the numbers until every project earns more than 25 percent!" At that impasse, it occurred to us to inquire about his capital budgeting process. He went on to describe what is a quite normal capital budgeting process. Any project that requests more than £1,000,000 had to have a formal net present value analysis.

"How many projects each year require the limit or even more?" we asked. "About 200," he answered.

Then we asked, "What percentage of your total capital spending is on projects that require less than the limit?"

After remarking that no one had asked such a question before, he paused to think about it and responded that perhaps 60 percent of total capital spending was made without formal review—made via the annual budgeting process. "And what about the 200 projects that you *do* review? What happens to them? There are about 250 working days per year. Do you evaluate roughly one project per day?"

"Actually, we carefully review only a dozen or so project requests—the big ones," he replied.

Continuing, we asked, "How do you challenge the engineering assumptions?"

He said, "It is not a level playing field. We are accountants and economists, and cannot in general overrule the engineers' judgment." Then he smiled weakly and confessed, "Our capital budgeting system is totally out of control!"

The fact of the matter is that nearly every company has an out-of-control capital budgeting system.

Seven Symptoms of an Out-of-Control Capital Budgeting System

This section of the chapter can be used as a self-audit. If one or more of these symptoms can be found at your company, then you are probably wasting capital.

Symptom #1

Budgeted spending is defined as spending that results from the annual budget, not from specific project-level review. Figure 6.1 shows the breakdown of total capital spending of an electric utility. Notice that 61 percent of the total is budgeted spending for small projects where there is usually no specific set of controls. If your company has 50 percent or more of

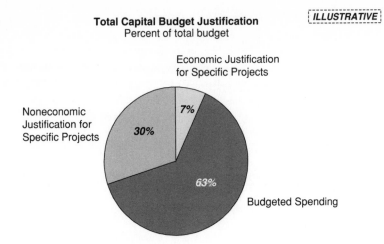

FIGURE 6.1   Symptom #1—Budgeted spending.

annual capital spending derived from the annual budget, your capital spending program is very likely out of control.

Symptom #2

Seasonal spending. Graph capital expenditures by quarter. If the result is anything like Figure 6.2, there will be very high capital spending during the fourth quarter, relative to the other three quarters. This happens as managers begin the year by underspending on capital, then play catch up in the fourth quarter because they are fearful that if they do not use up all of this year's budget, then there will be a reduction in next year's budget. Often this practice leads to wasteful spending.

Symptom #3

An integrated approach allows managers to slide expenditures from their operating budget to their capital budget so long as they keep to their budgeted total. It also allows discipline to break down and capital spending overruns to occur frequently.

Symptom #4

Myopic planning. Figure 6.3 shows a typical pattern. The blanket spending at a utility was allocated into two primary categories: connections and sys-

Project Expenditures by Quarter

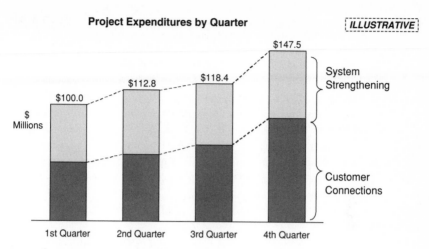

FIGURE 6.2 Symptom #2—Entitled spending.

tem strengthening. The original budgeted amount of capital spending was $346 million, and eventually $479 was actually spent—an overrun of $133 million, or 38 percent. This was not an isolated event. It happened year after year in project after project. Everyone began to expect overruns and adjusted for this self-delusional behavior. But it is not a good idea to begin with biased expectations and then have to correct for them.

Expenditures vs. Budget

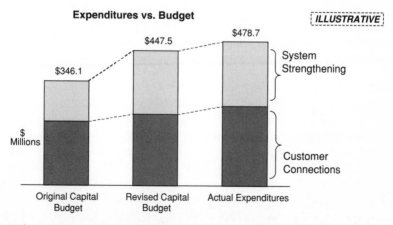

FIGURE 6.3 Symptom #4—Myopic spending.

Symptom #5

Tradeoffs not well understood. There are many types of tradeoffs, but we cover just a few here. The first is the tradeoff between the reliability of engineering and the extra capital that is required for better reliability. A favorite story comes from an experience at a telecommunications company. We asked why the cables were buried two meters underground—why not one meter? We know that it would be a lot cheaper. The head of network engineering answered that a depth of two meters was required to protect the network from the "thermonuclear magnetic impulse effect." He went on to explain that when a hydrogen bomb goes off over the ground it creates a strong magnetic wave impulse that destroys cables unless they are covered by two meters of earth. The depth assured that the network would survive.

We then asked, "Where are your customers after the bomb goes off?"

Today the company saves about $80 million per year (even after the "backhoe effect," i.e. cables are dug up more often) by burying its cables only one meter deep. The tradeoff between reliability and capital cost had not been well understood.

Another example of a tradeoff that is not well understood is between lower profits and higher capital expenditures. We had been studying the engineering of the distribution system of an electric utility and discovered that is was built to be much stronger than the specifications required. The poles were thicker and closer together, and the wires were also thicker than required. We asked why. The answer was that there were violent wind storms in the area and tree limbs often broke the wires during a storm—resulting in dangerous and expensive repairs. We responded by suggesting they consider trimming the tree limbs further back from the wires. They refused, saying that the extra costs would decrease their profits. The burden of proof was then back in our court, so we estimated the extra trimming costs from now to infinity on an after-tax basis, then capitalized them by discounting them back to the present. Then we compared the capitalized cost of tree trimming with the extra capital expenditures necessary to strengthen the distribution system. The capitalized tree trimming costs were much lower. Now the company trims the trees.

While this chapter is primarily about reducing capital spending, if you understand tradeoffs well there may be times where it is more profitable to increase capital spending. As an example, we met a bottler and distributor of Coca-Cola products in China who believed that with extra capital spending support from Coca-Cola he could more than offset (in present value terms) the incremental capital costs with the extra profits from volumes sold in currently underserved markets. Such profits would go disproportionately to Coca-Cola and so this distributor had little incentive to spend the capital himself.

Most managers, and engineers in particular, are not equipped to readily make tradeoffs between income statement and balance sheet implications of their actions.

Symptom #6

Badly aligned incentives are contributory to poor judgment when it comes to increasing the value of a firm. If engineers are asked to focus solely on profit (i.e., on the income statement), then capital spending becomes a free good. Any amount of capital spending is justified if it can increase profit—even if the increase is trivial. We took on a capital efficiency project at a pharmaceutical company, focusing exclusively on working capital. Managers were compensated on their profit contribution to the firm and there was no charge for capital employed. At orthopedic appliances (i.e., artificial arms and legs), we found a three-year supply of inventory when the longest delivery time for any artificial limb was only six weeks. They never lost a sale, but they also had periodic inventory write-downs.

Symptom #7

Failure to conduct a postmortem. When all is said and done, even the most careful capital budgeting process is fallible. That's why managers need to supplement budget supervision with regular audits of each business unit's capital spending. Not only should an audit team take a look at the lessons learned from large projects; it should also study budgeted spending. Such audit results should be widely available rather than restricted to only those directly involved in a project.

The audits should not be confrontational. To avoid situations where a finance team cross-examines the business unit team in a confrontational manner, the audit team should include employees from the departments being reviewed. The audit team should come up with recommendations for change—not merely criticize what went wrong. Finally, budgeted expenditures can best be analyzed by grouping small items. They can add up to big money. For example, we remember an executive at a chemical company—he was blind—who had his staff construct a detailed scale model of a new chemical plant. Having reviewed the design in three dimensions, he and his team reduced the cost of the plant by 10 percent by rerouting the pipes to save on expensive elbow joints. There were many of them, and together they added up to big savings.

Seven Cures for Capital Inefficiency

This is not a complete list of ideas for how to correct inefficient use of capital, but it is a good start. Once you get the idea that there is a lot of free cash flow tied up in net property plant and equipment, operating working capital, and goodwill, you will find creative ways of being frugal with capital.

Get the Right Information

When it comes to reviewing large projects, the net present value work-up is almost always a justification for the spending. After all, how many negative net present value projects are submitted for review? The problem with major capital requests is that the work-up often does not ask for information about the next best alternative. It might be outsourcing. It might be installing used equipment that can be purchased at a significant discount. Or it might be relocating facilities at significant savings.

In order to fight impulsive acquisitions of new machinery, companies should require business unit managers to run the numbers on alternative investment options open to them—including maintaining the existing assets or buying used ones. If the economics of buying a new machine is acceptable, then often the economics of these alternatives will be even better. Alternative investment options need not be restricted to capital investment—is it lower cost, for example, to substitute operating expenses for capital equipment?

Eliminate Bureaucracy

Bureaucracy causes misallocation of resources by slowing down decision making.

An example taken from a telecommunications company had to do with better switch allocation. The company owned thousands of switches—computers, really that routed signal traffic. In any local geography the traffic density, and therefore the demand for switches, varied up and down as new companies entered an area or left. Priority at the administrative level was getting new (purchased) switches to the areas of need as fast as possible. But this meant that less effort was concentrated on the forecasting of declines in switch demand and the availability of used switches for relocation to growth areas. As shown in Figure 6.4, forecasted disconnects were 90 percent lower than actual, and the paperwork was so slow that scheduled disconnects could not be included in the current capital budgeting year. If one takes the switches that were reserved but no longer needed, those whose disconnection was past due, and scheduled disconnects in the current year, the total amounts to 70 percent of the needed switches. This meant that new switch purchases could have been cut substantially.

Measure Capacity Utilization Correctly

Budget massaging is common at large companies where senior management does not police capital spending beyond looking to see whether a

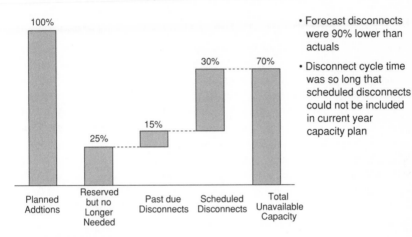

Capacity Unavailable for New Construction Planning | ILLUSTRATIVE |
Telecommunications Company Example

- Forecast disconnects were 90% lower than actuals

- Disconnect cycle time was so long that scheduled disconnects could not be included in current year capacity plan

FIGURE 6.4 Eliminate bureaucracy.

Note: Does not imply 1-to-1 substitution as demand does not correspond completely with spare capacity locations.

unit's spending matches its forecasts. In such companies, managers may be reluctant to propose reductions in their capital spending because they are fearful that the head office will not be generous when they need an increase; at the other extreme, they may be afraid that asking for too much money will provoke a close encounter with the company's internal auditors. So they try various ways of massaging the budget. Sometimes managers will shuffle expenditures between their capital and their operating budgets. Sometimes they will stack their capital expenditures into the fourth quarter. A dented fender, for example, becomes an excuse to buy a new pickup truck. And sometimes they encourage incorrect measurement of capacity utilization.

Capacity utilization can be tricky. There is a good Harvard Business School case called *The Super Project* that serves as a good example. A food company, General Mills, wanted to extend its currently successful Jell-O product line to introduce a new product that would be lighter and have fewer calories—the Super Project. As the analysis progressed, a debate arose about to handle the fact that the Super Project would, after only one year, use up the remaining 50 percent of a powder-fluffing machine called the agglomerator. One side said that the agglomerator was a sunk cost as far as the Super Project was concerned because the capital expenditure had already been made. The other side argued that the Super Project should be assigned agglomerator costs based on usage—the traditional cost accounting approach. It turns out that both approaches fail because they do not take the true marginal impact over time into account. Without the Super Project, the growth in Jell-O demand would require investment in more agglomerator capacity in three years. With the Super Project, a new agglomerator would be required in one year. Consequently, the Super Project should be charged with the present value of the difference between spending the capital one year rather than three years hence.

We see the same issue crop up in mergers and acquisitions. Excess capacity is often viewed as a synergy but it isn't—at least not all of it. What matters is only the timing difference between when excess capacity would be used up without the merger versus with the merger.

Sometimes capacity utilization is accounted for incorrectly. If measurement of utilization is not sufficiently fine-grained, managers can underestimate the amount of capacity that they actually have. This happened at a cable company whose capacity measures indicated that a bundle of optical fibers was fully utilized if only one fiber was lit. But each bundle held 11 fibers and since there were three bundles per cable, a line with 33 fibers could be counted as fully utilized with as few as three fibers actually in use

Eliminate Safety Chains

Every engineering department tries to build in a margin of safety and reliability. This is not unreasonable because their jobs depend on it and customers often value reliability. The problem arises when there are many stages of engineering in a project, and the small amount of extra capital spent at each level accumulates to a lot of capital. The incremental effect on reliability may be negligible, though the cost of redundant layers of safety margin can be significant.

At an electric utility we learned that the engineers who designed the transformers that "pump" electricity down the line had intentionally designed them to carry 30 percent greater load than was stated as standard. Next, the field engineers installed 40 percent extra transformer capacity, part of it anticipating demand that had not materialized yet. While no single transformer cost very much, they added up to be a significant part of blanket capital expenditures. Significant savings (every year) were achieved by managing this safety chain.

Lower Cost Solutions

Lower cost solutions are always to be desired, and are often missed. Often small items must be grouped to understand how to save. Figure 6.5 is an example taken from work done at a natural gas pipeline. The contractor suggested that the riser clamps that supported the pipeline above ground be

FIGURE 6.5   Cost reduction—Gas pipeline example.

spaced roughly 20 meters apart. The design engineers added their usual safety margin and suggested every 8 meters. Actual installation spaced them 5 meters apart. The cost of riser clamps per section of pipe rose from $400,000 to $1,000,000 as a result.

At the same company another example came up. The pipeline under construction (Figure 6.6) also required compressor buildings at a cost of

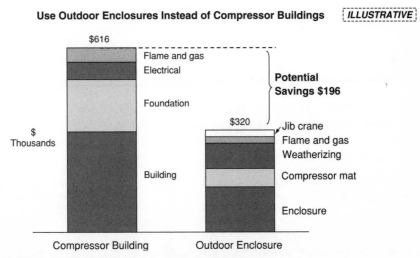

FIGURE 6.6   Cost reduction—Compressor building example.

$516,000 each. When management was challenged that a full enclosure was unnecessary because the pipeline was being constructed in a temperate climate, they decided to use outdoor enclosures instead, at a cost of only $320,000 per unit. Still another debate about the same project had to do with the thickness of the pipe walls and whether or not they too were over-engineered.

Better Planning

Better planning is also part of capital efficiency because it can help to reduce or eliminate wasteful spending. Figure 6.7 shows how a $20.3 million budget turned into a $22.7 million expenditure. As the year rolled on, it looked like the unit would spend only $8 million because of under-spending caused by padded budgets and nonspending due to projects that never materialized. Overspending on projects early in the year brought the shortfall to $7.3 million. But the unit, being determined to spend its allocation, came up with new projects that cost $9.7 million. Look at it this way: They overspent the first $8 million that was budgeted by $4.1 million—over 50 percent. We don't actually know whether they overspent the second $9.7 million or not, but they ended up exceeding their original budget by $2.4 million.

Wasteful spending and bad planning are usually symptoms of compensation design that focuses exclusively on the income statement at the expense of the balance sheet.

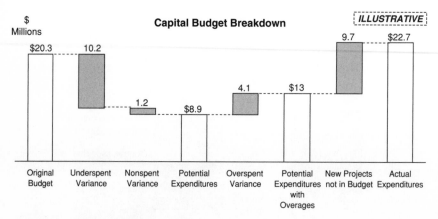

FIGURE 6.7   Need for better planning.

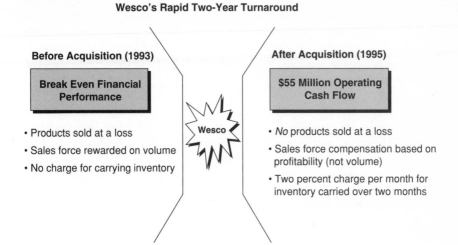

FIGURE 6.8   Better incentive design.

Note: Successful acquirers put the pace of change to capture value. For example, when Clayton, Dubilier, & Rice acquired Wesco in 1991, they insisted on dramatic change—quickly! The result was that operating income jumped from zero to $55 million within two years.

Source: Monitor analysis

Incentive Design

Incentive design that is linked to better balance sheet management as well as to better income statement management helps to focus managers on creating shareholder value. An example was provided by Chuck Ames, a former director of McKinsey & Co. and senior partner at Clayton, Dubilier, and Rice (CDR), one of the world's largest private equity investment firms. As he describes the success of Wesco—an acquisition from Westinghouse that CDR turned around from losses to substantial profits in less than two years—he emphasizes the role of getting the incentives right. See Figure 6.8.

Two key actions centered around incentives. CDR's first step was to create a measure of profitability by product line. Sales commissions were changed from a percentage of sales volume to a percentage of profit. No unprofitable product lines were sold. Second, there was a working capital problem that no one in top management could figure out. Instead, they simply charged business unit managers 2 percent per month for every dollar of receivables or inventory carried over two months. Says Mr. Ames, "The problem vanished after about six months—we still don't know exactly how."

In both cases, success resulted from linking incentives to better free cash flow management.

The Capital Efficiency Process

In the short term, capital efficiency is a little like being on a crash diet. Your whole being is trying to get down to a sustainable weight. In the long run you have to exercise and eat right—changing your mindset and your daily routine. Not a bad analogy, this two-step process is quite similar to how one goes about achieving capital efficiency. A swat team approach is followed by an Expectations-Based Management routine that sustains capital efficiency over time.

The Short Run

In the short run, several small teams are formed with the charge from the CEO that there is a great need and a wonderful opportunity to create value by getting rid of excess capital from the balance sheet. The first two boxes in Figure 6.9 are usually the focus of the short-term effort, namely to manage down the demand for capital and to search for lower cost alternatives (the supply side of the equation).

In order to challenge the conventional wisdom, these swat teams will often need to check engineering specifications for standard tolerances against what is actually happening and challenge the tradeoffs that are

Capital Management Effective Framework

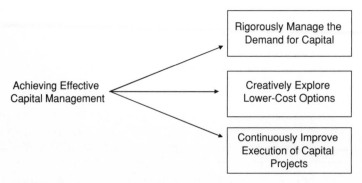

FIGURE 6.9   The capital efficiency process.

Source: Monitor analysis

being made between reliability, safety, and capital expense. It is also important to see if administrative procedures can be streamlined to move faster, and to contain the right amount and type of information. Each swat team should be charged with finding ideas that can cut planned capital expenditures by 10 to 25 percent—without reducing the quantity or quality of goods and services provided to customers. Team composition should include not only the top management of the business unit but also representatives of engineering, and of internal suppliers and customers of the unit.

The Long Run

In the long run, the continuous improvement shown in the third box of Figure 6.9 comes from establishing the three-part Expectations-Based Management system with the following:

- discounted cash flow models of the company and its business units
- business unit performance measured on an annual basis by the difference between actual and expected economic profit
- new investment required to earn more than the cost of capital
- daily operating value drivers.

But the EBM system requires training for new employees, a hot line to answer accounting and DCF questions, a set of common assumptions (e.g., what is the cost of capital?), and, most important of all, the continued support of management. In our opinion the most difficult part of EBM is understanding and setting expectations, both externally and internally. Remember, expectations are not meant to be stretch targets. Over a period of time one would hope that performance exceeds expectations about half of the time.

Since this chapter is about capital efficiency, another difference between the short run and the long run is that some capital savings are one-time events (e.g., selling a business), and other capital-saving ideas save money year after year (e.g., cutting plant construction costs by 10 percent). It is worth remembering that the value impact of the latter category is usually 5 to 10 times greater than the first.

Summary

This chapter is the last of three that have reviewed management of the investments of companies. EBM requires that we look at them in a new way. Maintenance investments, covered in Chapter 3, are built into expectations—both their amount and their expected rate of return. Therefore, maintenance investment has to earn more than expected in order to grow your stock price faster than the cost of equity. New investment, discussed in Chapter 4, is unexpected, and is not built into the stock price. It must earn more than the cost of capital. Finally, this chapter has suggested ways of "working your core assets harder"—how to stop wasting capital—and how to improve the capital spending process.

CHAPTER 7

Reverse Engineer the Value of Your Firm

Most companies that are listed on a major stock exchange are followed by one or more analysts whose job it is to obtain and analyze any and all available information about the forecasted future of the company. These analysts are categorized in two broad groups—buy side and sell side. The former are employed to give advice to their own company and the latter provide analysis to the public—often in the form of buy, hold, or sell recommendations that are accompanied by detailed reports. Analysts are certainly not the only ones who gather and study company information, but they are the most visible. They are leaders of market opinion and help to form expectations about company performance.

Who sets expectations? The answer has not changed—top management does, because it is best informed. But you would be surprised how well informed some analysts can be, and at the same time, how poorly informed others are. To help ward off self-delusional behavior, we recommend that top management not only engage in a two-way dialog with analysts, and read analyst reports; they should also make a concerted effort to understand what is driving the stock price—an effort that puts analyst expectations into a DCF valuation model to find gaps between analyst and management expectations. In short, reverse engineer your share price.

This chapter is organized to discuss the effect of analyst biases about forecasted earnings on the stock price, the steps in the process of reverse engineering, and what to do when you find information gaps—differences in expectations. By the way, reverse engineering stock prices is useful for investors, too. For example, see Rappaport and Mauboussin (2001), Chapter 5, that discusses how to estimate price-implied expectations.

Analyst Expectations Are Biased—What Should You Do?

A constant bias in any signal is easily corrected because it is expected. If you have a friend who loves only scary movies and you hate them, there is plenty of information in a reply that says she hated a movie that she saw very recently. You are reasonably sure that you will like it.

The academic literature is fairly convincing about the allegation that, indeed, analyst forecasts are unduly optimistic. According to Jegadeesh, Kim, Krisehe, and Lee,[1] Wall Street sell-side analysts overselect "glamour" stocks and underselect "value" stocks. Glamour stocks tend to be high growth, positive momentum, high volume, and relatively expensive. Analysts are quick to upgrade stocks with favorable news, but fail to downgrade quickly bad news stocks. The research of Jegadeesh et al finds that once other factors that explain stock returns are accounted for, the marginal predictive ability of analysts is not statistically different from zero. Nevertheless, favorably recommended stocks outperform those that have unfavorable recommendations, and changes in recommendations are stronger signals than the levels of recommendations (much like how changes in expectations more strongly relate to shareholder returns than the level of expectations).

Additional research by Barber, Lehary, McNichols, and Trueman[2] also studied sell-side analyst stock recommendations and found that with daily portfolio rebalancing based on an immediate response to changes in analyst recommendations, it was possible to earn an excess return of 4.13 percent from buying upgraded stocks and 4.91 percent from selling downgraded stocks. They also report that the excess returns are perishable. On the buy side, a one-week delay in trading cut the gross return to about two percent and a one-month delay cut it to less than one percent. These reduced returns were not statistically different from zero. The short sale portfolio gross rates of return stayed at four percent after one week and 2.5 percent after a month—all statistically significant. When returns net of transactions costs were calculated, however, no strategy produced excess returns that were significant.

The take-away from all of this is that analysts are better informed than the market but are biased toward quick upgrades of glamour stocks and tardy downgrades of value stocks. The market is reasonably efficient, however, because delays in trading quickly devalue the information contained in rating changes, and returns net of transactions costs are small—not statistically different from zero.

---

[1]See Jegadeesh, N., J. Kim, S. Krische, and C. Lee, "Analyzing the Analysts: When Do Recommendations Add Value?" *Journal of Finance*, Vol. 59, No. 3, 2004, pp. 1083–1124.
[2]See Barber, B., R. Lehavy, M. McNichols, and B. Trueman, "Can Investors Profit from the Prophets? Security Analyst Recommendations and Stock Returns," *Journal of Finance*, Vol. 56, No. 2, 2001, pp. 531–582.

Couple these results with the apparent success of insider trading (reported in Chapter 8) and it seems reasonable to conclude that management, having insider information, is the best informed group, analysts are the next-best informed group (by collecting information on their own and by having superior analytical skills), and shareholders at large stand at the end of the information queue. Nevertheless, it is a challenge for management to fully communicate with potential investors. To be successful at this, management must understand what the analyst community correctly understands, what it is missing, and what it has misunderstood.

The Process of Reverse Engineering Your Stock Price

The process of Reverse Engineering, illustrated in Figure 7.1, can be used to infer the impacts of analyst expectations on the value of your company and that of a competitor. The first step, of course, is to obtain the necessary data. Two large data bases, IBES and Zacks, compile analyst forecasts of earnings per share for most listed companies for the current year, one year ahead, and long-term earnings growth (a three- to five-year forecast). More specific forecasts of value drivers, such as revenue growth, operating margins, and capital expenditures, can be found in individual analyst reports, as well as from the *Value Line Investor Survey*. Management-initiated surveys may also be used to obtain a more consistent and comprehensive set of expectations metrics across a broad set of analysts. Such a survey should ideally obtain buy-side analyst expectations as well, though such analysts may be reluctant to share information even with management due to the proprietary nature of their models and a desire to maintain information advantage.

Differences between analyst and management expectations are highlighted by a discounted cash flow valuation exercise:

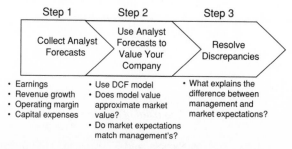

FIGURE 7.1   The process of reverse engineering.

Source: Monitor analysis

Once the data have been obtained, there is the problem that the market expectations may be biased or noisy. One good way of testing this proposition is to put the analyst forecasts into a discounted cash flow model. If the resulting estimate of the value of the stock is approximately the same as the current market value, it is possible to conclude that current expectations are reasonable and are baked into the stock price.

If the market's expectations produce a DCF (discounted case flow) value quite different from the market price of the stock, then the discrepancy begs for an explanation. It might be that management has its own expectations different from those of the market, and that when they are substituted for the analyst expectations, a DCF value results that is closer to the market. One cannot argue that the market price is always right because it has been known to be founded on bad information and rumor. The opposite is also possible—because management forecasts have also been known to be wrong. Once you fully understand which is the best set of forecast assumptions and their impact on the intrinsic value of the stock, it is only then that you can make informed decisions.

A Case Example—Home Depot and Lowe's

Pretend that it is April 2001 and we have just entered the new millennium. The terrorist events of 9/11 have not transpired; in fact, they are quite unimaginable. Two companies in the home improvement business are slugging it out. Given the publicly available information at the time, what were the market's expectations? How likely would it be that they could exceed those expectations? And at a more basic level, what drove the share prices of these competitors?

Step 1—Obtain the Data

Home Depot and Lowe's are competitors in the home improvement business, which experienced double-digit growth in the late 1990s that continued until (at least) the mid-2000s. Their products range from plumbing and painting supplies to gardening and carpentry equipment. Table 7.1 shows the actual earnings per share, revenue growth, operating margins, capital turns (revenue per dollar of capital invested), and return on invested capital. Note that the actual data for 2001–2003 was not available in April 2001.

It is fairly easy to see that at the end of 2000, Home Depot was winning. Its return on invested capital was higher every year by at least 4.3 percent, its operating margins are higher every year, and so were its capital turns. The only close race was for revenue growth. Home Depot averaged 23.1 percent growth over the first two years while Lowe's averaged 24 percent—a trivial difference. Over the entire 5-year period, as it turned out

Table 7.1 Home Depot versus Lowe's, Key Statistics, 1999–2003

Home Depot Actual Performance					
	1999	2000	2001	2002	2003
Revenue growth	27.2%	19.0%	17.1%	8.8%	11.3%
Operating margin	9.9%	9.2%	9.3%	10.0%	10.6%
Capital turns	4.46×	3.99×	4.06×	3.04×	2.99×
ROIC	19.7%	17.9%	17.6%	19.9%	22.6%
Earnings per share	$1.00	$1.24	$1.32	$1.52	$1.90
Lowes Actual Performance					
	1999	2000	2001	2002	2003
Revenue growth	29.9%	18.1%	17.7%	19.8%	16.4%
Operating margin	7.4%	7.5%	8.1%	9.6%	10.4%
Capital turns	3.89×	3.31×	3.03×	2.99×	2.42×
ROIC	13.8%	12.4%	12.4%	15.6%	16.8%
Earnings (FY 1/31)	$0.92	$0.50	$1.30	$1.75	$2.25

Source: Monitor analysis, Compustat

later, Home Depot's yearly average growth was 16.7 percent, while it was higher (20.3 percent) at Lowe's.

Next, take a look at Figure 7.2. It shows the total return to shareholders for both companies from December 1998 through June 2004. By April 2001 the cumulative returns of the two companies were about the same, in

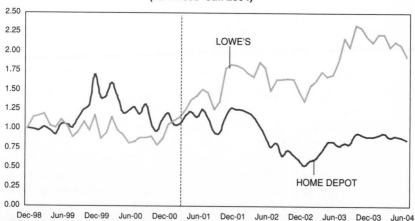

**Home Depot vs. Lowe's Total Shareholder Returns
(Jan. 1999–Jul. 2004)**

FIGURE 7.2   Cumulative total return to shareholders.

Source: Monitor analysis

Table 7.2 Home Depot versus Lowe's, Analyst Expectations, 1999–2003

Home Depot Expected Performance					
	1999	2000	2001	2002	2003
Revenue growth	20.8%*	24.9%	21.0%	15.7%	10.1%*
Operating margin	9.0%*	10.1%	8.8%*	9.7%	10.3%*
Capital turns	3.74x*	4.58x	4.09x	4.14x	3.06x
ROIC	17.5%*	20.1%	16.2%*	19.2%*	18.7%*
Earnings			$1.50	$1.52	$1.40
Lowes Expected Performance					
	1999	2000	2001	2002	2003
Revenue growth	25.0%*	20.1%	17.7%*	18.7%*	16.3%*
Operating margin	7.6%	7.7%	8.2%	8.6%*	10.3%*
Capital turns	3.69x	4.09x	3.31x	3.01x	3.04x
ROIC	14.2%	12.8%	12.1%*	12.4%*	15.2%*
Earnings			$1.30	$1.50	$1.75*

*Designates years when actual performance (Table 7.1) exceeded expected performance (Table 7.2)

Source: Analyst reports, Monitor analysis

spite of Home Depot's superior financial performance. After that point in time (up to June 2004), total return to shareholders of Lowe's increased about 95 percent while shareholders of Home Depot experienced around a 25 percent decline.

It should be obvious by now, halfway through the book, that if we dig further we are going to find that Home Depot failed to meet expectations while Lowe's exceeded expectations. Take a look at Table 7.2. It provides analyst expectations of the key value drivers and of earnings.

If we look at revenue growth expectations, for example, both companies exceeded expectations in 1999 and neither did in 2000. Then Lowe's exceeded expectations in each of the three following years (2001–2003)—while Home Depot did not in 2001–2002, and did so only by 1.2 percent in 2003. Both companies exceeded return on invested capital (*ROIC*) expectations in 2001.

Figures 7.3 and 7.4 show the evolution of earnings and analyst consensus earnings expectations for Home Depot and Lowe's, respectively, overlaid with the total returns to shareholders. Look at 2001. At Home Depot, two years earlier, in January of 2000, analysts were forecasting about $1.50 earnings per share, but revised the estimate down to about $1.30 by December 2001. Earnings for 2002 and 2003 came in roughly according to expectations. Home Depot failed to exceed earnings expectations in any year 2001–2003. The Lowe's results for 2001 came in as expected, but the

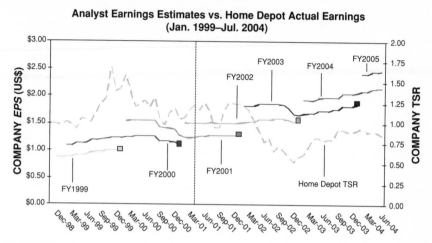

FIGURE 7.3   Consensus analysts expectations of Home Depot earnings.

Note: Boxes denote actual EPS before extraordinary items; lines that end in boxes denote consensus analyst estimates for the current and next fiscal year.

Source: IBES, CRSP, Monitor analysis

2002 earnings, which in December 2000 were expected to be roughly $1.50 per share, actually were $1.75 per share—a fact that caused upward revisions in analyst expectations throughout 2001 and 2002; actual earnings exceeded expectations by roughly $0.50 per share in 2003. Lowe's exceeded earnings expectations in two of three years.

To summarize, Home Depot turned in better absolute performance between 1999 and 2003 in every category except for revenue growth. It had higher return on invested capital than Lowe's every year, higher operating margins and capital turns every year, and roughly the same geometric average sales revenue growth. But starting in 2001, Lowe's began to exceed earnings expectations while Home Depot failed to meet or just met expectations.

Step 2—Use the Data in a DCF Valuation[3]

Using the analyst estimates of revenue growth, operating margins and capital expenditures, we developed free cash flow forecasts that started in 2001 and ended in 2010, plus an estimate of the present value of all cash flows from 2011 on (a number that we call the "continuing value" but

---

[3]For detailed instructions on creating a DCF valuation model, see Copeland, T.E., J. Murrin, and T. Koller, *Valuation: Measuring and Managing the Value of Companies*, 3rd Ed., John Wiley & Sons, 2000.

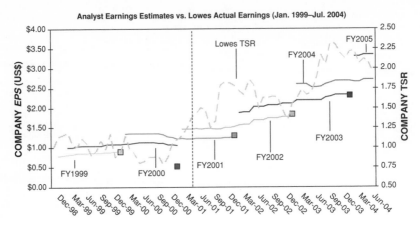

FIGURE 7.4   Consensus analysts expectations of Lowe's earnings.

Note: Boxes denote actual EPS before extraordinary items; lines thus end in boxes denote consensus analyst estimates for the current and next fiscal year.

Source: IBES, CRSP, Monitor Analysis

which is also called the "terminal value"), calculated the weighted average cost of capital, and finally discounted all cash flows as well as the continuing value. The resulting DCF estimate of the entity value was adjusted by adding the value of nonoperating assets (e.g., excess marketable securities) and by subtracting debt and other liabilities in order to get the estimate of the equity value of the shares outstanding. Our results seemed to indicate that, indeed, the market's expectations were baked into the stock price, because it was no stretch of the imagination to see that the discounted cash flows were very close to the actual market values. The market price of Home Depot at the time of valuation (April 2001) was $47.10 while the DCF value was $42.69—a 10.3 percent difference. Similarly, the market price of Lowe's was $31.50 and the DCF estimate was $35.10—a 10.2 percent difference in the other direction.[4] Figure 7.5 shows the valuation summaries, key assumptions, and free cash flows for both companies.

---

[4]Note that reverse engineering share price expectations is not an exact science. Due to the inherent noise in key inputs such as the weighted-average cost of capital or long-run expected growth, a DCF value that varies by 5 to 10 percent away from share price is not unusual.

Home Depot Inc
Valuation Summary

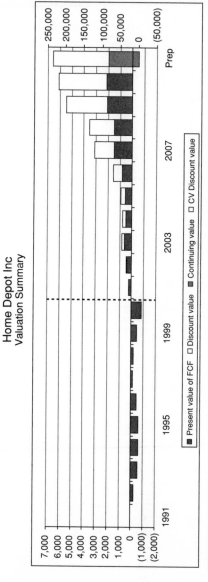

■ Present value of FCF □ Discount value ■ Continuing value □ CV Discount value

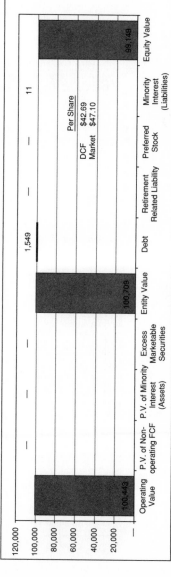

FIGURE 7.5A DCF valuation summaries, April 2001.

Source: Monitor analysis, Compustat data

Lowe's Valuation Summary

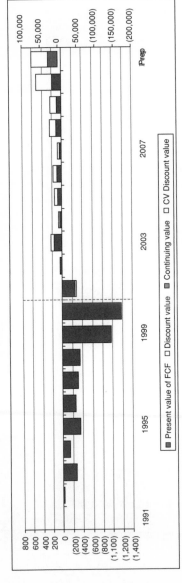

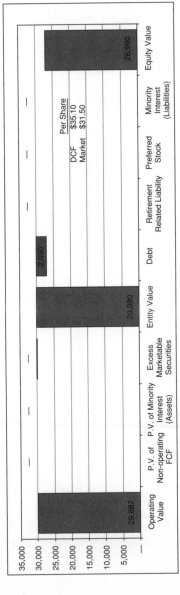

FIGURE 7.5B Lowe's valuation summaries.

Source: Monitor analysis, Compustat data

It is also useful to study the value drivers that lie behind the economics of the companies. The three highest-level value drivers are revenue growth (but only if it is profitable growth),

$$g_R = \frac{R_t - R_{t-1}}{R_{t-1}}$$

the return on invested capital,

$$ROIC = \frac{EBIT(1-T)}{IC} = \text{operating margin times capital turns}$$

$$ROIC = \frac{EBIT(1-T)}{\text{Sales}} \times \frac{\text{Sales}}{IC}$$

and the weighted average cost of capital,

$$WACC = k_b(1-T_m)\frac{B}{V} + k_s\frac{S}{V}.$$

Figures 7.6 and 7.7 show these value drivers for Home Depot and Lowe's, respectively. Note that revenue growth, while forecasted to be high in the next few years, was expected to decline to roughly 15 percent for both firms by 2010. The biggest difference is in their *ROIC*. At Lowe's it was expected to stay around 16 percent while at Home Depot it was expected to stay at 22 percent. This is driven by a higher operating margin and higher capital turnover at Home Depot, possibly a consequence of leased versus owned facilities.

Both companies had strong balance sheets in April 2001. Home Depot had a AA bond rating while the rating for Lowe's was A. At the bottom of the value driver figures we see that the weighted average cost of capital was 10.35 percent at Home Depot and 11.07 percent at Lowe's.

The heart of the matter is what one believes about the ability of these competitors to raise their return on invested capital. Figure 7.8 plots net property, plant, equipment (NPPE), and inventory (and their sum) as a percentage of total revenues. Note that their sum as a percentage of sales is very much the same. The breakdown of this figure into net property, plant, and equipment over sales indicates that Lowe's has less sales per dollar of investment in NPPE than does Home Depot. However, Home Depot has more inventory per dollar of sales.

We could try to figure out why Home Depot has better utilization of NPPE and worse utilization of inventory—possibly because Lowe's owns a higher percentage of its buildings than Home Depot, and because Home Depot has fewer stock outs because it carries more inventory. However,

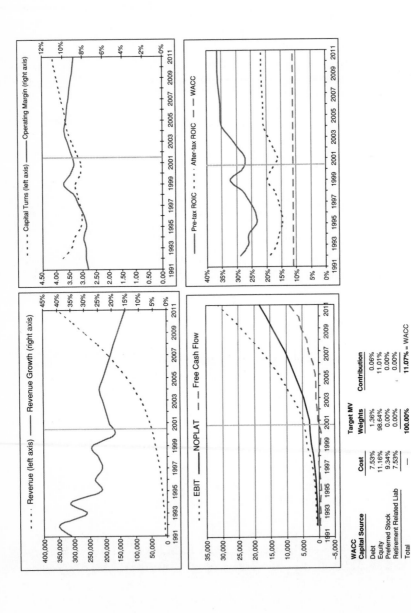

FIGURE 7.6 Key value drivers at Home Depot.

Source: Monitor analysis, Bloomberg, Compustat

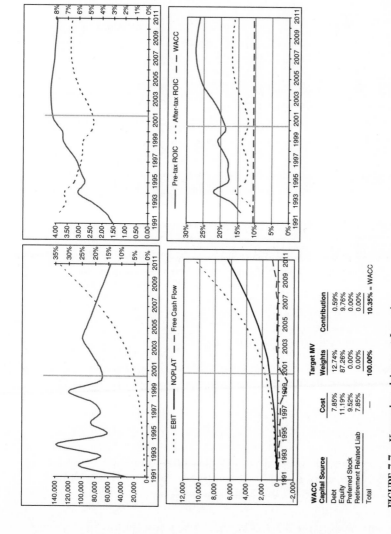

FIGURE 7.7 Key value drivers at Lowe's.

Source: Monitor analysis, Bloomberg, Compustat

WACC Capital Source	Cost	Target MV Weights	Contribution
Debt	7.85%	12.74%	0.59%
Equity	11.19%	87.26%	9.76%
Preferred Stock	9.52%	0.00%	0.00%
Retirement Related Liab	7.85%	0.00%	0.00%
Total	—	100.00%	10.35% = WACC

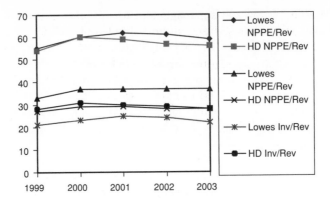

FIGURE 7.8   NPPE and inventory as a percentage of revenues.

Source: Monitor analysis, Compustat data

Expectations-Based Management asks a different question—namely, which company is more likely to exceed expected performance and on which value driver?

It seems that 2002 was a pivotal year. Analysts expected revenue growth to be 15.7 percent at Home Depot and 18.7 percent at Lowe's. Instead, Home Depot grew at only 8.8 percent, a full 6.9 percent below expectations, while Lowe's grew 1.9 percent above expectations—at 18.7%. Analysts lowered their earnings growth forecast at Home Depot from 15.7 percent in 2002 to 10.1 percent in 2003.

Step 3—Identify and Resolve Discrepancies

There could be many sources of discrepancy. The market value might be out of synch with the analyst expectations, for example. Using the expectations that were developed in 2001, we found that the implied discounted cash flow model was quite close to the market value. Therefore, it seems that in April of 2001, the market was expecting Home Depot to grow revenues faster than at Lowe's in 2001—21.0 percent and 17.7 percent, respectively. Lowe's came in with exactly the expected growth, but Home Depot disappointed the market with 17.1 percent growth, 3.9 percent less than expected. A similar pattern followed in 2002. The market modestly raised its expectation of Lowe's to 18.7 percent and Lowe's beat it with 19.8 percent. Expectations of Home Depot sales growth fell to 15.7 percent and the company grew only 8.8 percent—a second disappointing year.

We do not know what management was expecting at the time. It, too, may have been surprised and disappointed. But we do know from our reverse engineering exercise that relatively ambitious sales growth expectations were baked into Home Depot's stock price.

Did Home Depot earn positive and increasing EVA during the 2001–2003 interval? Yes it did. Did its earnings grow? Again the answer is "yes." Was its total return to shareholders positive? Sadly, the answer is "no", because it failed to exceed expectations. As the market was disappointed, the stock price fell.

What Should Be Done About Gaps in Expectations?

Remember that management has the best information about the destiny of the firm. But there is a lot of noise and management has been known to engage in self-delusional behavior—hockey stick forecasting, for example. But analysts have been known to be wrong and there is no guarantee that the market does not have speculative bubbles or what we prefer to call information mirages.

Most of the time reverse engineering will shed some light on the subject. The discounted cash flow valuation tells you what assumptions or expectations are consistent with the current market price. When these seem too high or too low vis-à-vis management expectations, then try to identify the specific source of the discrepancy by interviewing analysts, examining analysts' written opinions, and carefully listening to analysts on earnings conference calls and similar events. If they expect, for example, that sales are going to be more robust than your management team expects, and if you believe that your team is right, then you might issue new shares, but even more likely, the best thing to do is to deflate their estimates. This will probably bring their expectations down and pull the stock price down with them. But it will also bring less noise and greater credibility to the market. The stock price would have dropped later anyway, when circumstances revealed the firm's underlying weakness. But the greater noise associated with the unexpected and uncommunicated fall might drive the stock price down even further as management loses credibility.

It may be that the market is right and management is wrong. Perish the thought, of course.

Summary and Conclusions

Reverse engineering of a company's stock price is a process that uses time-tested discounted cash flow valuation methodology to see whether analyst expectations give back the market price when they are imbedded into the model. If so, and it usually is so, then it is reasonable to assume that the company has to meet or exceed those expectations in order to experience a total return to shareholders that is equal to or greater than the cost of equity.

Reverse engineering a competitor's stock price is also instructive, as we saw when we compared Home Depot to Lowe's.

Reverse engineering is all about uncovering beliefs and expectations of management, analysts, and investors, and figuring out the difference between what management thinks it can achieve and what the market and analysts expect—then doing something about it. This might mean better external communications between management and analysts on specific issues—e.g., performance on a value driver might imply sale or repurchase of shares, or it might imply action vis-à-vis a competitor.

Appendix—Tips for Reverse Engineering Stock Price

We've found the following tips helpful in reconciling share price with analyst and/or management expectations.

- Make sure to survey as many analysts as possible to get the most representative sample of market sentiment. Check which analysts have been more successful with their prior forecasts. And don't forget about debt securities analysts who often have a more conservative (or cautious) outlook.
- Check for consistent definitions. Some analysts forecast gross capital expenditures, others forecast capex net of depreciation and asset sales. Some analysts include cash in working capital, others treat cash as a financing item.
- Build as complete a set of financial statement forecasts as possible. While it is possible to build a DCF valuation model based solely on expected operating cash flows, forecasting a complete balance sheet and income statement can help in evaluating the reasonableness and consistency of assumptions.
- Where analysts do not provide specific forecasts, use historical benchmarks or economic rules of thumb to develop a forecast. For example, if analysts do not provide long-run growth estimates, one can use a forecast based on long-run (20+ years) historical industry sales growth or expected national or global economic nominal growth.
- When assumptions must be substituted for unavailable analyst forecasts, triangulate using different methods as much as possible. This is especially important for continuing value (terminal value) estimates, as they comprise a large proportion of total firm value.

CHAPTER 8

Investor Relations

OK, by now you have the idea—expectations count. Performance measurement should be assessed relative to expectations. But who should set expectations? Who has the best information about the future of the company? Is inside information valuable to investors? What sources do investors use to form their expectations? Where does market "noise" come from? For that matter, what is noise? These are the questions that matter to executives formulating an investor relations strategy. In this chapter we turn to these questions and show an EBM approach to the external communications problem.

Some of the points we'll make in this chapter are that top management has the best information about the firm and therefore is best situated to set expectations, reduce market uncertainty, and act to correct market mispricing. Top management must be professional about investor relations. We cannot forget, however, that there are other ways of closing the gap between the management and market views of the firm—decisions that have boardroom implications. This chapter discusses these boardroom decisions—namely, signaling via share repurchase or by issuing new shares. Next, it turns to focus on investor relations and the regulation of the flow of information between management and the public. Finally, we make some recommendations about management conduct when it communicates with potential investors.

Investor Relations

It is worth starting with a few thoughts on what investor relations is all about—or rather, what it *should* be about. In the organizational structure of most firms, the investor relations function has had a dotted line to senior management. Investor relations officers have frequently been appointed due to their relationships with the CEO or CFO, their experience in public relations, or because they possessed a knowledge of finance and capital markets. We're generalizing a bit here, but until only recently it was not too much of a leap to say that investor relations was viewed as a specialized communications function.

We believe this view is too myopic—and indeed there is plenty of evidence that companies are placing more credence in the importance of investor relations.[1] External communications should be about getting the stock price to be correct—i.e., to accurately reflect the fundamental value of the company. This may go against the intuition of many who have seen the goal of market communications to "talk up" a stock.

Of course, hyping a stock can get you into trouble by trapping management into a misguided or myopic approach to value creation. The so-called "earnings game," described in great detail in *The Value Reporting Revolution*, is one such trap. Management sets (quarterly) earnings targets that it believes investors want to hear and then makes operating and investing decisions to ensure that short-term expectations targets are hit.

A variant of this "earnings game" is the expectations treadmill. This is a point of view that critiques Expectations-Based Management with an example of a hypothetical company that exceeds earnings expectations by five percent in the first year. Not wishing to again underestimate next year's earnings, the market builds in an extra five percent of earnings growth into its expectations, and the company beats that, too. Year after year expectations rise until at last the expectations treadmill collapses. After all, even the most high-flying companies come back to Earth at some point. A corollary is that this earnings treadmill will lead every company to the point where expectations cannot be met.

The authors of the expectations treadmill hypothesis need to review the theory of rational expectations. No one said the market is perfectly rational, but to prevent too many people from becoming fabulously wealthy from selling short the stock of companies caught on the alleged expectations treadmill, we point out that, on average, expectations are rational. This means that if the revenue growth of a small company is much higher than normal, its expected growth will decline as it follows the typical "S-curve" for growth. Or a cyclical company will be expected to have bad years as well as good years. We do not believe investors would irrationally continue to ratchet up expectations in spite of all the information they have (see Figure 8.1).

---

[1]For a number of examples of companies that have restructured their approach to external communications, see Robert G. Eccles, et al., 2001.

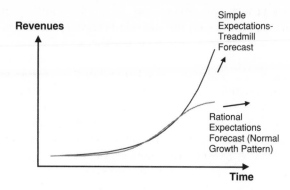

FIGURE 8.1   Expectations treadmill versus rational expectations.

If the market follows common-sense rules of forecasting, the expectations treadmill is a myth. Yet some managers have become caught in this vicious circle without much prompting. There has been much speculation about the role of management hubris in the Enron scandal. Consider the circumstances. In 1990 Jeff Skilling resigned as a McKinsey director to head Enron energy and trading. At the time, the New York Mercantile Exchange was reviewing the creation of natural gas futures contracts but had not finalized its plans. Enron has the most extensive natural gas pipeline in North American, had gas in the ground, and had the best real-time information system regarding the spot prices of natural gas anywhere in the United States and Canada. Skilling was able to create an active market in trading forward contracts in natural gas. Eventually, it became so active and so profitable that it made up nearly half of Enron's total profits.

The market expectations of Enron earnings were enormously exceeded during the early years of his tenure at Enron and the stock price shot up (from $45 in 1990 before he started there to a peak of $90 in 2000). The ride was exciting and Skilling became a multimillionaire. He wanted an encore, and tried to create markets in blocks of electric power (something that is hard to store), in fiber-optic telecommunications cable, and even in computer chips. Each time as Enron spent money to make these dreams come true, he went before the public to sell ideas that had a very low probability of success. Resources were squandered, predictions failed, earnings growth was manufactured from smoke and mirrors, and the company went bankrupt.

Putting aside the alleged fraud and accounting irregularities behind Enron's demise, there is a more fundamental story about a management team that became convinced that it had to continue its exponential growth indefinitely. It is certainly plausible that Enron could have transformed itself from a fast-growth company to one that grew at a rate closer to long-term energy industry growth rates. Excess cash could have been paid out as dividends rather than squandered on new, uneconomic ventures.

Management needs to view investor relations in the proper context. The "game" is not set by outsiders, and there is no predefined set of ever-increasing expectations to follow. The only rule—if we were to call it that—is to help investors value the company rationally. Manage the share price to reflect underlying value, and be prepared for it to move both up and down as fundamentals change. Hiding the truth from investors only delays the inevitable adjustment that must take place, and introduces undue noise/volatility that is harmful to shareholder value.

Getting the Message Out: The Signal to Noise Ratio

Our research (as reported in Chapter 2) indicates a strong and statistically significant link between the market-adjusted returns to shareholders and two types of variables—namely, changing expectations about earnings as well as changes in the level of noise. Roughly 50 percent of the cross-sectional variation of returns can be explained this way. Others' research confirms our findings. Our research also established that changes in expectations about long-term earnings have a significant, immediate impact on share price. Others have shown that long-run shareholder returns are correlated with actual long-run earnings growth.

What are the implications of this research for external communications? From the point of view of an investor, all new pieces of information about a company have two components—a signal and noise. Signals need to be relevant and material. Noise needs to be minimized. Investors interpret signals only in the context of the surrounding noise—i.e., the signal-to-noise ratio determines how the market reacts to news.

Management then has two goals in communicating with investors. First is to report not only the history of events at the company, but also its opinion of the future. We have established that higher expected earnings, especially long-term earnings growth, have a positive effect on the current return to shareholders. Thus, signals need to focus on long-term earnings potential (as well as any short-run factors that may have significant impact on value). The second goal of investor relations is to minimize noise so that investors fully receive the signal and factor it into share price.

Table 8.1 provides a taxonomy of different types of signals (and noise) and their sources. This is by no means comprehensive, but provides a good sense of just how many signals and sources of noise investors must manage. Because they have the best information about the firm (a point we discuss below), managers need to ensure that the signals they give to investors are not only right, but are heard through the noise.

TABLE 8.1 Signals and Noise

Source	Signals	Noise
Management	• Financial disclosures and earnings reports • Investor relations communications • Communications related to operations (e.g., product-related press releases) • Insider ownership stakes • Capital structure, dividends, and share repurchases	• Internal consistency of message • Consistency of message across managers • Depth and relevance of financial disclosures • Forecast bias • Consistency of signaling policies
Investors	• Share price • Bid and ask prices • Ownership stakes • Short-sold positions	• Share price volatility • Bid-ask spread* • Trading volume* • Divergence of expected future earnings
Analysts	• Buy/sell recommendations • Earnings forecasts • Investment opinions and research	• Divergence of opinions across analysts • Uncertainty of opinions
Other External Sources	• Prices of industry peers' stocks • Industry and macroeconomic news	• Volatility of industry peer's stock prices • Volatility of industry statistics (e.g., volume sold) • Differences of opinion about future industry fundamentals

* Bid-ask spread and trading volume primarily reflect liquidity, but also reflect market noise, that is driven by differences in expectations (see Copeland and Galai, 1983). For example, investors seeking to sell shares may quote an asking price significantly away from quoted bid prices if buyers and sellers have widely divergent opinions on the stock's value.

Getting the Signal Right—Management Has the Best Information

Research has shown that insiders have the best information about the value of a company. Insiders are defined as management, owners of five percent or more of the outstanding shares, members of the board, and advisors such as lawyers, consultants, investment bankers, and bankers. Insiders who trade a company's securities are required by the Securities and Exchange Commission (SEC) to register all trades. After a period of time these insider trades are released by the SEC to the public with the date and terms of transaction made a matter of public record. This makes it possible for academics to study the returns made by insiders, who are, of course, better informed than the public.

Jaffe (1974) was one of the first to study insider trading. He collected data from *The Official Summary of Security Transactions and Holdings*, published by the SEC. He then defined an intensive trading month as one during which there were at least three more insiders buying as selling and vice versa. If a stock was intensively traded during a month, it was included in either of two intensive trading portfolios—buy or sell. For 861 observations during the 1960s, abnormal rates of return, above the market, of five percent were observed during the eight months following the intensive trading event, with three percent occurring in the last six months. These returns are statistically significant and are greater than transaction costs. Jaffe concludes that, being better informed, insiders can and do earn excess returns.

A somewhat later study by Finnerty (1976) corroborates Jaffe's conclusions. The major difference was that the Finnerty data was not restricted to an intensive trading group. By testing the entire population of insiders, his empirical findings allow evaluation of an "average insider." His data set includes over 30,000 individual transactions between January 1969 and December 1972. Abnormal returns indicate that insiders are able to "beat the market" on a risk-adjusted basis, both when buying and selling.

A study by Givoly and Palmon (1985) correlates insider trading with subsequent news announcements to see if insiders trade in anticipation of news releases. The surprising result is that there is no relationship between insider trading and news events. Although insiders' transactions are associated with a strong price movement in the direction of the trade during the month following the trade, these price movements occur independently of the subsequent publication of news. This leads to the conjecture that outside investors accept (perhaps blindly) the superiority of the knowledge of insiders and follow in their footsteps.

The above discussion makes clear that the market perceives insiders as having superior information about the firm. Although we think management should listen to the market and understand its expectations for the firm—a point we will return to later—management needs to be at the forefront of shaping investor expectations. Its primary vehicles for doing so are traditional disclosures statements, conference calls, and communications. Equally important, however, are signals the firm can make to demonstrate positive or negative expectations about the future.

What Signals Can Management Use When It Believes Its Stock Is Mispriced?

For the time being, forget how management reaches the conclusion that its stock is mispriced. Actions speak louder than words. As we noted in Table 8.1, management has quite a few actions available to send a signal to investors. The strongest signal they can send would be through their own personal purchases/sales of stock (or exercise of options). We put aside such actions that benefit management directly and focus on financial signals the company can send. Such actions include the issuance/repurchase of securities, changes in dividends, and/or leverage-changing recapitalizations.

If management believes the market price is too low, then it can act directly to repurchase shares by using excess cash (that otherwise might have been paid out as dividends) or borrowing the desired funds (thereby increasing the riskiness of shares outstanding). If it believes the share price is too high, it can do the opposite. It can sell new shares (or use shares as currency in an acquisition).

There are two types of share repurchase programs that are useful when management believes the stock is undervalued—tender offers and open market repurchases. Stock prices rise upon the announcement of either type of repurchase, but the average announcement effect is greater for tender offers (averaging 15.8 percent) versus open market repurchases (averaging five to six percent) because tenders offer greater certainty that the stated number of shares will actually be repurchased and because they usually involve a greater percentage of the shares outstanding.

Tender Offers

Tender offers to repurchase shares are usually significant corporate events. Dann (1981) reports that, for a sample of 143 cash tender offers by 122 firms between 1962 and 1976, the average cash distributions proposed by the tender represented an average of 20 percent of the market value of the company's pre-tender equity value. The announcement effects of tender offers on the market values of corporate securities have been studied by Masulis (1980), Dann (1981), and Vermaelen (1981). There are several separate, but not mutually exclusive, hypotheses for share repurchase programs. The most popular among them is that repurchases are a management signal of improved expectations regarding a company's cash flows.

The tax code treats share repurchases as a dividend if the repurchases are pro rata across all shareholders. Consequently, insiders are usually ex-

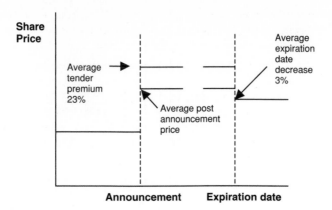

FIGURE 8.2   Share price changes around tender offers.

cluded from participating. This implies that the company repurchases shares from outsiders, and the direct result is that the percentage of insider ownership increases. The market knows this and the price of the shares goes up on *the announcement date*. Figure 8.2 provides a schematic based on the research of Vermaelen (1981) that was corroborated by Dann (1981) and Masulis (1980).

The average tender price is set 23 percent above the pre-announcement price. If all shares tendered were actually purchased by the firm, then the tender price would equal the post-announcement price. But because of pro rata repurchases, given that tenders are typically oversubscribed, we observe that, on average, the post-announcement price is eight percent less than the tender price. Thus, the post-announcement price (when the shares are allocated) is an average of 15 percent higher than the pre-announcement price. Finally, the average expiration date price is only three percent lower than the post-announcement price. Vermaelen (1981) found that the average wealth effect was an increase of 15.7 percent and that only 10.7 percent of all tender offers experienced a wealth decline.

What causes an average 15.7 percent wealth gain to shareholders from tender offers? Personal tax savings (versus dividends) are a possibility but are too small to explain the large wealth gain. For example, if 20 percent of the value of the firm is repurchased and if the marginal investor's tax rate is 40 percent, then the tax savings would imply a four percent return at most. This is too small to explain what we observe.

Some suggest that if the tender is financed by borrowing, there may be a tax gain from the tax deductibility of the interest on debt. If so, shareholders would benefit. Both Masulis (1980) and Vermaelen (1981) find evidence consistent with a gain from leverage. Masulis divided his sample into offers with more than 50 percent debt financing where the average announcement return was 21.9 percent and offers with less than 50 percent debt where the average announcement return was only 17.1 percent. Vermaelen finds similar results and concludes that while it is not possible to reject the leverage hypothesis outright, it is possible to conclude that it is not the predominant explanation for the observed returns.

The best explanation for the shareholder wealth gain from tender offers is that they represent favorable signals from management to the market. Vermaelen finds that the per-share earnings of tendering firms is above what would have been predicted by a time-series model using pre-announcement data. Also, the size of the tender premium, the fraction of shares repurchased, and the fraction of insider holdings are all positively related to the wealth gain and explain roughly 60 percent of its variance. These results are all consistent with the tender as a favorable signal.

Dittmar and Dittmar (2002) empirically investigate the motives behind decisions by firms to repurchase stock over the 1977–1996 time period. In general, they find that firms repurchase stock to take advantage of under-valuation and to distribute free cash flow. Grullon and Michaely (2002) report what seems to be an increasing propensity to prefer repurchases over dividend payout as a means of delivering cash to shareholders, though the recent cut in U.S. dividend tax rate may slow or even reverse this trend.

Open Market Repurchases and Dividend Payout

Open market repurchase programs have a similar motivation but are smaller and less definite than tender offers. To enact an open market repur-chase program, the board authorizes the CFO to repurchase up to a given number of shares on a discretionary basis during a pre-established period of time. Usually, less than the given amount is actually repurchased. There-fore, it is not surprising that open market repurchases have announcement effects that, although statistically significant, are smaller than tender offers—only in the range of four to six percent. Furthermore, the board can deliver cash to shareholders in the form of dividends as well. In many tax regimes, dividends are taxed at the ordinary income rate of the recipient while share repurchases in the open market raise the stock price, thereby creating a capital gain that is taxed at a lower rate. When the effective tax on cash delivered as capital gains is lower than the same cash delivered as divi-dends, the preferred delivery mechanism is repurchases.

Jagganathan, Stephans, and Weisbach (2002) point out that manage-ment treats repurchases of stock, especially open market repurchases, as more flexible than dividends. Repurchases are pro-cyclical while dividends in-crease steadily over time. Dividends are chosen by firms with higher "per-manent" operating income, while repurchases are chosen by firms that have more volatile income with a larger "temporary" component. In gen-eral, firms tend to increase dividends following good performance. Guay and Harford (2000) find similar results. Firms use dividends to distribute rel-atively permanent cash flows, and use repurchases to distribute transitory income. After controlling for payout size and for market expectations about the permanence of cash flows, the price reaction to positive dividend increases is greater than the reaction to repurchases.

What are the implications for management signaling the market? Tender offers should be used when management strongly believes that share price is undervalued. The wider the gap between management expectations and the market's, the more management should turn to a tender offer over open market repurchase programs. Open market repurchases should be used to signal to investors that performance is likely to exceed expectations temporarily—for example, because of a windfall caused by unexpectedly poor competitor product offerings. Of course, such repurchases also signal to investors that management believes cash from such temporary windfalls is best returned to investors rather than reinvested in the business (i.e., a signal of fewer real investment opportunities at the margin). Last, unexpected dividend changes should be used as a signal of changes in expectations about future cash flows—for example, due to regulatory or technological changes expected to change industry profitability on a permanent basis. Note that dividend changes should be thought of in terms of the growth rate of dividends, the percent of earnings paid out, or the targeted dividend yield on the stock price rather than in terms of the absolute amount of dividends. To reinforce the signaling aspect of tender offers, open market repurchases, and dividend policies, management should explain to investors the reasoning used to justify these policies.

Capital Structure Changes as a Signal to Investors

Payments to equity holders through dividends and repurchases are not the only financial signaling device available to management. Almost any financial decision sends a message to investors. In general, the use of greater leverage in the capital structure is viewed as a bullish signal to investors. Why? Because investors know that increased debt increases the riskiness of the firm—for example, through raising the probability of bankruptcy (see Chapter 5). Investors reason that management would only be willing to increase the firm's risk if management had confidence in their expectations of future returns. The academic literature has well established that leverage-increasing changes in capital structure are associated with positive share price reactions. The only exception to this is in the case of firms already burdened with too much debt.

Exploiting Perceived Stock Mispricing to Shareholder Advantage

While management can provide signals to correct perceived mispricing, actions can also be taken that exploit that mispricing. An extreme form of such actions occurs in the case of management buyouts. In these cases management believes in its expectations to such an extent that they can earn a large return by taking the company private.

Our concern, however, is for actions that can benefit existing shareholders. In this regard management can pursue M&A and divestitures in ways that allow shareholders to benefit from the apparent mispricing. Consider the case of a perceived overvaluation. Management holds expectations for future cash flows at levels below what the market currently values the firm. Using stock as currency in transactions allows management to underpay, in effect, for real assets. One usually thinks of acquisitions paid for with stock as the primary example of this. In hindsight it is easy to see AOL's acquisition of Time Warner in this light—an overvalued firm used "inflated currency" to purchase another firm with strong expected cash flows. Similar actions that exploit over-valued share prices can include share issuances and partial IPOs.

The same principle applied in stock-based acquisition can hold in using stock as compensation to others—for example, as part of employee compensation. We are not necessarily advocating paying stock to employees as compensation only when the firm is believed to be overvalued—after all, that would violate common-sense rules of decency. But management should at least recognize when the use of stock in incentive compensation plans is "expensive" and when it is "cheap." We'll discuss stock-based incentive compensation in more detail in Chapter 9.

In cases of perceived undervaluation—especially those that do not correct themselves in response to share buybacks or other management signals—management may need to pursue external options to correct the perceived mispricing. Private equity investors and other acquirers may have (or obtain) the information necessary to form the same value opinion as management has for the firm. While many may view asset sales as a symptom of financial distress, we think they should be considered by management also when the firm is being undervalued by investors.

While the above discussion may seem intuitive, we should note that there is an increasing amount of research showing that managers take perceived stock price mispricing into account in making investment decisions. For example, Loughran and Vijh (1997) report that acquirers paying in cash earn positive long-run returns while acquires paying in stock earn negative long-run returns, consistent with the view that stock-based acquisitions are made at times when share price is overvalued.

Noise

In Chapter 2 we described our research findings that showed that shareholder returns were related to changes in the level of noise. That is, if there was an increase in uncertainty about the future prospects of a firm, shareholder returns would decrease. Our findings related to noise are complemented by the research of others who have found that, especially for small firms, higher levels of noise lead to lower future returns.[2] The reasons for this relationship are not yet well established. We conjectured a market with informed and uninformed traders, where increases in noise raised the cost of acquiring information. In such a setting, more investors will choose to be uninformed if the level of noise increases. The market adjustment leads to decreased shareholder returns. Miller (1977) argued that a divergence of opinion with a short sale constraint leads only to optimistic opinions reflected in price. If share prices are biased upwards when there is significant noise, then it follows that shareholder returns will decrease subsequently. Others have found supporting evidence in shareholder returns around the lifting of short-sale constraints imposed at the time of IPOs. Whatever the mechanism whereby noise affects returns, it is increasingly evident that noise is an important factor relating to shareholder returns.

How do we measure noise? In Chapter 2 we discussed noise and the signal-to-noise ratio. Noise was measured as the standard deviation of analyst forecasts for a growth stock. Thus, sell-side analyst projections recorded on Zacks and IBES provide useful data that is used to measure the volatility of expectations.

Where does noise come from? At the most basic level, noise derives from the underlying uncertainty of a business. The unpredictability of consumer demand, input costs, and competitor actions all intersect to drive overall unpredictability. This manifests itself as fluctuations in financial results.

A second source of noise is communications from management. Firm history, management's financial track record, and quality/depth of financial disclosures. Third parties may also provide factual data about the firm—market shares, customer satisfaction rating, etc.—but there may be uncertainty about the quality or relevance of such information. External communications about management's expectations may be noisy due to bias, variability, or inconsistencies across managers or time.

A third source of noise is external information about the industry. Industry statistics are frequently available only with a lag. In our experience, these data are also often available only at substantial financial cost that many investors may not incur, leading to differences of available data across investors.

Some Stylized Facts about Noise

The following are some general observations about noise. They serve to orient you in our discussion, but are not intended to be comprehensive.

---

[2]See, for example, Karl Diether, C. Malloy and A. Scherbina, "Differences of Opinion and the Cross Section of Stock Returns," *Journal of Finance*, 2002.

You are encouraged to read more on the topic and to investigate how noise affects your firm in particular.

- Expectations for small firms are noisier than for larger firms. This may be a function of either their age (lack of track record), focus (lack of diversification), or lack of deep analyst coverage (lack of information).
- Less profitable firms are noisier—the financial results of firms at or near break-even are very sensitive to slight changes in performance. Forecasts for such firms are therefore that much more difficult to make.
- Noise varies across industries. Some industries are inherently noisier due to the volatility of demand or supply (e.g., commodities). Others are noisy due to the random nature of significant events—e.g., small biotechnology firms are very sensitive to R&D trial results. Noise *within* an industry may also change through time—for example, with fluctuations in economic growth (consumer products) or interest rates (financial services).
- Analyst forecasts tend to cluster together. Analysts are likely to provide outlier forecasts only if they are very confident in their prediction. If an analyst is wrong, it is better (for him or her) to be near the consensus average. If this is indeed the case, we would expect analyst forecasts to display less divergence of opinion than that of the broader investor community.
- Stock price volatility—a particular type of noise—has been studied extensively. Karolyi (2001) provides a useful summary of the relevant facts about volatility:
  - There has been no increase in total stock price volatility through time.
  - Nevertheless, stock price volatility tends to "cluster"—volatility is relatively predictable because periods of low volatility tend to be followed by additional low volatility, and periods of high volatility tend to be followed by additional high volatility.
  - There has been an increase in firm-specific volatility as a proportion of total volatility (as distinct from systematic volatility as stock prices covary with the overall market).
  - Trading activity tends to drive volatility—that is, the arrival of significant news that causes increases in trading volume also tends to increase volatility.
  - Stock price volatility is asymmetric—it increases more around bad news than good news.

Reducing Noise

Can management mitigate noise? If so, how? The answers depend on what kind of noise one it talking about. Management will have the most control over noise it directly causes, but much less control over noise coming from external sources. Take stock price volatility, for example—management will have very little influence over this, but can at least influence it at the margin by managing the public float and ownership structure in ways that may encourage more dispersed share ownership. Noise that stems from liquidity problems can be influenced by choice of listing exchange.

Noise stemming from divergence of opinion across analysts or uncertainty of individual analyst forecasts is addressed directly through management communications. Of course, this presupposes a set of information common across analysts that would lead them toward greater consensus. It may simply be the case that different analysts interpret the same set of information differently. That is why management can only seek to understand analysts' information needs and fill information gaps wherever possible.

Noise generated by management is addressed through a rigorous investor relations process, similar to the one introduced further below. Rigor is required to ensure a consistent message, lack of bias, and timeliness of information conveyed to the investors. We address these points in more detail below.

External Communications Case Studies

The extent and quality of external communications from top management to the outside world varies enormously. The various constituencies are led by investors—current and potential—and by analysts. Of course, the competition is listening, too. But there are many others, including bond rating agencies, regulators, and the public at large. Let's take a look at a few examples of external communicators.

Berkshire Hathaway

A good example, is set by Warren Buffett, chairman of Berkshire Hathaway, who is recognized as someone who plays his cards close to his chest. Commenting on this is Lou Schuler on the Amazon.com Web site:

> *Warren Buffett has a policy of seldom commenting on stocks he owns— he feels that public pronouncements will lead only to the public's expectation of more public pronouncements...*

Yet when it comes to investor relations, Berkshire Hathaway gets it right. Mr. Buffett personally leads an annual shareholders meeting in Omaha, where the company is headquartered. Let's take the 2001 meeting as an example. There is good documentation of what management said and additional documentation of what Oak Value Fund (a large investor) heard.

Berkshire Hathaway is a diversified holding company that owned interests in insurance companies (General Reinsurance and GEICO), airlines (Executive Jet), food and beverages (Sees Candies, Dairy Queen, and Coca-Cola), financial services (American Express, Moodys', H&R Block, and Wells Fargo), and energy (76 percent of MidAmerican Energy).

When you read the chairman's letter to shareholders dated February 28, 2001, it is easy to see why Mr. Buffett is a good communicator:

- *Candor* is evident throughout his presentation. For example, his first sentence is "Berkshire's *loss* in net worth during 2001 was $3.77 billion…" Four paragraphs later he says, "Though our corporate performance last year was satisfactory, my performance was anything but. I manage most of Berkshire's equity portfolio, and my results were poor, just as they have been for several years. Of even more importance, I allowed General Re to take on business without a safeguard I knew was important, and on September 11, this error caught up with us."
- *There is evidence of detailed knowledge of each business* and clear communication about the idea for sustaining a competitive advantage. The detail on Berkshire's insurance operations is impressive.
- *Good incentive design.* Managers at Berkshire Hathaway have skin in the game. Mr. Buffett says, "Additionally, I will keep well over 99 percent of my net worth in Berkshire. My wife and I have never sold a share, nor do we intend to." His managers are expected to subscribe to the same incentive design. At MiTek, a company acquired in 2001, "…we arranged for 55 members of the MiTek team to buy 10 percent of the company, with each putting up a minimum of $100,000 in cash. Many borrowed money so they could participate."
- *Savvy acquisition policy* is evident from Mr. Buffet's tactics. When he became convinced that better management could improve operating profits at Fruit-of-the-Loom, an apparel company, he stepped into the bankruptcy proceedings to make a proposal to creditors.

What is there to criticize in Berkshire Hathaway's investor relations? Not much. Does management get its message across? It seems that they do. We turn to Oak Value Fund's report entitled "Reflections on the Berkshire Hathaway 2001 Annual Meeting."

One might worry that Mr. Buffett is the secret to the success of Berkshire, but Oak Value puts this concern to rest by saying that the management competitive advantages are "…structurally inherent in the organization and exist irrespective of who occupies the chairman's position."

In what was a year of relatively poor performance, Berkshire Hathaway was able to maintain the confidence of its shareholders. Oak Value notes that "Berkshire's value will be determined largely by the effectiveness of their insurance operation." According to the chairman's letter, insurance

operations lost over $4 billion in 2001. How did management talk its way
out of this corner? It was frank about the losses, and focused its shareholders on a long-run strategy. What Oak Value came away with was the
impression that "…reinsurance pricing discipline is absolutely religious fer-
vor at Berkshire. They will not write insurance business that does not represent compelling economic sense." The message that management wanted
had been transmitted.

Microsoft

Consistently biased reporting policy does no harm. Microsoft is well-known
for its conservative estimates of earnings expectations. Company management is consistent in its policy of constant reminders that future growth
cannot compare with the past. As of June 30, 1999, Microsoft had cash and
short-term investments of $17 billion, and assets totaling $37 billion. When
asked about the large cash balances at a panel discussion held at the
University of Washington, CEO Bill Gates explained:

> *The thing that was most scary to me was when I started hiring my
> friends, and they expected to be paid. And then we had customers that
> went bankrupt—customers that I had counted on to come through. And
> soon I came up with this incredibly conservative approach that I
> wanted to have enough money in the bank to pay a year's payroll, even
> if we didn't get any payments coming in. We have about $10 billion
> now, which is pretty much enough for the next year.*

As Professors Dawn Matsumoto and Robert Bowen of the University of
Washington comment in their case on Microsoft's reporting strategy, the
pessimistic attitude at Microsoft may have been simply an attempt to
manage analyst expectations. The idea is to lower analyst expectations
via conservative forecasts, then exceed those expectations. But they go on
to quote Wendy Abramowitz, a securities analyst at Argus Research Corp.,
who comments that "A lot of companies lowball estimates. Microsoft has
been doing that for a long time." In fact, up to June 1999 Microsoft met or
exceeded analyst expectations in 52 of 53 quarters since going public. Of
course, this biased behavior came to be expected and few were surprised
when once again, Microsoft exceeded expectations.

Microsoft was conservative in two other key aspects. It expenses software
development costs as incurred. Also, its revenue recognition was extremely
conservative, recognizing only 80 percent of the revenue on software products on date of delivery and 20 percent over the life of the product. By the
end of 1999 this unearned (deferred) revenue account totaled $4.2 billion.

In our opinion this is exemplary behavior and, due to its consistency
over an extended period of time, was viewed by the analyst community as
a constant bias that is easily adjusted.

During one conference call with analysts Microsoft announced that the company was under investigation by the SEC. According to Matsumoto and Bowen (2000), the SEC's action was prompted by a wrongful dismissal suit filed by the company's former head of internal auditing. The suit alleged that Microsoft regularly manipulated reserve accounts to smooth earnings. Court transcripts reported that an email from the CFO to Bill Gates stated: "I believe that we should do all that we can to smooth our earnings and keep a steady earnings model." The announcement of the investigation had little impact on analysts. Rick Sherland at Goldman Sachs was quoted in the *Wall Street Journal* as saying, "If the SEC wants to force Microsoft to be less conservative, Wall Street will just increase earnings projections for the company."

The investigation came to nothing—as it should have. When it comes to reporting earnings, a consistent policy—one that smoothes earnings (within legal constraints) and reduces noise—is a good policy.

Enron

The Enron collapse exemplifies the failure of external reporting, management hubris, and the flaws of incentive design. It is alleged, and may be proven in court, that top management deliberately misled the market with pronouncements of rapid earnings growth, then invented schemes for manufacturing profits from smoke and mirrors. We may never know whether management hoped to fool the investing public or whether it believed its own story. Figure 8.3 shows the shareholder return history of Enron from 1992 to 2001 and analyst short-term expectations of earnings and actual quarterly earnings.

On December 2, 2001, Enron, the Houston-based natural gas and energy trading company, filed for bankruptcy protection. That day its stock price closed at $0.72 per share down from $75.00 less than a year earlier. It was at that time the largest bankruptcy in United States history with $62.8 billion in assets, nearly double the size of Texaco's filing in 1987 when it had $35.9 billion in assets. Less than a month before seeking the protection of Chapter 11, Enron management stated that accounting errors had inflated earnings by nearly $600 million since 1994. The list of allegedly responsible parties and their collaborators includes top management, the audit committee, the auditors at Arthur Andersen, Enron's outside law firm, and investment advisors. But contributory was the market environment that fueled the flames of management hubris.

With 20/20 hindsight, we can look back at the unfolding of events. In Figure 8.3 the consensus analyst forecasts of earnings in October were $1.76 per share for 2001 and $1.93 per share for 2002. One month later, in November, they had declined sharply to $1.50 and $1.26, respectively. There is no mistake: The earnings drop for 2002 was $0.67 and the drop for 2001 was $0.26. Figure 8.4 shows forecasts of long-term earnings growth

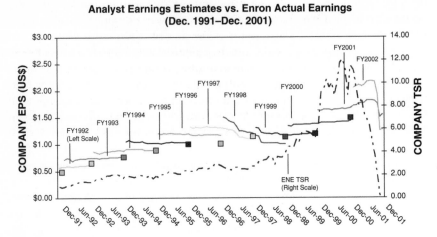

FIGURE 8.3   Short-term analyst expectations on Enron earnings.

Note: Boxes denote actual EPS before extraordinary items; lines that end in boxes denote consensus analyst estimates for the current and fiscal year.

Source: IBES, CRSP, Monitor analysis

that continue to rise until a few weeks before bankruptcy. There is no doubt that the analyst community was fooled.

At the beginning of the 1990s Enron was primarily a natural gas pipeline and supplier of natural gas. It had the largest and most extensive pipeline in the United States, extending from the Pacific Northwest down

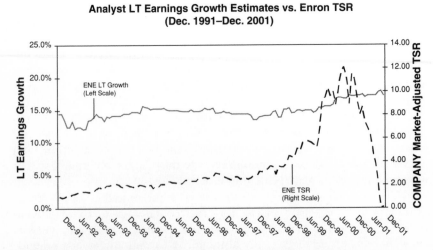

FIGURE 8.4   Analyst expectations of long-term growth for Enron.

Source: IBES, CRSP, Monitor analysis

through California, into the South Central states and then into Florida and up the East Coast. Only the North Central states were left uncovered. In 1990, Jeff Skilling resigned as a director of McKinsey & Co. and joined Enron as head of Enron trading. It was his idea to use Enron's commanding information advantage about the real-time price of natural gas and its ability to supply natural gas to fill short positions, to develop a forward market in natural gas—thereby adding a new business to the base that Enron already had. This enterprise proved to be enormously successful—so successful that by 1996 it was contributing roughly 38 percent of total profit.

The challenge was what to do for an encore. The model that seemed to work was to acquire a "foundation" in a profitable business endeavor, then create a trading market on top of it by using Enron's newly developed trading acumen. Newspaper headlines began to hit the streets. July 25, 1998: Enron announces a £1.36 billion cash bid for Wessex water of the United Kingdom. March 16, 1999: Enron plans an IPO of Azurix, its global water and wastewater subsidiary. May 21, 1999: a plan is announced to create a market in the trading of bandwidth on Enron's fiber-optic network. July 12, 2000: A new division called Enron Net Works will attempt to become a "new economy" player. These announcements indicate attempts to expand into water and fiber optics. There was also expansion into electric power generation and an attempt to trade block power. On December 14, 2000, Jeff Skilling was named CEO, but only eight months later, on August 14, 2001, he resigned.

Bad news started to surface in May of 2001. There is a dispute with the Indian government about unpaid bills, and in the same month, Enron pulls out of a $10 billion Dolphin gas export project in the Persian Gulf. In June, Enron pulls out of its 15 percent participation in an energy field development project for Saudi Arabia. In July, it announces it wants to sell its interest in the Indian power plant.

The bad news affected the third quarter of 2001. Enron took a $1.2 billion charge against equity. The week of October 25, Enron's price fell 40 percent and its CFO, Andrew Fastow, was replaced. By December 2, 2001, Enron was bankrupt.

It is a matter of record that Skilling gained $15.6 million by selling 500,000 shares of Enron on September 17, 2001, four weeks after he resigned as CEO. He allegedly racked up $200 million in total between 1998 and 2001. Yet during a March 2001 conference call with analysts he is quoted as saying, "I know that this is a bad stock market, but Enron's in good shape."

In an interview with *Business Week* correspondent Stephanie Anderson Forest one week after Skilling's resignation, chairman of the board and former CEO Ken Lay, said "There are absolutely no accounting issues, no trading issues, no reserve issues, no unknown problem issues. The company is probably in the strongest and best shape it has ever been in." When asked if the fundamentals of the business remain solid, Mr. Lay replied "Yes. We think the company is on solid footing and we're looking forward to continued strong growth."

What went wrong? What caused this debacle?

- *Bad business decisions* were the primary cause. The pressure to follow the initial success of Enron trading with an encore was tangible. Consequently, Enron rushed ahead into bad ventures in broadband fiber optics, acquisitions of power companies, and water companies.
- *Manufacturing earnings* was a deliberate and clever effort to distort reported earnings by using questionable accounting practices. In one deal, $100 million of dark fiber optic cable was allegedly sold to a joint venture (JV). The value of the deal was sweetened for Enron's JV partner in two ways. First, Enron gave up a put option that allowed its partner to sell back the assets at an undisclosed price. Second, Enron guaranteed a loan to its JV partner. In return for these sweeteners, the partner agreed to pay an extra premium (reputedly $30 to $40 million) on the deal. Enron then was able to report a gain on sale, but did not report the contingent liability in its footnotes.
- *Flawed incentive design* was a major contributing factor that spurred top management to take risks, and to falsify information given to the public. Stock option plans should not vest until after a waiting period of three to five years, or else the board of directors should be empowered to "claw back" gains from fraudulent behavior.

Even if Enron had narrowly avoided bankruptcy, the credibility of its top management would have been destroyed due to a lack of confidence. In this case the best thing to do would have been to replace management and continue with a team capable of restoring confidence.

Gillette

Gillette, headquartered in our hometown of Boston, provides an interesting example of a company that fell into the expectations treadmill trap discussed at the start of the chapter. In the early 1990s, Gillette's earnings grew at a steady 18.4 percent annual rate. Over the same time period, from 1990 through 1996, the company's share price increased over 30 percent at a compound annual rate. Figure 8.5 shows that as the company was able to sustain its earnings growth, management and investors raised their expectations for the future. Analyst-consensus estimates for five-year earnings growth increased from 15 percent in 1990 to over 17 percent in 1996.

In the late 1990s, the company faced some serious financial pressures from both external and internal sources. Externally, a strong dollar decreased the value of overseas sales (a majority of the company's sales were outside

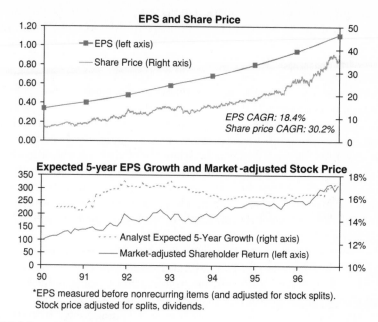

*EPS measured before nonrecurring items (and adjusted for stock splits).
Stock price adjusted for splits, dividends.

FIGURE 8.5   Gillette, 1990–1996

Source: Zack's, Reuters, Monitor analysis

the United States). Weak demand in Europe hit its Braun product lines particularly hard. In their core shaving product segment, new competitor product offerings limited pricing flexibility. And newly acquired Duracell faced intense price competition in the battery market from lower-cost competitors like Rayovac.

Internally, the company had poor management of working capital, allowing receivables and inventories to increase well outside industry norms. Aggressive growth targets were also causing channel-loading, building up excess inventories downstream. The integration of Duracell into the company also did not proceed well, with a large part of senior Duracell management reportedly leaving the company after the acquisition.

What was Gillette's response to these pressures? First of all, the CEO kept up the pressure to produce strong earnings growth, promising investors over 15 percent earnings growth. The target was aimed primarily at managers that were thought to need stretch targets to improve performance. The market was told through "whisper" numbers disseminated by Investor Relations that lower, more achievable, earnings targets were likely to occur. Analysts reacted to the combination of repeated quarterly earnings misses and the inconsistent message from CEO and investor relations by ratcheting down earnings expectations and increasing the amount of noise as measured by the dispersion of analyst forecasts (see Figure 8.6).

At times the relationship between analysts and the company seemed to be almost antagonistic. In response to Gillette's claim that slowing sales in 1997 was caused by a deliberate inventory destocking process in anticipation of the launch of a new razor (the Mach 3), a Salomon Smith Barney analyst wrote in January that it was simply unrealistic to go through a six-month destocking process. A Bank of America analyst in 1999 responded to continued promises of double-digit earnings growth: "It is often foolhardy to set up too-high expectations." And in a Q1 2001 earnings conference call an analyst complained that "[management] repeatedly said inventory is fine…But again and again it is just out of control…[management's] explanation does not hold much water. I have heard it for six quarters….is it also because management are not honest and are still trying to push for quarterly earnings?"

Indeed, management was pushing for short-term earnings. The clearest sign of this was the decrease in advertising spending as a percent of sales from 1995 through 2000 while spending on promotional spending increased. As early as 1997 a Bear Stearns analyst noted that earnings growth targets were being hit by cuts in ad spending. By 2001 an A.G. Edwards analyst noted the "well-chronicled inconsistencies in marketing

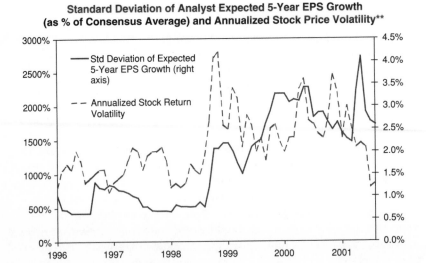

**Stock Price volatility equal to standard deviation in daily total return to shareholders (90-days)

FIGURE 8.6   Gillette—Noise Indicators, 1996–2001

Source: Zack's, Reuters, Monitor analysis

support and reliance on promotional spending." According to this analyst, the shift from advertising to promotion "compromised Gillette's future sales and earnings power."

In early 2001 Gillette's board hired a new CEO, Jim Kilts, to turn the company around. Kilts had successfully turned around Nabisco. Upon taking the reins of the company, he instituted a portfolio review wherein poorly performing units were evaluated for divestiture or salvage. The White Rain unit was sold off having been deemed "non-core." Incentive structures and turnaround programs were used to correct channel-loading behavior and to improve the company's working capital position. Core brands were targeted with reinvestment in the form of new product development and significant advertising dollars.

Kilt's approach to investor relations was first to stop providing short-term earnings guidance. From analyst comments in the first few quarters this was resisted by analysts, but eventually they adjusted to the new approach. At a six-month strategy review conference call, Kilts did provide long-term guidance, indicating the sustainable rate of growth the company could achieve (in the single digits). Communications also moved from detailed discussion of quarterly earnings and targets to discussion of business unit strategies and honesty about the company's past shortcomings. Note that this turnaround in investor relations strategy may go back to the good example Warren Buffet provided, considering that he was a large investor in Gillette and sat on the company's board.

As we write this, the turnaround at Gillette is well established. Expected five-year earnings growth rebounded from a low of 9.6 percent in July 2001 to 11 percent by the middle of 2002. Shareholders earned significant returns from mid-2001 to the end of 2004. Just recently Proctor & Gamble announced an acquisition of Gillette at a price of approximately $54 a share, over 120 percent higher than the low price of $23.68 in April 2001.

The Gillette example illustrates both sides of an expectations mindset applied to investor relations. The company fell into the trap in the late 1990s of setting unrealistic targets and talking to the street in a way that damaged management's credibility and created noise. Thinking that investors demanded earnings growth at the cost of long-term viability was the fundamental mistake of previous management. Investors complained about short-term earnings only as a signal that they were concerned about the implications for long-term health. Rather than pursue a turnaround, previous management further damaged the company's prospects by cutting ad spending. Investor relations was turned upside down during the turnaround. Investor relations no longer included short-term earnings targets at all. Instead, management's focus on in-depth conversation about strategy, long-term results, and an honest approach to analyst communications restored credibility, decreased market noise, and helped the turnaround in share price as results followed.

What Do Others Say about External Communications?

Noise, Earnings Smoothing and Financial Disclosures

Fischer Black, coinventor of the Black-Scholes option pricing model, addressed the American Finance Association in 1986 by delivering a speech entitled "Noise." It was one of his favorite themes—and one of ours, too. We had debates about the economic ramifications of noise on more than one occasion. One of the points that he made during his talk was that although the smoothing of earnings by management is often criticized by regulators, it is not at all clear that smoothing is bad. Most scholars of valuation would assert that the market price of equity is based fundamentally on expectations of the distribution of uncertain cash flows in the future. If these expectations are extremely diffuse one might conjecture that the stock price would be discounted more heavily by potential investors. If earnings are smoothed not to deceive investors, but rather as an honest effort to reduce the amount of noise in the earnings signal that management sends to the market in its published reports, then smoothing earnings serves a socially useful purpose.

A paper by Graham, Harvey, and Rajgopal (2004) surveys 401 financial executives and conducts in-depth interviews with an additional 20. Its central findings are that (1) the majority of firms view earnings per share (not free cash flows) as the key metric for outsiders, and (2) they are willing to sacrifice economic value to meet short-term earnings targets. Their preference for smooth earnings was so strong that 78 percent said they would give up economic value in exchange for smoother earnings. They also find that managers make voluntary disclosures to reduce information risk associated with their stock, but try to avoid setting a disclosure precedent that will be difficult to maintain.

Al Rappaport, former professor of accounting at Northwestern University, told us that he likes to think of earnings as parsed into three categories. First, revenues and expenses are booked during the current accounting period and known with absolute certainty. Next, accrued revenues and expenses are very likely to eventuate. He has no problem putting these two items onto the income statement and balance sheet. The third category is contingencies. In Europe, a special liability called "reserves" and an expense called "provisions" are permitted as part of financial reporting and are used primarily to smooth earnings. For example, for the nine-month period preceding the listing of Daimler on the New York Stock Exchange, according to German accounting standards, the company lost $400 million. According to U.S. GAAP, however, it lost $1.2 billion. Most of the difference was caused by provisions and reserves. In the United States there is a movement afoot that would require the expensing of the market value of executive stock options on the date of original issue. The problem is that payoff on a stock option is a stochastic event that may happen at different times during the life of the option—or it may never happen at all. If an expense is charged to the income statement at the time of issue, then what happens if the option expires worthless? Does the company record a profit? Suppose there is a class action lawsuit that has a low but unobservable chance of succeeding. Should the company put the present value of the potential settlement profit onto its income statement at this time, or some later date? Should the amount be the size of the claim or of the expected settlement?

Rappaport's point was that reporting contingent claims on the income statement only increases noise. Attempts to do so should be avoided. Disclosures of the type and relevant features of contingent claims is sufficient. For example, detailed footnotes setting out the parameters of employee options would be sufficient—after all, sophisticated investors will take notice of these footnotes when they materially affect value. The requirement that these options, for example, be valued in particular ways or expensed on the P&L does not significantly reduce noise—but it does raise the cost of compliance (more on this in Chapter 13).

Firms can and should put more into the footnotes that reflect the current state of the business—e.g., detailed descriptions of hedging policies and instruments, or a listing of all existing litigation and probable payouts for lost lawsuits. Of course, what EBM requires—additional disclosure details about forward-looking expectations—is exactly what opens up firms to litigation. In spite of the safe harbor provision of the PSLRA,[3] it is still the case that management shy away from announcing their own expectations in any level of detail that is meaningful to investors. Some have taken to giving no guidance at all—a mistake, we believe, that will do nothing to lessen investor noise.

Investor Relations as a Marketing Challenge

It has become fashionable for some to view investor relations as a marketing problem—whereby management "sells" its stock to investors. This analogy leads to viewing investors as consumers. Different investors have different preferences, and therefore management needs to provide information that matches investors to the stocks that best suit them. For example, a company that wants retail investors under the belief that such investors tend to be less speculative in their trading behavior might structure a communications strategy that reaches out to such investors and addresses their

---

[3]The PSLRA is the Private Securities Litigation Reform Act of 1995, which, among other things, limited liability for forward-looking statements made subject to various requirements.

concerns about dividend policies, capital structure, and so on. Some consultants have taken the marketing approach a step further by advocating a detailed analysis of how individual investors are likely to react to news, and therefore how stock price is likely to react.

We think the marketing approach is ill-conceived. It assumes that if some aspect of a company's value equation changes that the firm needs to find the right investors to buy the stock rather than assuming that investors will "find" the stock that suits them on their own. A "market segmentation" approach to investors—whether looking at groups of investors or key individual investors—cannot change the fundamental value of the company. If management believes the stock is mispriced, the problem is not one of finding the right investors, but of knowing what information investors lack to properly value the shares.

Value Reporting

In the chapter introduction we mentioned a work called *The Value Reporting Revolution*, written by Robert Eccles, former Harvard Business School professor, and his colleagues from PricewaterhouseCoopers. They argue that the stock market is inefficient due to incomplete information and an excessive short-term focus on the "earnings game." They agree with our general point made in Chapter 1 that traditional performance measures like earnings per share (EPS) do not provide the right kind of information to investors. Due to inadequate corporate reporting systems, Eccles argues that information gaps develop between the quality, quantity, and type of data management provides to the market as compared to what investors want to know. They advocate greater transparency of corporate reporting, emphasizing the following:

■ Broadening the metrics reported to investors, with particular attention to metrics investors use to assess value. These metrics may include special emphasis of intangible assets not captured by traditional financial disclosures.
■ Integrating the explanation of strategy with financial disclosure data.
■ Presenting more forward-looking information.
■ Maintaining credibility through transparency, honesty about bad results, and timely reporting.

Value Reporting is a good first step that companies can take to improve investor relations. It helps managers think about the relationship between strategy and financial metrics, and encourages the development of tracking and reporting systems. But Value Reporting falls short in at least three respects. First, Value Reporting treats external communications as a one-way street. That is, by focusing on reporting information to the market, it neglects the need to listen to investors. The dialog with investors should be a two-way street. Second, Value Reporting does not by itself provide a structured way to communicate expectations. For that management needs an understanding of valuation models and how their expectations relate to stock prices. Last, Value Reporting focuses on disclosures and explicit communications to the possible detriment of signaling through other mechanisms. Indeed, actions such as changes in capital structure may often be necessary to reinforce the credibility of management's expectations communicated to the market through investor relations.

An EBM Approach to Investor Relations

Expectations-Based Management suggests the following management behavior regarding communication externally with investors and analysts.

Principles

- *Unbiased.* While a constant bias—whether it be optimism or pessimism—is easily adjusted by the market, a variable bias just increases noise, thereby reducing shareholder returns.
- *Timely.* No news is bad news. A study by Professor Maureen McNichols of Stanford (1988) looked at delays in annual reports from the date that the market expected them to be published. Most companies release their annual reports the same day each year (e.g., the third Tuesday in February). She found that total returns to shareholders are increasingly negative the longer the delay relative to expected release date.
- *Complete.* It is not enough to merely report earnings. People want to know why it is going to be higher or lower and when the changes are expected to happen, whether they are temporary or permanent, and the competitive dynamics involved.
- *Verifiable.* Current management is not the only source of information. Never underestimate the amount of information that analysts can obtain on their own. We were once asked to interview the top ten banking analysts during the commercial real estate crisis that took place in the Northeast in the early 1990s. Most of them obtained a good picture of the extent of troubled loans at individual banks without actually talking to the bank in question. They contacted the real estate developers and contractors who were in default, talked to banks that did not have troubled loans, and spoke to regulators and, sometimes, former employees. Before they went to interview management at the bank of interest, they already had a good estimate of the dollar amount of troubled loans. What they wanted to know was what plans the bank had for workouts of the loans.

Verifiable information not only provides analysts and investors an alternative source for data used to form expectations, but also lends credibility to management's own forecasts. To the extent that management itself relies on specific external data sources—industry analysts, consumer surveys, and so on—sharing such data reinforces for investors that management's strategic thinking was sound and was based on hard data.

- *Consistent.* Most members of the top management team have the occasion to represent the company at one time or another. Our advice is that they confer with each other in a deliberate and coordinated effort to be consistent. Inconsistency only increases noise and that drives down shareholder returns. Inconsistency that is deliberate is, of course, the worst of all. At one company we visited, the head of investor relations recounted to us how the ex-CEO had advised the market of one expected EPS growth rate while asking him to put forth to analysts "whisper numbers" that more accurately reflected what the company could achieve. The CEO's intention was to motivate management by putting forth stretch targets. Instead, line management was bewildered by unachievable targets and outside analysts were confused at the mixed messages they were receiving.

- *Focused and relevant.* Often the analyst community has a specific area of concern that management has overlooked. Remember, no news is bad news and garbled news is no winner either. Management should conscientiously research through interviews and study the information needs of analysts. Management should patiently supply analysts with missing information and educate them about what information is relevant. Just as a large merger or asset sale will have a data room for potential buyers, so should the investor relations department keep a constantly updated set of files of both financial and operating data of importance to investors.

- *Selective secrecy.* One cannot forget the caveat that some information should be kept secret. Even shareholders would agree that it does not do any good to let the competition know too much. We caution, though, that much of what managers have thought are competitive secrets are really common knowledge within an industry. We've worked with managers that have had detailed information of competitors' market offerings, cost structures, and organizational forms. Such knowledge was obtained either through firsthand experience having formerly worked for competitors, through industry-specific technical knowledge, or through careful analysis of public information (e.g., product displays at trade shows, engineering specs, and marketing brochures). Moreover, we know from our own experience that most information that competitors are interested in learning can be obtained in one way or another. Therefore, the burden is on management to know when information is material for investors while not necessarily a "secret" from companies.

A Two-Way Dialog

It is true, of course, that managers listen to investors—they do so indirectly through sell-side analyst comments and questions, as well as directly. But such listening tends to be narrow and episodic. It is narrow in the sense that managers' attention usually focuses on large, institutional investors—for example, the investors who may take part in a financing roadshow discussion. It is episodic in that management listens to the market most when seeking financing through bond, stock, or other securities issuances.

There is room for an approach that involves more listening so that management can track changes in investor sentiments. Actions management would take to learn to listen to investors better includes:

- *Tracking analysts and listening to their questions and concerns.* All companies with sell-side analyst coverage actively track analyst opinions and forecasts. Fewer systematically evaluate analyst reports and conference calls to identify information analysts have that may contradict or supplement internal data and management's expectations. At times, analysts engage third-party researchers or conduct original primary research (e.g., customer and supplier interviews) that provides valuable information not only to investors but to management as well. Effort should also be made to understand analysts' financial forecast logic—for example, what are the factors considered to determine expected long-term growth and margins?
- *Periodically surveying buy-side analysts.* The information available from buy-side analysts may be less available than that from the sell-side, but it is arguably more valuable due to the potential bias in sell-side forecasts. Buy-side analysts will be unwilling to share proprietary valuation models, but may be willing to answer questions about the value drivers they track, their chosen valuation methods, assessment of company strategic choices, and information they would like to know.
- *Evaluating stock price reactions to announcements.* Also consider canceling actions viewed negatively by the market. The academic research is inconclusive as to whether managers actually do listen to stock market signals. Jennings and Mazzeo (1991) find no impact of stock market reactions to proposed M&A deals on managers' subsequent actions closing the deals. Both Luo (2003) and Kau, Link, and Rubin (2004), however, find that managers tend to cancel investments viewed negatively by market reactions. Kau et al also find that managers are more likely to respond to market signals in the presence of more outside

firm monitors and higher pay-performance sensitivity. In a 1987 Harvard Business Review article, Al Rappaport makes a compelling case for the value of managers reading signals from the market.

An EBM approach to external communications should revise managers' attitude about stock price. Most managers we've talked to about the subject seem to view stock price as disconnected from fundamental value, about which they know much more than investors. But in truth there is always something to be learned from market signals. Management should try to remain open to the possibility that their assessments are incorrect—due to faulty analysis or bias—and that reading the stock price tea leaves can help them improve their expectations.

Role of the Investor Relations Officer

EBM envisions an expanded role for the investor relations officer (IRO). Traditional responsibilities of interacting with investors will go unchanged. Additional responsibilities will include taking on an advocacy role internally. The IRO should present the investors' perspective within the strategy, budgeting, and investment decision processes. The IRO will also need to do more in the way of financial research—analyzing stock market trends, volatility, and securities price reactions to significant news announcements. Such analysis should not be restricted to the company's own shares, but also that of all major competitors. Finally, the IRO needs to be the point person for maintaining message discipline—ensuring consistency across communicators. In the latter regard, it may be advisable for the IRO to have at least monitoring rights, if not approval rights, related to all major external communications. They need not read every single press release, but those that describe significant events (like a product launch) should be coordinated with investor relations.

An EBM External Communications Process

We have said earlier in the book that EBM has three integrated parts. These parts are performance measured by value drivers on a daily basis, economic profit vis-à-vis expectations at the business unit level, and the DCF of the company at the board level. Refer to Figure 1.3, for example. Now let's talk about what management should do with a narrow focus on investor relations.

Here are the actions that we believe should be part of a world-class external communications program. Parts of this process were covered in Chapter 7, and are summarized again here. Figure 8.7 illustrates these processes graphically.

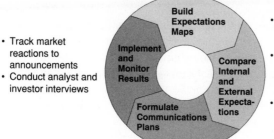

- Reverse engineer share price
- Survey analysts and investors
- Understand value driver expectations
- Tie expectations to strategic planning

- Track market reactions to announcements
- Conduct analyst and investor interviews

Build Expectations Maps

Implement and Monitor Results

Compare Internal and External Expectations

Formulate Communications Plans

- Identify expectations biases
- Find gaps in expectations between internal and external
- Understand sources of noise/ differences of opinion

- Define communications message
- Create signaling and monitoring plan
- Coordinate communications with both line management and investor relations

FIGURE 8.7   An EBM approach to investor relations.

Source: Monitor analysis

1. *Build expectations maps.* Reverse engineer a DCF model of your company and your competitors (see Chapter 7) to determine whether the expectations that analysts and investors currently have are consistent with the DCF model. Survey analysts and investors, and catalog investment analysis in analyst reports. Strive to understand what the current market expectations are regarding the value drivers of your stock price. Tie these expectations maps back into the strategic planning and budgeting processes.

2. *Compare internal and external expectations.* Compare the market's beliefs with those of top management and line management, and where they differ, study the sources of difference. Understand sources of noise in the market—what causes analysts to have differing opinions about the company's short-term and long-term prospects. Identify levers that can be used to address analysts' specific information needs to reduce noise as much as possible.

3. *Formulate communications plans*
   a. If the market is undervaluing your stock, either it is too conservative about your future or your management team is too optimistic. Before making any decision, figure out what is realistic. If you conclude that the market has it wrong, then you have several signaling options available. You can repurchase more than the expected number of shares (via tender offer or open market repurchase). You can

also present your case to analysts and investors, being careful to be specific about verifiable facts.

   b. If the market overvalues your stock, there is the temptation to do nothing. But you run the risk of increasing the amount of noise about your stock, and will eventually lose credibility (at least relative to the alternatives). You can communicate the bad news to the market. This seems to be a foolish choice, but it will do wonders for your credibility and will decrease noise. Stronger action involves issuing new shares in a secondary offering or perhaps to finance an acquisition.

In either the case of perceived under- or overvaluation, communications plans need to span across all layers of management that interact with the public. Press releases, financial disclosures, and analyst conference calls all have to present a consistent message to investors.

4. *Implement and monitor results.* If you have chosen to correct the "information gap" between management and market expectations via better communications, follow up with additional interviews to understand how beliefs have changed. Track changes in sell-side analyst reports, consensus expectations metrics, and buy-side investor sentiment.

    Monitoring external communications also involves in-depth analysis of market reactions to major announcements. Make sure both senior and line management are aware of the reaction, what caused it, and whether there is anything to learn from the reaction. Should plans be revised or reconsidered in light of shareholder reactions?

The first two steps were covered in Chapter 7. Steps 3 and 4 were covered in greater detail in this chapter. When there is a difference between the market's expectations and those of management, we have found that either party can be wrong. Management must be realistic and recognize that market opinions may be better founded in fact than management opinions. In these instances, it is management that must change rather than the market.

Summary and Conclusions

This chapter discussed the important topic of setting expectations externally. There is plenty of hard empirical evidence that top management, in possession of inside information, has better informed expectations than outside investors and analysts. There is also hard evidence that the market reaction to management external communications depends on the signal-to-noise ratio with the implication that (1) constant bias (e.g. conservative earnings forecasts) can easily be reversed by the market, and (2) changing bias, once discovered by the market, results in negative stock returns. As

FIGURE 8.8   Two-way top management communication.

Source: Monitor analysis

P. T. Barnum once said, "It is possible to fool all the people some of the time." As the Enron case proved, it is possible for stock option plans to catalyze management hubris that can mislead the investing public, bankrupting a major company. Thus, incentive design, external communication, and internal performance measurement are all linked together. Later in the book, we shall revisit this crucial triad.

In addition to jawboning investors and analysts, top management can obtain board approval to take more direct action to close perceived information gaps. A company that is undervalued by the market can repurchase its shares via tender offer or by announcing an open market repurchase plan. If its shares are overvalued, a company can issue new shares or can use its shares as currency for acquisition.

As illustrated in Figure 8.8, top management communications must be effective internally as well as externally. First, incentive design should linearize the pay-for-performance schedule in order to remove any incentive to lie. This is not easy, but can be accomplished by presetting salary and expected bonus (the intercept of the linear pay-for-performance function) before discussing the bounty for performance (the slope of the line). Once the budgeted expected performance is separated from pay so that gaming is removed from the budgetary process and there is no incentive to lie, then the budget and planning system can work.

CHAPTER 9

Incentive Design

There is never any doubt that executive compensation is a "top-of-mind" subject for shareholders and managers alike. The board of directors almost always has a compensation committee that represents shareholder interests in this matter. The list of relevant issues is long and complex. We start with the theory of the case, expressed as what has come to be called the principal-agent problem—namely, with the separation of ownership by shareholders (the principals) from decisions made on their behalf by managers (their agents). Exactly what form of incentives maximizes shareholders' wealth? We then argue that the agent's performance raises the share price when it exceeds expectations. Next, we link performance measurement to incentive design in a single-period setting, then discuss extensions to a multiperiod setting. Later sections cover incentive design for staff versus line, whether compensation should be based on absolute or relative performance, and what portion should be pay-at-risk. Finally, we state our recommendations and contrast them with common practices.

We recommend that any changes in your company's incentive design take place after having already implemented an Expectations-Based Management system. It is tempting to try to use incentives to facilitate compliance with EBM, but you run the risk of having a rebellion on your hands. People are conservative when it comes to change. Consequently, it is better to let them see the usefulness of EBM before trying to change the way they get paid at the same time you are trying to get them to think differently about the way they manage the company.

The Heart of Incentive Design—The Principal-Agent Problem

In a world of specialization, the separation of ownership and control allows people whose consumption is less than their income to invest in the ownership of assets that they do not necessarily know how to manage. For this purpose they hire professional managers who can control the assets and earn higher returns on them than they can. This form of specialization can increase productivity.

The agency problem arises because both the owners and the managers usually behave in their own self-interest. If an owner-manager decides to play golf on Wednesday afternoon rather than work, there is no problem because the owner and manager are the same person who maximizes his/her own utility. But as soon as ownership is separated from management of assets, perquisites, such as playing golf instead of working, become a principal-agent problem. The agent can consume perquisites, shirk responsibilities, or otherwise extract value at the direct expense of the owner.

The principal must choose and the agent must accept an incentive design that works for both. Monitoring costs play an important role. If the agent's actions are observable and monitoring is costless, the principal-agent problem vanishes. The cost of perquisites can be charged directly to the agent, and the principal can be sure to take away exactly the desired output. We shall see what happens in a variety of other situations: assuming that the outcome is not observable, or that only the final outcome is observable, and assuming that there are multiple actions that the agent can take.

Who Sets Senior Management Compensation?

The principal-agent problem is mediated at the most senior level of the company by the board of directors, whose job it is to oversee the firm's governance on behalf of shareholders. As executive compensation grows to previously inconceivable levels, it has become fashionable to assume something is broken in the compensation setting process—some sort of market failure. A variety of compensation-related facts are perceived by some as examples of potential market failure, including the extremely high levels of CEO pay, low correlation between CEO total compensation and TSR, the extent of perquisites given to management, or the fact that most options are granted at-the-money.

Two of the most dominant of the many theories proposed to explain how management/CEO compensation is set are the optimal contracting approach and the managerial power approach.[1] The former assumes an

---

[1]The optimal contracting approach is typified by the research of our colleague Michael Jensen who pioneered agency theory and its application to compensation. The

efficient market for CEO labor and seeks to explain anomalies with economic theory. For example, high levels of CEO pay may be explained by such simple observations as the scarcity of CEO-level skills, especially for organizations with multiple lines of business. Another example is a recently proposed explanation of lavish perks as a cheap way to confer status in hierarchical organizations or as a way to enhance productivity in companies located in remote or difficult locations (e.g., helicopter to optimize CEO work time). The optimal contracting approach basically takes the view that CEO pay is set in arm's-length transactions that should maximize value to shareholders. The managerial power approach examines the workings of boards of directors to find excessive influence by managers who are able to shape their own compensation to the alleged detriment of shareholders. Managerial power researchers note that board members have incentives to support management and that companies often go to great lengths to disguise the extent of CEO pay to avoid public "outrage."

Boards of directors try to act in the interests of shareholders, but may lack the information or skills to do so adequately. If CEO compensation is to be set relative to expectations (as we argue below), this requires board members to become that much more knowledgeable about the economics of the business and the capabilities of the organization. However, management will always have better information than board members have with which to form expectations.

Our focus for the remainder of this chapter is about the form of compensation rather than the process by which it is set. We assume rationality in how compensation is set, and focus on its impact on managerial incentives and behavior. We allow that lack of understanding, insufficient information, and other factors may allow suboptimal contracting. Corporate governance improvements—for example, the NYSE's listing requirement that compensation committees be independent from management—may correct some of the occasional suboptimal compensation decisions. We hope our discussion, as well as that of others in the field, will further narrow the gap between optimal contracting and current practice.

Linear Pay-for-Performance

Linear Pay-for-Performance schedules like that shown in Figure 9.1 are optimal in a one-period setting when the agent's actions are observable. By way of contrast, more typical bonus schemes, such as that illustrated in Figure 9.2, create conflicts between the agent and the principal. The illustrated incentive design system has a floor—for example, the agent's salary with no bonus—and a cap, represented by the maximum bonus. The kinks

---

managerial power approach has a wide set of proponents, most recently typified by the work of Lucian Bebchuk and Jesse Fried (2004).

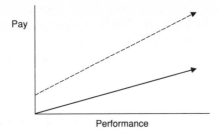

FIGURE 9.1   Linear pay-for-performance.

Source: Monitor analysis

in this compensation schedule cause conflicts between the principal-owner and the agent-manager of the company.

Performance is usually measured over an interval of time—a year, for example. If the executive does well and exceeds the level of performance where his or her compensation is capped, there is a natural tendency to slack off because further effort cannot improve his or her pay. Therefore, a cap on the executive's bonus is suboptimal from both the agent's as well as the principal's point of view. On the downside, if the end of the year is approaching and the executive is still near the lower end of the bonus range, he or she will be tempted to undertake riskier activities because there is much to gain on the upside and little to lose on the downside. A linear pay-for-performance schedule eliminates these problems.

"Skin-in-the-Game"

"Skin-in-the-game" is an expression that implies commitment. In incentive design it means asking the top executives to place a significant portion of

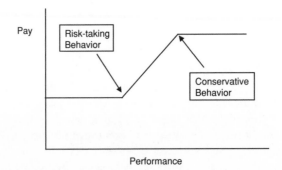

FIGURE 9.2   Kinked pay-for-performance creates conflicts.

Source: Jensen, M., "Paying People to Lie: the Truth about the Budgeting Process," *European Financial Management,* Vol. 9, No. 3, 2003, p. 386

their personal wealth at risk by investing in the firm. In other words, mitigate the principal-agent problem by turning agents into principals. There are at least two important questions, without getting into the effect of taxation. First, which is the best type of "skin-in-the-game?" Second, how much is optimal?

What Type?

To minimize the agency problem, shareholders would like a significant fraction of each top executive's wealth to be ownership in the firm. The alternatives are phantom stock, executive stock options, or actual ownership of common shares. To discuss the pros and cons of each, recall that when major investment decisions are made, there may be a difference between the effect of a decision on shareholders' wealth and on the stock price.[2]

Phantom stock. Managers who own phantom stock that receives no dividends would be anxious to make investments that increase share price, even if the optimal decision is to pay a dividend instead. Actual shareholders would recommend that management should not make the investment, however, because if they receive the cash that is not invested, they can reinvest the money at the same expected risk/return as the weighted average cost of capital (*WACC*). (This was discussed in Chapter 3 as the Overinvestment Trap.)

Suppose that the market believes the firm (which has a book value of $1,000) will have an expected return on invested capital, *E(ROIC)* equal to five percent, but management knows that all future investments will earn *ROIC* equal to eight percent, which is less than an assumed 10 percent *WACC*. When management undertakes investments, it believes that the stock price will rise. If management does not make the investment, it will return the cash to all ordinary shareholders who can do whatever they please with it, but nothing to holders of phantom stock, i.e., management itself. Let's see what happens:

Before any decision: $V_0 = E(ROIC)I\,/\,WACC$
$= .05(\$1,000)\,/\,.1 = \$500$

If an investment of $500 is made: $V_1 = .08(\$1,500)\,/\,.1 = \$1,200$

---

[2]For example, if the expected return on replacement capital becomes greater than the market expected *ROIC* but is still below the *WACC*, the stock price will rise as the market expected *ROIC* is revised upward—even though the optimal decision from a shareholder wealth perspective is to pay a dividend rather than reinvest at a rate below the *WACC*.

Phantom Stock: $V_p = \$1,200$

If the \$500 is paid $V_2 = .08(\$1,000) / .1 + \$500 = \$1,300$
  to shareholders:

Phantom Stock: $V_p = .08(\$1,000) / .1 = \$800$

No matter what happens, the market will soon discover that $E(ROIC)$ will rise from five to eight percent, it's only a matter of time. Note that shareholders are better off if the firm refuses to invest whenever $ROIC < WACC$, i.e., $V_2 > V_1$. However, phantom stockholders are better off if the firm does invest when $WACC > ROIC > E(ROIC)$, i.e, $V_{P1} > V_{P2}$. Thus, phantom stock that receives no dividends does not solve the agency problem, and should be avoided.

Most phantom stock plans pay out "capital gains" as annual cash bonuses. As a result, managers may have an incentive to take actions that temporarily boost the phantom stock price (much as senior executives may have incentives to boost share price as their options mature). We discuss elsewhere the use of bonus banks, clawbacks, and vesting features as ways to control such myopic behavior.

If a phantom stock plan is used, there are two plan features that can alleviate its pitfalls. First, dividends should be paid commensurate with the business's dividends. But the dividend payment must be tied to the business unit rather than the corporation as a whole. Phantom dividend yield can be estimated as a business unit's free cash flows to equity (after making appropriate assumptions about debt service) as a percent of phantom stock value. Phantom dividends should earn the firm or business unit's (market-adjusted) cost of equity until paid out as a cash bonus—this allows managers to adequately compare investments against shareholder's alternative investments. Second, phantom "capital gains" should either be subject to normal long-term incentive restrictions such as clawbacks or bonus banks, or be paid in additional phantom shares subject to long-term vesting schedules.

Stock options. Stock options may have their virtues in the overall scheme of incentive design, but linear pay-for-performance is not one of them. When viewed in isolation from other incentives, call options have payoffs that are linear on the upside but have a floor on the downside as shown in Figure 9.3. Therefore, call option grants induce risk-taking behavior by themselves because the downside payout is limited. We recognize, however, that options may have other features such as tax effects that could outweigh the downside of nonlinear incentives.

If one argues that base compensation, i.e. salary, is like a risky bond, which pays a fixed amount if the firm does well but pays out less and less as the firm deteriorates, then some combination of salary and call op-

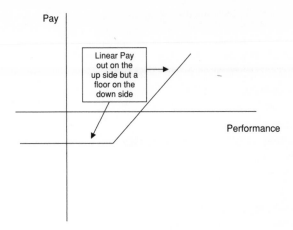

FIGURE 9.3   Call option pay-for-performance is nonlinear.

tions will produce stock-like changes in wealth. Hypothetically, just the right amount of call options might linearize the pay-for-performance incentive structure, but in fact, habitual use of large option grants has created situations similar to what is seen in Figure 9.3.

Vesting schedules are thought to be a solution to the nonlinear payout of option prices: Managers must keep the share price up long enough to realize the gains from their options. With a long enough vesting schedule, so this logic goes, managers will take actions in shareholders' best interest. The problem with this logic, though, is that it actually exacerbates the nonlinearity of the option payout problem. For the time period until options vest, managers have little to no downside. After the vesting date, managers may have only a short window (say, a few years) in which to realize their gains. Managers may thus take even more risks as they approach the vesting date for their options than they would if their options remained exercisable for the duration of the options' maturity.

Share ownership. Given the drawbacks of phantom stock and call options, share ownership seems desirable. Owners of regular shares receive dividends as well as capital gains, therefore their cash payout opportunities are the same as other shareholders. Furthermore, at least for those top managers who can directly affect the company's performance, there is a linear relationship between pay and performance.

How Much Skin in the Game?
No one knows the answer to how much equity top management should own. However, it is not what percentage of the firm's equity that matters.

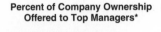

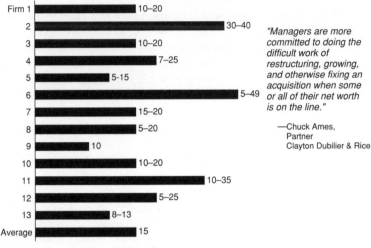

*Percentages vary mostly because of total size of buyout

Figure 9.4   Percent of LBO'd companies owned by top management.

Source: Interview notes. Anslinger and Copeland (1988)

Rather, it is the percentage of management's net worth invested in the firm's shares that indicates whether or not their wealth is where their heart is.

While doing research for their *Harvard Business Review* paper entitled "A Fresh Look at Growth through Acquisition," Anslinger and Copeland (1988) found that the incentive design at companies owned by private equity investment associations (LBO associations) was much more linear than at diversified acquirers that wee shareholder-owned. Figure 9.4 shows that typically 10 to 20 percent of the company is owned by top management.

This requires top management to put skin into the game. If the company fails, their personal wealth is at risk. Their wealth goes up and (especially) down linearly with the wealth of shareholders. There are companies today that require senior management to maintain an equity stake in the firm itself—above and beyond that paid to them through stock options and share bonus plans. We think these requirements are good, especially when those executives that have skin in the game are also those who directly affect the outcome of the game. It should be remembered, though, that managers have incentive to diversify this risk. In the wake of Enron it is now painfully obvious to lower-level managers that they should avoid having their retirement wealth tied to the same fortunes as their labor income (salary plus bonus).

The Weak Link Between the Principal's Wealth and the Agent's Performance

It is not difficult to grasp the common sense of a linear relationship between pay and performance. But there must also be a strong link between performance and wealth creation for the owners of the firm. Most of the research on this finds poor alignment between CEO pay and shareholder returns.

Graef Crystal (1988), for example, studied the top 100 of all Fortune 500 companies in the United States, ranked by sales revenue. He found that CEO pay varies with a number of reasonable factors. The problem is that the total return to shareholders is not one of them. Figure 9.5 shows his results. CEO compensation includes salary, bonus, value of perquisites when available, and 20 percent of gains from long-term incentives (e.g. stock options). Company performance is measured with an index that is a weighted average of profits, a five-year average return on book equity, the market-to-book equity ratio, and the historical five-year average total return to investors. The performance index had the greatest impact on CEO pay, yet it was not correlated with the total return to shareholders during the pay period. If the results of Chapter 2 of this book mean anything, we should not be surprised by the lack of correlation because none of the factors that went into the performance index had any information about expectations.

Meredith (1987) measured relative company performance as average annual total shareholder return over a five-year period minus the median industry return. This measure of relative performance was then correlated

Factor	Definition/Comment	Effect of a 10 percent Increase on CEO pay
Company Size	Index combining sales, assets, book equity, and number of employees	+2.0%
Company Performance	Index based on profits, 5-year average ROE, market-to-book value of equity, and 5-year average total return to investors	+31.0%
Company Risk	Beta	+5.0%
Government Regulation	Regulated companies pay less	N/A
Tenure of CEO	Longer tenure results in relatively lower pay	−1.2%
Location	More pay in high-cost-of-living areas (e.g., +7% for New York, and 10% for Los Angeles)	N/A
CEO Age	No effect on pay	0.0%
Shares Owned by CEO	No effect on pay	0.0%

FIGURE 9.5   Factors that affect CEO compensation.

Note: CEO compensation includes salary, bonus, value of prerequisites when available, and 20% of realized gains from long-term incentives (e.g. stock options).

Source: G. Crystal, *Fortune,* "The Wacky, Wacky World of Executive Pay," June 1988, Copyright © 1988 Time Inc. Reprinted by permission.

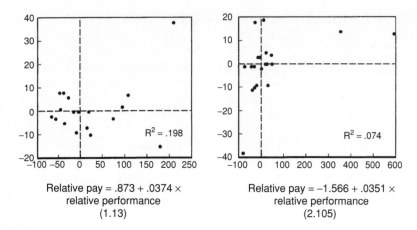

FIGURE 9.6   Relationship between CEO pay and performance, relative to industry and adjusted for size (1986).

Source: David Meredith, "Getting the Right Bang for the Buck: Are CEOs Paid What They Are Worth?", *Chief Executive*, September/October 1987.

with relative CEO pay, measured as the annualized present value of salary, bonus, and long-term incentives such as stock options, minus predicted CEO pay based on company size. The correlation between relative performance and relative pay was very low, as shown in Figure 9.6. The problem with Meredith's analysis is the same as with Crystal's—namely, that performance is not measured relative to expectations. In the "Salary and Bonus" section of this chapter we attempt to resolve this problem by studying what we shall call "pay at risk"—the difference between actual and expected compensation. Once again, we find that expectations matter.

The body of research concludes there is a weak link between company performance, CEO pay, and the total return to shareholders. Unfortunately, the research that we could find all uses inadequate measures of performance—measures that do not take changes of expectations into account. To illustrate what we mean, reconsider the Intel example introduced in Chapter 1. Recall that in October of 1998, Intel announced that its earnings were up 19 percent over the year before, and the stock price fell six percent on the announcement. The reason was that analysts were expecting a 24 percent increase and were disappointed by the announcement. In short, Intel failed to meet expectations and therefore underperformed. If pay is linked to performance then Intel's top management would not have received the highest possible bonus.

The Multiperiod Problem—Is Budgeting Just an Excuse to Lie?

Expectations-Based Management asks that managers communicate in an unbiased fashion with as little noise as possible in order to make the signal-to-noise ratio as high as possible. This is true with external and with internal communication.

External Communication

The importance of superior insider information for incentive design arises from the fact that top management is often heavily compensated with stock or stock options and, therefore, actually may have an incentive to lie. If the stock price can be "talked up" by management pronouncements that are overly optimistic, then they can sell their stock or options before the bubble (that they caused in the first place) bursts. There are no restrictions on insider trading if the executive reports all trades to the Security and Exchange Commission, and if there is no trading on special insider information. There are, however, requirements to disclose material information in a timely manner, and not to transact on it while it is insider information.

In spite of the requirements of Sarbanes-Oxley, it may still be possible for managers to influence results through what the public would consider "lies." Even within the limits of the new law, there still remains great latitude in accounting standards. While materially misleading financials may now carry a greater penalty, Sarbanes-Oxley does nothing about the "management" of earnings—e.g., manipulation of estimates of asset-depreciable lives, the use of accruals and reserves, or even revenue-recognition policies. Over the long-run, the kinds of errors introduced by playing around with accounting recognition will cancel each other out: In the long run, only cash flows matter. But our concern is not only the long run—it is also the short- to medium-term, where managers are most interested in boosting the share price to reap share price option gains.

There is also another type of "lie" and it is one that is incapable of being found out by even the most stringent accounting controls. This is the "lie" caused by manipulating actual performance in a way that presents investors with a distorted picture of the company. We see this, for example, when sales reps pull sales forward from the next period to this period in order to earn their commission sooner (this may be done without any fraud involved through careful manipulation of customer incentives). Timing and placement of advertising revenues or R&D expenses may also affect short-term results. One company we studied told investors that the level of advertising expenses had remained unchanged—what they did not tell investors was that advertising had been shifted away from brand image (more long-term focus) toward trade promotion (short-term incentives like store coupons), though a careful reading of SEC Form 10-K footnotes might have revealed this shift. This type of shift in advertising dollars is not required to be disclosed to investors. However, investors see the real increase in volume and may be fooled into believing this revenue bump was more than a short-term effect of a shift in ad spending. As these examples make clear, relying on penalties for lying from Sarbanes-Oxley will do little for investors concerned about preventing management from lying in the broader sense of the term.

Stephen Ross (1976) demonstrated that one way to prevent lying was to create a penalty large enough to dissuade improper actions in the first place. It is really common sense that if the probability of getting caught in a lie is high and if the gains from lying are removed and a penalty imposed, then no rational person would lie. The government took a role in this matter via the Sarbanes-Oxley law. Now the CEO and CFO can be held criminally liable for misstatements of the financial health of their company. But there are additional actions firms can take.

Clawbacks and vesting Schedules are two types of action that a company can take on its own to discourage prevarication. First, stock or options grants may require a period of time before they vest. Delayed vesting seemingly separates the consequences of a bonus award from the time that the award can be consumed. Thus, insider information becomes stale before options can be exercised, for example. The second type of action is called a "clawback." When enacted, it gives the board of directors the authority to take back the gains from the sale of stock or options. Executives are required to escrow any funds received from the sale of stock or options, or the exercise of options. The timing and the extent of clawbacks are at the discretion of the board.

A bonus bank is sometimes suggested as a solution to the multiperiod problem. Similar to setting up a vesting schedule, the idea is to escrow bonuses earned this period in a "bank" where they earn interest, with withdrawals being allowed after a prespecified period of time. For example, a $90,000 bonus might be withdrawn at the rate of $30,000 per year over a three-year period. This idea can solve the multiperiod problem if the bonus can be clawed back when performance does not materialize.

Internal Communication

Planning and budgeting are at the intersection between expectations setting and performance measurement. The budgeting process has been criticized as an excuse to lie—and it is, of course. The budget is intended to be an expression of the most likely, that is, the *expected* outcome. There is nothing inherent in the budgeting system that prevents the pay-for-performance schedule from being linear. There is, however, an incentive for the lower-level employee to understate her expected performance to receive a higher bonus. To prevent this from happening, senior management has to be well informed about the performance that can be expected of junior management. Information must be gathered and compiled from every possible source. Look at benchmarks set by competitors. Look at the history of performance at your own business unit. Look at the track record of the manager with whom you are discussing budget targets. Look at the economic environment. Talk to peers and subordinates of the individual being evaluated. Don't be shy. Be frank and open. Then set reasonable targets. Remember that along with achievement of an expected target comes an expected bonus. If stretch targets are used (though we counsel against them), pay for achieving such targets should be significantly more than the expected bonus.

Hockey stick forecasts, like those illustrated in Figure 9.7, are a typical problem with budgeting and planning. As managers try to game the budgeting and planning process, they often underforecast next year's performance and overforecast longer-term performance. If this is done year after year, the picture looks like a row of hockey sticks.

There are several ways of confronting the hockey stick problem. One way is to compute this year's bonus on the difference between actual and expected performance for this year forecasted at the beginning of this year, plus the difference between actual performance this year and expected performance for this year forecasted last year, plus another difference based on expected performance for this year forecasted two years ago. Suppose that we refer to Figure 9.7 as an example. In Year 3 the manager would have three pieces to his bonus. His actual performance in Year 3 was greater than expected—a positive piece. But this actual performance is significantly lower than his Year 1 and Year 2 forecasts, so these pieces would reduce his bonus. Depending on the weights assigned, they could make the bonus zero or even negative.

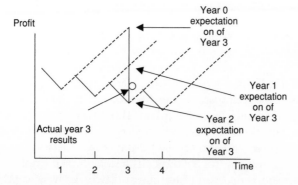

FIGURE 9.7   Budgeting and forecasting hockey sticks.

Another way to confront the hockey stick problem is the use of biased forecasts to value the business unit. If hockey sticks are present, the value that is based on management forecasts will be much higher than the market value and higher than valuation that is based on analyst forecasts. If biases are believed to be constant, then the upward bias in value will carry forward from one period to the next. Bonuses can then be tied to changes in valuation in a way that bypasses the impact of upward bias. Alternatively, forecasts can be adjusted downward to ensure that valuations are consistent with external, unbiased benchmarks.

Often the question of the timing of budget cycles comes up. How often should the budget be revised? If the operating environment does not change then the budget will never require an update. However, if competition, regulation, technology, or any other significant part of the business system change, then the old budget becomes outdated and a new budget must be prepared to reflect new expectations.

More and more companies are using real options to make major decisions. In a *Harvard Business Review* article coauthored with Peter Tufano (2004) and titled "A Real-World Way to Manage Real Options," we suggest changes to the budgeting system to accommodate the additional decision-making requirements that accompany the use of real options. As we described in Chapter 4, most real options are various types of flexibility that managers have in making decisions about large capital projects. For example, suppose you are asked to manage the construction and subsequent operation of a General Motors automotive assembly plant. You have already conducted a standard net present value analysis that forecasts the expected cash flows, discounts them back to the present at the weighted average cost of capital, then subtracts out the initial capital expenditure. This analysis fails to value the future decisions—all real options—that can be made. If the plant does worse than expected (perhaps due to a fall in demand), you can scale it back, close it down with the intention to reopen, or abandon it altogether. If it does better than expected, you can extend its life or expand its scale. Finally, you have the option to defer the start of the project until circumstances become more favorable. The definition of a real option is that it is the right, but not the obligation, to take an action (at a fixed cost called the exercise price) for a predetermined period of time called the life of the option. Real options have trigger points that must be part of the budgeting process—and, by extension, the compensation process. When, for example, the demand for automobiles falls below a predetermined threshold, then the plant should be shut down and then reopened when demand subsequently rises to surpass another trigger point. Considerable value can be lost if the correct decision is not made in a timely way when the trigger point is reached. The implication for the budgeting system is that there are time variances as well as price and volume variances that must be monitored. Similarly, business unit-level compensation needs to account for real options—for example, by encouraging the exercise of options, even if such options include project abandonment.

Long-term compensation methods go beyond the short-term mentality of one-year bonuses. They are probably most useful for top management because compensation, or at least part of it, is deferred until the goal is achieved. A bonus bank or a vesting schedule also can serve as golden hand-cuffs because the accrued or unpaid portion may be forfeited by a departing executive. For middle management, a promotion-based system that works over an entire career helps to keep each executive's mind focused on the long term. Continuous improvement plans that provide bonuses for hourly workers help to keep them focused on the long term as well.

Salary and Bonus—Pay at Risk

Most studies of compensation divide the total into salary, assumed to be fixed, and bonus that is supposed to be based on performance.

$$\text{Total Compensation} = \text{Salary} + \text{Bonus}$$

We believe that this is not the right way to think about it, and would like to introduce the concept of "pay at risk." If one asks about how executives think about their pay, the role of expectations cannot be ignored. They divide their pay into an expected component that is the sum of their salary and their expected bonus, and a residual component that we call pay at risk.

$$\text{Total Compensation} = \text{Expected pay} \pm \text{Unexpected pay} = \text{Salary} \\ + \text{Expected bonus} \pm \text{Unexpected bonus}$$

The unexpected part of compensation is as likely to be positive as negative. An executive will interpret a bonus that is less than expected as a negative signal, and will view receipt of the expected bonus as simply average—which it is meant to be. If the executive always receives her expected bonus, then no signal about her performance is being communicated.

We were curious about the percentage of total compensation that is really pay at risk for the CEOs of the largest companies in the United States. We used the Forbes compensation database that covers the compensation of 800 CEOs. The data covered five years (1994–1998) and broke total compensation into salary, bonus, other compensation, and realized stock gains. We would have liked to look at the value of stock and stock option grants during the year of the award, but such data was unavailable.

Table 9.1 explains total compensation in the current year as the function of the market capitalization of the company, the percent of stock owned by the CEO, and last year's total compensation. The *r*-squared was

TABLE 9.1   Expected Total Compensation

Variable	Median	Coefficient	t-test
Ln Total Compensation	7.584 ($1.966 mm)	—	—
Constant	—	1.264	9.411
Ln Market Cap	8.478 ($4.528 bn)	0.127	10.023
% Stock Owned	.2%	−732	−3.253
Ln Total Compensation Previous Year	7.421 ($1.671 mm)	0.714	39.348

Note: r^2 = 62.0%, F-test = 843.6, 1,552 observations

Source: Forbes data, Monitor analysis

62 percent and was highly significant. This regression was used to estimate expected total compensation. "Pay at Risk" is the difference between actual and expected compensation:

$$\text{Pay at Risk} = \text{Actual Total Compensation} - \text{Expected Total Compensation} \qquad (9.1)$$

When the absolute value of pay at risk was measured as a percentage of actual total compensation, our calculations indicated that the (absolute value of) average pay at risk was 17 percent of expected compensation.

To test for a relationship between pay and performance, we used ten years of data (1992–2001) from the Execucomp database and defined total compensation as annual salary plus bonus. We then estimated expected compensation for the CEO of each company as predicted by the time series linear regression.

$$TC_t = a + b(\text{Year}) + e_t$$

Pay at risk was defined as the difference between actual and expected total compensation, divided by expected total compensation. Thus, pay at risk is the percent of total compensation that is discretionary. We regressed pay at risk against the total return to shareholders during the concurrent year (Table 9.2) and the prior year (Table 9.3). The results show a statistically significant relationship between pay at risk and contemporaneous total return to shareholders in seven out of ten years, but the correlation is quite low. At least the relationship was positive, with the result that executives did, in fact, earn more than expected in years when the TRS was high.

TABLE 9.2 Pay at Risk Regressed Against Concurrent TRS (1992–2001)

Year	Sample Size	Interest	*t*-test	Slope	*t*-test	*R*-Sq.	*F* (Sig.)
1992	273	0.02468	1.20	0.001	0.02	0.000	0.00 (0.99)
1993	688	0.1310	1.17	0.002	0.10	0.000	0.01 (0.92)
1994	917	0.00803	1.15	0.060	2.90	0.009	8.41(0.004)
1995	984	−0.05537	−7.28	0.115	8.35	0.066	69.77 (0.00)
1996	1045	−0.04451	−5.60	0.137	7.36	0.049	54.13 (0.00)
1997	1129	−0.02644	−2.94	0.099	6.49	0.036	42.05 (0.00)
1998	1142	−0.01468	−1.90	−0.000	−1.03	0.001	1.06 (0.30)
1999	1138	−0.00811	−1.02	0.065	5.87	0.029	34.46 (0.00)
2000	1120	0.01027	1.28	0.070	6.17	0.033	38.08 (0.00)
2001	993	−0.05823	−6.90	0.110	6.50	0.041	42.21 (0.00)
Average	943			0.066		0.26	

Source: CRSP, Execucomp, Monitor analysis

However, the slope coefficient is quite low, indicating that pay-at-risk is not very responsive to TRS.

Although we believe this rudimentary analysis is useful because it does show a direct relationship between unexpected pay and unexpected return to shareholders, the results are too weak to be conclusive.

When measured as a percentage of actual total compensation, our calculations indicated that the (absolute value of) average pay-at-risk was 17 percent of expected compensation.

How does one set the appropriate level of salary and bonus? Salary should be set at a level that enables your company to attract and retain the quality of executive who can meet or exceed the expected level of performance that is built into your stock price. The higher are the expectations of the shareholders the higher should be the expected compensation of top management. Recall, for example, our comparison of Wal-Mart versus Sears in the 1994–1997 time period. The level of expected higher performance was built into Wal-Mart's stock price and Wal-Mart actually did perform better than Sears. Without knowing what all of Wal-Mart's middle and senior level managers were actually paid, we hypothesize that their salaries were higher than at Sears, which attained a lower level of performance.[3] The

---

[3]Annual proxy statement disclosures for Sears and Wal-Mart indicate that the top five executives at Sears were paid more in annual compensation in 1994 than the top five managers at Wal-Mart. By 1998 Wal-Mart's top five managers were paid substantially more in annual compensation than that of the top five managers at Sears. Valuation data were unavailable to compare long-term compensation paid, for example, through option grants.

TABLE 9.3   This Year's Pay-at-Risk Regressed Against Last Year's TRS

Year	Sample Size	Intercept	t-test	Slope	t-test	R-Sq.	F (Sig.)
1993	286	−0.0197	−1.16	0.0849	2.07	0.015	4.26 (0.04)
1994	700	0.01064	1.18	0.01538	0.81	0.001	0.65 (0.42)
1995	932	−0.02346	−3.45	0.06629	3.37	0.012	11.35 (0.00)
1996	988	−0.02778	−3.14	0.03177	1.98	0.004	3.93 (0.05)
1997	1034	−0.00670	−0.73	0.07383	3.45	0.011	11.89 (0.00)
1998	1132	−0.0335	−3.59	0.0549	3.41	0.010	11.60 (0.00)
1999	1136	0.00143	0.18	0.00007	0.17	0.000	0.03 (0.87)
2000	1121	0.01396	1.74	0.05364	4.75	0.020	22.56 (0.00)
2001	993	−0.04959	−5.55	0.00701	0.55	0.000	0.31 (0.58)
Average				0.043		0.008	

Source: CRSP, Execucomp, Monitor analysis

idea is that salary should be linked with the expected level of performance. Bonus compensation should be linked (linearly) to expected performance. If performance exceeds expectations then the bonus should be higher than expected, and vice versa. Because Wal-Mart executives underperformed expectations during the period that we studied, they should have received less than the expected bonus.

We have not been able to find any literature on the income elasticity of the bonus. If performance exceeds expectations by 10 percent, for example, just how much should the bonus increase as a percentage of what was expected? One thought is that it should be more sensitive to the market-adjusted return to shareholders when the company has more volatility—as a compensation for risk.

Absolute or Relative Performance?

For top management, absolute performance implies accepting responsibility for everything. This actually makes sense to a certain extent because top management can change the portfolio of businesses that a company owns. Warren Buffet is responsible for the fact that Berkshire Hathaway has invested heavily into insurance companies. Westinghouse, over a period of years, transformed itself from a manufacturer of consumer durables into a media company. When Chevron decides to explore for and to extract oil from Kazakhstan, it accepts risk beyond its control in the form of possible political instability. Many of the bets that top management must decide upon involve risks over which they have no control except for whether to make the bet in the first place. What logically follows is the necessity of taking responsibility for absolute performance—simply because management agreed to play the game. Therefore, there are many advocates of the point of view that top management performance should be linked directly to the share price—not to the movement of the stock price relative to the market.

There are advocates of the opposite point of view as well. They argue that top management, especially the CEO, have too short a time in the job to be held responsible for the business that the company is in. If you are the CEO of a steel company, with the requisite set of skills, why would anyone expect you to transform the steel company into a farm products company?

If one takes an agnostic point of view about whether the responsibility of top management is absolute or relative, then some combination like that shown in Table 9.4 may be appropriate. On the horizontal scale is the company stock price performance relative to an index constructed from its peers, and on the vertical scale is the market movement this year. Two regressions are run:

$$\text{Total return on company's shares} =$$
$$a + b(\text{Total return on peers}) + \text{residual}(1)$$

$$\text{Total return on company's shares} =$$
$$a + b(\text{Total return on market}) + \text{residual}(2)$$

If both residuals are positive it means that your company exceeded expectations because its stock returns were higher than expected given returns on the market and peer company indices. When the stock market goes up and the company does worse than the industry, i.e., when residual 1 is negative and residual 2 is positive, then top management would receive a modest bonus but less than expected. If the market is down (residual 2 negative) but the company performance is better than peers (residual 1 positive), then executives receive a good bonus, better than expected.

As an example, we analyzed the returns from 10 large-capitalization pharmaceutical companies in 2003. Based on five years of historical data we estimated each firm's beta against the S&P 500 and against an equal-weighted index of the other nine firms. For simplicity the analysis is conducted on share price returns only rather than total shareholder returns. Table 9.5 summarizes our results. Six firms outperformed both the market and their industry peers: Pfizer, GlaxoSmithKline, Bristol Myers, AstraZeneca,

TABLE 9.4 Bonus Payoff Matrix Relative to Peers and to the Market

	Positive residual(1)	Negative residual(1)
Positive residual(2)	Top Bonus	Modest Bonus
Negative residual(2)	Good Bonus	No Bonus

Source: Monitor analysis

TABLE 9.5 Pharmaceutical Industry Performance Relative to Peers and to the Market (2003)

	Actual Return	Market Beta	Peer Index Beta	Market Return	Peer Index Return	Excess Return Against Market	Excess Return Against Peers
Abbott	17.6%	0.4	0.7	23.4%	14.5%	7.8%	7.6%
AstraZeneca	34.2%	0.5	0.8	23.4%	12.6%	23.0%	24.5%
Aventis	21.7%	0.4	0.4	23.4%	14.0%	13.2%	16.2%
Bristol Myers	25.6%	0.6	1.0	23.4%	14.3%	11.3%	11.0%
Eli Lilly	12.4%	0.4	1.0	23.4%	15.0%	3.5%	–3.0%
GlaxoSmithKline	25.3%	0.4	0.6	23.4%	14.5%	16.7%	17.2%
Johnson & Johnson	–2.1%	0.5	0.9	23.4%	17.3%	–13.8%	–17.5%
Merck	–11.9%	0.6	1.1	23.4%	18.5%	–25.4%	–32.6%
Pfizer	16.3%	0.7	1.0	23.4%	15.0%	0.7%	1.4%
Schering Plough	–21.1%	0.7	1.3	23.4%	17.3%	–36.7%	–43.2%

TABLE 9.6   Pharmaceutical CEO Annual Compensation (2003)

	2003 Annual Comp	2002 Annual Comp	% Change
Abbott	3,399	2,813	20.8%
AstraZeneca**	1,790	1,479	21.0%
Aventis**	2,779	2,007	38.4%
Bristol Myers	3,225	1,100	193.2%
Eli Lilly	2,753	2,135***	28.9%
GlaxoSmithKline**	2,787	2,452	13.7%
Johnson & Johnson	4,409	3,092	42.6%
Merck	2,958	2,983	−0.8%
Pfizer	6,670	5,335	25.0%
Schering Plough*	1,395	1,523	−8.4%

* Schering Plough changed CEOs between 2002 and 2003.

** In local currency.

*** Eli Lilly CEO voluntarily took almost no annual salary or bonus in 2002; 2001 compensation used instead.

Abbott, and Aventis. We would expect managers at these firms to receive large bonuses as a result. Eli Lilly outperformed the market but not its peer index, meriting a modest bonus. Merck, Johnson & Johnson, and Schering Plough failed to outperform both the market and their peers, meriting no bonus (or a low bonus relative to managers' expectations).

How does this compare with the actual bonuses? Table 9.6 examines just CEO bonus payments for each firm according to SEC annual proxy statement for U.S. firms and Form 20-F for overseas-based firms.[4] For comparability we examine only annual incentive plan payouts rather than long-term incentive plans. We've also excluded benefits and other compensation. Though we have not adjusted these compensation amounts for pay at risk (i.e., for management's expectations), we can make some rough conclusions simply on the basis of growth in total annual compensation.

Johnson & Johnson stands out as a firm that should have merited little or no bonus based on stock price performance. Instead, the company paid annual compensation over 42 percent higher than the prior year. By contrast, GlaxoSmithKline's CEO may have been underpaid, considering the company's good relative performance against both the market and peers, yet compensation grew only 13.7 percent—low compared to the growth of compensation of several peers. We also see that Merck and Schering Plough CEOs' annual compensation fell, which is in line with the relative share price performance approach stated previously.

---

[4]It would be even better to use pay at risk.

Excess Performance Relative to Peers

		30%	20%	10%	0%	−10%	−20%	−30%
	30%	190%	170%	150%	130%	110%	90%	70%
	20%	180%	160%	140%	120%	100%	80%	60%
Excess	10%	170%	150%	130%	110%	90%	70%	50%
Performance	0%	160%	140%	120%	100%	80%	60%	40%
Relative to	−10%	150%	130%	110%	90%	70%	50%	30%
Market	−20%	140%	120%	100%	80%	60%	40%	20%
	−30%	130%	110%	90%	70%	50%	30%	10%

FIGURE 9.8   Bonus payout as percent of expected bonus.

In practice, the bonus payoff matrix can be translated into a more continuous payout scheme. For example, there might be a payoff matrix for senior management that looks something like Figure 9.8. The percentages in the grid correspond to the percent of *expected* bonus paid to managers. If performance is exactly as expected, after adjusting for both peer and market effects, then bonus is expected as well. The payouts here are structured so that greater weight is given to performance relative to peers, though this need not be the case for all firms.

The responsibility for absolute performance dissipates when we shift our attention to the business unit level. For example, the head of operations for Chevron in Kazakhstan had no choice. He is there as a condition of employment. Since he is not responsible for the Chevron investment, he is responsible for making it better (or worse) than expected. For this reason, business unit performance should be measured relative to competition and to forces at work in the economy.

Should Goodwill Be Charged Against Business Unit Incentive Targets?

It may be the case that a business unit was acquired recently with a considerable amount of goodwill created on the balance sheet as a result. Often a debate results about whether the goodwill should be added to invested capital at the corporate level or at the business unit level. At the time of the acquisition, it is a new investment and goodwill is part of the total capital invested. The expected rate of return on invested capital including goodwill must exceed the cost of capital in order for the acquisition to create value. But the instant the acquisition has been made, and therefore baked into expectations, it makes no difference whether the goodwill is allocated to the business unit or not. The job of the business unit manager is to exceed expectations. If goodwill is allocated to his business unit, his expected return on invested capital target is lower, and if goodwill is not allocated, his target is higher. Therefore his performance depends on beating expectations—whether goodwill is or is not allocated is irrelevant.

We can't stress enough the need for more rigor by managers in using EBM to think through the implications of the incentive targets they choose. At one firm we heard of internal discussion about the very question of goodwill we concluded above as being irrelevant. At this firm, business unit managers were compensated on return on invested capital including goodwill. In response to the annual accounting impairment test for goodwill on one subsidiary's balance sheet, business unit management argued for writing off as much as possible (in order to boost return on capital). Senior management looked at it differently, thinking the write-off would be seen by investors as a negative signal of management's ability to execute acquisitions. Actually, they are both mistaken—the market had already assimilated the fact of the goodwill paid at the time of the acquisitions, and had also adjusted its expectations for return on capital accordingly. Writing off this goodwill would make absolutely no difference in business unit managers' ability to meet expectations targets. Arguing over an accounting allocation was wasting senior management's time. This particular problem was so difficult for managers to get beyond because *ROIC* with goodwill was not only used to measure business unit performance, but also to pay managers their bonus. Who wouldn't spend time arguing over an accounting allocation as long as they could influence their own pay in so doing?

Line versus Staff Compensation

We would be remiss if we did not discuss the relationship between the review process and the ability to monitor and measure the relationship between the effort that an executive puts into a job and the effect that effort has on output. In some cases output is easy to measure and pay-for-performance can be determined largely with a formula approach. However, when output is difficult to measure, a subjective review process becomes necessary. Table 9.7 shows the relationship between the review process and the two key dimensions that help to determine it—namely, the impact that the job if done well can have on shareholder value, and the ease of observing the link between input and expected output.

Incentives and Middle Management

So far we implicitly assumed that incentive design is only for top management, and this oversight must be corrected. Promotion is a powerful incentive for middle management—more important than bonuses. Medoff and

TABLE 9.7   The Balance Between Objective and Subjective Reviews

		Ability to Impact the Stock Price	
		High	Low
Ability to Measure Output	Nebulous	*Extensively a Review Process* (CFO, Treasurer, head of HR, R&D, sales)	*Intermittent Review and Straight Salary* (legal staff, engineers)
	Relatively Clear	*Largely Formula driven but with careful judgment* (CEO, COO, BU heads, key sales mgrs.)	*Formula driven with Periodic checks* (Plant Managers, lower level sales, field engineers)

Source: Monitor analysis

Abraham (1980) studied two companies: The first had 4,788 managers and the second had 2,841. Table 9.8 shows that the bonus system paid salary premiums that differentiated among ratings by an average of 2.5 percent (on a $40,000 base this amounts to a $1,000 bonus). Note also that at Company A, 94.5 percent of all ratings were either good or outstanding, and at Company B, 95 percent were good or superior. Some would argue that clear messages at Company A were being sent to only those 5.5 percent of all managers who fell into the other ratings. At Company B clear messages were sent only to the 1.2 percent who were ranked as satisfactory (none were minimum acceptable or unacceptable), and to the 3.8 percent who were ranked excellent. Two comments are helpful. First, the performance ratings could be forced ranked with a predetermined percentage of managers in each rating. But there is a caveat—namely, that the predetermined distribution is not useful unless it matches the actual distribution of performance. The second comment is that although the bonuses are relatively small differences between performance ratings, they may be signals of potential for promotion if the distribution of ratings is communicated so that people know where they stand.

Jensen, Baker, and Murphy (1988) found that vice presidents of U.S.-based corporations receive average pay increases of 18.8 percent upon promotion compared to 3.3 percent (bonuses) during the years that they stay in the same position. From this we can conclude that bonuses for middle-level management, while too small to be significant on a current period cash basis, are best interpreted as signals of the potential for promotion—an event that when built into expectations makes the bonus an effective signal. Remember though, the signal cannot be easily interpreted unless the entire distribution of ratings is communicated to all managers.

If promotion, rather than bonuses, is the motivator for middle-level management, then it makes sense to be sure that you have high-quality review processes in place. In academia, promotion to tenure depends heav-

TABLE 9.8   Typical Bonus Systems for Middle Management

Performance Rating	Bonus Relative to Lowest Performance Rating	Percent of Sample Receiving Performance Rating
Company A (4,788 managers)		
Not acceptable	0.0%	0.2%
Acceptable	1.4	5.3
Good	5.3	74.3
Outstanding	7.8	20.2
Company B (2,841 managers)		
Unacceptable	0.0	0.0
Minimum acceptable	0.0	0.0
Satisfactory	0.0	1.2
Good	1.8	36.6
Superior	3.6	58.4
Excellent	6.2	3.8

Source: Reprinted from "Experience, Performance and Earnings," by J. Medoff, and K. Abraham, *Quarterly Journal of Economics*, December 1980, by permission of the publisher. Copyright © 1980 by Massachusetts Institute of Technology. All rights reserved.

ily on letters of recommendation that are written by faculty at other schools and chosen by the evaluation committee, not by the candidate. There are two advantages of this "external review" process. First, it reduces the threat that the evaluation committee might be biased against (or for) the candidate, for whatever reason. Second, it requires that the candidate for promotion actually attain a respectable reputation outside of his or her own campus, thereby providing external validity.

Although we have not seen many examples of similar promotion review processes in industry, we believe that most internal review processes are too dependent on feedback within the hierarchy.[5] There is more than a little truth to the statement that promotion is impossible if your boss does not like you. We suggest that every executive be reviewed every year (whether she is due for promotion or not) by top management in her own business unit and by a committee that spans business units. Furthermore, her evaluation should be based on feedback from her superiors, her peers, and her subordinates, as well as from people outside and within her own business unit. In some cases, surveying external stakeholders may provide the most useful information—e.g., customer satisfaction surveys for positions with line of sight to the customer.

---

[5]The closest we have seen to industry using external evaluations of managers is the use of client surveys in evaluating the performance of senior-level professional services employees.

Remember that there is an upper limit to the span of control in the promotion process. It is determined by the degree of association among the people who are being evaluated at a given level. They have to know each other well enough to be able to understand why one of the group of peers was promoted while others were not. When the relevant peer group becomes too large, so that they do not know each other very well, paranoia and superstitious behavior begin to creep into their behavior—not a good thing. Rumors begin to replace logic. People begin to believe in mentorship that is inappropriate, e.g., "work for Jim because he has the clout to get his people promoted."

The relationship between the rate of growth of your company and the rate of promotion should be understood due to its effect on the incentive design of middle management. It too, is important. Table 9.9 illustrates the problem. Company A has twice the growth rate of Company B, but have the same first-year sales. They also have the same ratio of sales to employees and the same ratio of executives to employees. The number of executive promotions, however, is roughly four times greater in Company A. Look at Years 2 to 3, for example. Company A starts with 2,000 units of sales, 20 employees and two executives, but by the end of the year has grown to need four executives (therefore, two promotions). Company B starts with 1 executive and grows to need 2—requiring one promotion. As high-growth firms slow down, this example illustrates that promotion will slow down even faster, and this will be likely to demotivate junior-level management because their expected (lifetime) income stream decreases in value. Slower growth firms, however, may still deliver on shareholder expectations, for example through higher dividend yields rather than capital gains. Middle managers in these firms should be compensated in ways that recognize their contribution to meeting shareholder expectations. As growth rates fall, then, junior-level compensation should tilt toward bonuses rather than promotions as reviewed for exceeding expectations.

TABLE 9.9   The Relationship between Growth and Promotion

		Year 1	Year 2	Year 3	Year 4	Year 5	Total
100%	Sales	1,000	2,000	4,000	8,000	16,000	
Growth	Employees	10	20	40	80	160	
	Executives	1	2	4	8	16	
	Promotions		1	2	4	8	15
50%	Sales	1,000	1,500	2,250	3,275	5,063	
Growth	Employees	10	15	22	33	50	
	Executives	1	1	2	3	5	
	Promotions		0	1	1	2	4

Hourly Workers

Hourly workers usually are the single largest pay category. Pay-for-performance can extend below management levels right down to hourly wage earners. In a comprehensive article, Mitchell, Lewin, and Lawler (1990) conclude that productivity gains of 10 to 25 percent are common when incentive pay is used properly. Table 9.10 summarizes their multiple regression results. They had no direct measure of productivity, therefore they used the (natural logarithm of) employees' hourly wage as a proxy for productivity, assuming that in the long run there is a strong relationship between productivity and the hourly wage.

A second major consideration for the incentive design of hourly workers is the risk they take regarding the stability of their employment across time. In some countries, hourly workers at large companies expect that they will not be laid off if demand for the company's products falls. This is made possible without forcing bankruptcy because a much higher percentage of their annual income is bonuses. When bonuses are tied to company profitability, they become a form of profit-sharing and provide incentives for hourly workers who benefit when the company does well. On the downside, bonuses are cut dramatically rather than laying off workers. Table 9.11 shows a table constructed from the work of Hashimoto (1990) showing salary versus wage compensation in various countries in the late 70's/early 80's.

From the company's point of view, either approach reduces operating risk. When there is an economic downturn, total wages paid can be cut either by layoffs or by cutting bonuses. However, the determining factor may be the specificity of the skills of the work force. If hourly workers have company-specific skills, it is costly to fire and rehire them. They may not come back. Therefore, it is better to keep them during a downturn, but cut way back on their bonuses. The problem with this approach, though, is that shortfalls may be due to secular/structural factors rather than cyclical

TABLE 9.10   Productivity and Incentives for Hourly Workers (Eleven Industries, 1979–1986)

Dependent Variable	Logarithm of hourly wage	
Constant	1.76	significant at the 1% level
Proportion of workers with incentives	−0.07	significant at the 1% level
Incentive plan	0.14	significant at the 1% level
R-squared	.68	
Number of observations	716	

Source: Mitchell, Daniel; D. Lewin, and E. Lawler, 1990. Reprinted by permission from The Brookings Institution, 1775 Massachusetts Ave NW, Washington DC 20036. (202) 797-6000, Fax (202) 797-6004, E-mail Brookings: webmaster@brookings.edu.

TABLE 9.11 Fixed and Variable Compensation as a
Percent of Revenues

Country	Wages and Salaries	Bonuses
Japan (1978)	56.7%	20.3%
Belgium (1982)	56.4	12.0
West Germany (1981)	57.7	9.1
Italy (1981)	54.4	8.9
Netherlands (1981)	57.8	8.8
France (1981)	56.6	5.4
United Kingdom (1981)	71.8	0.7
United States (1977)	74.4	0.4
Canada (1971)	83.1	0.2

Source: Hashimoto, 1990. Reprinted by permission from
The Brookings Institution, 1775 Massachusetts Ave NW,
Washington DC 20036. (202) 797-6000, Fax (202) 797-6004,
E-mail Brookings: webmaster@brookings.edu.

factors. In such cases it is preferable to shed employees rather than hold
on to many who may all be collectively hoping (expecting?) bonuses to
return shortly. There may certainly be a relationship between different
economies' levels of structural unemployment and the prevalence of relying on variable pay to defer layoffs.

Expected performance of hourly workers is set most often in terms of
value drivers. In an earlier chapter we talked about the need to extend the
ROIC tree down to the value driver level by focusing on those value driv-
ers that were most closely tied to the business issues of the company.
Another thing to keep in mind is the relationships among value drivers.
Illustrated in Figure 9.9 is the tradeoff between two value drivers in a wood

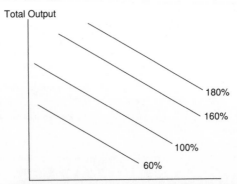

FIGURE 9.9   Iso-value lines determine tradeoffs between value drivers.

mill. The vertical axis is total dollar volume of products sold, and the horizontal axis represents the percent of sales in the most profitable product. The straight lines are iso-value lines that measure combinations of total volume and product mix that give the same increase in value. Bonus percentages are tied to the iso-value lines.

Summary

It is no simple job to piece together all aspects of incentive design. The owners of the company should protect their own interests by trying to linearize the pay-for-performance relationship at all levels and pay grades throughout the firm. This can be done via stock grants. Also, the multi-period problem must be addressed. For top management this requires skin-in-the-game, i.e. bonuses that are paid for beating the competition, but loss of personal wealth if expectations are not met. In addition, when the bonuses are vested over time, are banked, or can be clawed back, then the incentive to provide biased forecasts is considerably reduced.

When it comes to consideration of whether top management compensation should be relative or absolute, we lean toward relative performance. Salary and the expected bonus should be based on the level of relative performance while pay at risk should depend on exceeding expectations. Expectations should be reasonable. Stretch targets are often demoralizing. Management must be well informed to be able to set reasonable expectations, both internally and external to the firm.

Middle management look to promotion and to the quality of the evaluation system for their primary motivation. Bonus differences among ratings are usually much smaller by comparison. The use of promotion rather than bonuses, however, needs to be limited, in slower growth firms.

Hourly workers should be evaluated on the basis of their ability to continuously improve the value drivers under their control, and do better when they can share in the resulting profit improvement. Also, careful thought should be given to the way that the variable portion of aggregate hourly compensation is managed. Should people be laid off or should bonuses be cut instead?

CHAPTER 10

Implementing an EBM System

What are the elements of an Expectations-Based Management system? How do you bring about the cultural change in your company in a way that empowers management? What training procedures are best? What type of organizational support do you need? How does an EBM approach affect strategy, planning, and budgeting?

The worst thing that can happen is "value veneering." You don't want people simply going through the motions without any real impact on their behavior or on the return to shareholders. You do want to implement for impact—to change decisions, to generate new ideas, and to change behavior in a way that increases the value of your company.

The contents of this chapter are directed mainly at large, multibusiness, multinational companies. They are the most complex and have the most layers of management. Their strategy, planning, and budgeting processes are well established. But they are also the firms that can benefit the most from EBM. However, we have not forgotten smaller firms and family-owned businesses. A section of this chapter focuses on their special needs.

Three-Part EBM System

The span of control of a well-functioning EBM system reaches from the beliefs of current and potential investors that establish your company's stock price to board-level decisions that affect the value of the entire company, to business unit–level decisions, all the way down to daily operating decisions. Furthermore, the value of the firm depends on tradeoffs between current and future decisions. EBM is the golden thread that extends from

243

operating value drivers at the greatest level of specificity all the way to the long-term strategy and the stock price of your firm.

To span these assorted activities over multiple time periods, EBM has three measures of performance that are integrated into one system. At the highest level, the tool that has the strongest link with your stock price is a discounted cash flow (DCF) model of your firm. Embedded in it are the expectations of the market (on one hand) and the expectations of management (on the other hand)—with the implied assumption that the two points of view are complementary.

The second level of performance measurement is actual versus expected economic profit—an annual measure of performance, and therefore limited. But as we clearly demonstrated in Chapter 2, it has much higher correlation with the total return to shareholders than measures that fail to contain expectations (e.g., earnings growth and EVA growth). The best way to use actual versus expected economic profit is to set expectations within the framework of a DCF valuation. Moreover, for those able to construct credible estimates of longer-term expectations, changes in expected economic profit can be monitored not just for current year performance, but to gauge the impact on the long term.

A war story helps to paint a picture. In the late 1980s we were developing a value-based management system for the retail bank of a large money center bank. The planning system of the bank asked for forecasts of the return on equity (ROE) over the next three years as its criterion for making large investments. Even today, roughly 15 years later, many banks continue to use this type of decision rule. The retail bank had been losing market share—called "share of wallet." It devised a plan that required $100 million of investment to recapture its market share by refurbishing branch banks, installing new automated teller machines, aggressively advertising, and training clerks and tellers in customer relations skills. Figure 10.1 shows the forecasted return on equity for the two strategies. The current policy was named the "harvest strategy" and the $100 million strategy was called the "aggressive growth strategy."

If the top management team were to have used ROE over the next three years, they would have concluded that the aggressive growth strategy should be rejected. Due to the up-front expenditure of $100 million, its ROE is well below that of the harvest strategy during the first year, roughly equal the second year, and only a little bit better the third year.

If top management were to calculate the DCF values of the two strategies, they would base their decision on a very different picture—as shown in Figure 10.2. Now the two projects are compared on the basis of their expected cash flows over a long horizon. Because the aggressive growth strategy is expected to earn a greater ROE in the fourth year and beyond, its value was estimated to be 124 percent more than the value of the harvest strategy.

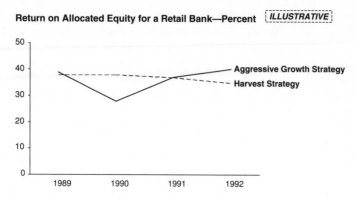

FIGURE 10.1   Three-year ROE forecasts for two strategies.

Top management checked the assumptions of the DCF analysis carefully and quickly adopted the aggressive growth strategy. It turned out to be a great success, recapturing share of wallet even faster than expected. The important take-away is that measures of performance that are not guided by the multiperiod perspective of DCF valuation are myopic.

The third level of performance measurement is operating value drivers. In Chapter 7 we described high-level or generic value drivers that are

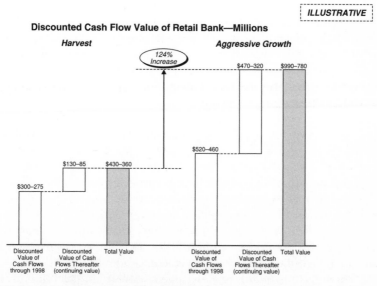

FIGURE 10.2   DCF estimates of two strategies.

common to all companies and all business units. Operating value drivers are similar but are driven down to the level of daily operating performance. At a bank, examples might be the ratio of deposits to employees, average time a customer stands in line, the ratio of teller to ATM transactions, or the amount of money per transaction. Later on in this chapter, we discuss the art of creating an ROIC tree that drives down to the set of value drivers that focus on the most relevant business issues.

Figure 10.3 illustrates the three interlinked parts of a comprehensive EBM system. It starts with operating value drivers at the lowest level and the most limited time frame, continues with the difference between actual and expected economic profit at the business unit and corporate level with a quarterly and annual time frame in mind, and then concludes with a DCF valuation model at the corporate and business unit levels and with an infinite time horizon.

The most important thing to remember is that expected annual performance must be guided by the expected performance over time that is embodied by the DCF valuation. Most projects have low or negative rates of return (*ROIC*) during their early years, followed by rates that increase as the capital invested depreciates. This pattern is well known in advance and can easily be built into expectations if management takes a multiperiod point of view. Without a long-term perspective, however, almost anything can happen—most of it resulting in myopic behavior.

Guiding Principles

Put yourself in the place of a CEO or CFO who wants to overhaul a flawed planning and budgeting system. You believe that an EBM system will prevent short-sighted behavior and will help the top management team to focus on exceeding what are currently low expectations about long-term earnings growth. What are the guiding principles that will help you avoid the land mines that might prevent success?

Management Understanding and Support

Top management understanding and support is absolutely necessary. We were once invited to sit in and to comment on the first value-based strategic plan of a large regional telecommunications company. For almost three hours, we listened to a discussion of methodology—how the cost of capital was calculated, how free cash flows were estimated—one boring detail after another. At the end when asked to comment, we complemented the planning staff on an excellent presentation, but asked, "Which heads of operating units did you interview to understand their challenges and reflect

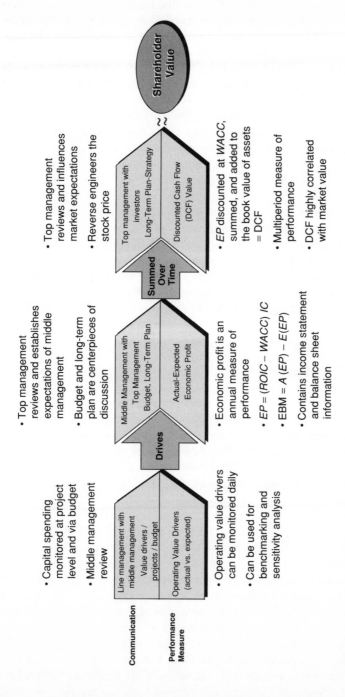

Communication

Line management with middle management
Value drivers / projects / budget

Drives

Middle Management with Top Management
Budget, Long-Term Plan

Summed Over Time

Top management with investors
Long-Term Plan-Strategy

Shareholder Value

Performance Measure

Operating Value Drivers (actual vs. expected)

Actual-Expected Economic Profit

Discounted Cash Flow (DCF) Value

- Capital spending monitored at project level and via budget
- Middle management review

- Top management reviews and establishes expectations of middle management
- Budget and long-term plan are centerpieces of discussion

- Top management reviews and influences market expectations
- Reverse engineers the stock price

- Operating value drivers can be monitored daily
- Can be used for benchmarking and sensitivity analysis

- Economic profit is an annual measure of performance
- $EP = (ROIC - WACC) \, IC$
- $EBM = A \, (EP) - E \, (EP)$
- Contains income statement and balance sheet information

- EP discounted at $WACC$, summed, and added to the book value of assets = DCF
- Multiperiod measure of performance
- DCF highly correlated with market value

FIGURE 10.3 The three-part EBM system.
Source: Monitor analysis

247

them in the plans?" When they confessed that they had not engaged business unit chief operating officers in any way, we suggested that their efforts were merely a paper exercise and would remain so until they communicated with operating management and obtained their support.

One good way of building support for a change to EBM is to value the company using various sets of mutually consistent expectations, i.e., scenarios that illustrate competing strategies that the company is considering. One good example is the discussion centered around Figure 10.2, in which the harvest strategy was shown to be of lower value than the aggressive growth strategy.

Adequate Accounting Data

Adequate accounting data are a prerequisite. This means complete income statement and balance sheet information, because management is responsible for resources found on both. When Bob Allen was named CEO of AT&T, the company was organized functionally. Given this setting, it is possible to implement EBM at the corporate level, but difficult to apply for functions. For example, there was a single general manager of production, another for sales, one for marketing, and so forth. It is a stretch of the imagination to discuss return on invested capital at this level. Given AT&T's size and complexity, Mr. Allen decided to reorganize into customer-facing business units such as the business communications group (BCG) and the consumer communications group (CCG). These were broken down into sub–business units (SBUs). For example, the CCG was subdivided into roughly 20 SBUs, such as operator services, college and university services, submarine cable, language line, telemarketing, universal credit card, and so on. At first, these units had only income statements as guidelines. It was not until 1992 that cost accounting had finished allocating electrons flowing through a network. Finally, the SBUs had balance sheets and at that time it became possible for the firm to manage capital utilization at the SBU level. Hundreds of millions of dollars were saved as a result. While the up-front cost of setting up such accounting systems can seem daunting (e.g., due to the expense involved in building systems or the time required to obtain consensus on capital allocations), the value-improvement opportunities of having such information at the business unit level are enormous.

If a company is organized along functional lines instead of business units, it is still possible to extend an EBM system down into the organization—although it is somewhat more complicated. Suppose that your company has a sales and marketing function, a production function, administration, delivery, and procurement. You want to evaluate the effect of a just-in-time inventory system. To do so you will need to estimate its impact on all of the functions that it touches, then aggregate the changes into a new forecast of the free cash flows of the company. Functional groups may also be assessed through careful use of transfer pricing, though such pricing must appear fair to all parties involved (e.g., bear some resemblance to what it would cost to outsource the particular function).

Management Reports

Management reports that are comprehensive but relatively short (25 pages or less) are an aid to communications. They should contain the strategy of the business unit, state expected performance, benchmark it against competition, estimate the discounted cash flow value, tie it to budgeted performance, and justify capital expenditures. Management reports should be resubmitted any time that competitive and regulatory information changes. Requiring managers to update these reports on a real-time basis ensures that business unit managers have a handle on the business and how it shapes their expectations. At AT&T, for example, top management could call for a revised report with as little as 24 hours notice.

Effective Feedback and Support

Effective feedback and support also make a huge difference. Management reports are not meant to be one-way communication, not meant to be something that is done once a year whether they are needed or not, and not meant to be devoid of strategy. Headquarters has the obligation to reply quickly as reports are submitted, and to coordinate among them. And this two-way communication needs to extend straight on down the line. We've had the opportunity across a wide range of companies to see how the lower levels of the organization act in the annual planning cycle. It is not uncommon to hear line managers complain about how their budget was cut "because management needed to trim some costs." Just as we'd advocate a two-way dialog between SBU management and the CEO/CFO to establish high-level strategic operating and capital plans, we would also expect a two-way dialog between line managers and SBU management. It is only when the chain extends all the way down the line that plans get built on a solid understanding of competitive dynamics and operating conditions.

High-Impact Training Program

A high-impact training program builds morale because decisions get made quickly and early wins can be held out as examples of value creation. It is important that training be much more than a paper tiger. Train for impact. Train for lasting cultural change. Get people excited about training. Ensure training is built around customized content that resonates with managers in a way that off-the-shelf training never can. There will be more on this theme later in the chapter.

Value-Based Resource Allocations

Value-based resource allocations are like fresh meat to a tiger—they are often incentive enough for your employees. Approval of a capital spending plan is a real morale builder for most employees. They get new toys to play with. To make it really exciting, the last step should be to tie compensation design to performance measurement.

Incentive Design

Incentive design is a powerful motivator, but is usually the last major change in an EBM system—last because everyone usually wants to try out the new system before putting their pay at risk in a system that has not been stress-tested yet.

EBM for Strategy

Remember that Chapter 2 confirms that the largest impact on current stock price was caused by changes in expectations about three- to five-year earnings growth—a useful proxy for expected long-term earnings growth. Think about what this says about the importance of strategy—the long-run future of your company. Figure 10.4 provides a framework we first introduced in Chapter 2.

EBM asks two questions relating to strategic choices. About existing assets the question is: "What is the likelihood of exceeding expectations? And of new investment the question is: "Can you create value by putting new capital into the business?" If the answer to both questions is "yes," then you are in the upper left-hand box of Figure 10.4 and you should not only keep the business—you should commit more investment to grow it. If the

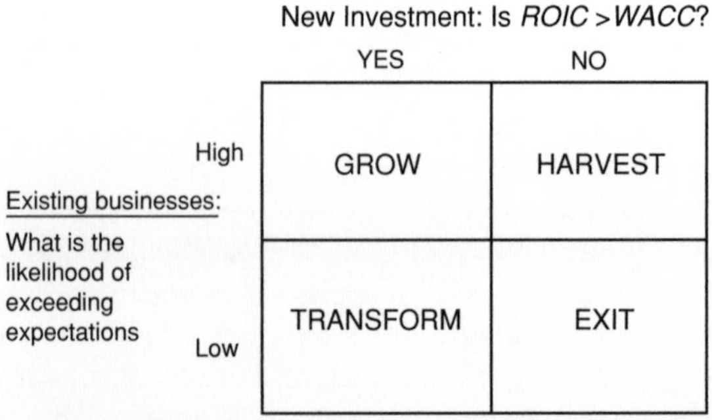

FIGURE 10.4 An EBM framework for strategy.

answer to both questions is no, it means that you cannot extract value with a turnaround, nor can new investment earn the cost of capital. Therefore it is best to exit the business either by selling it to someone who can manage it better than you, or by closing it down.

The interesting boxes in Figure 10.4 are in the lower left and upper right corners. If the business cannot earn more than the cost of capital on new money invested in it but can still exceed expectations, then it can be harvested. Remember, however, that this implies no reinvestment unless it can earn more than the cost of capital.

If the existing business seems unlikely to exceed expectations but new capital can be invested profitably, then a transformation is taking place. This situation is found when there are rapid changes in technology or the competitive environment. Polaroid film, for example, was a tremendous success due to its instant film development capability. But when digital cameras began to have sufficient resolution to allow the photographer to instantaneously view the picture and to print it, the obvious conclusion was that Polaroid had to transform by investing in new technology. It failed to do so and went bankrupt. In the same industry Kodak radically restructured itself and invested in the new digital technology, doing better than expected. More recently Kodak pursued niche imaging fields, such as medical imaging, where it can garner higher returns.

Most managers have little difficulty understanding what it means to earn more than the cost of capital on new investment. But what does it mean to exceed expectations? There are two sides to the issue—whose expectations, and what does it mean to exceed them? First, let's talk about who sets expectations. Top management does. Expectations are the best estimate of what can be achieved with sustainable effort, i.e., average performance. Not a stretch target, it is a target that you can beat about half of the time and fail to beat the other half of the time. And the expected value of anything is its average. Expectations are neither stretch targets nor underestimates. Your team should be able to beat expectations about half the time. What do we mean when we ask "Can you exceed expectations?" in Figure 10.4? Of course you can exceed expectations—but only half the time—so that is not the point. What we have in mind is the ability to exceed expectations in a way that really has a major impact on the value of your firm. These opportunities are some combination of the size, feasibility, and risk involved—which combine to make up value.

Once again, the subjective nature of EBM is made evident. A risk to one manager is an opportunity to another. The bigger the risk, the bigger the opportunity on the upside and the greater the potential for failure. When considering two opportunities, top management must weigh the potential to exceed expectations along the three dimensions that we discussed earlier. First, if the project ends up in the high end of expectations, how much value will it create? Second, what must be achieved to obtain these results? Does your company have the people and resources to do the job? Finally, how feasible is it to achieve Can your firm pull it off? These are the subjective issues that one must wrestle with when making a decision.

Phases of Implementation

Too often EBM is a staff-captured exercise that has little or no impact on decision making by operations managers. The reason for implementing value creation as an objective for all the management of your company is that it is the best criterion for what is meant by a "sustainable competitive advantage." Ultimately the issue boils down to the impact on the value of the firm. Therefore, implement for impact. Proceed in the three stages shown in Figure 10.5.

First, design the approach by building a preliminary valuation model of the firm—one that consolidates headquarters operations with those of business units. You will have to decide which headquarters costs are to be allocated to the business units, decide on transfer pricing guidelines among business units, and figure out what common assumptions will be necessary (e.g., the methodology for the cost of capital). You will need to coordinate the timing and content for management reports submitted by each business unit as part of the planning process. And perhaps most important, you will need to decide on the training process and who will be trained.

Management reports are one of the primary formal ways of communicating the strategy and the value drivers of business units. The information that they contain should be an integral part of your planning system, and they should always be ready, on 24 hours notice, to be updated as the competitive environment changes. At one company, a new manager who was just starting as the CEO of a business unit said to us that the management report outlined in Figure 10.6 (about 25 pages long) contained exactly the right amount and kind of information to save him weeks of time in becoming familiarized with the unit.

From experience, we can say that the most important but also the most abused section of the management report is the strategy statement. It is supposed to be a clear exposition of how the business unit is going to create and maintain a sustainable competitive advantage. What usually comes back from business units is a mission statement instead of a strategy. For example, "Our strategy is to gain market share," or "Our strategy is to develop a brand name." These are mission statements. If your mission is to gain market share, you need to flesh out the value that it will create, and the actions that must be carried out to beat competition and to beat expectations. A strategy statement should make tradeoffs explicit—what actions are *not* being taken? A strategy statement is useless without good compet-

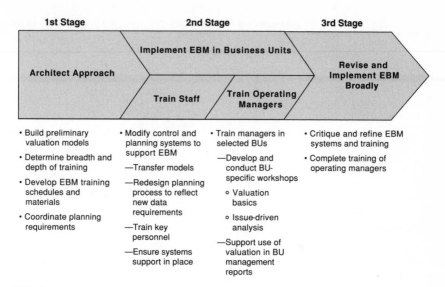

FIGURE 10.5 Three stages of implementation.

itive intelligence about what competition is doing to win, and without any thought about what can be done to defeat competition.

To answer the question "What is the value creation potential of your strategy?" it is necessary to provide a discounted cash flow valuation of each business unit and, therefore, a valuation of its strategy. Both the strategy and its valuation require a multiyear (in fact, an infinite) horizon. Value becomes a way of making tradeoffs between higher profits in the short term and lower profits in the future, such as the retail banking example given at the beginning of this chapter. Having a valuation of your business unit also makes it possible to work out the value created from better performance on value drivers.

Another use for valuation is that it becomes necessary to understand what was behind the changes in value from one time period to the next. Which expectations were exceeded and which were unfulfilled? What were the differences between actual and expected performance on value drivers? How and why did expectations for the future change? The conversations that result from these (and related) value-creation questions generally sharpen management's understanding of strategy and improve decision making.

The management report also documents all major resource requests. The business unit must provide justification for its major capital spending requests, but it must also plan several years ahead to forecast its human resource needs as well. Also, headquarters can aggregate all business unit plans to better plan funds requirements and to know how to reallocate

Management Report Design

Section	Contents
Strategy summary	• Mission and strategic intent • Detailed market assessment • Key value drivers • Threats and opportunities • Key planning initiatives
Valuation results	• Value • Key assumptions • Changes from previous submissions
Resource requirements	• Near- and long-term resource requirements (both physical and human capital) • NPV of incremental investments

Plan forecast summary	• Financial overview of 10-year forecast
	  —ROIC
	  —Revenue
	  —Market size and share
	  —Unit costs and revenue
	  —Operating margin
	  —Capital turns

ROIC/ROE diagrams	• Business projections • Key competitor comparisons
Sensitivity and scenario analysis	• Value-driven sensitivities • Value impact of threats outlined above
Key performance metrics	• Projections for performance • Proposed process for auditing performance
Cross-business issues	• Discussion of key issues between business units
Detailed financial statements	• 10-year income statement, balance sheet, and cash flow statement

FIGURE 10.6 Suggested management report.

excess human and capital resources in one area to other areas where growth makes these resources scarce.

The plan forecast summary contains 10-year forecasts of the financial statements of the business unit with explanations of the high-level value drivers such as revenue growth, market size and share, the return on invested capital, operating margin, and capital turns. It should also provide as much competitive intelligence as possible about comparable company performance on these value drivers.

The report should also contain sensitivity analyses of how the value changes when operating value drivers change. But even more important are various strategic scenarios. Each one should be a consistent set of assumptions based on a specific threat or opportunity. For example, suppose that your company is a gold mine that has hedged against fluctuations in the price of gold, and the price of gold goes up. What will happen to your stock price relative to the price of competitors who have not hedged? How will the price change affect production and maintenance/investment decisions? Will capital spending increase or decrease, and with what effect on long-term expected cash flows?

Finally, the management report should contain cross–business unit problems; otherwise they can easily be overlooked. For example, is one unit cannibalizing the sales of another unit, or is transfer pricing fair?

Implementing EBM for Impact

Impact means making better value-creation decisions immediately. This means that training must transition to decision making even before the training has ended.

Most training programs use abstractions to teach principles that may (but probably will not) be used at a later date. The instructor, in an attempt to keep preparation time to a minimum, usually chooses highly stylized cases to work on. They are good cases, of course—but they are not your cases, not your people, and probably not even your business. To find immediate impact, driven by low-hanging fruit, it requires some careful work ahead of time. In most cases the trainees will expect that nothing will happen as a direct result of the training program—that it will be a paper exercise. That is exactly what you do not want to happen.

Somehow an implementation team has to be selected. The quality of management on the team is a huge signal about the importance of EBM to top management. If the CEO is serious, the team will be led by a respected manager, preferably an operating manager rather than a staff person. Training for impact starts with the right decision about who gets trained and in what order. This can be a thorny problem in large multibusiness companies with several layers of management—e.g., corporate, group, division, business unit, and sub business unit. Remember that buy-in at the top of the organization comes first and is necessary. But at the end of the day, the EBM system will have little or no impact and no sticking power unless middle- and lower-level operating managers believe that it helps them maximize the value of the firm.

Once top management support has been achieved, then a training program for the firm should be designed for maximum impact. We recommend training the financial and planning officers first. They usually have the right accounting and math background to quickly master the most complex of the three-part system—the discounted cash flow valuation.

Training kicks off with an introduction to EBM by the corporate CFO, to whom the trainees have direct reporting responsibility. Next, there is a review of the three components of the EBM system using corporate level data. They are shown how the company was valued using analyst forecasts, and this is compared with management forecasts. The trainees are shown the effect of exceeding expectations for each of several key value drivers. And there is a discussion of how comparable companies are performing. During the afternoon of the first day they work through a hands-on valuation of the company in order to become familiar with the spreadsheets, the cost of capital, the continuing value, and so on.

The next training step is usually separated from the first by one or two weeks. It is attended by the business unit financial officers and planning staff, who are required to present a valuation of their business unit in front of their peers. (There is nothing like peer pressure to motivate a homework assignment.) One thing that often happens during these presentations is that the business units get to know each other better. Sometimes this reveals issues that need immediate attention—for example, the strategy of one unit may unintentionally cannibalize the strategy of a sister unit.

Once the financial officers are trained, they are asked to facilitate the preparation for a one- or two-day training event for the key decision makers that affect the value of their business unit. The first decision centers around who should attend the training. It is essential that the top management of the business unit be there and that they set the agenda. It may, depending on the circumstances, be advisable to invite other company employees from business units that are either suppliers or customers of the business unit holding the training.

In order to have impact, about four to six weeks of preparation are necessary. This is because the agenda will typically look like Figure 10.7. Training starts with an introduction delivered by the business unit head. At some companies the CEO of the entire company does this in person or in a videotape. Either way the message is clearly stated that the company is implementing a planning and performance measurement system. This system is directed at increasing the market value of the company, and is intended to be driven all the way down to the grass roots of the business units by using value drivers. Before very long, compensation will be tied to value creation.

Following the introduction there is an overview of Expectations-Based Management and valuation concepts—a presentation that is kept simple and straightforward, and that shows how to do a rough-cut valuation on the back of an envelope. Next the business unit finance staff shows off the results of the four to six weeks of preparation. They present the value of the business unit—often this is the first estimate that any of the employees have seen. The BU officers present the management report they have prepared, and discuss the operating value drivers that will, if changed, have the

Business Unit Operating Manager EBM Training
Typical Schedule

Time	Activity	Lead
8:00–8:15 AM	Introduction	BU head
8:15–9:30 AM	Overview of value-based planning	Corporate Staff
9:30–10:30 AM	Valuation concepts	BU Finance Staff
10:30–10:45 AM	Break	
10:45–11:30 AM	Preliminary BU valuation and management report	BU Finance Staff
11:30–12:30 PM	Targeted valuation issues and discussion	BU Finance Staff
12:30–1:30 PM	Lunch	
1:30–2:45 PM	Value improvement brainstorming • Introduction • Breakout group discussions • Overall synthesis	Breakout groups
2:45–4:45 PM	Valuation and prioritization of ideas • Key assumption brainstorming • Preliminary modeling • Idea prioritization	Breakout groups
4:45–5:00 PM	Wrap-up	BU head

FIGURE 10.7 Typical agenda for business unit training.

greatest impact on the value of the firm. They provide a clear understanding of the expectations that are already baked into the value of the business unit and what will happen to that value if expectations are not met.

All of this is interesting and definitely concrete. It is focused directly at the hopes and plans of the unit. But the exciting part takes place next.

The assembled group is broken down into small teams whose task is to brainstorm new ideas—not ones contained in the management report that had been discussed in the morning. These new ideas are ranked by their feasibility and impact as shown in Figure 10.8. For examples, at a regulated telecommunications company, a fairly large business unit was providing operator services to assist international phone calls—services that required special language skills. Callers were billed a surcharge for the operator and translation assistance, and all minutes of service were billed at the same rate. Yet some language skills also required additional expertise and, being rare, were in high demand. At the brainstorming part of training, an executive observed that although the fee for a minute of telecommunications was regulated, the fee per minute of translator services was not. Why, then, did the company not charge a greater fee for the rarer operator services rather than turn customers away or subject them to long queues? When the team worked out the value impact, the idea turned out to be worth several hundred million dollars. What was fun about being an observer to this event was seeing the instant application of the knowledge of people in the

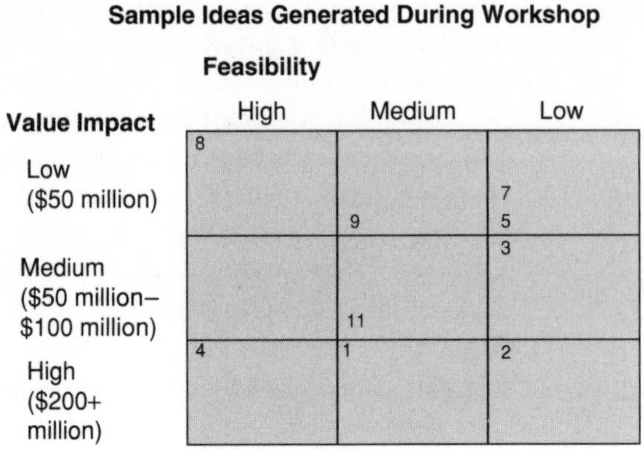

Sample Ideas Generated During Workshop

Feasibility

Value Impact	High	Medium	Low
Low ($50 million)	8	9	7 5
Medium ($50 million– $100 million)		11	3
High ($200+ million)	4	1	2

FIGURE 10.8   Value creation ideas parsed by impact and feasibility.

room to a new opportunity—and the excitement that it generated. The business unit CEO immediately formed a task force to pursue the idea. Even better, rumors spread throughout the company that EBM training was actually better than having a root canal.

Figure 10.8 is a simple screening device to keep the idea generation realistic. Big ideas were those that had the potential for raising the value of the business unit by 10 percent or more. And the feasibility of the idea was also challenged. Big ideas were no good if, for example, they required passage of a new amendment to the Constitution or a unanimous Supreme Court opinion.

The new ideas frequently center on managing the balance sheet better because, often for the first time, business unit managers are asked to be responsible for managing uses of capital as well as sources of income. Chapter 6, on managing capital efficiency, dwells on better balance sheet management as a source of value, but to whet your appetite, let's discuss a few more examples here. At a paper mill, success was measured in terms of speed—the number of meters of paper per second through the mill. But a new perspective that increased value was a simple change to the number of meters of *finished product* per second. Stated this way the management problem becomes obvious. Faster throughput resulted in more breakdowns and more defects. Greater value resulted from running somewhat slower.

CSX, the railroad company, hauled freight through the Rocky Mountains at night using three engines (two at the front and one at the back) to move enormously long trains at 36 miles per hour. Speed was the objective. But when value creation became the objective, they changed to two locomotives per train, running at 24 miles per hour. The trains still got to their destination in time to unload the next day, and the company was able to spend one-third less capital on locomotives.

The feasibility of a project is entirely a subjective opinion, but it plays an important role in Expectations-Based Management. The lower the feasibility of a project, the lower are the expectations about it. Projects with the greatest potential not only have a major impact on the value of the company, but they are feasible—that is, highly likely to succeed.

EBM training can be a classroom exercise where participants learn the theory and where there is very little impact. Or it can be a type of cultural change process with high impact that follows from the pre-work by a small team that prepares a management report and develops value drivers for discussion.

The Art of Using Value Drivers

Part of the preparation of each training session is the identification and use of operating value drivers. This is a simple concept that is tricky to implement. Let's start with one of the key performance measures of EBM—namely, the difference between actual and expected return on invested capital (*ROIC*). Figure 10.9 provides a generic *ROIC* tree that breaks down *ROIC* before taxes into operating margin and capital turns.

Think of operating margin as the profit before taxes that your business unit earns and capital turnover as the profit per dollar invested. Together, when operating margin is multiplied by capital turnover, they determine the return on invested capital. The difference between the expected *ROIC* and the actual *ROIC* measures your business unit's contribution to the value of the company. Often, the segment-based reporting found, for example, in a company's SEC Form 10-K gives enough information to calculate the return on assets employed, if not the *ROIC*.

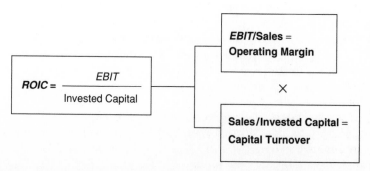

FIGURE 10.9   A generic *ROIC* tree.

The difference between return on assets and *ROIC* is that assets include nonoperating assets, such as marketable securities and cash, and may exclude operating liabilities, such as accounts payable. Invested capital includes net operating working capital, goodwill, net property plant and equipment, and deferred taxes. In spite of the difference between assets and invested capital, it is useful to search out competitive benchmarking data to compare your business unit *ROIC* with other companies and with itself over time. Has your *ROIC* been rising or falling over time? How does your *ROIC* compare with that of comparable companies?

It has been our experience that managers quickly digest the concept of value drivers, but are rarely experienced enough to create an operating value driver tree that addresses the challenges that confront them in a useful way. Standardized cost accounting systems easily and mechanically churn out hundreds of useless financial value drivers. The art of using value drivers successfully requires that we find just the right twist to link the value drivers to the issue at hand.

A Case Example

What follows is a disguised case example where value drivers were used to solve the challenge of turning around a company, and created a little over $500 million dollars of value. Trilink was the earth station provider of satellite dishes that uplinked signals to and downlinked signals from geosynchronous satellites. An example of everyday use is what happens when you make a credit card purchase at a shopping mall. When your card is swiped, the electronic information goes to a transmission dish located atop the mall and from there to a satellite. It then relays the signal to a receiving dish at your credit card company where authorization is processed and beamed back to the satellite, and from there back to the dish at the mall and back to the store—all in a few seconds. There were only a few competitors in the satellite dish industry. Hughes had about 50 percent of the market, Trilink had about 10 percent, and Scientific Aerials had about 15 percent. The remainder was held by smaller companies including Gilco, an Israeli company.

Trilink was losing $9.9 million before taxes and was thinking of selling itself. Its pro forma income statement and (beginning-of-year) balance sheet are given in Figure 10.10.

The return on invested capital at the time was

$$ROIC = EBIT/\text{Sales} \times \text{Sales}/\text{Invested capital}$$
$$= -4/201 \times 201/(\text{NPPE} + \text{Operating working capital})$$
$$= -.0199 \times 201/(40 - 2 + 50 \times 33 - 16)$$
$$= -.0199 \times 201/109 = -.0199 \times 1.84$$
$$= -3.67\%$$

INCOME STATEMENT		
Price per unit		
High-tech dish		6,000
Low-tech dish		2,700
Number of units		
High-tech dish		20,000
Low-tech dish		30,000
Total revenue		201,000,000
COGS		164,000,000
SG&A		37,000,000
Depreciation		4,000,000
EBIT		-4,000,000
Interest expense		5,900,000
EBT		-9,900,000
Taxes @ 35%		0
Net Income		-9,900,000

BALANCE SHEET (BOY)		
Cash		2,000,000
Inventory		50,000,000
Accts. Receivable		33,000,000
Gross PP&E		80,000,000
Accum. Depr.		-40,000,000
Net PP&E		40,000,000
Total assets		125,000,000
Accts. Payable		16,000,000
Short-term debt		40,000,000
Long-term debt		19,000,000
Common stock		20,000,000
Retained earnings		30,000,000
Total liabilities		125,000,000

FIGURE 10.10   Trilink pro forma income statement and balance sheet.

The generic *ROIC* value driver tree is illustrated in Figure 10.11. Because Trilink's operating margin was negative, it was obvious to everyone that it had to be improved.

The challenge was either to sell the company for what it would fetch given its current and expected performance, or to turn it around and then decide whether to sell it or keep it. We can extend the *ROIC* tree analysis one or two levels as shown in Figures 10.12 and 10.13, but they are still too generic. We want to fix the operating margin, but how? The tree must be extended further and linked to specific actions that will improve the margin.

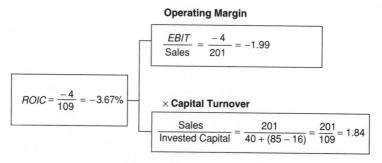

$EBIT$ = Earnings before interest and taxes

Invested capital = Net property, plant, and equipment + Operating working capital

FIGURE 10.11   Trilink's generic *ROIC* tree.

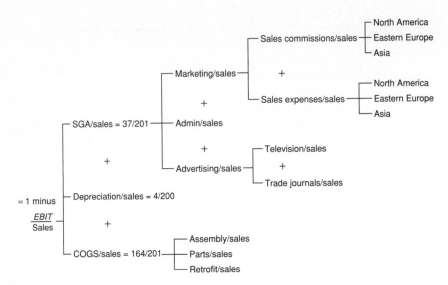

FIGURE 10.12 Operating margin for Trilink.

We were invited to hear a presentation at the company that suggested the key value driver was economies of scale in production. Figure 10.14 graphs the cost per satellite dish against the annual total number of dishes sold. Two broad categories of dishes were produced in the industry. For simplicity we have called them high-tech and low-tech. Only high-tech production costs are plotted in the figure. The cost per unit was obtained by dividing each company's cost of goods sold by the number of units produced. Note that Hughes has a much lower cost of goods sold per unit— $2,800 per dish versus $3,700 at Trilink. If Figure 10.12 were redone using Hughes costs, then Trilink's *EBIT* would increase by $900 per unit multiplied by 30,000 units of high-tech production—that is, by $27 million. This would improve Trilink's operating margin to 11.44 percent, i.e., $23/$201,

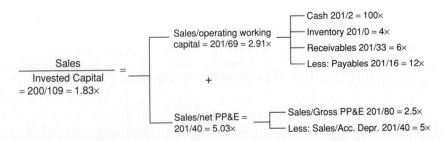

FIGURE 10.13 Capital turnover for Trilink.

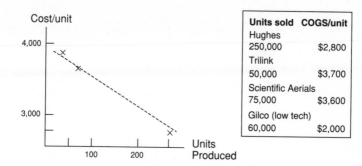

FIGURE 10.14   Cost per unit versus number of units produced.

and its *ROIC* to 21.05 percent. Unfortunately, in order to achieve this result, Trilink would have to sell 250,000 units, and to slash the sales price per unit to capture market share.

Economies of scale was rejected as a value driver because it was impossible to capture the market share and still become profitable. Another set of value drivers had to be uncovered.

In the next few weeks the team learned a few more significant facts. First, Trilink had won multiple awards for having the best quality of equipment in the industry. Second, it produced about 30,000 high-tech and 20,000 low-tech units per year. And third, the defect rate on high-tech units was 10 percent on average. It did not seem to make sense. Why would the company with the highest-quality equipment also have such a high defect rate?

Then the team saw the light. Trilink was primarily an assembly operation where technicians put together a batch of dishes using an instruction manual. For small batches, the instructions were complicated and it was easy to make mistakes at first—mistakes that would be eliminated with practice. But with small batches, it took too long to learn to avoid costly mistakes. Table 10.1 shows the relationship between batch size and defect rates on satellite dishes.

TABLE 10.1   Defect Rates, Batch Size and Retrofit Costs at Trilink*

	Batch Size	Number of Dishes	Defect Rate	Retrofit Cost	New defect Rate
High-tech dishes	< 50	5,000	20%	$2,500	NA
	51–200	15,000	10%	$2,500	NA
Low-tech dishes	> 200	10,000	5%	$2,500	3%
	< 200	20,000	5%	$500	3%

*Illustrative

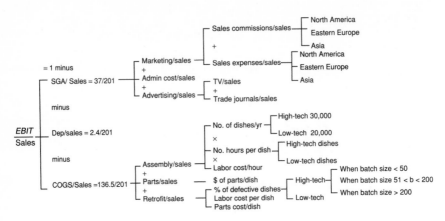

FIGURE 10.15 New operating margin for Trilink.

The team also realized that Gilco was better able to achieve low-cost production of the low-tech dishes than we were. Therefore, we decided to examine the cost and feasibility of setting up an outsourcing arrangement with Gilco. Before long it became clear that they could deliver low-tech dishes (all 20,000) at a cost of only $2,200 with a two percent defect rate and similar retrofit costs.

Figure 10.15 shows a new operating margin tree for Trilink, assuming that the minimum batch size would be 200 units, and that all low-tech dishes would be outsourced with Gilco. Since two-thirds of our high-tech demand was batches of less than 200 per order, we were concerned about the effect that a 200-unit minimum might have on sales. The results of a marketing study indicated that sales would not decline because the lower defect rate would increase sales enough to make up for units lost from low batch size purchasing requirements.

The analysis of batch size as a key value driver starts with the result of the marketing study that affirms the assumption that batch size does not affect sales revenues. It does, however, affect the cost of goods sold, decreasing it from $164 million to $158.55 million. There are balance sheet effects, too. First, there is an inventory reduction of $6.25 million because fewer defective units are returned for retrofitting. There is also a reduction in accounts receivable of $2.07 million because a higher percentage of dishes are paid for rather than being returned for retrofit. We assumed that these reductions in operating working capital are applied to reducing the amount of short-term debt outstanding (this year) and that, consequently, interest payments are down by $831,866.

The decision to outsource the low-tech units to Gilco resulted in a direct reduction in cost of goods sold of $22,100,000 ($500 per unit times 20,000 units and additional savings due to no defect responsibility). On the

INCOME STATEMENT	
Price per unit	
High-tech dish	6,000
Low-tech dish	2,700
Number of units	
High-tech dish	20,000
Low-tech dish	30,000
Total revenue	201,000,000
COGS	136,450,000
SG&A	37,000,000
Depreciation	2,400,000
EBIT	25,150,000
Interest expense	3,675,100
EBT	21,474,900
Taxes @ 35%	0
Net Income	21,474,900

BALANCE SHEET (BOY)	
Cash	2,000,000
Inventory	30,317,164
Accts. Receivable	30,931,343
Gross PP&E	48,000,000
Accum. Depr.	–24,000,000
Net PP&E	24,000,000
Total assets	87,248,507
Accts. Payable	19,502,488
Short-term debt	17,750,995
Long-term debt	19,000,000
Common stock	20,000,000
Retained earnings	10,995,025
Total liabilities	87,248,507

FIGURE 10.16   Revised Trilink pro forma income statement and balance sheet.

balance sheet, the effect was seen to be an increase in accounts payable of $3,502,488, an inventory decrease of $13,432,836, and a sale of $16 million for net property plant and equipment for $4 million. The net capital amount can be applied to payoff of short-term debt and the consequent reduction of interest expenses ($1,393,035). Figure 10.16 shows the revised income statement and balance sheet.

The effect of increasing the batch size (and consequently lowering the defect rate and the cost of goods sold) and of outsourcing the assembly of low-tech units was to raise net income from a loss of $9.9 million to a profit of $21.5 million. This was accomplished in a little over a year's time.

Not only did the profit get better; considerably less capital was employed. Figure 10.17 shows that the effect was to raise the before-tax return on invested capital from –3.7 percent to positive 37.1 percent.

This example serves to illustrate five important points:

1. Generic financial *ROIC* trees are not very useful unless they are driven down to the level of specific operating value drivers.
2. Value drivers must be selected so that they are tied to the real issues of the company. In this case, economies of scale, a common value driver, was inappropriate for solving Trilink's problems. Instead, batch size and outsourcing proved to be the key value drivers.
3. Value drivers have both income statement and balance sheet ramifications. They change operating margins as well as capital turns when affecting *ROIC*.

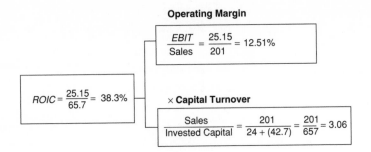

$$EBIT = \text{Earnings before interest and taxes}$$

Invested capital = Net property, plant, and equipment + Operating working capital

FIGURE 10.17   Trilink's new generic *ROIC* tree.

4. There are tradeoffs among value drivers that cannot be ignored. These tradeoffs may show up in a single period or across periods.
5. A value driver tree is not a good way of capturing the multiperiod aspects of decisions. In the Trilink case, for example, the cash from selling excess capacity reduced debt once and only once, but the higher operating margin was permanent.

EBM for Small Companies and Family-Owned Businesses

There is not really much different about the way EBM is managed in small or family-owned businesses except that it is easier to fall into the trap that external communication should be between management and current owners only. Potential investors are what give the company its value, and that value is the wealth of the family shareholders. Management information may be restricted from dissemination to the open market at the request of current family owners. Still, all owners must be prepared for the day when shares are sold to the public. Because the number of owners is usually quite small, it is much easier for management to understand their expectations in order to exceed them. There can be direct communication between owners and managers.

Another piece of advice is to separate cash flows earned from operations from those earned on excess marketable securities. Family-owned businesses often build up a large balance of excess marketable securities whose interest and divided income are commingled with the operating income of the business. When the financing flows of the securities are separated, the company's return on operating invested capital is often low and in need of improvement.

Summary

As with any other management system, EBM will survive the enthusiasm of current management much better if:

- It is kept as simple as possible.
- Support and training are provided.
- It really does help to create value, and internal performance measures are highly correlated with the market-adjusted return to shareholders
- It is linked to incentive design.

If line managers are not enthusiastic about EBM, then it will not survive new fads and their blushing popularity.

All too often new performance measurement systems fail because measured internal performance is not adequately linked to the returns to shareholders. EBM has been proven to have the necessary link. Nevertheless, it too will fail unless operating managers are confident that the new EBM system will result in better decisions. Implementation cannot be a staff-captured exercise. It should be implemented in a way that has immediate tangible impact on the value of each business unit—by improving the performance on value drivers, or simply by generating new ideas, and by doing so at the training sessions early on in the implementation process. The last step is to tie performance measurement to EBM-based incentives.

PART III

Other Points of View

This third section is still written with management in mind, but it turns the perspective around to view Expectations-Based Management from the other side of the looking glass—the investor's point of view (Chapter 11) and with an eye toward public policy (Chapter 13). It also tries to provide a frank comparison of the most popular value-based management systems with Expectations-Based Management, the new kid on the block (Chapter 12).

CHAPTER 11

Investor Relations: Understanding the Investor's Perspective

Most of this book is written from the perspective of top management. The lessons to be learned from this chapter are still intended for top management; however, we turn the telescope around and look in from the other end—from the investor's perspective. The issues are the same, but we believe that there are a few things that can be learned if top management steps away from the daily concerns about performance measurement, planning and budgeting, incentive design, and communications. Management needs to understand just how hard it is to beat the expectations of investors. Management also needs to understand how investors are able to access company-specific information (without ever talking to the company). And management needs to understand how investors are clientele that cannot affect the value of the firm in some instances, and are crucial in other cases. So put on your investor's hat, step out of your management shoes, and take a walk outside of your normal frame of reference.

We establish three principles in this chapter. First, it is not easy to exceed investor expectations year after year. Understand this reality and avoid setting aspirations unreasonably high. Second, realize that regardless of whether performance is expected to be above or below industry norms, a company's total return to shareholders is expected to be the same as the cost of equity if performance meets expectations, so set targets accordingly. Third, most corporations have investor clienteles that are attracted to some aspect of the company—maybe its dividend policy, maybe its growth potential, or maybe its environmental awareness. The reality is that it doesn't matter who your investor clientele is because a change in policy will attract a new clientele without necessarily changing the value of the firm. For example, there is no evidence to support the assertion that a change in dividend policy will change the value of the firm, even though it may change your investor clientele.

Once these principles are grounded in facts, we proceed to the process of doing something about it by implementing a better investor relations plan.

First Principle—It Is Not Easy to Exceed Expectations

The average life of a company is actually shorter than the life of the average person (although there are a few exceptions), and during a company's life it may exceed expectations roughly half of the time. Taken together, these facts imply that it is hard to put together a string of years of superior market performance. Read on to learn just how hard it is.

Queen and Roll (1987) published a paper in the *Financial Analysts Journal* where they introduced a mortality table for companies. It is a simple but fundamental concept. Companies are born, they grow, get married (via merger and acquisition), divorce or separate (via divestiture or spinoff), and pass away (via bankruptcy). Suppose that we ask a few basic questions. If listing on a major exchange is not the actual birth of a company (witnessed in the owner's garage), it is at least a form of baptism. Once listed, what is the life expectancy of a company? How long will it be on average before it acquires or is acquired? How long until it has a major divestiture or spinoff?

Queen and Roll's sample starts with all firms listed on the NYSE and AMEX as of July 1, 1962, then follows them for 23 years, up to 1985. Table 11.1 shows the survival rates when the companies are rank-ordered by size (market capitalization). There is a strong relationship between firm size and survival. Eight percent of the companies in the smallest decile fail to survive the first year, roughly 50 percent disappear within 12 years, and two-thirds fail to survive 23 years. The largest firms have much higher survival rates. Only one percent fail in the first year and roughly 80 percent survive 23 years. Still, it may come as a surprise to many readers that 20 percent of America's best known companies fail to last two decades.

Over the first ten years of the sample period, the smallest firms were seven to eight times more likely to fail as the largest firms. The cumulative failure rate is six to seven times greater in ten years than during the first year.

Total return to shareholders is positive (relative to the market) if expectations are met. During its life we might ask how a company performed. Of course, this brings us right back to the question about how to evaluate performance. From an investor's point of view, the first thing to remember is that he or she cannot put price earnings ratios into the bank. The only thing that matters is the total return—dividends and capital gains—that the investor can put into the bank. When we discuss total return to shareholders (TRS), there are two very important guiding principles to remember:

1. *The expected risk-adjusted performance of all actively traded securities is the same.* This is a fact, not an assertion, but it is hard to swallow at

TABLE 11.1   Total Corporate Mortality Based on Size (1962–1985)

Size decile	Total Cumulative Mortality After N Years						
	1	5	10	15	20	23	
1	8.0%	29.9%	45.9%	55.8%	63.1%	66.9%	↔ Smallest
2	5.5	26.2	43.9	56.8	64.5	67.6	
3	5.7	25.3	41.1	50.8	65.0	69.0	
4	4.8	22.0	37.8	50.1	61.4	66.2	
5	4.5	21.2	36.6	47.7	58.7	64.8	
6	4.9	21.4	34.0	44.6	58.2	62.1	
7	3.8	18.1	28.4	38.8	52.8	56.6	
8	3.2	13.2	21.8	30.3	42.1	45.5	
9	1.8	8.2	13.4	20.7	27.3	32.4	
10	1.0	4.2	7.1	9.2	15.8	20.0	↔ Largest

Source: Queen, M., and R. Roll, "Firm Mortality: Predictions and Effects," *Financial Analysts Journal*, May/June 1987, p. 23. Copyright © 1987 by CFA Institute. Reproduced with permission of CFA Institute in the format trade book.

first. At any point in time all securities are priced so that they are all held by someone. The implication is that $1,000 invested in bonds is worth the same $1,000 invested in stocks at the same point in time, even though, due to differences in risk, the two investments have very different expected rates of return. For example, had you invested $1,000 in a 90-day Treasury bill and rolled over this position (with no transaction costs) between 1963 and 2002, you would have earned an average of 2.5 percent per year. The same $1,000 invested in large-capitalization equities (with reinvested dividends) would have averaged 10.5 percent per year. At any point in time the choice of how to spend $1,000 is a matter of indifference from a market point of view. This implies that we cannot compare the total returns on securities without first adjusting for differences in risk. As shown in Table 11.2, in the long run, riskier securities earn higher returns.

TABLE 11.2   Risk and Return, U.S. Securities, 1963–2002

	Geometric Return	Standard Deviation
Small companies	19.6%	41.8%
S&P 500	10.5	16.6
Long-term corporate bonds	8.4	3.2
Long-term U.S. government bonds	7.0	3.1
Short-term U.S. Treasury bills	2.5	2.5

Source: Monitor analysis

2. *It is very difficult to exceed expectations.* Take the S&P index of 500 companies, for example. It was created in 1957. Forty years later, in 1997, only 74 of the original 500 remained. Remember though, that from an investor's point of view, to earn excess returns a stock has to do well vis-à-vis the return on the market and well relative to expectations about the company itself. We took a random sample of 100 companies listed on the NYSE at the beginning of 1993 and tracked them to the end of 2002—ten years in total, covering a bull and a bear market. Table 11.3 shows that only 60 out of the original 100 companies survived all 10 years. Of the survivors, only one company had positive returns every year, and no company beat the market every year. In fact, only three out of the 100 companies beat the market five years in a row starting in 1993, and only 16 out of the original 100 beat the market in any five years.

The sobering facts are that 37 percent of medium-sized companies fail within ten years (Table 11.1), that three percent of a randomly selected sample of companies beat the market five years out of ten (Table 11.3), and no company beat it seven consecutive years out of ten (Table 11.3). For management the lesson is the practicality of expectations setting. The CEO who asks his management to double the stock price in the next three years is setting them up for a very low chance of success—because they must exceed investor expectations by a wide margin each year. If there is a 50–50 chance of exceeding expectations, then there is only a 12.5 percent chance of success in this case.

Unfortunately, it is not uncommon to have CEOs put forth unreasonable objectives. One company we worked with had the goal of doubling its market capitalization within two years. The company's share price already reflected short-term expected earnings growth of 20 to 25 percent.

TABLE 11.3   Distribution of Returns (1993–2002) for 100 Randomly Chosen Companies (Chosen in 1993)

Year	Survived	TRS > 0	TRS > Mkt
1993	100	67	46
1994	95	33	25
1995	93	24	9
1996	88	16	5
1997	84	15	3
1998	80	11	1
1999	74	5	0
2000	68	3	0
2001	62	1	0
2002	60	1	0

Source: Monitor analysis

With only a modest dividend payout, this firm could only have increased its market cap by approximately 25 percent if it met these expectations (earning roughly its 12 percent cost of equity for two years). We calculated that with only limited potential to raise long-term growth expectations, this same firm would need to produce roughly 40 to 45 percent earnings growth to meet its share price targets. While this was not unheard of given the industry's history, it was in the ninetieth percentile of industry performance. Although the company still espoused an aspiration to double share price, it adjusted its incentive plans to allow for payouts for reasonable performance below this target.

What TRS Targets Are Reasonable?

Consider the case of Ralston Purina (as written by Campbell and Wansley [1999]). In 1986, the board of directors of Ralston Purina announced that 491,000 shares of stock would be awarded to the company's 14 top executives (160,000 to the CEO) if the stock price closed at or above $100 per share for 10 consecutive days during the next 10 years. The stock price at the time was $63. An increase from $63 to $100 would represent a gain of $811 million for shareholders, and the stock awarded to management would be 6.05 percent of the total. At first glance this seems to be a win-win incentive structure where both management and shareholders benefit.

This would not be a book about Expectations-Based Management unless we asked, "What was the expected stock price performance at the time of the award?" Campbell and Wansley use the Capital Asset Pricing Model to estimate the cost of equity. If all expectations are met, then the stock price should grow at the cost of equity if no dividends are paid, and at the cost of equity minus the dividend yield if they are paid out. Based on this principle, Campbell and Wasley estimated that if Ralston Purina merely earned its cost of equity, it was expected to reach the target of $100 per share in four years and ten months. It actually took four years and five months. During this time period, Ralston's return to shareholders was below the S&P 500 and much below comparables. Figure 11.1 shows Ralston's cumulative performance relative to the index for the five years before the award in 1986, then (starting at zero again) its cumulative performance starting at the award date and covering the following five years. As you can see, Ralston exceeded expectations prior to the award but fell below expectations thereafter.

During the four years and five months that it took to earn the award, Ralston announced share repurchases seven times, with total repurchases amounting to $1.541 billion. As we discussed in Chapter 8, share repurchase programs tend to force the stock price up. Taken together, dividends and repurchases at Ralston averaged 140 percent of net income between 1987 and 1990. The moral of the story is that performance should be set relative to expectations. In this case, management received a handsome reward for earning less than its cost of equity. Figure 11.1 shows very clearly that shareholders did not earn higher-than-expected total returns during the period of time that the incentive scheme was in place.

What might have been done better? The first problem is that the incentive scheme was not linearly related to performance. The deficiencies of "kinked" pay-for-performance plans were discussed in Chapter 9. If the stock never achieved the required $100 benchmark, the executives would still receive their base level compensation. The incentive design had no downside pay at risk. Second, the scheme was more a gift than an incentive plan, because the probability of not achieving the $100 per share benchmark within 10 years was very low. For example, suppose the cost of equity at Ralston was 15 percent and its dividend yield was five percent. Then the stock price would be expected to grow at 10 percent per year. Table 11.4 shows its expected growth path over a 10-year period. By Year 10 Ralston's stock price is expected to be $163.41. Suppose the standard deviation around this is roughly the average for NYSE stocks, i.e. 20 percent, then the 95 percent confidence interval is between $229 and $98. Thus, there is only a two to three percent chance that the company's stock price will be below $100 per share 10 years from now. That is why we say that the incentive scheme was more a gift than a stretch target.

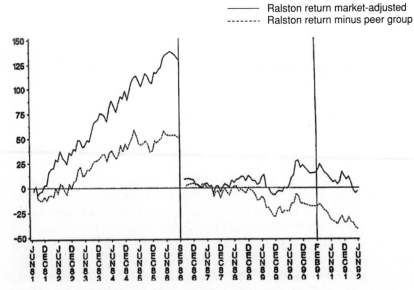

FIGURE 11.1   Cumulative excess returns on Ralston Purina.

Source: Reprinted from *Journal of Financial Economics*, Vol. 51, C. Campbell, J. Wansley, "Stock Price-Based Incentive Contracts and Managerial Performance: The Case of Ralston-Purina Company," pp. 195-217, Copyright © 1999 with permission from Elsevier Science.

TABLE 11.4   Expected Growth Path of Ralston
Purina Stock

Year	Expected Price with 10% Growth	Expected Price with 15% Growth
1986	$63.00	$63.00
1987	69.30	72.45
1988	76.23	83.32
1989	83.85	95.82
1990	92.24	110.19
1991	101.46	126.72
1992	111.61	145.72
1993	122.77	167.58
1994	135.05	192.72
1995	148.55	221.63
1996	163.41	254.87

Source: Monitor analysis

The stock incentive plan was nominally tied to the stock price and, of course, the management and shareholders were both better off the higher the stock price. But as it turned out, the top management got 6.05 percent of the company and the shareholders got normal, expected performance.

Perhaps the plan might have been a stronger incentive if the management was required to put up some of their personal wealth to buy the incentive shares, thereby exposing them to downside risk. Perhaps the incentive shares might have been constructed so that their value was adjusted for expected performance given a benchmark (e.g., given movement in the market or given the returns of competitors.) For example, the target share price might have changed each year (or even each month) as shown by the last column in Table 11.4. Note that the award threshold at the beginning of the fourth year is $110.19 and by the end of the fourth year it rises to $126.72. Ralston did not achieve this level of performance. These aspects of incentive design, how to engineer them, their tax consequences, and a discussion of their pros and cons are found in Chapter 9.

What are the implications so far? Expectations-Based Management requires a realistic understanding of the investor's point of view. The price that an investor is willing to pay for a share of stock is set so that he or she expects to receive the same risk-adjusted return as all other investments of equivalent risk. Your growth in earnings might be eight percent starting at a level of $10 per share and a competitor might be expected to have four percent growth starting at $5 per share, but if the risk-adjusted return is 10 percent, investors will pay

$$S = \$10/(.1 - .08) = \$500 \text{ per share}$$

for your company, and

$$S = \$5/(.1 - .04) = \$83.33 \text{ per share}$$

for the other company. It is tempting, of course, to conclude that owners
of the first company are better off than owners of the second, and they
are if the same amount of money was invested sometime in the past
when the share prices were equal. But a new investor with $100,000 to
spend will be indifferent between the two because the expected return
on them (i.e., 10 percent) is the same. If their growth rates turn out as
expected, then the investor's wealth at the end of the first year with the
first firm is the sum of the dividends received plus the end-of-year value
of 200 shares:

$$\begin{aligned}
S_1 &= 200 \text{ shares } (\$10/\text{share}) + [\$10.80/(.1 - .08)]200 \text{ shares} \\
&= \$2,000 + \$108,000 \\
&= \$110,000
\end{aligned}$$

The same amount of money buys 1,200 shares of the second firm,
which provides the following end-of-year value:

$$\begin{aligned}
S_1 &= 1,200(\$5/\text{share}) + [\$5(1.04)/(.1 - .04)]1,200 \text{ shares} \\
&= \$6,000 + \$104,000 \\
&= \$110,000
\end{aligned}$$

This simple example illustrates that if two firms have the same required
return, and if they meet expectations, they will create the same amount of
wealth for shareholders regardless of their growth rates.

Later on, we shall discuss tax clientele effects that would lead high–tax
bracket individuals to prefer the first firm to the second if capital gains taxes
are higher than taxes on dividends. However, we shall also provide evidence that if a firm changes its dividend policy there is no effect on its
stock price—just a change in clientele.

The market's expectations handicap the performance of companies by
adjusting their stock prices so that on a risk-adjusted basis, they are all
equivalent bets. That is the first step. The second step is that once the
stocks are handicapped (somewhat like a horse race), it becomes quite difficult to pick a winner. It is hard enough to exceed expectations two years
in a row, and virtually impossible to exceed expectations, say, 10 years in
a row. All of this adds up to a better understanding of how to link goals
for the firm to success in the stock market.

Management must beat expected performance in order for shareholder
returns to exceed the cost of equity. Remember that these returns are based
on market prices, not book values.

Second Principle—Learn from the Market

What types of information do investors want? How do they obtain it? How do they act on it? What can you learn from what they know?

In Chapter 2 we reported that changes in analyst expectations about long-term earnings growth had a higher impact on today's share price than any other variable. If the average holding period is less than three years, why should most investors care about long-term earnings growth? The answer is found in the story of a young man who found a small firm to invest in, and every time he bought the stock price went up. For weeks he bought and bought until one day he called his broker and said, "The price has reached a new all-time high—please sell my shares." With a wry smile his broker replied, "To whom?"

If an investor plans to hold a stock for the short run, there is still the problem of what he or she can sell it for. His or her successor stands in an infinite chain of holders, each being concerned of the eventual sale price. In this way, today's price depends on cash flows far into the future—cash flows that must be anticipated when the stock is bought today. This is the reason why a discounted cash flow model of the value of a firm is the most sensible among the many valuation approaches that we might select—and why it is an integral part of an Expectations-Based Management system.

Wall Street Insight

Investor and analyst expectations provide the background for understanding exactly how stock prices are set. Top management is one of many sources of information, not the only source. Even so, top management must communicate to the outside world, both current and potential investors, information about the inner workings of the company that is relevant and useful. Inside the company, top management plays a crucial role in setting the expected performance targets of lower-level management.

Top management stands in the middle between the information needs of investors and the expectations of lower-level management. It can use this position—in the middle—to do a little reality checking, a process that we have nicknamed "Wall Street Insight." The steps in the process are illustrated in Figure 11.2, which is virtually identical to Figure 8.4.

The idea is to figure out how well the value of the company that uses analyst forecasts aligns with the value of the company that uses management forecasts, and to understand the sources of any differences. Often this comparison reveals the important discrepancies that need to be communicated to the market if management believes its vision of the future is better. Revision in the other direction may also be appropriate, because sometimes the market knows better. One such example, based on real experience, can

FIGURE 11.2   Wall Street insight.

be described in the following vignette. At noon one Friday, we received a call from the CEO of a large mineral extraction company who told us that his firm had just been offered to buy the equity that represented controlling interest in a competitor—and there was no premium being asked. We valued the company over the weekend and estimated that its market value was "fair," i.e., that the company was trading at neither a premium nor a discount. A key assumption in our analysis was that, according to the futures prices of the commodity, the market was indicating that the commodity price would rise. The CEO's staff believed the opposite, and he believed them rather than the market. Consequently, he turned down the offer. CEOs get paid to make tough calls, and this was one of them. You may be wondering what happened to the commodity price. It went up as predicted by the market. It has been our experience that when it comes to predicting future spot prices of commodities where there are many players, the forecast implied by market prices is usually quite reasonable—and a better forecast than that made by any individual.

Companies are better at forecasting their own results than the market is. But the market is better at forecasting such things as future interest rates, commodity prices, and the like. Professional analysts spend most of their time digging up high-quality, company-specific information.

Where Do Analysts Get Their Information?

Analysts often get their information from a variety of sources in the economy without asking management first. Analysts are skilled in the art of competitive intelligence. Too often, top management summarily dismisses their opinion as naïve or uninformed. Our experience with them is quite the opposite. Analysts obtain a great deal of their information about a firm from sources other than the firm itself—from customers, suppliers, competitors, industry associations, the government, and even former employees. They are resourceful, too. One analyst told us a story about an occasion where he wanted to estimate the headquarters cost of a company. To do so, he was able to get, as a matter of public record, the CEO's compensation. He then got the annual report and got a list of the other corporate officers and directors and ratioed their pay to the CEO's. He found that the top three floors of the HQ building were filled by HQ staff; by dividing the average num-

Forecast Assumptions for TELECOM CP NEW ZEALAND -ADR						
Cash Flow	**2003**	**2004**	**2005**	**2006**	**2007**	**2008**
1. Revenue Growth	12.3%	−2.3%	−1.5%	0.5%	4.6%	4.8%
2. Operating Margin	28.1%	28.9%	29.1%	27.7%	28.2%	27.8%
3. Capital Spending / Revenues	11.5%	12.3%	15.3%	18.3%	21.3%	22.3%
4. Net Working Capital / Revenues	−2.7%	−2.7%	−2.7%	−2.7%	−2.7%	−2.7%
5. Cash Tax Rate	34.8%	34.8%	34.8%	34.8%	34.8%	34.8%
6. *WACC*	7.8%	7.8%	7.8%	7.8%	7.8%	7.8%

Cash Flow	**2009**	**2010**	**2011**	**2012**	**2013**	**Perpetuity**
1. Revenue Growth	5.4%	6.0%	5.7%	6.6%	5.8%	5.8%
2. Operating Margin	27.6%	27.3%	27.0%	26.7%	26.4%	26.1%
3. Capital Spending / Revenues	23.3%	24.3%	25.3%	25.3%	25.3%	25.3%
4. Net Working Capital / Revenues	−2.7%	−2.7%	−2.7%	−2.7%	−2.7%	−2.7%
5. Cash Tax Rate	34.8%	34.8%	34.8%	34.8%	34.8%	34.8%
6. *WACC*	7.8%	7.8%	7.8%	7.8%	7.8%	7.8%

FIGURE 11.3 Salient assumptions used in valuation.

Source: Monitor analysis

ber of square feet of office per person into the total number of square feet, he estimated the size of the staff. You get the idea. It turned out later that his estimate was within 10 percent of the actual HQ cost.

It is not surprising that analysts can get most of the information that they want without speaking directly with management. Their efforts at cross-checking and verifying the facts makes it even more important that management be prepared to speak informatively on its point of view concerning its value drivers.

Having established that the information in analyst forecasts is useful, we suggest that it is a beneficial exercise for top management to compare the assumptions in analyst forecasts and to see how close the model DCF is to the market price given the consensus analyst forecast.

Use analyst forecasts to value your firm. Figure 11.3 shows the consensus analyst assumptions for Telecom New Zealand ADRs in 2003.

These assumptions were assembled from a variety of sources: analyst forecasts from Morgan Stanley and Merrill Lynch, forecasts published by IBES, and Bloomberg. Although these assumptions do not always agree with each other, and may produce a valuation far different from the market value, they do seem reasonable in this case. Consequently, the DCF equity value is close to the actual market value—only seven percent different. (See Figure 11.4.)

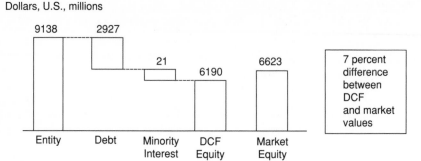

Dollars, U.S., millions

FIGURE 11.4   DCF estimate of New Zealand Telecom ADRs.

Management-Implied Assumptions

The next step is to assemble forecasts made by your own management team, and to put them into the same DCF model that was used to determine the value of your firm given analyst forecasts. Hockey-stick forecasts that are overly optimistic are fairly common. But so, too, is market undervaluation of stock. How do you decide whether the market is right or whether your management team has greater insight? One way to nibble away at the problem is to decompose it into its value driver components and ask a few questions about the generic value drivers that are illustrated in Figure 11.5.

When assessing corporate or business unit performance, the questions are: *Can you exceed expectations? Will your actual return on invested capital exceed what the market expects? Will sales growth exceed expectations? What about capital turnover, i.e. the dollars of sales per dollar of capital invested?* You should contrast the expectations of your management with those of analysts for each of the value drivers. You should also benchmark yourself vis-à-vis competition. Then you can identify information gaps between your beliefs and those of the market in light of what actions you can take given the competitive environment.

Information Gap

The last step is to figure out exactly where the important differences are between analyst and management expectations. This starts with collection of all the published data about your company, its competitors, its suppliers and their competitors, its customers and their competitors, the government, and foreign governments. Read analyst reports, magazine articles, newspaper clippings, search the Web, and talk to people. Interview analysts and

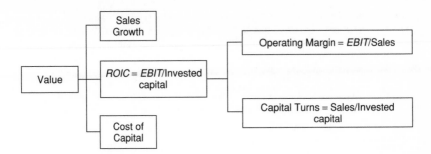

FIGURE 11.5   Value driver tree.

writers. Find out where you disagree with the specifics, and plan to address these information gaps during your next meeting with the analysts.

Third Principle—Listen as Much to Potential as to Current Investors: Clientele Effects

A CEO who stands before an open meeting of shareholders is exposed to direct contact with the company's *existing* shareholders. Communication tactics are usually also focused on current shareholders. They are the current clientele of the firm. They are its owners. But they do not, by themselves, determine its stock price. They are not the only audience nor are they the only investors with whom the management must communicate. *Potential* investors are important, too.

Put yourself in the shoes of an investor who is looking for a good company to invest in. Professional fund managers are constantly searching for good investments, and there is a constant demand for fresh information. There are many different portfolio strategies. Some want high dividend yield, others want low. Some will prefer high-growth and high-risk stocks. Some want momentum stocks, others want value stocks.

Whatever the financial policy a firm adopts there is a set of investors that will like it—at the right price. For example, some gold mining companies do their utmost to hedge against fluctuations in the price of gold. Other companies in the same industry do not. It is not surprising that investors who seek exposure to gold prices choose to invest in those gold mining companies that are unhedged. Other, more risk-averse investors choose hedged gold mining firms. Each company has its own clientele. If either firm were to change its hedging policy, its current shareholders would be very likely to protest, and might even sell the stock. The net effect, however, would be negligible, because as one clientele walks out, it is replaced by another that appreciates the firm's newly changed policy.

There are two lessons to be learned by top management. First, on issues where there are multiple clienteles, it does not make any difference which policy is adopted by your firm because one clientele quickly replaces another. Shareholder protestations are often a tempest in a tea-pot—amounting to nothing. Be careful, though: Investors are unanimous about many issues. For example, they all prefer more cash flow over time to less. Second, it is necessary to communicate with potential investors as well as to existing investors.

Clientele effects are found to be related mainly to financial issues—dividend policy, capital structure, and hedging policy. Perhaps the best researched among them is the dividend policy clientele effect. Miller and Modigliani (1961) were among the first to describe it:

> *If, for example, the frequency distribution of corporate payout ratios happened to correspond exactly with the distribution of investor preferences for payout ratios, then the existence of these preferences would clearly lead to a situation whose implications were different, in no fundamental respect, from the perfect market case. Each corporation would tend to attract to itself a "clientele" consisting of those preferring its particular payout ratio, but one clientele would be as good as another in terms of the valuation it would imply for firms.[1]*

Academic research has provided evidence consistent with dividend and debt (financial leverage) clientele effects. Usually shareholder clienteles form around tax effects of debt or dividend policy. Low–tax bracket investors prefer higher dividend payout and lower use of debt in the firm's capital structure. Higher–tax bracket investors prefer capital gains to dividends and more debt to less.

The earliest comprehensive study of tax clientele effects that result from dividend policy was conducted by Elton and Gruber (1970). They reasoned that the price decline on the day that a stock goes ex dividend could be used to estimate the marginal tax rate of the marginal investor in the stock. Suppose that you are a current shareholder of a stock and that the value of the stock the instant before it goes ex dividend, is $S_b = \$20$. If you were to sell the stock at this point in time, you would pay a capital gains tax, t_g, on the difference between the original stock price, S_o, and the current price, S_b. Your other choice is to hold the stock through the ex dividend date. In this case, you receive the price of the stock after it goes ex dividend, $S_a < S_b$, and pay taxes on the capital gain (or loss) as well as on

---

[1]Miller, M. H. and F. Modigliani, "Divided Policy, Growth, and the Valuation of Shares," *Journal of Business*, 34, October 1961, pp. 411–433. Published by permission of publisher, The University of Chicago Press.

the dividend received, leaving you with the after-tax amount of $D(1 - t_p)$. To prevent arbitrage profits, the payout from either course of action must be the same, as shown below:

$$S_b - (S_b - S_o)t_g = S_a - (S_a - S_o)t_g + D(1 - t_p)$$

Solving this no-arbitrage condition for the percentage decline in the stock price on the ex dividend date, we obtain a relationship with the marginal investor's tax rates:

$$(S_b - S_a)/D = (1 - t_g)/(1 - t_p)$$

Using over 4,000 observations from 1966–1967 of the actual decline in the stock price on the ex dividend date, Elton and Gruber found the average decline in the stock price as a percentage of the dividend was 77.7 percent. This implied an average marginal tax rate of 36.4 percent, a number that made good sense at the time. When they partitioned their sample into deciles from the lowest to the highest dividend payout, they found that the implied tax bracket of the marginal investor declined as the dividend payout increased—strong evidence of dividend clientele. Their results are given in Table 11.5.

Pettit (1977) also finds evidence of dividend clientele effects by examining the portfolio positions of 914 individual accounts handled by a large brokerage house from 1964 to 1970. He finds that stocks with low dividend

TABLE 11.5   Dividend Yields and Implied Tax Brackets

Decile	Mean D/S_b	Mean $(S_b - S_a)/D$	Implied Tax Bracket
1	.0124	.6690	.4974
2	.0216	.4873	.6145
3	.0276	.5447	.5915
4	.0328	.6246	.5315
5	.0376	.7953	.3398
6	.0416	.8679	.2334
7	.0452	.9209	.1465
8	.0496	.9054	.1747
9	.0552	1.0123	N/A
10	.0708	1.1755	N/A

Source: Reprinted from "Marginal Stockholders' Tax Rates and the Clientele Effect," by E. Elton and M. Gruber, *Review of Economics, and Statistics,* February 1970, p. 72, by permission of publisher. Copyright © 1970 by Massachusetts Institute of Technology. All rights reserved.

yields are preferred by investors with high incomes, who are younger, whose ordinary and capital gains tax rates differ substantially, and whose portfolios have high systematic risk. Lakonishok and Vermaelen (1986) postulate that trading volume increases significantly around ex dates and that it is more pronounced for high yield stocks—consistent with tax arbitrage induced by clientele effects.

There is also evidence of debt clientele effects. Harris, Roenfeldt, and Cooley (1983) used the Elton-Gruber methodology and partitioned the data to see if firms with high financial leverage have investors with low tax rates, and vice versa. They found that implied tax rates are strongly negatively correlated with leverage, and concluded that the evidence was consistent with a leverage clientele effect.

The important thing about understanding clientele effects is that although they seem to exist, there is little or no evidence that a change in dividend or debt policy actually has much effect on the value of the firm. Therefore, if top management announces a change in dividend policy (i.e., the target percentage of earnings that will be paid out), current shareholders may express their displeasure, but will be replaced (if they sell their shares) by a new set of shareholders who are content with the new policy. The net effect on the company share price is nil.

Summary

The investment community is constantly searching all possible sources for any information that will help to establish the best set of expectations about the future prospects of your company. Although competing companies (with the same risk) may have very different growth rates and profitability, they will be priced (i.e., handicapped) by the market in such a way as to have the same expected rate of return to shareholders. To beat this return, your company must exceed investor expectations. It is worth the time and effort to reverse engineer the discounted cash flow valuation of your company, to study analyst reports, and to interview existing and potential investors in an effort to better understand the "market's expectations." Understand where these expectations are merely clientele effects—where changes in financial policy (e.g., dividend payout) have no impact on the value of your firm—and which expectations are really value drivers. Then work on your value drivers. Which do you need to communicate better to the market? Which can you target as candidates for exceeding expectations?

Be careful to set targets for performance in a way that will beat investor expectations but keep your targets realistic. Remember that it is difficult to ring the bell year after year. And remember that the expectations of potential investors count as much as the expectations of current investors.

CHAPTER 12

Comparison of Value-Based Management Systems

As you consider adoption of a value-based management system, you will be confronted with and have to choose among a variety of approaches that all claim to link your performance measurement and compensation systems to your goal of maximizing the wealth of shareholders. Nearly every consulting firm has a spiel. McKinsey, Boston Consulting Group, Accenture, Monitor, Bain, Booze Allen, Marakon, LEK (that acquired ALCAR), and especially Stern Stewart all claim to have approaches that maximize shareholder value. This chapter first compares three main approaches that purport to measure shareholder value directly: EVA, CFROI, and EBM. EVA is the trademark of Stern Stewart, an early pioneer and strong advocate of shareholder value management systems. ALCAR, founded by Al Rappaport and Carl Nobel, was also an early leader of "creating shareholder value." CFROI is an approach developed at HOLT Value Associates and described in *CFROI Valuation*, a book written by Bartley J. Madden. It has been used by Boston Consulting Group and Credit Suisse First Boston. EBM is a trademark of Monitor Group, located in Cambridge, Massachusetts. At the close of the chapter we discuss an alternative approach, the Balanced Scorecard, advocated by Robert Kaplan and David Norton. The Balanced Scorecard is a performance management system that balances among metrics covering four perspectives: financial, customer, internal business process, and learning/growth. We will do our best to describe each approach and their claims in a unbiased manner. To avoid the risk of being misunderstood we shall base our comments on analysis that is replicable and try to ask questions rather than make judgments. We are, of course, advocates of EBM; however, we recognize that any of these systems might represent an improvement for companies starting from square one.

General Principles

The list of recommended attributes of a Value-Based Management (VBM) system that is given below is our list—not yours—and not necessarily a list that other proponents of a VBM system would subscribe to.

- Decisions, performance measurement, and compensation should have as strong a link to the total return to shareholders as possible.
- Performance measurement on an annual basis should include balance sheet as well as income statement information—i.e., it should be founded on free cash flows. Where possible, it should also adjust for risk (opportunity costs).
- Performance measurement should be as simple as possible (i.e., there should be few adjustments to numbers normally available from accounting and control systems).
- Multiperiod tradeoffs should be made using a discounted cash flow approach (this includes real options).
- Every aspect of the process should be transparent—no black boxes.
- External benchmarking should be as easy as possible (not tied to only internally available information).

When asked, consultants reluctantly but firmly claim that their approach is best for whatever it is that ails you. With Value-Based Management, the claim is usually that the particular flavor of performance measurement touted by the consulting firm visiting you today is correlated with value creation. This chapter shows the qualifications that bring out the truth.

The greatest hubris of all are those firms that claim responsibility for increases in the stock prices of their clients—as if all the increase were the direct result of a program in Value-Based Management. For example, we wish that higher export sales could be traced back to EBM, rather than to devaluation of the dollar—but we are not as bold as others. Sometimes luck, coincidence, and other external factors are as important as deliberate efforts to create value. Value-Based Management systems most likely have their greatest impact at the margin—by encouraging investment in that one additional NPV-positive project, or by helping managers refine their approach to working capital management.

Three Competing VBM Systems

It is important to keep in mind that three of the competing approaches, EVA, CFROI, and EBM all have three-part systems that start at the grass roots level with value drivers. They are linked to a measure of periodic performance and then are tied to valuation models that are similar in spirit, if not in execution. We will not repeat the three parts of the EBM system here—the rest of the book has already done that. However, we will describe EVA and CFROI here, and the Balanced Scorecard in a section by the same name.

Economic Value Added

Economic Value Added is defined on an annual basis as

$$EVA = (ROIC - WACC)(\text{Invested capital})$$

and given that we are dealing with a perpetuity, the discounted expected EVA when added to the beginning-of-period book value, BV, will equal the standard discounted cash flow value of the firm. To prove this result, start with the definition of enterprise free cash flow:

$$FCF = EBIT(1 - T) + \text{depreciation} - \text{investment}$$

then write down the value of the company as a perpetuity

$$V = FCF / WACC$$

Next, we discount EVA at $WACC$ and add the enterprise book value, BV.

$$V = (ROIC - WACC)(\text{Invested capital}) / WACC + \text{Invested capital}$$
$$= ROIC(\text{Invested capital}) / WACC$$
$$= EBIT(1 - T) / WACC \text{ because } ROIC = EBIT(1 - T)/(\text{Invested capital})$$

Thus, the DCF approach to valuation and the discounted EVA approach (often called the residual income approach) are mathematically identical (even for growing cash flows and even when $ROIC > WACC$).

There are a few other details to remember. First, one can use the model with nominal cash flows discounted at the nominal discount rate, or real cash flows discounted at a real rate. But if one chooses to use real cash flows and discount rates, then care must be taken. After we describe the CFROI approach, we shall go into a detailed description of the landmines involved in using real cash flows and real rates.

Cash Flow Return on Invested Capital (CFROI)

CFROI is a model that discounts net cash receipts (NCRs) denominated in real terms at what is called the market rate. In Chapter 3 of his book, Bart Madden defines NCR from the point of view of the firm and its twin, the same NCR from the point of view of suppliers of capital. Both are defined

TABLE 12.1 CFROI Model definition of Net Cash Receipts

Entity Perspective	Financial Flows
Net income	Interest expense
+ Depreciation expense	− Debt principal repayment
+ Interest income	− Dividends
= Gross cash flow	− Share repurchases
− Capital expenditures	= Cash to suppliers of capital
− Increase in working capital	− New debt
	− New equity
	= Cash from suppliers of capital
= Net cash receipts (NCR)	Cash to − Cash from suppliers of capital = NCR

on a before-tax basis (so we are not sure whether the discount rate is before taxes, too). Table 12.1 provides the definition of NCR from both points of view. Table 12.1 is after-tax.

Note that these are real (inflation-adjusted) cash flows and that there is no mention of how to handle goodwill or its amortization, nor how to deal with changes in accrued taxes. Other than these omissions, the definition of net cash flows in the CFROI model is roughly the same as in the DCF and residual income approaches, except that it is built up from the bottom of the income statement. To use it appropriately we need to forecast interest income and expenses, as well as cash from operations. Consequently, we must forecast future interest rates on debt and the firm's capital structure as well if we are to take the definition literally.

There is also the issue of exactly how to inflation-adjust the NCR forecasts (and the history as well). Bart Madden's book suggests that the book value of net property plant and equipment be adjusted to current dollars by using the GDP deflator index. This is discussed in detail later on in this chapter.

To estimate the market discount rate, the CFROI approach is said to be forward-looking and market derived. The methodology finds the internal rate of return that equates the present value of the aggregated NCRs of 1,438 firms forecasted in real terms to the aggregated current market values (debt plus equity) of the companies. This "market discount rate" is a real rate and is a weighted average of the costs of debt and equity (on a pre-tax basis). In September of 1997 this rate was 4.8 percent, while the nominal yield on 10-year Treasury bonds was 6.2 percent. If we assume that the market expected three percent price inflation, the real yield on treasuries was approximately 3.2 percent, implying a market risk premium of approximately 1.6 percent (somewhat low compared to most practitioner estimates of the market premium).

The CFROI methodology adjusts the market discount rate for the financial leverage and size of individual companies. This is done by rerunning the aforementioned procedure at the individual company level to obtain the rate, K, that equates the present value of the forecasted company NCRs to the market value of the debt plus equity of the company. The firm's apparent risk differential APR is then estimated as the difference between K and the market discount rate. These risk differentials were then sorted into deciles based on the size of the company and its financial leverage (debt to debt plus equity). For example, the estimated discount rate for Emerson Electric in September of 1997 was

$$\text{Discount rate} = \text{Size differential} + \text{Leverage differential} + \text{Market discount rate}$$
$$= -0.4 - 0.5 + 4.8 = 3.9\%$$

If valuation is done this way several questions come to mind:

- Does it make any difference whether or not the cash flows are estimated properly? Apparently it does not because the discount rate compensates and still conforms the present value of the NCRs to equal the market value of the company.
- If the size differential is important, then doesn't it make sense to merge two small firms that have no synergies with each other and no restructuring opportunities? Size may be a proxy for the "track record" of a company that is a reflection of its reliability.
- Why does the same leverage differential apply to all industries in the same way? In practice we observe that within some industries (such as pharmaceuticals) the bond rating is quite sensitive to changes in financial leverage, while in others (such as electric utilities) it is much less sensitive.

Expectations-Based Management

Expectations-Based Management does valuation by using what has come to be accepted over the years as the "standard" discounted cash flow approach. It is more or less the same approach used by Stern Stewart, McKinsey, Marakon, and Accenture. As was proven earlier, it is mathematically identical to the residual income (EVA) approach.

What differentiates EBM is that the impact of an action (or inaction) on a firm's stock price is determined by the change relative to expectations (of management as communicated to the market) and not relative to the cost of capital. The reasons for the EBM approach and the extensive empirical evidence that supports it have already been discussed in the preceding chapters of this book.

EBM defined on an annual basis measures performance as the actual economic profit minus the expected economic profit of a company and its business units:

$$
\begin{aligned}
\text{EBM} &= A(EP) - E(EP) \\
&= [A(ROIC) - E(ROIC)](\text{Invested capital}) \\
&\quad - [A(WACC) - E(WACC)]\,(\text{Invested capital}) \\
&\quad + [ROIC - WACC]\,[A(\text{Invested capital}) - E(\text{Invested capital})]
\end{aligned}
$$

These three terms imply that shareholder value is created by working existing assets harder to earn an *ROIC* that is greater than expected, by lowering the weighted average cost of capital more than expected, and by investing more than expected in projects that earn more than the cost of capital.

The Race for Highest *R*-Squared

Perhaps the most highly debated aspect of competing VBM systems is the claims made by each concerning the correlation between its measure of performance and some measure of shareholder value creation. Every advocate has charts that convey the impression that their measure of VBM is highly correlated with shareholder value creation. If you are not trained in econometrics it is hard to know what questions to ask. Furthermore, most of the competing approaches have not been subjected to a rigorous review process as is necessary for publication in a respected academic journal. Here are a few questions and answers that should help you evaluate these claims.

What Is the Best Choice of a Measure of Shareholder Wealth Creation?

First, what are the choices? Stern Stewart prefers to use MVA (market value added), defined as the change in the entity market value minus the change in capital invested. This measure has been popularized by *Fortune* magazine, which annually publishes MVA rankings. Second is the total return to shareholders, TRS, defined as the (split-adjusted) price per share at the end of the year minus the price per share at the beginning of the year plus any dividend payments during the year, all in the numerator, divided by the price per share at the beginning of the year. Third are various market-adjusted measures of return that remove the general market movements and leave company-specific performance relative to the market as the variable of interest.

What is the best choice? We believe that the unadjusted total return to shareholders is the single best measure of the performance of the action (measured relative to the TRS without the action), but that market-adjusted returns are the best measure of company-specific performance. Why don't we recommend MVA? Mainly because it confounds performance with the sheer size of the firm. In a good year a large firm with a healthy return will be high on the list of top-performing firms, and in a bad year it will be near the bottom of the list. Shareholders choose the weighting of stocks in their portfolios by the rate of return expected of a stock, not necessarily by the size of the company.

Market-adjusted returns, *MAR*, are defined as the ratio of the TRS to the market return, R_m:

$$MAR_{i,t} = (1 + TRS_{i,t})/(1 + R_{m,t})$$

The expectations-based model of the total return to shareholders says that the TRS is equal to the cost of equity plus the unexpected market return plus any unexpected company performance relative to the market:

TRS = Cost of equity
      + Unexpected market return
         + Unexpected company performance relative to the market

Therefore, if the market return turns out as expected and if there is no unexpected company performance, then the TRS will equal the cost of equity. This is because the current stock price is set by taking into account investors' current expectations of company and market performance—and set so that if expectations are met, the gain in price plus expected dividends is just equal to the cost of equity when divided by today's price.

What Does Grouping the Data Do to the Interpretation of the Results?

Grouping is a device used to eliminate noise in the data and therefore to improve the *r*-squared of the regression.

In *The Quest for Value*, Bennett Stewart reports that when using 613 companies, grouped into bundles of 25 companies in 1987–1988, there is a 97 percent *r*-squared when averages of change in market value added are regressed against their average 1987–1988 change in economic value added. Grouping is a technique that usually improves the *r*-squared over what would be obtained were the regression to use ungrouped data. Also, Stewart reports that "pre-Z" companies were excluded from the sample.[1]

---

[1]A "pre-Z" company is an early-stage firm that is earning substantially less than its cost of capital (negative EVA) while growing rapidly through investment. These companies are characterized by rapid sales growth and valuations dependent on future rather than current cash flows.

TABLE 12.2   Ungrouped Results of Regressions of EVA on MVA

Regression	Sample	R-squared	F-test
MVA = 7726.4 + 4.2 (EVA)	6,204	0.016	99.11
MVA = 7756.9 + 11.6(ΔEVA)	5,271	0.042	229.49
ΔMVA = 1179.4 + 4.2(ΔEVA)	5,271	0.049	271.53
$\Delta MVA/S_{t-1} = 0.30 + 2.08[\Delta EVA/S_{t-1}]$	3,790	0.052	208.87
$\Delta MVA - R_m S_{t-1}/S_{t-1} = 0.086 + 2.08[\Delta EVA/S_{t-1}]$	3,790	0.052	209.06

Source: Monitor analysis, Stern Stewart data

We purchased the Stern Stewart database covering the 1991–1998 time interval. It contains their estimates of MVA and EVA for individual companies during this period. To study the effect of grouping we ran ungrouped and grouped regressions (excluding outliers in both cases). To be consistent with Stewart's sample selection, so-called pre-Z companies were also excluded. They were those companies that experienced capital growth of 25 percent or more but with very low returns—at least 2.5 percentage points less than the cost of capital. These are often smaller firms that are investing for future profitability whose current value is high while current return on invested capital is low but is expected to improve.

Table 12.2 shows the results of various regressions when individual company data is not grouped.

Although the regressions are all statistically significant, the *r*-squared statistics are very low (one to five percent). Remember, the *r*-squared statistic is a measure of the percentage of the variability in the left-hand variable that is explained by the variable or variables on the right-hand side of the regression. Only about five percent of the change in MVA is explained by the change in EVA in Table 12.2. Is this relationship strong enough to use to measure performance of a company? You decide for yourself.

By way of comparison, Chapter 2 presents ungrouped results where the *r*-squared between the market-adjusted returns of the same set of ungrouped companies and changes in expectations ranges between 42 and 50 percent.

Table 12.3 shows the results of our effort to improve the results using grouping techniques similar to Stern Stewart. Our first step was to calculate an average standardized measure of performance for each company using five years of data. For example, we took data from 1994 to 1998 and divided EVA by invested capital each year, then averaged the five years. Then we repeated the process using the 1993–1997 and the 1992–1996 data. The five-year averages were then ranked based on EVA divided by invested capital, and 25 groups were formed within each of the three (overlapping) time periods. The dependent variable was the change in MVA for each company in a group averaged across companies in that group. The

TABLE 12.3   Grouped Results: Regression of ΔEVA on ΔMVA

Years	Sample	Regression Intercept	Regression Coefficient	R-squared	F-test
1996	26	3,725.8	11.254	0.594	35.11
1997	26	5,870.8	11.886	0.462	20.63
1998	25	7,537.2	23.478	0.784	83.27
1996–1998	77	5,632.1	17.722	0.570	99.30

Source: Monitor analysis, Stern Stewart data

r-squared from grouping rises by a factor of 10 from roughly five percent in Table 12.2 to 57 percent in Table 12.3.

Do Any of the Approaches Amount to Curve Fitting?

Let's start with a definition—what the heck is curve fitting? In econometrics it means that the number of variables that are used to explain a number of data points increases until they are equal. In this event the number of unknowns to be explained equals the number of equations and there is an exact solution for every variable. For regression analysis to have any meaning the number of observations should be much larger than the number of variables used to explain them.

This is not the case with the CFROI approach to valuation. As Madden explains in his book, the cost of capital is calculated from one equation that has one unknown, the cost of capital. Because the market value of the company is one of the known input variables, and the expected NCRs are the other input variable, then at the company level the CFROI valuation is fit to the market value. Madden does not apply his methodology at the company level, however, because he first aggregates all companies to solve for a real market discount rate, then adjusts it by the size and leverage of each company to attain a company-specific cost of capital. This is still curve-fitting, however.

Suppose the definition of NCR were to change significantly. Because the discount rate is chosen to equate the expected NCRs to the current market value, the CFROI valuation approach would still fit the market price equally well.

Adjusting for Inflation

The philosophy of both EVA and EBM is to use nominal free cash flows and to discount them at the nominal cost of capital because management thinks in nominal terms (with the exception of chaotic hyperinflationary periods). However, real numbers are used in the CFROI approach with the

TABLE 12.4   Inflation-Adjusted Returns Destroy Relative Prices

Business Unit	Nominal Return	Price Deflator	Inflation-Adjusted Return
Automotive parts	15%	8%	7%
Oil refining	20%	15%	5%
Exploration and development	40%	32%	8%
Machinery	25%	10%	15%

hope that it will result in asset growth rates and discount rates that will result in a performance/valuation model useful on a worldwide basis.

Our point of view is that *if the inflation adjustments are done correctly,* then valuation is the same in real and nominal terms and so, too, is performance measurement. At the end of the day, we find onerous the extra work required to make all the adjustments and almost always opt for doing valuation and performance measurement in nominal terms.

Let's study performance measurement first, then move on to valuation. Back in the early 1980s we had lunch with the CFO of a large conglomerate who was concerned with the effect of double-digit inflation on his ability to determine the real performance of his business units that included automotive parts, oil refining, oil exploration and development, and machinery (among others). Concerned about inflation-related distortions, he was preparing to subtract inflation from the nominal returns of each business unit to compare them on a real basis. Table 12.4 provides a hypothetical example. Inflation clearly affected different sectors of the economy at different rates. Increases in energy prices were driving general inflation and we can see from Table 12.4 that the largest inflation was in crude oil prices and that exploration and development experienced a 32 percent price rise, followed by oil refining with a 15 percent price rise.

The key question is which business unit created the most value for shareholders. We believe that it is performance relative to expectations that counts. For the sake of argument, suppose that expected inflation was five percent for all of the businesses. If so, then exploration and development clearly exceeded expectations by the greatest margin and created the most value for shareholders. This conclusion is warranted because the relative price of oil went up more than anything else. In terms of cash flow to shareholders it exceeded expectations the most. The example in Table 12.4 serves to demonstrate that decision making is based on relative prices, not real prices.

Madden (1999, p. 109) focuses on a different type of problem in his book *CFROI Valuation.* He says that

The capital suppliers' perspective requires that all monetary values—all cash-in/cash-out accounts—be measured in monetary units of equivalent purchasing power.

If one were to adopt this philosophy, it would become necessary to make many adjustments to the GAAP income statement and balance sheets. A few are defined below:

■ Adjusted gross plant starts with gross plant less land and construction in progress and makes a gross plant inflation adjustment that is based on the GDP deflator index. Frankly, it is a mystery to us why one would use the same GDP deflator for all types of plant and equipment—let's say a computer system and a 20-megawatt generator.
■ Intangibles are also adjusted for inflation.

Now we use an example to illustrate inflation's impact on financial ratios and valuation. Table 12.5 shows the nominal cash flows forecasted for four years (five points in time) and the real cash flows for the same four years. The inflation for the first three years is 20 percent and for the last year it is 10 percent. In nominal terms revenue grows from $1,000 to $1,901, but in real terms it stays constant at $1,000.

Note that inflation distorts certain ratios. For example, the return on invested capital (*ROIC*) rises through time because its numerator, earnings before interest and taxes (*EBIT*), grows with inflation, but its denominator, invested capital, remains relatively constant because it is based on historical costs. By contrast, if *ROIC* is based on real dollars, it remains constant at 18 percent. The CFROI approach adjusts the *ROIC* ratio by using the GDP price deflator to gross up the book value of invested capital so that the denominator grows with inflation and keeps up with the numerator.

EBM handles the inflation effects (and the aging effects as well) on key ratios such as *ROIC* by making no adjustments. Instead, if 20 percent inflation is expected, then the expected *ROIC* changes from 18 percent the first year to 21 percent the second year, and so on. Remember that with EBM, performance is measured relative to expectations, not relative to the cost of capital. As long as expectations properly anticipate inflation, the distortions caused by using historical cost accounting should not be a problem.

To discount the free cash flows we match a real cost of capital, assumed to be eight percent per year, with the real cash flows and the nominal cost of capital with the nominal cash flows. If inflation is 20 percent and the real rate is eight percent, then the nominal discount rate is

$$1 + (\text{Nominal } WACC) = (1 + .08)(1 + .20)$$
$$\text{Nominal } WACC = 29.6\%$$

We also have to estimate the continuing value (CV). The usual approach can be applied to the real numbers, namely[2]

$$CV = NOPLAT_{t+1}[1 - (\text{Real growth rate}/\text{Real } ROIC)]/[WACC - g]$$

However, when using nominal cash flows the distortion in ROIC makes it meaningless for valuation purposes. The following formula makes the necessary adjustment[3]

$$
\begin{aligned}
CV = NOPLAT_{t+1} \\
\times [\text{Real } NOPLAT \text{ margin}/\text{Nominal } NOPLAT \text{ margin}] \\
\times [1 - (\text{Real growth rate}/\text{Real } ROIC)]/[\text{Nominal } WACC \\
- \text{Nominal growth}]
\end{aligned}
$$

The NOPLAT margin is defined as EBIT after cash taxes divided by revenue. Nominal NOPLAT must be adjusted to reflect true profitability and therefore is reduced by multiplying it by the ratio of the real NOPLAT margin over the nominal NOPLAT margin. If we substitute the assumptions of the nominal cash flow approach, we get a CV estimate of:

$$
\begin{aligned}
CV &= [235(1.1)](.096/.124)[(1 - (0/.20))/(.296 - .2)] \\
&= 258.5(.77)/(.096) = 2{,}073
\end{aligned}
$$

Note that the adjusted real NOPLAT margin is taken from Table 12.6. Now we can compare the valuation results of the nominal approach with the real approach. The free cash flows are shown in Table 12.5, and the valuations are given in Table 12.7. Surprisingly, the two approaches give different answers. The real approach overvalues the company.

There are two errors in the valuation that discounts real cash flows at the real cost of capital. First, the depreciation tax shield is constant while taxes are based on growing EBIT. One can say that inflation has the effect of increasing real taxes on capital-intensive firms (unless the tax code allows firms to revalue their property, plant, and equipment—which is not the case in this example). Therefore, the unadjusted real cash flows underestimate taxes and overestimate value. To understand the effect on cash flows see Table 12.6, which is an adjusted real statement of free cash flows. For example, look at taxes in Year 2. Depreciation expense remains at $80, the same as Year 1, but nominal income has increased to $280 so that taxes are now $140. In real terms this must be adjusted by the 1.2 inflation factor to obtain adjusted real taxes, i.e. $140(1/1.2) = $117.

---

[2]Net Operating Profit Less Adjusted Taxes (NOPLAT).
[3]Copeland, Koller, and Murrin, 2000, p. 378.

TABLE 12.5   Nominal and Real Cash Flows for a Company (5 years)

	Nominal Dollars					Real Dollars				
	Year 0	Year 1	Year 2	Year 3	Year 4	Year 0	Year 1	Year 2	Year 3	Year 4
Revenues	1,000	1,200	1,440	1,728	1,901	1,000	1,000	1,000	1,000	1,000
EBITDA	300	360	432	518	570	300	300	300	300	300
Depreciation	(80)	(80)	(83)	(90)	(99)	(80)	(80)	(80)	(80)	(80)
Operating income	220	280	349	429	471	220	220	220	220	220
Taxes @ 50%	(110)	(140)	(174)	(214)	(235)	(110)	(110)	(110)	(110)	(110)
Net Income (also, *NOPLAT*)	110	140	174	214	235	110	110	110	110	110
Real net income (*NOPLAT*)	110	117	121	124	124	110	110	110	110	110
Net working capital	200	240	288	346	380	200	200	200	200	200
Beg Net PPE	400	400	416	448	497	400	400	400	400	400
Depreciation	(80)	(80)	(83)	(90)	(99)	(80)	(80)	(80)	(80)	(80)
Capital expenditures	80	96	115	138	152	80	80	80	80	80
End Net PPE	400	416	448	497	549	400	400	400	400	400
Net income		140	174	214	235		110	110	110	110
plus: depreciation		80	83	90	99		80	80	80	80
less: change in working capital		(40)	(48)	(58)	(35)		—	—	—	—
less: capital expenditures		(96)	(115)	(138)	(152)		(80)	(80)	(80)	(80)
Free cash flow		84	94	108	148		110	110	110	110
Real cash flow		70	66	63	78		110	110	110	110
Average inflation rate/index		20%	20%	20%	10%	1.00	1.20	1.44	1.73	1.90
Net working capital/revenues	20%	20%	20%	20%	20%	20%	20%	20%	20%	20%
PPE/ Revenues	40%	35%	31%	29%	29%	40%	40%	40%	40%	40%
Capital expenditures/revenues	8%	8%	8%	8%	8%	8%	8%	8%	8%	8%
Depreciation/previous PPE	20%	20%	20%	20%	20%	20%	20%	20%	20%	20%
ROIC	18%	21%	24%	25%	25%	18%	18%	18%	18%	18%

Source: Valuation: Measuring and Managing the Value of Companies, 3rd Ed., by McKinsey & Company Inc., Tom Copeland, Tim Koller, Jack Murrin, Copyright © 2000, McKinsey & Comany, Inc. Reprinted by permission of John Wiley & Sons, Inc.

Another type of inflation tax is the effect that inflation has on working capital requirements. Net working capital is 20 percent of revenues in nominal terms. In Table 12.6 we see that in nominal terms, inflation requires an increase in working capital of $40 in Year 2, $48 in Year 3, and so on. Unadjusted real numbers do not capture this net increase in working capital, which is another form of inflation tax. Once again, this means that valuation in real terms will overstate the DCF value of the company. In fact, it overvalues the company by 22 percent. Note that the real cash flows have been adjusted in Table 12.6 to account for the effect in real terms of the need for extra working capital. In Year 1, for example, the $40 net increase in nominal working capital translates into $40/1.2 = $33 in real working capital.

This example points out that correct valuations can be obtained either by discounting nominal cash flows at the nominal rate (and adjusting the CV formula for distortions in *NOPLAT* and *ROIC*) or by adjusting real cash flows downward to account for the inflation "tax" effects on *EBIT* and on

TABLE 12.6   Nominal and Adjusted Real Cash Flows

	Nominal Dollars					Adjusted Real Cash Flows				
	Year 0	Year 1	Year 2	Year 3	Year 4	Year 0	Year 1	Year 2	Year 3	Year 4
Revenues	1,000	1,200	1,440	1,728	1,901	1,000	1,000	1,000	1,000	1,000
EBITDA	300	360	432	518	570	300	300	300	300	300
Depreciation	(80)	(80)	(83)	(90)	(99)	(80)	(80)	(80)	(80)	(80)
Operating income	220	280	349	429	471	220	220	220	220	220
Taxes @ 50%	(110)	(140)	(174)	(214)	(235)	(110)	(117)	(121)	(124)	(124)
Net Income (also, NOPLAT)	110	140	174	214	235	110	103	99	96	96
Real net income (NOPLAT)	110	117	121	124	124	110	103	99	96	96
Net working capital	200	240	288	346	380	200	233	267	300	318
Beg Net PPE	400	400	416	448	497	400	400	400	400	400
Depreciation	(80)	(80)	(83)	(90)	(99)	(80)	(80)	(80)	(80)	(80)
Capital expenditures	80	96	115	138	152	80	80	80	80	80
End Net PPE	400	416	448	497	549	400	400	400	400	400
Net income		140	174	214	235		103	99	96	96
plus: depreciation		80	83	90	99		80	80	80	80
less: change in working capital		(40)	(48)	(58)	(35)		(33)	(33)	(33)	(18)
less: capital expenditures		(96)	(115)	(138)	(152)		(80)	(80)	(80)	(80)
Free cash flow		84	94	108	148		70	66	63	78
Real cash flow		70	66	63	78		70	66	63	78
Average inflation rate/index		20%	20%	20%	10%	1.00	1.20	1.44	1.73	1.90
Net working capital/revenues	20%	20%	20%	20%	20%	20%	23%	27%	30%	32%
PPE/ Revenues	40%	35%	31%	29%	29%	40%	40%	40%	40%	40%
Capital expenditures/revenues	8%	8%	8%	8%	8%	8%	8%	8%	8%	8%
Depreciation/previous PPE	20%	20%	20%	20%	20%	20%	20%	20%	20%	20%
ROIC	18%	21%	24%	25%	25%	18%	16%	15%	14%	13%

Source: Valuation: Measuring and Managing the Value of Companies, 3rd Ed., by McKinsey & Company Inc., Tom Copeland, Tim Koller, Jack Murrin, Copyright © 2000, McKinsey & Comany, Inc. Reprinted by permission of John Wiley & Sons, Inc.

net working capital. In either case, it is necessary to start with nominal cash flows in order to estimate the proper adjustments to the real income statement and balance sheet. Therefore, in our opinion it is easier to use a nominal approach rather than going to all of the extra effort and added complexity of using real cash flows.

The CFROI approach to valuation attempts to make adjustments by using the GDP deflator to increase estimated capital expenditures. It is not clear (to us, at least) that this method is correct. First, the GDP deflator is not company-specific and cannot differentiate between the increasing relative cost, for example, of real estate and the decreasing relative cost of computer equipment.[4] Second, the replacement cost approach fails to capture inflation's impact on taxes (due to constant depreciation) and working capital requirements.

_____

[4] A possible counterargument is that a homogenous price deflator helps to preserve relative prices.

TABLE 12.7 Discounted Cash Flows

| | Free Cash Flows | | | Discount Factors | | Present Values | | |
	Nominal	Real	Adjusted Real	Nominal	Real	Nominal	Real	Adjusted Real
Year 1	84	110	70	0.772	0.926	65	102	65
Year 2	94	110	66	0.595	0.857	56	94	56
Year 3	108	110	63	0.459	0.794	50	87	50
CV	2,073	1,375	1,200	0.459	0.794	952	1,011	952
Value						1,123	1,375	1,123

Adjustments to the GAAP Accounting Numbers

Expectations-Based Management requires no adjustments. It does require, however, that expectations appropriately take into account whatever distortions are caused by the use of accounting information (for example, the inflation distortions of *ROIC* discussed in the previous section).

In his book entitled EVA, Al Ehrbar of Stern Stewart says (1998, P. 164) that "The first step in calculating EVA for any one company is to decide on which adjustments to make to the GAAP accounts." He cautions that "…the correct answer is far fewer than you might expect…" but goes on to note that "Stern Stewart, for example, has identified more than 160 potential adjustments to GAAP…" He focuses on eight major adjustments: research and development, strategic investments, accounting for acquisitions, expense recognition, depreciation, restructuring charges, taxes, and balance sheet adjustments.

The previous section of this chapter discussed a few of the adjustments made by the CFROI approach and some that it should make but doesn't.

We understand the appeal of making adjustments to accounting numbers. As economists we recognize that accounting profits are very different from economic profits. Given the current state of GAAP rules there is odd mixture of historical and market-based cost measurement. For example, if the market value of an asset increases, its balance sheet value and depreciation rate remain unchanged. But if the market value of an asset decreases, the company may be required to write down the value of that asset to reflect its lower market value. This sort of approach to asset values (and depreciation) reflects the inherent bias of accounting toward conservatism, but is clearly skewed in terms of the information financial statements tell us about economic value.

Should you use a VBM system that adjusts accounting information? While that is a matter of preference, we think there are three benefits of using accounting information that may outweigh the benefits of making adjustments to reflect economic factors not otherwise captured by accounting data. First, accounting-based metrics are easily compared across firms due to the (general) consistency of accounting practices across firms, and especially across firms within the same industry. Second, managers are used to using accounting information—there is little need for incremental training or systems. Third, accounting rules generally do not rely on arbitrary rules of thumb or subjective judgment. For example, it is fairly arbitrary to use a particular macroeconomic price index to adjust the market values of various assets for inflation. Another example would be the choice of how to capitalize and amortize R&D costs through time—over how many years? Straight-line or accelerated amortization? All R&D or development spending tied to specific products?

The Balanced Scorecard

In their book *The Balanced Scorecard: Translating Strategy into Action,* Robert Kaplan and David Norton present a performance management system that does not tie back to a single overarching measure of value creation. Instead, they advocate a balanced set of metrics intended to link strategic objectives with tangible financial and nonfinancial measures that can serve as the focal point for planning, target setting, performance evaluation, and feedback/learning. They suggest that managers identify metrics from four strategic perspectives: financial, customer, internal business process, and innovation and growth. The authors see this approach as a way to counter the tendency for financial metrics like *ROIC* to reward current returns over future growth.[5]

Properly implemented, the Balanced Scorecard is used at the level of a strategic business unit to capture the elements of a consistent, logical strategy. Specifically, every measure on the scorecard should reflect a "chain of cause-and-effect relationships" for each unit, i.e., one that conducts activities across the entire range of the value chain and has easily identified economic linkages to the rest of the organization. The scorecard should reflect management's understanding of the business. This need to measure cause and effect implies that the scorecard should encompass both performance outcomes as well as performance drivers (much as EBM advocates the use of valuation measures together with operating value-driver metrics). Much as we've described an *ROIC* tree as a way to connect operating value drivers to financial value, so does the Balanced Scorecard require causal mapping between drivers and outcomes.

The Balanced Scorecard approach at first blush seems appealing, as it encourages managers to consider all the various aspects of their business strategy. The metrics used in scorecards focus on both results and inputs, and cover a wide range of both operational and strategic perspectives. But one should consider some questions that the Balanced Scorecard raises in our minds:

---

[5]As an aside, it is interesting to note that Kaplan and Norton's underlying premise is that existing systems encourage short-term behavior to satisfy investors' demands. Without this underlying premise, it is not apparent why a financial metric that quantifies shareholder value creation, for example, must be "balanced" against nonfinancial metrics. However, our research (described in Chapter 2) and the research of others have found that the stock market generally does place more weight on long-term economic performance.

What is the relevance of the Balanced Scorecard's assumption that management has fully thought through the tradeoffs between different strategic objectives?

Kaplan and Norton say that proper use of the scorecard requires a set of consistent metrics. Such consistency would imply that pursuing higher levels of performance on one metric does not trade off against worse performance on another metric. It is easy to see, however, that such tradeoffs are quite common: For example, higher customer satisfaction may come at the expense of profitability if the firm allows customers to capture all the value created by the firm's products or services. Kaplan and Norton fail to present a methodology whereby managers can be assured that their metrics do not trade off against each other. Instead, they trust that a (mostly) qualitative process of mapping cause-and-effect relationships ensures consistency. But such mapping exercises do no more than codify management's hypotheses about the business. Only through rigorous financial modeling and valuation exercises that reverse engineer stock price can managers know whether their understanding of the business is right.

Even when managers are aware of tradeoffs between different metrics, the scorecard approach does not give any guidance on how to make specific decisions. There is a presumption that translating strategic plans into a logical set of initiatives that supports Balanced Scorecard objectives will necessarily optimize investment and budgeting decisions. But this need not be the case. If a growth strategy requires, for example, development of a specific production capability to meet customer demand, the Balanced Scorecard gives no guidance as to how best to pursue that capability: through acquisition, greenfield investment, joint venture, etc.

How should managers place weights on various metrics? What is the impact such weighting systems might have?

There is no specific guidance that Kaplan and Norton give about determining weights. However, they do advocate policies that would force managers to pay attention to all metrics—for example, by tying incentive compensation to a minimum level of performance across all metrics.[6]

Arbitrary weightings given to different scorecard metrics implicitly favor one behavior over another. Assuming the possibility of tradeoffs between scorecard metrics, the nature of those tradeoffs need not be linear. For

---

[6]Note how such an approach would create nonlinear incentive compensation schedules, leading to suboptimal managerial performance as described in Chapter 9. For example, if management is unlikely to earn any bonus at all due to the failure to achieve adequate performance on a single Balanced Scorecard metric, they will take short-term actions that will maximize the likelihood of earning a bonus in the next period.

example, using customer service spending to raise customer satisfaction ratings from some low figure like 25 percent satisfied to moderately high satisfaction of 75 percent might result in improved financial performance. But if customer satisfaction were to rise from, say, 95 percent to 99 percent, it is possible that the incremental customer services costs could destroy value. Where such nonlinear tradeoffs exist, the use of fixed weights across multiple metrics will give managers improper incentives. The use of a single metric that encompasses such nonlinearity does not suffer from the same pitfall.

How does the Balanced Scorecard handle uncertainty and change?

Scorecards are tied to strategies and an understanding of the underlying economics of the business that would allow such a strategy to succeed. But what if the strategy is ill-conceived, or, more likely, inappropriate once external conditions change? In such a setting, the scorecard metrics may encourage the wrong operating and investing decisions. Only when financial underperformance persists are managers likely to go back to the drawing board to rewrite their strategy and the scorecard metrics that go with it.

Recall from Chapter 4 our discussion of real options as applied to strategy. While it is true that some strategies may require commitment (inflexibility), others may require flexibility to change course as new information arrives. New technologies, regulatory regimes, or competitive conditions can all lead to fundamentally different strategic and operational choices. Strategies that fail to anticipate such changes will be slow to react, and thereby leave money on the table by failing to exercise in a timely fashion the option to redirect the business. The scorecard does not encourage such flexibility—in fact, it discourages it by tying managers to a given set of metrics. Kaplan and Norton are very clear that they are aiming for a system that encourages long-term pursuit of a strategy. While it is important to be consistent in the pursuit of any strategy, it is equally important to recognize when it is time for new strategies and metrics.

Are these questions and our answers related to the Balanced Scorecard important? Context likely matters. We know of organizations that have cultures and processes that are so ingrained that only through explicit adoption of a multiperspective set of metrics can senior management get the organization to focus on new goals. The scorecard is certainly appealing in its transparency—there is no explicit need for valuation models, though we suspect such models would be useful to help managers navigate the inevitable tradeoffs that arise.

Comparison of the Four Approaches to VBM

Three of the competing systems mentioned in this chapter all claim that they:

- facilitate the creation of shareholder wealth
- are highly correlated with changes in shareholder wealth in the stock market
- are a multipart system that includes valuation, annual performance measurement, and operating value drivers
- should be the basis for determining top management compensation

These approaches as well as the Balanced Scorecard approach also claim that they:

- link performance measurement directly to strategic and operating planning systems
- are better than the competing approaches

No one believes that all of these claims are valid for all VBM systems. Here are some of the key differences as we see them:

- *Linkage to the total return to shareholders.* On an ungrouped—i.e., company-by-company basis—the correlation of EVA or the growth in EVA (scaled by the price per share) is five percent or less. The correlation of CFROI values is irrelevant because the cost of capital is solved to fit NCRs to the current market prices. However, the EBM measures of changes in expectations have a 40 to 50 percent correlation with the market-adjusted returns of individual (ungrouped) companies. The Balanced Scorecard makes no direct claims about linkage to TRS.

    One careful distinction we have made throughout the book is the difference between value and value creation. Note that any of the three metric-based approaches can adequately explain the current *level* of stock price. Ultimately, though, value creation requires generating returns either through dividends or stock price appreciation. This is why we have focused on TRS over other measures of value such as MVA (discussed above).

- *User dependency on the vendor* varies considerably. Users of CFROI must rely heavily on their consultants because of the complexity of estimating the real market discount rate, an exercise that must be completed periodically. Users of EVA are less dependent but still need assistance on how to make the many adjustments to accounting statements required to make EVA relevant. EBM makes few if any adjustments; therefore, it is easy for the user to independently operate and maintain the system. The Balanced Scorecard does not rely on outside vendors for data, but often requires consultants to help formulate a consistent, logical set of metrics—an exercise that may need repeating any time a business unit's strategy changes.

- *Comparability and benchmarking* against peer firms become more difficult when the reported GAAP financial numbers are modified by adjustments that, while easy enough to make within the firm, are difficult to calculate for other firms due to the lack of enough public information at the right level of detail. The Balanced Scorecard approach actually discourages comparisons, presumably because of a belief that each firm (or business unit) requires its own unique set of metrics. Keep in mind that investors and analysts are very interested in being able to make comparisons across firms; therefore metrics that either are not easily compared or are not relevant across firms or industries cannot help in external communications.
- *Simplicity* is the hallmark of a good performance measurement system. Due to its transparency and its use of unadjusted numbers, EBM is easily the simplest of the approaches. Depending on the number of metrics chosen, the Balanced Scorecard may be easy to implement, but can create some confusion if there is insufficient guidance as to how to make tradeoffs should conflicts arise between the various scorecard metrics.
- *Business unit performance measurement* as provided by the different systems is different. The potential for serious misallocation of resources makes it time to get serious about which system you choose. Table 12.8 compares EBM with EVA measures of performance for a company with four business units.

Obviously, the market was disappointed and as a result, the stock price adjusted downward. EVA, however, measures performance as positive and predicts erroneously that the stock price will go up. By failing to measure performance against expectations, CFROI will make a similar mistake.

The Balanced Scorecard, unfortunately, does not give any help at all in comparing actual or expected future performance across business units. Therefore, its use at the corporate level in managing the portfolio, allocating capital, and communicating with investors is quite limited.

TABLE 12.8   EVA and EBM Give Different Answers

Business Unit	Actual ROIC	Expected WACC	Expected ROIC	Capital	EVA	EBM
A	30%	10%	40%	5,000	1,000	−500
B	10%	15%	5%	10,000	−500	500
C	20%	10%	15%	8,000	800	400
D	20%	8%	40%	20,000	2,400	−4,000
Total (weighted average)	19%	10%	27%	43,000	3,700	−3,600

- *The ease of implementation* is also worth serious thought. All three metric-based VBM systems (CFROI, EVA, and EBM) require an accounting system that produces both income statements and balance sheets at the business unit level if the system is to be used below the corporate level. Sometimes the intermediate step of extending the accounting system is appropriate. If you already have the needed information then you can proceed rapidly. The information required for the Balanced Scorecard will vary depending on the particulars of its implementation. All approaches, including the Balanced Scorecard, require some upgrades to systems to be able to identify and track value drivers—operating-level metrics that tie to the higher-level metrics used to judge performance.

    If you already use EVA then the change to EBM is simple because all of the data is already there. But management's mindset has to change from earning more than the cost of capital to earning more than a hurdle rate based on expectations. The definition of victory changes from earning positive EVA to earning EVA that is greater than expected.

Summary and Conclusions

One of the breakthrough ideas in artificial intelligence was the realization that a hallmark of human intelligence is its ability to anticipate what will happen—not prescience, but thinking through the implications of causality. Expectations setting and performance to exceed expectations are as much a part of the human psyche as is humor. In fact, one of the indications of intelligence is a sense of humor. Many, or even most jokes, are funny because they have a punch line that is unexpected in one way or another. That's what makes us laugh.

Is it surprising, then, that expectations govern the pricing of stocks, the betting odds at a horse track, and the planning and budgeting systems of today's complex multinational, multibusiness enterprises? It is not, however, surprising that some very clear thinkers have missed the mark because they have ignored the role of expectations in decision making. Many people think of management as part science—and as a science it is assumed that objective factors are key to our understanding of how to manage a business. Expectations, however are subjective. Expectations-Based Management puts subjectivity back into performance measurement.

The alternatives to EBM have their advantages and disadvantages. The various books and articles available on each clearly describe the purported advantages of each. This chapter aimed to raise a few questions. Our aim was not to dismiss the alternatives outright, but to identify possible pitfalls for each and to provide our thoughts on how the approaches should be evaluated.

CHAPTER 13

Expectations, Noise, and Public Policy

This book has primarily been for management; to a lesser degree, it is for investors. We have put forth ideas for improving a firm's ability to measure and manage shareholder value creation and, in so doing, dramatically improve the relationship between the firm and capital markets. Our research also has lessons outside the boardrooms and inside the halls of regulators, standard setters, and politicians. While we do not propose any wholesale revamp of public policy, we do believe some of the lessons of EBM inform some of today's most contentious regulatory and policy debates. The level and composition of CEO pay, expensing of stock option costs, and the composition of corporate boards are all front and center in this post-Enron environment. We believe that public policy decisions about these top management issues should be grounded in a clear understanding of how businesses and capital markets work.

A critical component of EBM is how to communicate with the market. We therefore begin this chapter with a discussion of issues related to firm disclosure requirements. We present ways to think about this problem as well as implications for today's accounting standards. We then turn to the question of investor research, as our view of "noise" in the market has important implications for the distribution of effort between buy-side and sell-side analysts and corporate insiders. We then address the management of governmental (or quasi-governmental) entities to show how EBM concepts can improve their policies. We conclude with some modest observations about the role of "noise" in the context of setting and implementing macroeconomic policies such as monetary and fiscal policies.

A Market Equilibrium for Information

In Chapter 2 we described the impact of noise on shareholder returns, specifically, that an increase in noise is associated with a decrease in returns. Why might this be the case? Our approach is based on a theory of a world with both informed and uninformed investors who trade anonymously. We assume that informed investors pay higher costs for information and are able to generate higher gross returns, but that in equilibrium the returns of informed and uninformed investors are equal net of the costs of obtaining information.[1] If informed investors earned higher net returns, more investors would choose to become informed either through purchasing research from analysts or conducting their own research. If uninformed investors earned higher returns, informed investors would realize that their purchase of information is not valuable, and so would curtail their research activities.

What does this mean for public policy? Later in the chapter we will discuss the merits of having more or fewer informed investors. Here we focus on what corporations can or should do to affect the market through their information disclosures—and in so doing, how this equilibrium may be affected.

Note that corporations bear much of the cost of reporting information to investors. This cost includes accounting and financial systems, investor and public relations departments, and management time and attention. But the corporation is merely a legal entity and, consequently, owners of the corporation ultimately bear these costs.

One might take the view that there should be *no* regulation of corporate disclosure because it is in the shareholders' interest to monitor firm disclosures. Firms that fail to disclose enough to reduce investor fears of fraud and share price manipulation would have their stock prices deflated simply from the fact that their disclosures are inadequate. For example, if a clean audit opinion were optional, we might expect that most companies would obtain one anyway because investors would assign higher risk—and lower stock prices—to those without such opinion letters. Deregulating disclosure rules would also allow firms to concentrate their disclosure resources on information most valuable to investors in their firm- and industry-specific situation. For example, a retail firm that relied heavily on leased stores might disclose more information about such leases, while a competitor that owned real estate might disclose the estimated market values of owned properties. However, we recognize that there are public interest reasons to prevent uninformed investors from being taken in by fraudulent companies, and so we will assume from here forward that a

---

[1]Evidence from experimental market research that also supports the equality of net returns can be found in Copeland and Friedman (1992).

minimum level of disclosure is required for all firms, regardless of industry- or company-specific strategies. The questions that matter in a world of uniform minimum disclosure rules revolve around how much and what types of disclosure should be required.

Before we turn in that direction, a few more words need to be said about "noise." In the broadest sense of the term, noise is investor uncertainty about the firm's value. This may derive from uncertainty about facts such as current period earnings or uncertainty about truly unknowable things like what revenues will be in the future. Disclosure rules need to distinguish facts from projections. Historically, disclosure requirements focused on accounting results—facts about which there may be disagreement over reporting rules, but are nevertheless derived from actual, measurable firm performance.

The line between disclosure of recorded facts and of forward-looking projections is starting to blur. There has always been a tension in the field of accounting between conservatism and relevance. Conservative accounting tends toward reporting of historical facts, while what investors truly care about is expectations for the future—what we call relevant accounting. Thus, we see Financial Account Standards Board (FASB) rules, for example, being expanded over time to include more and more value-focused measures. Acquisition of goodwill is no longer amortized over 40 years, but instead is subject to impairment tests based on forward-looking valuation estimates performed by management. Likewise we see today the march toward inclusion of stock options "costs" on the income statement—even though there are both factual and forward-looking elements to these costs. We will explore both issues further as examples of how EBM can inform required disclosure rules.

Disclosing facts will always reduce investor uncertainty, though not necessarily in a material way if the fact is irrelevant to investor concerns. Forward-looking estimates may either decrease or increase uncertainty, depending on such factors as management credibility, the verifiability of the underlying data and logic for the forecast, or the consistency of a forecast with other signals received by investors. We discussed these factors in Chapter 8 on investor relations. When something is truly uncertain and management has no better handle on the situation than outsiders, reporting such information will do little to reduce noise and may even confuse some investors. As you read the following discussion, keep in mind the idea that some disclosures, while costly to report, do nothing at all to reduce noise or improve share prices.

Disclosure Requirements—Too Much of a Good Thing?

In the wake of Enron, WorldCom, and other high-profile accounting scandals it became fashionable to argue that firms need to disclose ever more details. Thus, we find ourselves in the midst of a wave of changes to accounting disclosure standards such as impairment of goodwill, disclosure of off-balance sheet items, and expensing of employee stock options. Not to be outdone by the FASB, Washington and New York regulators have required management to certify under penalty of law the veracity of the firm's financial statements. There has also been a vast expansion in the number and type of disclosures that public firms are required to report in SEC filings (e.g., Forms 8-K). All this comes on the heels of a major change to the whole practice of investor relations in the form of Regulation FD (fair disclosure).

There are two central questions that should be addressed in any discussion of disclosure requirements. First, how much disclosure should be required? While better disclosure has obvious benefits for the efficient pricing of assets in capital markets, there are costs as well, e.g., those generated by the firm's reporting function or the cost of revealing critical information to competitors. Balancing the benefits and costs of disclosure is a critical part of finding the right level of disclosure. Second, what is the right mix of disclosures? What information is truly informative to investors? How does the mix of disclosed information interact with the overall level of information required? Shouldn't the mix of information vary by firm and industry context?

From an economist's perspective, the optimal level and mix of firm disclosures should be a function of costs and benefits. There are two types of benefits that public disclosures provide. The first is a check on management to control insider self-dealing. This benefit is essentially an avoidance of the costs incurred when those in the know can shift value from those who are not. Generally this is the motivation behind insider trading rules. This benefit is mostly a matter of fraud avoidance—and as such, EBM adds little to the issue.

The second benefit of firm disclosures is the reduction in noise regarding firm value. We noted in Chapter 2 that greater levels of noise—e.g., uncertainty or disagreement about a firm's expected future cash flows—lead to lower values. The idea behind additional disclosures is to improve market values.

It is this second benefit that we believe needs to be more carefully considered against the costs of disclosure. These costs are clear and tangible—unlike the benefits that are diffuse and difficult to quantify. The costs include internal accounting costs, internal and external audit costs, costs of board review and approval, and, as noted above, the potential loss of competitive edge through disclosure of critical information.

One-Size-Fits-All Disclosure Rules?

One of the difficulties of crafting disclosure requirements is that the value of different types of information can vary significantly across a range of dimensions. In some cases, whole industries require unique disclosure requirements—for example, companies with activities to explore and develop oilfield properties need to disclose estimates of the size and value of both known and potential oil reserves. Financial service firms also have unique disclosure requirements, owing to their central role in the monetary mechanisms that allow the economy to function. Industry-specific disclosure rules developed either through regulatory needs (e.g., in the case of banks) or because investors are particularly interested in specific pieces of information (e.g., detailed R&D information for pharmaceutical firms).

The type of information that is valuable can also vary within an industry. In a retail environment, one firm may directly own its retail chain while its competitor uses a franchise system. For the firm with wholly owned retail outlets, investors may find it valuable to know, for example, the lease obligations and/or real estate value of owned facilities. The franchisor, however, would benefit investors by disclosing important franchise agreement terms that could affect growth, profitability, or brand image—e.g., in what ways and to what degree is the franchisor able to customize the consumer experience in its stores?

Examples of Compliance Cost versus Value to Investors

FASB 142—Goodwill Impairment Charges

In 2001 the Financial Accounting Standards Board implemented FASB 141 and 142. FASB 141 changed the way firms could account for acquisitions/ mergers, with the most significant change being the elimination of pooling-of-interests accounting for mergers. Goodwill created in acquisition would no longer be written off over time through regular amortization expenses (typically over 40 years). Instead, goodwill would remain on the balance sheet until such time as it was "impaired," and then it would be written down to reflect the then-current value of the acquired company. Other intangibles (e.g., the value of acquired patents) could still be amortized over their useful economic life. FASB 142 requires firms under GAAP accounting to conduct annual impairment tests, where the estimated market value of an acquired company is compared with its carrying value on the books. If the market value is less than the carrying value, goodwill is impaired.[2] These annual tests can never be used to write up the value of goodwill.

---

[2]It is possible that other assets besides goodwill could be impaired—e.g., the fair market value of property, plant and equipment could also be written down as a result of this annual impairment test. For our purposes here, however, we focus on the write off of goodwill.

The idea behind FASB 142 was to make the expensing of goodwill more relevant to investors. In spite of the protestations of managers who continued to focus on earnings dilution from goodwill amortization, investment practitioners were well aware of the resounding academic evidence that such amortization was irrelevant for valuation purposes. *Goodwill amortization under the old scheme was a non-cash expense, did not affect cash flows via tax effects, and provided no new information to investors. In our EBM terminology, goodwill amortization simply did not affect expectations of cash flows.*

While goodwill impairment charges do not affect taxes and cash flows, it is possible now that they may affect expectations by partially revealing management's forward-looking view of the firm. The annual impairment test requires management to conduct a forward-looking valuation of the cash flows associated with the acquired business. It is therefore possible that an impairment charge could reveal information to the market about management's expectations for the future. However, as we note later, this is rarely the case. Before we turn to the problems with goodwill impairment from an EBM perspective, though, it is worth pointing out the costs imposed by this rule change.

These costs involve significant time and effort on the part of management to develop the cash flow forecasts used in their impairment test valuation models. This cost is often multiplied by fees paid to consultants and outside valuation experts for their assistance. In addition, there are the associated audit costs for verifying that the impairment test was conducted according to GAAP standards. These are all the direct costs, but there are also indirect costs such as the resources diverted toward identifying the acquired company's financials: immediately after an acquisition this may be easy, but once an acquired company is integrated into the firm's operations it can be quite difficult to tease out its unique financials. In some cases, the need to conduct impairment tests may lead management to avoid integration of accounting and control systems so that direct measurement of the acquired entity can continue with ease. Another indirect cost is management time and effort diverted to managing the impairment charge process and making related decisions.[3] These costs of complying with FASB 142 can

---

[3]At one company facing a potential goodwill impairment charge, countless hours were spent in discussions between line and corporate management to determine whether an impairment charge should be taken and if so, how large it should be. Line management wanted to write off as much as possible because they were compensated on return on capital, including goodwill. Corporate management wanted to avoid any write off at all—we speculate that it was to avoid admitting to investors that the acquisition did not go as planned. Of course, neither position makes any sense from an EBM perspective. With respect to line management's

be quite substantial. At one company we are familiar with we estimated well over $1 million in direct costs alone.

The costs of complying with FASB 142 can be high and the benefits are minimal:

- The market value of the company often already reflects the decline in value of the firm's assets—whether obtained through ongoing investments or acquisitions. In many cases, then, the write off of goodwill is more for the sake of accounting catching up with market expectations than the reverse. Although the evidence is inconclusive, there is no systematic pattern to share prices declining on the news of a goodwill impairment charge.[4]

- It is unclear what information investors can glean from an impairment charge that they cannot obtain more easily and directly through other means. To the extent the impairment test is based on forward-looking estimates of cash flows, investors either already have such estimates, or management can provide more direct guidance specifically addressing the various components of cash flow.

- The value of the information inherent in the impairment test is further diminished by the flexibility afforded management in conducting their valuation tests. As every good financial modeler knows, it can be quite easy to manipulate a valuation model to create higher or lower valuations by slight changes in key inputs like the discount rate, expected long-term growth rate, or expected future tax rate—all while staying within the boundaries set up by GAAP rules and financial theory. Investors know this and therefore put less stock in management's valuation estimates. Investors would rather have the inputs to the valuation model shared than the value estimate itself.

---

position, writing off goodwill does not change expectations of future performance one bit—management is being compensated against the wrong metric. With respect to corporate management's position, investors likely already knew what the acquired unit was worth in light of the then-prevailing industry downturn. Writing off goodwill would do little to convince investors otherwise.

[4]The relationship between shareholder returns and goodwill impairment is difficult to study definitively because most goodwill impairments are reported the same time as earnings. Therefore, disentangling the share price reaction to earnings from the reaction to goodwill impairment is a difficult, if not impossible, task. While some recent studies have found negative share price reactions to impairment charges, these studies fail to control fully for simultaneous announcements of earnings. In spite of inconclusive evidence that share prices decline *after* an impairment charge, there is clear evidence that share prices decline *before* these charges.

As we've seen, at many companies the costs of complying with FASB 142 very likely exceed the benefits afforded to investors. An EBM perspective reminds us that it is expectations of future performance that count the most, and that information disclosed to the market needs to be meaningful in a way that reduces noise. It is not clear that FASB 142 impairment tests do this for investors.

Expensing of Stock Options

Another area where current accounting standards are changing is the new requirement to expense stock options. As of this writing, the FASB has decided that employee stock options must be recognized as an expense on the income statement at the time of issuance, with appropriate expenses incurred as the fair value of those options changes through time. The expensing requirement would require either market-based pricing of such options (usually unavailable) or option-pricing model valuations. The latter use either oversimplified closed-form solutions, such as the Black-Scholes formula, or more flexible solutions, like lattice-based models, that allow more accurate modeling of some of the restrictive conditions imposed on employee options (e.g., vesting periods and the expected time to exercise). While the U.S. Congress has thus far not responded to industry calls to legislate different rules that would not require such expensing, the FASB has delayed the required implementation of this rule and so the final version to be implemented may yet change due to industry lobbying.

Putting aside all the technical discussion about which is the best method for expensing employee stock options, it is important to keep in mind that the debate can really be boiled down to a disagreement on whether investors focus on earnings or value. The earnings perspective argues that investors only care about the income statement when they value a firm: Having more earnings leads to higher valuations, no matter what happens on the balance sheet or even off-balance sheet. The value perspective believes that investors need to know enough information to form their value estimates, regardless of whether that information is in the income statement, balance sheet, footnote, proxy statement, or press releases.

In this debate we are squarely in the value camp, although we know this puts us at odds with many well-regarded practitioners and influential academics such as Nobel laureate Robert Merton. The most important information about employee options had already been disclosed in most, if not all, company footnotes. Firms disclosed the number of options, their weighted-average exercise price, estimated values today, and a number of other data. It is true that these disclosures could stand to include more detail, such as the distribution of exercise prices (rather than simply the weighted average), the vesting schedule for various tranches of outstand-

ing options, and the firm's historical data on the rate at which employees
exercise options prior to maturity.[5]

While this disclosure could have been improved, we see several reasons
why the purported benefits to expensing of options are not worth the costs.
First, the costs of compliance are likely to rise as firms turn to consultants to
conduct valuation estimates and need auditors to validate the results. Second,
as noted previously, it is unclear that expensing such options provides any
new information to investors not already disclosed in the footnotes. Third,
there is the inherent bias in the requirement to expense a contingent liability when other contingencies—both assets and liabilities—are left off the
income statement. In fact, other contingencies may have an impact on firm
value that is orders of magnitude greater, but are not included in the P&L
(e.g., litigation and regulatory contingencies). Fourth, this line item will need
even more footnote disclosures to explain the methodology used or to
explain the differences between expenses for options issued in the current
period versus adjustments for the ever-changing value of options issued in
prior periods. Finally, if options are expensed at the time of issue, shouldn't
the firm record a gain if they expire worthless? Last, and certainly not least,
as we noted in Chapter 8, there is reason to believe that putting any contingent claim on the income statement will increase the noise inherent in earnings figures—as options expire or as share price changes, earnings will need
to adjust in ways that cannot be predicted. Management's inability to set
expectations about options costs is probably the soundest reason to avoid
expensing options.

Co-Co Craziness

Another area of changing accounting standards is the FASB's recent decision to force companies to calculate diluted EPS using the implied shares
created if contingent convertible debt (so called "Co-Cos") were to be converted. General Motors' CFO recently complained that this change in
reporting would significantly dilute the company's earnings on both a historical and forward-looking basis (the new rules would require restatement
of prior years' earnings).

Does this reporting change matter? Investors already know which companies have Co-Cos, and can factor that into their valuations—especially if
the values of such bonds could be directly observed from debt markets.

---

[5]Other employee option–related information that might be valuable to investors
includes conditions for repricing options, the distribution of options between
different divisions or layers of management, or the amount of options that may
be issued in the future as a result of incentive compensation plans.

Reporting EPS differently does nothing to change the economic cost of these securities. If companies are acting rationally, they have used Co-Cos because they find their cost, flexibility, or other features economically beneficial relative to other available forms of financing. A simple reporting change cannot alter that in any way. If, however, companies are using Co-Cos simply to play accounting games, then there may be some benefit to forcing their inclusion in EPS calculations, as companies may turn back toward less costly forms of financing.[6] In our opinion this is all a non-issue. While the benefits from adjusting the EPS figures are likely small, the costs of doing so are also small. Adding to these costs is the cost of increased noise from adding contingent claims into earnings, discussed earlier in the context of stock options.

Disclosure Given an EBM Perspective

This book—and much of the existing finance literature—shows that value is a function of expected future cash flows. How we account for current and past performance should not materially change those expectations. But the truth is that expectations are in part formed by our understanding of where a company is today. It is one thing for managers, with in-depth understanding of their operations and competitive situation, to make informed judgments about a firm's potential future cash flows without regard to accounting concerns. It is an entirely different matter for investors who rely on such historical information to inform their expectations. Thus, it goes without saying that financial statements must present an accurate picture of the firm's financial condition.

But accuracy need not require "completeness." After all, a complete picture of a firm's financial condition would reveal intimate details such as the firm's detailed cost structure, composition of its customer base, or the project-level details of R&D spending. These details would, of course, improve investors' ability to discern the firm's value. But such details would also provide information to competitors that might be used to engage in costly competitive behavior such as price cuts or selective poaching of critical customers.

We think regulators of financial disclosures need to keep these things in mind—just as managers, investors, and analysts do. Several principles for

---

[6]Due to their quasi-equity nature, the cost of Co-Cos must be somewhere between the firm's cost of debt and its cost of equity. The closeness to the firm's cost of debt will be determined by the distance of current share price to the Co-Cos conversion price. While the cost of Co-Cos will be between the cost of debt and equity, their cash costs can be lower than straight debt coupon payments--and therefore may provide benefits to cash-strapped companies.

disclosure rules present themselves to us as we use our EBM lens to view the issues:

■ *While accounting financial statements may affect value, they are not the sole means by which information is conveyed to the market.* Policy decisions such as whether to expense stock options need to be informed by a thorough understanding of what information needs to be disclosed, and what is the lowest-cost way of disclosing that information. It is better to report the salient terms of options and to let the shareholder figure out their value than it is to report an estimate made by management (with unreported assumptions and an unknown model).

■ *The method of reporting is less important than the fact of its disclosure.* For years the smart money spent time analyzing the company's financial statement footnotes, for here is where the details were revealed. Forcing more information into the main statements is unlikely to materially change investor behavior or stock valuations.

■ *Accounting disclosures are likely to be more costly to shareholders than other forms of disclosure.* Auditors, independent valuation experts, and related direct expenses raise the cost of using financial statements as a means to disclose information. Whether those costs provide benefits of greater value is entirely another matter.

■ *Reporting of contingent claims should be in the footnotes, not the income statement.* Management should be free to disclose information that would reveal material differences between its accounting balance sheet, for example, and a market value–based balance sheet. But the move to change existing balance sheets toward market valuations moves away from conservatism and begins to put forecasts onto the income statement and balance sheet. It is easy to mark-to-market liquid securities, but using forward-looking projections to measure the value of long-lived assets simply opens the door to abuse (just tweak the discount rate and anybody can avoid an impairment charge). Forecasts cannot be audited. The unpredictability of the earnings impact of contingent claims makes their inclusion in earnings a noise-increasing accounting measure.

Thoughts on Regulation FD

In 2000 the Securities and Exchange Commission adopted Regulation Fair Disclosure, commonly known as Regulation FD. This regulation requires firms to disseminate material information in a way that gives the general public access to that information at the same time as analysts and institutional investors. Any information that is accidentally revealed to a selective set of investors or analysts must be disseminated to the general public within 24 hours. A positive outcome of Regulation FD has been the creation of more capable investor relations functions. Internet sites and earnings release conference calls are now easily monitored by any investor with a phone or Web connection.

From the perspective of a manager applying EBM, Regulation FD simply reinforces the need to have a strong, credible story behind a company's stock. Rather than shaping the market's expectations through a select group of analysts, FD allows for—even requires—a much wider target set for the firm's investor relations.

Reg FD is a mixed bag for investors. On the one hand, it ensures that materially important information is released broadly to the market and therefore does not give any specific investor—institutional or otherwise— or any particular sell-side analyst an unfair advantage. On the other hand, Regulation FD makes it more difficult for investors to earn a higher return, having found out important information about a company—whether through interviews of senior managers or otherwise. Reg FD may have the perverse incentive to limit the amount investors spend conducting primary research. While sophisticated fundamentals-driven investors may still conduct research by talking to a company's customers or suppliers, the best source for information—management—becomes largely irrelevant (or inaccessible).

For management, Reg FD might be seen as a nuisance, requiring the firm to issue Form 8-K disclosure statements any time material information slips out of a senior manager's mouth. But in an EBM company, Reg FD may even be an obstacle to effective shareholder management. If managers and investors are both reluctant to engage in one-on-one conversations (investors, because they reap no significant advantage from it, and managers, because they risk violating FD), then there are fewer opportunities for management to learn firsthand what the market expects of their company and why. Without this knowledge, management may have only a cursory understanding of how their own expectations match against investors, gleaned, for example, from sell-side analyst reports or questions posed to management at investor conferences. This is hardly ideal, and requires explicit regulations to delineate the types of communications that not only fall outside the purview of FD, but that ought to be encouraged with the aim of having share prices better reflect management's informed opinion.

Sarbanes-Oxley

The Sarbanes-Oxley legislation was the U.S. government's reaction to the perceived need to address a rash of scandals to hit corporate America (e.g., Enron, WorldCom, Global Crossing, and Tyco). The intent was to reassure the investing public (in particular, smaller retail investors). While it remains to be seen how European regulators will react to their own scandals (e.g., Ahold and Parmalat), as of this writing Sarbanes-Oxley is the primary public policy response to these scandals. Its key requirements include:

- Establishing a public company accounting oversight board
- Segregating audit services from other consulting services
- Rotating the lead audit partner and reviewing partner
- Auditors report directly to audit committee
- Audit committee must be independent (cannot accept consulting or other compensation from the company or its subsidiaries), include at least one member who is a financial expert, have authority to engage independent counsel or advisors, and have funds for payment to auditors
- Forbidding personal loans to officers and directors, except if made on terms no more favorable than those made to the public
- Each annual and quarterly report must be certified by the CEO and CFO
- Annual reports to include internal control report
- Additional disclosures through SEC Form 8-K (discussed below)

What should be made of "Sarbox" from an EBM perspective? Sarbox focuses on assumed structural factors such as board composition. The academic evidence is certainly mixed on these factors, with the strongest evidence supporting only the need for board members with finance and/or accounting knowledge. These type of reforms are really focused on detection and punishment of fraud—detection supposedly enhanced by improved board and auditing structures, and punishment through penalties for certifying false financial reports. Though barring personal loans to officers and directors may remove some incentive to present false financial information, on the whole, Sarbox does not address the underlying drivers of financial fraud.

While the underlying drivers of fraud vary across circumstances, often management cooks the books because they may truly believe the firm will grow out of what is perceived to be a temporary earnings shortfall. For example, if management fails quickly to realize the synergies hoped for in a merger, they may cook the books in an effort to bide time while they continue to work the merger integration problems. This is nothing more than earnings smoothing taken outside the confines of GAAP standards.

An EBM-driven company may avoid this to the extent it follows our advice about investor relations—namely, the need to present credible, verifiable data about underlying value drivers to investors. Firms that present only the headline financial data without underlying details that investors can verify are the most susceptible to management's cooking the books. Investors can take the initiative to set up a credible dialog by requiring such detailed information from management. Public policy can support these types of dialogs by encouraging firms to disclose more detailed, relevant data to investors, and by protecting them from litigation problems for immaterial or reasonable errors in such data.

Other aspects of Sarbox, especially the requirement for stronger internal controls, raise the costs to companies and therefore investors.[7] While stronger controls are important to ensure accurate accounting, it is probable that managers hoping to mislead investors will simply shift their accounting mischief to factors outside the purview of accounting controls. As we know from our EBM research, the easiest way for managers to lie is to do so about the firm's future prospects rather than historical performance. Because value is disproportionately driven by expectations of the future, it follows that managers determined to artificially inflate their share prices will aim to shape those expectations regardless of what the firm's past performance has been.

To some extent, such lying is more likely to be discounted by investors who make their own assessments of the future. However, there are certainly cases where structural or other changes could do more to prevent lying even about the firm's future prospects. We examined at length in prior chapters the link between EBM and incentive design. While Sarbox at least prohibits loans to managers that may lead them to put their own interests ahead of shareholders, stronger controls on incentive pay structures could do even more to help investors. The key is to encourage—or even require—pay structures that are more in line with shareholder interests. At the very least, providing more detail to investors about management's pay structure could help. More extreme forms of control may require longer vesting periods and clawback features for incentive pay, whether or not it is paid in options, shares, or cash.

Revised 8-K Disclosure Requirements

Sarbanes-Oxley brought with it new requirements to disclose certain events through SEC Form 8-K filings, as well as an accelerated window in which such events must be disclosed. In August 2004 the SEC announced the items requiring disclosure under the revised Form 8-K. These include:[8]

---

[7]Others have already pointed to these higher costs imposed on companies as the primary reason for increasing numbers of public companies going private, and foreign firms avoiding listing shares on U.S. exchanges.

[8]The SEC is still considering disclosure rules for changes in outlook or rating from credit rating agencies. It also rejected a proposal to require disclosure of termination or reduction of relationships with customers.

- Entry into and termination of material definitive agreements (excluding letters of intent and other nonbinding agreements)
- Bankruptcy or receivership
- Completion of acquisition or disposition of assets
- Public announcements of material nonpublic information regarding operations or financial condition (Regulation FD)
- Creation of a material financial obligation such as debt, capital leases, or operating leases (as well as contingent, off-balance sheet obligations)
- Triggering events that accelerate or increase material financial obligations
- Costs associated with exit or disposal activities (disclosed when the firm commits to such activities, though allows for amended disclosures if cost estimates are not available at the time the decision is made)
- Material impairments (at the time a decision is made to impair an asset, but only if the impairment decision is made separate from preparations of normal quarterly or annual statements)
- Delisting, failure to satisfy a continued listed rule, or transfer of listing (except if the security is redeemed or matures under normal course of business)
- Unregistered sales of equity securities (if greater than defined levels of outstanding shares in any given class of stock)
- Material modification to rights of security holders
- Changes in auditing accountant
- Nonreliance on previously issued financial statements
- Changes in control
- Departure of directors or officers; election of directors; appointment of officers
- Changes to company bylaws, articles of incorporation, or fiscal year
- Temporary suspension of trading under employee benefit plans

Clearly this list is in the spirit of EBM, because it requires timely disclosures of many items that materially affect company value. However, the requirements are in some cases biased toward disclosure of negative events only—for example, there is a requirement to disclose increases in contingent liabilities, but no requirement to disclose decreases in such liabilities or the creation of contingent assets. While not required by the SEC, we think it worthwhile for EBM-driven companies to consider disclosing such items as well. While the SEC is focused on protecting investors on the downside, managers must also remember their obligation to bring positive news to the market, whenever appropriate.

Second, note that these SEC disclosure requirements are incomplete from an EBM perspective. Just as accountants lean toward reporting of facts rather than forecasts, so are the SEC requirements listed previously focused solely on facts. We think management ought to be encouraged to disclose more information related to how they form their long-term expectations. Notwithstanding the SEC's safe-harbor provisions that offer limited protection to managers and analysts who provide forward-looking information, companies are still reluctant to lay out their case completely for what the company's long-term prospect looks like.

Some managers have taken to giving analysts and investors *no* guidance rather than more detailed, longer-term oriented guidance. This seems to us to be a knee-jerk reaction that managers have taken to avoid being caught up in the quarterly earnings game. Of course, the smart money knows the quarterly earnings game isn't what matters—it is long-term expectations that matters, as we've noted numerous times in previous chapters. The problem with "solving" the quarterly earnings game by not providing earnings guidance is that now investors have *less* information with which to gauge the worth of a company. What is needed—and what SEC disclosure requirements could encourage—is more forward-looking guidance, not less. Instead of just quarterly and annual EPS targets, management should be encouraged, if not required, to provide such information as long-term revenue growth potential, long-term capital investment plans, projected rates of return on new investment, and so on. Perhaps this information could be added to the management discussion and analysis section of Forms 10-K and 10Q by including discussion of material changes in long-term outlook, whether driven by technological, regulatory, or competitive changes in the industry. Prospectus statements for new securities could similarly include multiyear forecasts and explicit discussion of management's long-term expectations that serve as foundations for the issuance of securities.

Simple Improvements to Current Disclosure Rules

Keeping in mind what we've said about the benefits and costs of additional disclosures, we believe there are at least three areas where additional disclosures could improve the ability of the market to understand firm value. These disclosures are all low-cost to provide and offer significant new information to the market in a way that can lower investor uncertainty.

Better Segment-Based Information

Current disclosure requirements for segment-level data are very limited. Most corporations with multiple lines of business provide segment-level data in the footnotes to their annual and quarterly reports (SEC Forms 10-K and 10-Q). Some firms report segment data every quarter, while others only provide it annually. Some provide both segment data and geographic data. These segment data are often very limited, including a select number of financial line items, typically including revenues, profit (either profit before tax or operating income), and total assets. Many companies also disclose the amount of segment capital expenditures and depreciation.

While segment-level data is helpful to investors attempting to estimate business unit valuations, it is clearly insufficient for investors to develop robust understanding of the economics of different lines of business. The following is a nonexhaustive list of additional segment-level disclosure data that could dramatically improve the market's understanding of firm economics. Note that some of this data may be information companies want to shield from competitors (e.g., inventory levels by segment); however, we doubt such aggregate statistics, even at the segment level, would materially hurt a company's strategic positioning.

- Percent of sales to inside versus external customers (currently investors may only see a corporate-level eliminations figure, rather than segment-by-segment estimates)
- Segment-based cost structure—e.g., cost of goods sold, SG&A, R&D, and other expenses as a percentage of sales
- Structure of net assets on the balance sheet
  - Mix between current and fixed assets
  - Inventory, receivable, payable, and accrual levels
  - Average age of fixed assets
- Composition of capital expenditures
  - Land, equipment, etc.
  - Whether capital expenditures are primarily related to replacement/maintenance or new equipment
- Significant off-balance sheet liabilities and assets (e.g., buyback guarantees provided to customers)[9]

Corporate and Line Management Compensation

Annual proxy statements are the primary means by which management and directors' compensation structures are revealed to the market. These proxy statements already provide good information on board compensation and

---

[9]An interesting example about segment-level off-balance sheet liabilities is demonstrated by DaimlerChrysler. The company's Freightliner division sold trucks with guarantees to repurchase the trucks later at some predetermined level. When the market price for used trucks crashed, customers exercised their options to sell their trucks back to Freightliner. Customers would sell at a high price and then purchase a used truck at a lower price, for a guaranteed profit. Through Freightliner, DaimlerChrysler was exposed to significant risk that investors could not have known about from existing disclosure rules.

usually detailed information about CEO compensation. However, there are ways in which the existing information can be improved and additional information provided. While some companies already provide such detailed information, we've found the availability of this information across companies to be quite limited:

- The composition and weighting between short-term and long-term components of compensation
- Vesting and clawback provisions (including explicit disclosure where such provisions are absent)
- Composition of "other compensation"—insurance, benefits, and perks
- Policies and procedures related to reevaluating executive compensation structure (e.g., under what conditions will the board vote to reprice executives' options?)
- Caps and floors on bonus payouts (which we've argued in earlier chapter can distort managers' incentives through "kinks" in their compensation curve)
- The composition structure for segment-level managers: metrics used, vesting and clawback provisions, caps/floors on bonuses, base versus bonus structure, etc.[10]
- Major determinants of lower-level line management and staff compensation: use of fixed versus variable pay, and types of metrics used

Indications are that the SEC is considering changes to compensation disclosure rules. The *Wall Street Journal* reported in February 2005 that the SEC has found executive compensation disclosures to be opaque.[11] Problems cited include lack of a single SEC filing in which all compensation is disclosed, lack of disclosure of tax benefits from deferred compensation plans, and lack of timeliness due to amendments and changes to pay packages that happen between annual proxy statement filings. The *Journal* went on to suggest a simple Form "PAY-K" that would, among other things, create a single place where all components of executive compensation would be disclosed along with a "total compensation" estimate. As compensation disclosure reforms proceed our hope (and advice) is for policy-

---

[10]Some may respond to the suggestion to disclose segment-level compensation structures that firms will be reluctant to share such information with their competitors (for fear of driving up labor market costs). In our experience, this fear is unfounded because such information is widely available in the industry anyway, either through compensation consultant surveys or through managers regularly sharing such information with headhunters, industry peers, etc. At times it seems like investors are the only ones who don't know such information.

[11]Eisinger, Jesse. "Follow the CEO's Money," *Wall Street Journal*, February 16, 2005, page C1.

makers to distinguish between improved disclosure versus other types of goals. It is not clear that disclosure will change the level or compensation of CEO pay. But it will help share prices better reflect reality.

Insider Transactions and Holdings

Academic studies have long established that news of insider buys and sells has a significant impact on share prices. This makes intuitive sense: When those with the best information about a company's future prospects are willing to put their money where their mouth is, it lends significant credibility to management forecasts. Current SEC regulations require disclosure by insiders through Forms 3, 4, and 5. Form 3 requires new insiders to declare their holdings within 10 days of becoming an insider. Form 4 requires disclosure of purchases and sales by insiders within two days of the transaction. Form 5 requires disclosure of transactions not otherwise reported on Form 4 (e.g., dividend reinvestments, merger-related trades); these are reported within 45 days of fiscal year-end.

As mentioned earlier, Sarbanes-Oxley drastically shortened the time window for disclosing insider transactions (now, within two days). While we believe there is no reason why disclosures cannot be made the same day as the transactions, this window is likely short enough to maintain the strength of signals read by the market. Note that some insiders do not file their Form 4 on a timely basis (executives are busy running their businesses, after all), and so perhaps there is room to shift the reporting burden from insiders to the brokers who execute their trades.

In addition to timely disclosures of purchases and sales, it would be helpful to investors if insiders were permitted (or even required) to publicly state the reasons for their purchases or sales. It would be helpful for investors to know, for example, if an insider is selling her holdings for personal reasons (e.g., needed liquidity or routine portfolio rebalancing) or for reasons related to the company's financial outlook. This added requirement need not be burdensome to managers and directors—e.g., a simple checkbox for various categories of reasons for buys/sells may suffice.

There is more, though, that can be done to improve disclosure of insider holdings. In particular, we believe more can be revealed about what insiders' net exposure is to the company's share price performance. While smart investors could, with time and diligent research, estimate how much wealth exposure managers have to a company, it would cost much less to have insiders disclose this information. This disclosure need not be so detailed as to reveal significant personal financial information to the world. Instead, it may suffice to simply have annual or quarterly disclosures indicating the estimated percent of financial portfolio holdings held by each manager. Or, for even greater privacy protection, insiders may be required only to report whether their holdings exceed some threshold percent of portfolio (e.g., 10 percent of their net worth linked to the company).

A last disclosure related to insider transactions and holdings would be to require managers to disclose significant financial transactions or holdings that either increase or decrease the risk of their company stock and options. For example, have insiders set up zero-cost collars to protect the value of their nonvested stock grants? Transactions related to competitors' stocks or industry/sector funds could also be used to decrease exposure to the company's share price fluctuations. It may even be the case that some transactions increase an insider's exposure (e.g., buying company stock on margin).

Who Should Do Securities Research?

While better disclosure rules and more voluntary disclosures by firms may reduce market noise, they cannot eliminate it. After all, expectations are forward-looking and therefore are inherently noisy due to different analysts' assessment of the future. In the face of noise, an enormous research industry has emerged to help investors form their expectations. While the various accounting and investment bank scandals of the past few years have focused attention on the independence of sell-side analysts, there are broader public policy questions related to research.

Buy-Side Research

Buy-side analysis is likely to stay as a tool used by large, well-funded investors to gain an edge over other investors regardless of various changes in market disclosure rules. Buy-side research is never published, though it is more valuable than sell-side research because investors are willing to put money at stake based on this research. Certainly the value of buy-side research has been slightly diminished by Regulation FD, but there remain many other avenues for investors to learn about a firm besides through discussions with senior management (e.g., interviewing customers or suppliers). While buy-side research needs to remain proprietary, there may be room to allow—even encourage—buy-side investors to share their research with management. For those already invested in a company, such sharing would give managers a better understanding of market expectations and would give investors greater voice in firms' strategic decisions beyond that already provided through board of directors' representation.

Sell-Side Research

We noted earlier policymakers' recent focus on sell-side analyst independence. While independence sounds like an unarguable goal, it is not clear to us as we survey the existing academic evidence that independence is necessary or even desirable. Note that sell-side analysts provide different types of information to the market including investment recommendations (buy, hold, sell), earnings forecasts, and background research on a company and its industry. While the recommendations of star analysts might influence share price, we are skeptical. Certainly average market recommendations have little influence on share price. And one can argue that the market's reaction to star analysts' changes in recommendation stem more from information provided about changes in earnings outlook than the recommendation per se.

Yes, there is substantial evidence that sell-side analysts are upward-biased in their estimates. But the market as a whole is adept at discounting this bias. Our research has shown that is not necessarily the level of long-term expectations that matter, but changes in those expectations. Thus, analysis that is consistently biased upward still provides important information to investors through changes over time. While no bias is ideal, consistent bias is not as bad as complete noise from analysts.

Some question whether it would be beneficial even to require the elimination of bias. To the extent analysts can contribute to investment bank profitability (beyond the limited value of research captured from brokerage customers), banks will be willing to provide coverage of firms, disproportionate to their importance in brokerage customers' portfolios. Thus we see today decreased coverage of smaller-capitalization firms as banks put up firewalls between research and investment banking that limit the implicit subsidy for covering smaller-cap firms. Market noise may be reduced overall by more analyst coverage, even with biased recommendations. Research reports provide more than just recommendations—they provide analysis of financial statements, research of industries and customer segments, and the evaluation of management's strategies and plans.

As we think about research, though, the bigger picture question is whether we want an equilibrium with more or fewer "smart" investors. With increasing requirements for company disclosure requirements and limits on sell-side analyst coverage, retail investors in particular may be left to rely solely on their own analysis. Large, institutional investors will be at a distinct advantage in this world, provided they have the resources to conduct their own buy-side research. This may or may not be an optimal outcome (e.g., this may not matter much so long as retail investors invest through funds that can afford them the benefits of such research). While the ultimate public policy choice decisions about research may focus narrowly on bias, we think the debate, at least, should be expanded to discuss the impact of research on investor returns and the extent and type of analyst coverage that is important to the general public.

EBM for Government

Managing based on expectations is not just for the private sector. There are many ways in which expectations can play a role in governmental organizations—e.g., in managing capital expenditures at an airport authority or measuring employee value contributions at a government service agency. Understanding *market* expectations is particularly important in agencies that intersect with the private sector—for example, regulators of private enterprise, insurers of last resort (e.g., the FDIC) or quasi-governmental agencies like Fannie Mae.

As we write this today, the U.S. Pension Benefit Guaranty Corporation (PBGC) is in the news. A record number of private sector defined benefit pension plans are in danger of defaulting on their obligations, with the airline industry a particular problem as of this writing. One of the problems with agencies that guarantee private sector risks is the inability of these agencies to track the market values of their obligations. While EBM by itself does not necessarily address the PBGC's problems,[12] it does suggest that government can be more proactive in using markets to price PBGC liabilities. At this point, the extent of the PBGC's liability can only be known from individual analysts' estimates—but which analyst, and whose assumptions should policy makers believe? While the PBGC has been raising its discount rate on its liabilities (thus, lowering their perceived value), the market's expectations may instead assign a risk-free discount rate to these liabilities due to the government's guarantee. Other assumptions besides the discount rate—e.g., the probability of payouts—are also obscured by lack of a market for the agency's risk.

A publicly traded PBGC would provide early and strong signals to policymakers about the extent of underfunding for its liabilities. Public trading would require at least some minimum level of disclosures that would allow investors to price the agency's risk (though as we've noted above, even for-profit publicly traded companies may not be currently *required* to disclose all material information used by analysts in market valuation). Second, private investors would have incentive to seek out additional information in order to reveal the inherent value of the agencies' net assets (e.g., by researching the assumptions behind guaranteed pension funds' calculated funding shortfalls). Third, a public market would provide a single place in which the above information can be combined with a wide range of analysts' assessment as to the probability of payouts to defaulting pension funds. Thus, as the market's assessment of the probability that an airline might go bankrupt changes, the market's valuation of PBGC's stock would change.

There are already examples of public agencies using share prices as signals of market expectations. Fannie Mae, for example, has come under fire recently because of its own accounting issues (driven by excessive earnings smoothing) and the market's uncertainty as to the extent of the

---

[12]These problems stem from agency costs and incentives to firms whose pensions are guaranteed by the PBGC.

agency's true exposure to mortgage market risks. The Fannie Mae example tells us that the public market can be a useful indicator—but also reminds us that public agencies with traded securities need to have extensive disclosure requirements if the market is to price their risks accurately. Just because they are government-sponsored enterprises does not mean they should be exempt from disclosure requirements.

The use of public expectations of behavior need not be limited to floating stock in government agencies. Regulators may also use prices of securities already traded in the market as signals to their own oversight function. The FDIC, for example, might look at the difference in pricing of insured and uninsured deposits across banks in order to measure the market's assessment of a bank's risk exposure.

Expectations, Noise, and Macroeconomic Policy

While this book has been very "micro" in its focus—detailing aspects of managing a firm or communicating with the market—it has not escaped us that some of the elements of EBM, when extrapolated across the economy, can have implications for macroeconomic policy makers.

Take, for instance, the firm's decision to invest. This is a critical element behind much of business cycle theories and the macroeconomic stabilization policies that flow from such theories. We will not attempt to rehash the well-covered debates between monetarists, Keynesians, and real business cycle theorists. Instead, we note that EBM tells us more about how investment decisions are (or, in most cases, should be) made and therefore how firms may react to various policies.

The discussion of real options in Chapter 4 showed the relationship between investment decisions and uncertainty. When uncertainty is high— and management's flexibility to react to changing information is also high—investments have more option value. It may frequently be the case that in times of high uncertainty there is value to the deferral option: Firms will wait and see rather than invest immediately.

In an economy where investment decisions are made on the basis of expected future cash returns and where uncertainty affects the timing of investments, fiscal and macroeconomic policies need to address factors that affect both expectations and the uncertainty of those expectations. Fiscal policies, for example, that offer tax incentives to encourage capital investment may actually reduce such investments if they are structured in a way that increases uncertainty in the form of policy instability.

In addition to paying attention to the impact of policy on noise, macroeconomic policy makers and advisers would do well also to focus on what expectations they are setting for the future. While there is always a degree of uncertainty about future policies, some expectations are more certain than others. Firms' expectations for future tax rates, for example, are weighted toward a belief that current tax rates will remain in place—it is more difficult for Congress to pass new tax laws than to let the existing ones remain in place. However, phased-in tax changes may lead investors to discount the probability that the policy changes will come to pass without any additional changes.

A last point about fiscal policy that EBM suggests is the need for discussions to be focused on long-term expectations. At least with respect to Medicare and Social Security there has been an increasing amount of debate over the government's unfunded liability. How that liability is funded or eliminated is, of course, up for discussion, but all can agree that the important elements in this discussion are long-term expectations for productivity gains, population growth, inflation rates, and so on. While there is disagreement on what a reasonable set of assumptions should be, at least the debate has shifted toward an expectations-based framework.

Unfortunately, the same cannot be said for more mundane budget decisions, which are subjected to arbitrary forecast horizons of, at most, 10 years. To the extent that some policies—for example, investments in fundamental technologies or tax incentives to provide startup capital—encourage longer-term economic decisions, a short-term look at the budget will never fully capture expectations related to these policy decisions. An alternative approach might be to score individual policy choices according to their respective "economic life"—how long will it take for there to be "payback" (if any) and how does that fit within the overall budget?

Summary

One way in which EBM informs public policy is by shedding light on regulatory policies that affect capital markets and corporate interactions with investors. Disclosure rules, accounting standards, restrictions on investment banking research, and other policies all affect the quantity and quality of information available to investors. Noise-reducing policies are ideal, but such policies must balance the value created from reducing investor noise against the costs of producing and disseminating such noise-reducing information.

A second aspect of EBM in public policy is the application of EBM principles to government policy questions. Using capital markets to price risk and measure expectations can bring new, important insight to budget decisions and public policy investments. Changing budget discussions from a focus on short-term (e.g., 10-year) outlooks to very long-term expectations highlights government shortfalls like that of the PBGC today, and avoids arbitrary sunset provisions that force budgets to balance in the short term. Macroeconomic policy may also improve through a focus on the EBM factors that drive corporate investment, such as long-term expectations and noise/uncertainty.

CHAPTER 14

Summary and Conclusions

As a way of wrapping up this book we want to go back and review some of the questions that we believe it has answered. But we also want to do two other things. We want to summarize the EBM story—what it is, why it is different, and its effects on managerial decision making. That is the second part of the chapter. But most important of all we want to say something about how companies can come up with the ideas that are generated within an EBM framework—about how implementation adds value. That is the third part.

Questions That Have Been Answered

Here are some of the questions we've heard from managers as they've reacted to the EBM ideas presented in this book. The answers provided serve as a useful summary of the key points we've made.

1. *Why doesn't our company's stock price react to growth in earnings?*
   Your stock price depends on the expected future cash flows that your firm can provide to its stockholders and not only on current earnings. In order to just hold wealth constant, the firm has to meet those expectations. The cost of (equity) capital is the expected total return to shareholders and will equal the actual total return to shareholders if the company exactly meets the return on invested capital and makes the capital investments that are expected of it. For example, if investors expect your firm to have a *ROIC* of 40 percent, that will already be factored into the stock price. If the cost of equity is 15 percent and you meet expectations by earning 40 percent *ROIC*, then the total return to

shareholders (after removing any unexpected movement of the market) will be 15 percent. But if your *ROIC* is less than expected—say, 30 percent—the price will fall because expectations were not met.

One way of determining what the market expects of your company is to reverse engineer your stock price using a discounted cash flow model based on a survey of analyst forecasts (see Chapter 7). It is always a good idea to understand any differences between your expectations as a management team and the market's expectations.

2. *Why did our stock price fall when we had growth in economic value added?* Economic value added (EVA) measures whether your *ROIC* this year exceeds your weighted average cost of capital or not. However, your stock price is driven by changes in expectations about both short- and longer-term performance. EVA does not use any information about expectations or how they change; therefore, it has a very low correlation with the total return to shareholders (five percent or less).

3. *What measure of performance makes the best tradeoffs between short- and long-term performance?* The answer is net present value analysis (including the present value of real options). It includes expected free cash flows, assuming that the correct decisions will be made in a timely manner in the future as new information arrives in the market. When discounted at the appropriate risk-adjusted rate, the present value of alternatives with different patterns of cash across time can be compared.

4. *Who sets expectations?* Management usually sets expectations. After all, management typically has better information than anyone else concerning the future prospects of the company. But this information must be communicated to current and potential investors as clearly and with as little bias as possible. Investors ultimately form their expectations by considering management's guidance, management's credibility and consistency, and information obtained independently.

5. *How should I measure the performance of our business units?* The best way is to set reasonable targets based on the best forecasting that you can do. Utilize incentives and improved planning processes and systems to minimize the amount of bias in your forecasts. Targets that are too high defeat their purpose and lower morale because stretch targets may be unachievable. Targets that are too low pay out incentive compensation for little or no effort. Senior management must accept a lot of responsibility for knowing a great deal about the operation of business unit managers below them in order to set appropriate targets that are neither too high nor too low.

6. *Should we have different hurdle rates for maintenance investments and acquisitions?* We once talked to the chief operating officer of a financial services company that had a cost of capital of 11 percent, but required an 18 percent internal hurdle rate on maintenance investments because the firm earned 18 percent year after year.

   They realized their mistake when they required 18 percent for a potential new investment in a large credit card portfolio that was up for sale. They underbid by about $1 billion, because the cost of capital—the required risk-adjusted rate of return on investments of the same risk—was about 11 percent. They did not distinguish between the rate of return required to meet investor expectations—namely, an internal hurdle rate of 18 percent—and the cost of capital of 11 percent, which was the hurdle rate for this new investment.

   Their second mistake was that their internal hurdle rate for maintenance investment was also 18 percent It should have been their cost of capital, namely 11 percent. They were correct in their belief that maintenance investment that earned less than 18 percent (but more than 11 percent) would cause their stock price to fall. Nevertheless it would fall even more if the maintenance investment were rejected and the cash were returned to shareholders who could earn only 11 percent (see Chapter 3 for examples). They had fallen into the underinvestment trap.

   It may help to think about the investment problem from investors' perspective—would they prefer you to return the cash to them or keep it invested in the business?

7. *Why shouldn't we use stretch targets?* Stretch targets can be self-defeating. It is better to set targets that are unbiased expectations of performance—with a 50–50 chance of exceeding them. For this reason we believe that setting easy targets (sandbagging) is also self-defeating. We've also seen that stretch targets can set up unproductive dialog with investors who are looking for a credible set of forecasts. It is not helpful to either constituency to be telling different stories to employees and investors.

8. *Even if I merely require that we meet market expectations, won't we get trapped on an expectations treadmill?* The expectations treadmill assumes the market and its participants are irrational. Investors supposedly set tough expectations, then when a company exceeds them, they raise expectations even higher—and so it goes with higher and higher expectations until it becomes impossible to meet or exceed them. The expectations treadmill is a fiction based on irrational expectations. Most investors expect regression toward the mean. A company that has above-average performance is expected to return to the average and vice versa. Management only gets trapped on this treadmill if

it buys into mistaken notions of what Wall Street expects. Careful guidance helps investors set their expectations in advance, sometimes by years. For example, management may expect rapid earnings growth due to a temporary upswing in demand or realization of cost-saving synergies during a merger integration; however, management is also aware of the temporary nature of such earnings growth and can therefore forecast the return to more normal growth rates in the medium term.

9. *How hard is it to exceed expectations?* The human mind is very good at forming expectations. It can handicap horse races, sports events, and set prices in the stock market. But there is a great deal of randomness in these expectations. We saw, in Table 11.3, that of 100 firms randomly selected in 1993, only 84 survived five years, only 15 had positive total return to shareholders all five years, and only three had TRS that exceeded the broad return on the market all five years. So it is very hard to beat the market's expectations year after year. However, winning companies, like champion athletes, know how to reach deep within themselves to surpass the performance that is expected of them—to beat the odds. Effective managers also know when their organizations are not up to the task and instead set expectations, targets, and strategic plans in a way that won't lead to sudden crashes should the organization fail to outperform expectations. Steady delivery on expectations can be even more valuable to long-term investors than exceeding expectations for a few years only to drastically miss expectations afterwards. Don't bankrupt the future in order to exceed expectations over the short term.

10. *What tips do you have about communicating expectations with the outside world and within my firm?* The empirical evidence presented in Chapter 2 suggests that when it comes to communicating with the market signal-to-noise ratio matters. It also is conclusive about the fact that longer-term expectations have a much more important impact on current shareholder returns than short-term expectations. Taken together, these facts imply that external communications with current and potential investors should emphasize long-term goals, be communicated with as little noise as possible, and should be consistent among the officers of the firm. Financial signals can reinforce the message communicated through direct communications. Noise can be reduced by learning in depth what information investors want or need.

Internal communications set expectations for future performance. Internal and external views should be reconciled via the process of reverse engineering your stock price, interviewing analysts, and having a robust internal planning process. Once top management reaches consensus about expected performance, a dialog with middle and lower management levels should establish performance goals that are neither too difficult nor too easy to achieve. Expected performance should be as reasonable as possible.

Turn investor relations into a two-way dialog. Learn from your investors as much as they learn from you. Understand their current expectations and the basis by which these expectations were formed. Listen to investor reactions and stock price movements in the wake of major financial, operational, or strategic announcements. Take heed to information gathered by analysts independently through their own surveys of competitors, customers, suppliers, technology advancement, and so on.

The EBM Story

The highest gains in the stock market—the big wins for shareholders—are difficult to achieve because the market uses whatever information it can get to handicap the stock. Great performers already have great stock prices and terrible performers have terrible prices. That is why, at any point in time, all securities are price-adjusted until they are all held by someone. In this way, the expectations of investors are continuously incorporated into the price of each stock. And if expectations turn out as anticipated, investors all earn the cost of capital on the stock.

EBM grew out of the desire to find a measure of company and business unit-level performance that has the highest practical correlation with the total return to shareholders (TRS). Measures that do not capture changes in expectations cannot and do not have useful correlations with TRS at the level of an individual company. Earnings and earnings growth, and EVA and EVA growth all have correlations with company-level, market-adjusted shareholder returns that are less than six percent. EBM that includes changes in analyst expectations of earnings, earnings growth, and noise has a 50 percent correlation with shareholder returns. The difference is not merely an order of magnitude—it is a level of meaning—one has such low correlation with shareholder return as to be meaningless, while EBM is actually useful.

The implications for management are that company and business unit performance should be measured relative to expectations rather than relative to the cost of capital. If the market expects a low rate of return on invested capital—say, two percent—then the company must earn more than two percent in order for its stock price to grow faster than its cost of equity—for example, 15 percent. When we use an EBM lens, an existing business that earns eight percent when it was expected to earn two percent is a business that creates value. New investments that are unexpected, however, must be expected to earn their cost of capital in order for shareholders' wealth to increase.

If changes in expectations are relevant then the details are, too. We mean expectations about the cash flows now and in the future—all discounted to the present and summed to estimate the amount of wealth they will create. Therefore, EBM is a three-part system. Closest to the market is the discounted cash flow value of the company; next, and also based on expected future cash flows, are the expected annual economic profits of the company. When the expected economic profits each year are discounted to the present at the weighted average cost of capital and added to the book value of assets, the result is equal to the discounted cash flow value of the company. This process links expected annual profit to the DCF value of the company and in turn to its market value. It also provides a way of making rational tradeoffs between cash flows in different time periods.

Finally, expected economic profit is the spread between the return on invested capital and the cost of capital. *ROIC* is the product of operating margin and capital turns—so that higher *ROIC* can be attained either by charging a higher operating margin or spending less capital to achieve the same sales. By working down to a finer level of detail, one comes to micro-level value drivers at the plant level that can align against the larger issues of the firm in order to find a new way of creating value.

What Do the Skeptics Say?

Our conversations with hundreds of managers have revealed three types of negative response to EBM. Many managers claim that they are already using it implicitly—just that they are not calling it EBM. From their perspective, EBM offers nothing new. Others claim that EBM is a nice theory, but impossible in practice because expectations are too shadowy, too fuzzy, and too subjective to manage. A third group is happy with whatever brand of value-based management that they spent considerable time and effort developing. They are not ready for another change.

"Nothing new" is a common response. EBM has a mildly revisionist flavor due to its subjectivity. Because performance against budget is much the same as performance against top management expectations, EBM looks and feels like the old budget (command) and control model of management. There are, however, some salient differences. First is that EBM asks that top management try to link external market/owner expectations with internal expectations of performance. Second, EBM stresses the importance of long-term expectations—not simply one-year budgets. Our empirical evidence indicates that long-term expectations have roughly 10 times the impact on current shareholder returns (versus one-year expectations). Consequently, EBM is about the long term as well as the short term. It asks that planning and budgeting be linked, that great care be spent on the long-run aspects of executive compensation and external communication. Third,

EBM provides a sensible rationale for understanding why investment must earn more than the cost of capital (relative to the alternative of not investing) but may cause the firm's stock price to fall when it fails to earn the expected return. Maintenance (i.e., expected) decisions, should earn the *ROIC* that is expected of the business unit to be sure to increase the stock price. New (i.e., unexpected) investments, however, should always earn at least the cost of capital.

"Expectations are too subjective to manage" is a comment that is almost completely opposite to "nothing new, we are already using it." Managers who find expectations too fuzzy to grasp have focused their anxiety on *external* expectations. They worry that EBM amounts to using outsiders' opinions to run the firm. They miss the point that, being better informed than the market, their own expectations set the course of action for the firm. Their own judgment, however subjective it might be, is quite tangible to them. But to make EBM work well, top management must inform itself about the operations of the firm (in order to guard against sandbagging). Moreover, there are many ways to inject rigor into subjective planning processes—for example, by forcing managers to make explicit to others the logic and assumptions underlying their forecasts. A degree of objectivity can be retained through careful use of outside advisors, disinterested internal plan evaluators, and a rich data set of benchmarks for judging the reasonableness of forecasts.

"We're happy with what we've got" is an understandable response. We've seen the amount of time, money, and effort that is needed to get a value-based management program up and running. The cultural change itself is quite daunting, requiring sustained efforts to obtain line management buy-in. Anyone that has gone through such a process recently can understandably be gun-shy about introducing more change. But EBM can be introduced slowly—for example, by starting with senior management spending more time understanding the market's expectations. Selected applications to performance evaluations or target setting helps line managers understand the shift in mindset. Also, though we have our own reservations about some of the metrics in use today (see Chapter 12), we think much is to be gained by simply adding an expectations perspective to existing metrics.

Implementing for Impact Ensures EBM Leads to Value Creation

It is not enough to know how to measure the creation of value—one must learn how to create—and this is a process, not a metric. A lot has to do with the inception—the first implementation of EBM at a company. It should be designed for maximum impact. But then it becomes necessary to maintain the momentum as long as possible, while being realistic about what results are achievable.

Implementing for impact means that management should prepare carefully for EBM training—or for any training. The objective of a training session is not just to learn a new concept. Rather, it is to come up with better ideas and to shed bad practices. Outsiders who are experienced (not necessarily with your company or industry) are useful because they come to the table unencumbered by habit. If they are good at pattern recognition, based on years (even decades) of experience, they will be able to draw from their deep well of experience to bring ideas from other working environments to help you.

Implementation should start with the valuation of the business and of the key value drivers that capture the economics of the issues that are central for success. Often it requires out-of-the-box thinking. Chapters 6 and 10 gave quite a few such examples. Challenge your business unit teams to apply valuation concepts to find news ways to add value. Search for trade-offs that do not add value—e.g., excessive capital spending—to ensure 110 percent reliability. Use these early wins in a public way to obtain additional buy-in.

EBM is a discipline that asks management to look at the long run as well as the short run, to manage the balance sheet as well as the income statement, and to realize that in an economic horse race you must exceed expectations in order to drive up your share price (beyond the amount it would naturally increase if expectations are met). But do not expect that you will win every race, or that you can exceed expectations year after year—that is nearly impossible. Instead, put together the best team—the one that sets the pace for others, is highly paid for being excellent, and exceeds itself and the market more than its fair share of the time.

Sustained value creation requires that a firm create an environment that stimulates its management team to surprise the market (i.e., owners). Here is a list of some of the things that help:

- Use EBM to link what you do (your generation of economic profit) to the total return to shareholders.
- Linearize top executive compensation, pay careful attention to the promotion of middle management, and reward others via value driver metrics.
- Understand owners' (the market's) expectations and communicate clearly with them. Reduce noise.
- Hire and retain the best management team.
- Provide an environment that stimulates innovation and quick, effective implementation.
- Turn your merger and acquisition (M&A) strategy into an acquisition and divestiture (A&D) strategy.
- Compare the market's expectations of your competitors with its expectations of your own company. Deal with gaps through signaling, communications, or changes in investment strategy.

Final Thoughts

Some economic concepts seem so intuitive and powerful that you begin to see their application well outside the world of business. We can see, for example, how risk aversion and proper incentives can work to motivate children to do their homework. We can see the value of flexibility and therefore encourage our children to learn a very wide range of general skills (e.g., math and reading) rather than specific skills like farming. So it is with expectations—once you start thinking in an expectations mindset, you'll see its relevance across a wide range of situations. Old debates will hopefully seem that much less relevant. It doesn't matter, for example, if stock options are expensed or business units are charged for goodwill once you remember that the market has already incorporated these factors into expectations.

EBM is a management tool that links performance measurement of businesses and therefore management decisions (and incentive design) directly to the total return to shareholders. There is strong empirical support for this linkage—and we think there is strong intuitive support for it as well. Seasoned managers know this—as they run their business on the basis of judgment applied to expectations. We hope at this point the basic concepts have been ingrained and you're ready to go out and try them with your business.

References

Dedication and Acknowledgments

Gordon, M., "Dividends, Earnings, and Stock Prices," *Review of Economics and Statistics,* May 1959, pp. 99–105.

Keynes, J. M., *The General Theory of Employment, Interest and Money,* Harcourt Brace, New York, 1936.

Lucas, Robert, "An Equilibrium Model of the Business Cycle," *Journal of Political Economy,* 1975.

Malkiel, Burton G., "Equity Yields, Growth, and the Structure of Share Prices," *American Economic Review,* 53, December 1963, pp. 1004–1031.

Marshall, A., *Principles of Economics: An Introductory Volume,* Macmillan, London, 1890.

Miller, Merton and Franco Modigliani, "Dividend Policy, Growth, and the Valuation of Shares," *Journal of Business,* 34, October 1961, pp. 411–433.

Rappaport, A., *Creating Shareholder Value,* The Free Press, New York, 1986.

Rappaport, A., and M. Mauboussin, *Expectations Investing,* Harvard Business School Press, Boston, 2001.

Samuelson, P., "Proof that Properly Anticipated Prices Fluctuate Randomly," *Industrial Management Review,* Spring 1965, pp. 41–49.

Preface

Copeland, T., A. Dolgoff, and A. Moel, "The Role of Expectations in the Cross-Section of Returns," *Review of Accounting Studies,* Vol. 9, 2004, Issue 2–3.

Marshall, A., *Principles of Economics: An Introductory Volume,* Macmillan, London, 1890.

Chapter 1

Copeland, T., A. Dolgoff, A. Moel, "The Role of Expectations In Explaining the Cross-Section of Returns," *Review of Accounting Studies,* Vol. 9, 2004, Issue 2–3.

Tuchman, Barbara, *The March of Folly,* New York, Ballantine Books, 1985.

Chapter 2

Ackert, L., and G. Athanassakos, "Prior Uncertainty, Analyst Bias, and Subsequent Abnormal Returns," *Journal of Financial Research,* 20, 1997, pp. 263–273.

Amir, E., B. Lev, and T. Sougiannis, "What value analysts?" Working paper, New York University, 1999.

Ball, R., and P. Brown, "An Empirical Evaluation of Accounting Income Numbers," *Journal of Accounting Research,* Autumn 1968, 159–178.

Bernard, V., and J. Thomas, "Evidence that stock prices do not fully reflect the implications of current earnings for future earnings," *Journal of Accounting and Economics* 13, 1990, pp. 305–340.

Biddle, G., R. Bowen, and J. Wallace, "Does EVA beat earnings? Evidence on associations with stock returns and firm values," *Journal of Accounting and Economics* 24, 1997, pp. 301–336.

Biddle, G., and G. Seow, "The estimation and determinants of association between returns and earnings: Evidence from cross-industry comparisons," *Journal of Accounting, Auditing and Finance* 6, 1991, pp. 183–232.

Collins, D., S. Kothari, J. Shanken, and R. Sloan, "Lack of timeliness and noise as explanations for the low contemporaneous return-earnings association," *Journal of Accounting and Economics* 18, 1994, pp. 289–324.

Copeland, T., A. Dolgoff, A. Moel, "The Role of Expectations In Explaining the Cross-Section of Returns," *Review of Accounting Studies,* Vol. 9, 2004, Issue 2–3.

Easterwood, J., and S. Nutt, "Inefficiency in Analyst Forecasts: Systematic Misreaction or Systematic Optimism?" *Journal of Finance,* 54, 1999, pp. 1777–1797.

Easton, P., and T. Harris, "Earnings as an explanatory variable for returns," *Journal of Accounting Research* 29, 1991, pp. 19–36.

Fama, E., and K. French. "The cross-section of expected returns," *Journal of Finance* 47, 1992, 427–465.

Foster, G., C. Olsen, and T. Shevlin, "Earnings releases, anomalies, and the behavior of security prices," *The Accounting Review* 59, 1984, pp. 574–603.

Jones, C., H. Latane, and R. Rendleman, "Empirical anomalies based on unexpected earnings and the importance of risk adjustments," *Journal of Financial Economics* 10, 1982, pp. 269–287.

Keim, D, "Size-related anomalies and stock return seasonality: Further empirical evidence," *Journal of Financial Economics* 12, 1983, pp. 13–32.

Kothari, S. P., J. Shanken, and R. Sloan, "Another look at the cross-section of expected returns," *Journal of Finance* 50, 1995, pp. 185–224.

Lim, T., "Rationality and Analyst Forecast Bias," *Journal of Finance,* 55, 2000, pp. 369–385.

Liu, J., and J. Thomas, "Stock returns and accounting earnings," *Journal of Accounting Research* 38, 2000, pp. 71–102.

Lundholm, R., and L. Myers, "Bringing the future forward: The effect of disclosure on the returns-earnings relation," *Journal of Accounting Research,* Volume 40, 2004, Issue 3.

Madden, Bartley, *CFROI Valuation,* Butterworth-Heinemann, Oxford, 1999.

Stewart, G. Bennett, *The Quest for Value,* HarperBusiness, New York, 1990.

Chapter 3

Brealey, R., and Myers, S, *Principles of Corporate Finance,* 7th edition, McGraw-Hill, 2002.

Campbell, C., and J. Wansley, "Stock Price-Based Incentive Contracts and Managerial Performance: The Case of Ralston-Purina Company," *Journal of Financial Economics,* Vol. 51, February 1999, pp. 195–217.

Copeland, T., "Cutting Costs Without Drawing Blood," *Harvard Business Review,* October 2000.

Copeland, T., J.F. Weston, and K. Shastri, *Financial Theory and Corporate Policy,* 4th edition, Addison-Wesley, 2004.

Jensen, Michael C. "Paying People to Lie: The Truth About the Budgeting Process," Harvard NOM Research Paper No. 01-01, and HBS Working Paper No. 01-072 (April 2001).

Chapter 4

Copeland, T., and V. Antikarov, *Real Options: A Practitioners Guide,* Revised Edition, Texere, 2003.

Copeland, T., and P. Tufano, "A Real-World Way to Manage Real Options," *Harvard Business Review,* March 2004.

Copeland, T.E., J. Murrin, and T. Koller, *Valuation: Measuring and Managing the Value of Companies,* 3rd Edition, John Wiley & Sons, 2000.

Martin, Roger, "Changing the Mind of the Corporation," *Harvard Business Review,* Nov–Dec 1993.

Chapter 5

Copeland, T., J. Murrin, and T. Koller, *Valuation: Measuring and Managing the Value of Companies,* 3rd Edition, John Wiley & Sons, 2000.

Cornell, Bradford, *The Equity Risk Premium: The Long-Run Future of the Stock Market,* Wiley, 1999.

Damodaran, A., working papers on estimating risk-free rates, risk premiums and risk parameters. Papers available online at http://pages.stern.nyu.edu/~adamodar/

Fabozzi, F., et al, *The Handbook of Fixed Income Securities,* 6th edition, McGraw-Hill, 2000.

Fama, E., and K. French, "The Cross-Section of Stock Returns," *Journal of Finance,* 1992.

Graham, J., and C. Harvey, "The Theory and Practice of Corporate Finance: Evidence from the Field," *Journal of Financial Economics,* Vol. 60, 2001, 187–243.

Ibbotson Associates, *Stocks, Bonds, Bills and Inflation (SBBI) Yearbooks,* published annually.

Ibbotson Associates, *Cost of Capital Yearbooks,* published annually.

Ross, Stephen A., R. Westerfield and B. Jordan, *Fundamentals of Corporate Finance,* 6th edition, McGraw-Hill, 2003.

Chapter 6

Copeland, T., "Cutting Costs Without Drawing Blood," *Harvard Business Review,* September–October 2000.

Chapter 7

Barber, B., R. Lehavy, M. McNichols, and B. Trueman, "Can Investors Profit from the Prophets? Security Analyst Recommendations and Stock Returns," *Journal of Finance,* Vol. 56, 2001, No. 2, pp. 531–582.

Copeland, T.E., J. Murrin, and T. Koller, *Valuation: Measuring and Managing the Value of Companies,* 3rd Edition, John Wiley & Sons, 2000.

Jegadeesh, N., J. Kim, S. Krische, and C. Lee, 2004, "Analyzing the Analysts: When Do Recommendations Add Value?" *Journal of Finance,* Vol. 59, No. 3.

Rappaport, A., and M. Mauboussin, *Expectations Investing: Reading Stock Prices for Better Returns,* Harvard Business School Press, 2001.

Chapter 8

Black, F., "Noise," *Journal of Finance* 41, 1986, pp. 529–544.

Copeland, T., and Galai, D., "Information Effects on the Bid-Ask Spread," *Journal of Finance,* 38, 5, December 1983, pp. 1457–1469.

Dann, L., "Common Stock Repurchases: An Analysis of Returns to Bondholders and Stockholders," *Journal of Financial Economics,* June 1981, pp. 113–138.

Diether, K., C. Malloy, and A. Scherbina, "Differences of Opinion and the Cross Section of Stock Returns," *Journal of Finance*, 2002, pp. 2113–2141.

Dittmar, A., and R. Dittmar, "Stock Repurchase Waves: An Explanation of Trends in Aggregate Corporate Payout Policy," Working Paper, Indiana University, 2002.

Eccles, Robert G., R. Herz, E. Keegan, and D. Phillips, *The Value Reporting Revolution: Moving Beyond the Earnings Game*, John Wiley & Sons, 2001.

Finnerty, J. E., "Insiders and Market Efficiency," *Journal of Finance*, September 1976, pp. 1141–1148.

Givoly, D., and D. Palmon, "Insider Trading and the Exploitation of Inside Information: Some Empirical Evidence," *Journal of Business*, January 1985, pp. 69–87.

Graham, J.R., C.R. Havey, and S. Rajgopal, "The Economic Implications of Corporate Financial Reporting," Working Paper, January 11, 2005.

Grullon, G., and R. Michaely, "Dividends, Share Repurchase and the Substitution Hypothesis," *Journal of Finance*, Vol. 57, August 2002, No. 4, pp. 1649–1684.

Guay, V., and J. Harford, "The cash-flow performance and information content of dividend increases versus repurchases," *Journal of Financial Economics*, Vol. 57, September 2000, No. 3, pp. 385–416.

Jaffe, J., "The Effect of Regulation Changes on Insider Trading," *Bell Journal of Economics and Management Science*, Spring 1974, pp. 93–121.

Jagganathan, M., C. Stephans, and M. Weisbach, "Financial Flexibility and the Choice Between Dividends and Stock Repurchases," *Journal of Financial Economics*, Vol. 57, September 2000, No. 3, pp. 355–384.

Jennings, R. H., and M. A. Mazzeo, "Stock Price Movements around Acquisition Announcements and Management's Response," *Journal of Business*, 1991, pp. 139–163.

Jensen, M., "Corporate Budgeting Is Broken, Let's Fix It," *Harvard Business Review*, pp. 94–101, November 2001.

Karolyi, G. Andrew, "Why Stock Return Volatility Really Matters," *Strategic Investor Relations*, 2001.

Kau, J. B., J. Linck, J. and P. Rubin, "Do Managers Listen to the Market?" Working Paper, October 2004.

Loughran, T., and A. M. Vijh, "Do Long-Term Shareholders Benefit from Corporate Acquisitions?" *Journal of Finance*, 1997, pp. 1765–1790.

Luo, Yuanzhi, "Do Insiders Learn from Outsiders? Evidence from Mergers and Acquisitions," *Journal of Finance*, August 2005.

Masulis, R., "The Effects of Capital Structure Change on Security Prices: A Study of Exchange Offers," *Journal of Financial Economics*, June 1980, pp. 139–178.

Masulis, R., "Stock Repurchase by Tender Offer: An Analysis of the Causes of Common Stock Price Changes," *Journal of Finance*, May 1980, pp. 305–318.

Matsumoto, D., R. Bowen, "Microsoft's Financial Reporting Strategy," *Harvard Business Review case,* 2000.

Miller, E. M., "Risk, Uncertainty, and Divergence of Opinion," *Journal of Finance,* 1977, pp. 1151–1168.

McNichols, M., 1988, "A Comparison of the Skewness of Stock Action Distributions in Earnings and Non-Earnings Intervals," *Journal of Accounting and Economics,* Vol. 10, July, No. 2.

Rappaport, A., "Stock Market Signals to Managers," *Harvard Business Review,* November–December 1987, pp. 57–62.

Schliefer, A., and R. Vishny, "Stock Market Driven Acquisitions," *Journal of Financial Economics,* 2003, 295–311.

Vermaelen, T., "Common Stock Repurchases and Market Signalling: An Empirical Study," *Journal of Financial Economics,* June 1981, pp. 139–183.

Chapter 9

Anslinger, P., and Copeland, T.E. "Growth Through Acquisition: A Fresh Look," *Harvard Business Review,* January–February 1996, pp. 126–135.

Baker, G., M. Jensen, and K. Murphy, "Compensation and Incentives: Practice vs. Theory," *Journal of Finance,* July 1988, pp. 593–616.

Bebchuk, L., and J. Fried, "Pay without Performance: The Unfulfilled Promise of Executive Compensation," *Harvard University Press,* 2004.

Copeland, T., and V. Antikarov, *Real Options: A Practitioner's Guide,* Texere, New York, 2001.

Copeland, T., and P. Tufano, "A Real-World Way to Manage Real Options," *Harvard Business Review,* March 2004, pp. 90–99.

Crystal, G., "The Wacky, Wacky World of Executive Pay," *Fortune,* June 6, Vol. 117, 1988, No. 12, pp. 68–78.

Hashimoto, M., "Employment and Wage Systems in Japan and Their Implications for Productivity," in Blinder, Alan, ed., *Paying for Productivity,* The Brookings Institution, Washington, D.C., 1990. pp. 245–294.

Jensen, M., "Paying People to Lie: the Truth about the Budgeting Process," *European Financial Management,* Vol. 9, No. 3, 2003, pp. 379–406.

Medoff, J. and K. Abraham, "Experience, Performance and Earnings," *Quarterly Journal of Economics,* December 1980.

Meredith, D., "Getting the Right Bang for the Buck: Are CEOs Paid What They Are Worth?" *Chief Executive,* September/October, 1987.

Mitchell, Daniel; D. Lewin, and E. Lawler, "Alternative Pay Systems, Firm Performance, and Productivity", in Blinder, Alan, ed., *Paying for Productivity,* The Brookings Institution, Washington, D.C., 1990.

Ross, S., "Options and Efficiency," *Quarterly Journal of Economics,* February 1976, pp. 75–89.

Chapter 11

Campbell, C., and J. Wansley, "Stock Price-Based Incentive Contracts and Managerial Performance: The Case of Ralston-Purina Company," *Journal of Financial Econonomics,* Vol. 51, February 1999, pp. 195–217.

Elton, E., and M. Gruber, "Marginal Stockholders' Tax Rates and the Clientele Effect," *Review of Economics and Statistics,* February 1970, p. 72.

Harris, J., Jr., R. Roenfeldt, and P. Cooley, "Evidence of Financial Leverage Clientele," *Journal of Finance,* September 1983, pp. 1125–1132.

Lakonishok, J., and T. Vermaelen, "Tax-Induced Trading around Ex-Dividend Days," *Journal of Financial Economics,* July 1986, pp. 287–320.

Rappaport, A., and M. Mauboussin, *Expectations Investing: Reading Stock Prices for Better Returns,* Harvard Business School Press, 2001.

Miller, M. H., and F. Modigliani, "Dividend Policy, Growth, and the Valuation of Shares," *Journal of Business,* 34, October 1961, pp. 411–433.

Petit, R. R., "Taxes, Transactions Costs and Clientele Effects of Dividends," *Journal of Financial Economics,* December 1977, pp. 419–436.

Queen, M., and R. Roll," Firm Mortality: Predictions and Effects," *Financial Analysts Journal,* May/June 1987.

Chapter 12

Copeland, T., T. Koller, and J. Murrin, *Valuation: Measuring and Managing the Value of Companies,* 3rd Edition, John Wiley & Sons, 2000.

Ehrbar, A., *EVA: The Real Key to Creating Wealth,* John Wiley & Sons, 1998.

Kaplan, R., and D. Norton, *The Balanced Scorecard: Translating Strategy into Action,* Harvard Business School Press, 1996.

Madden, B., *CFROI Valuation A Total System Approach to Valuing the Firm,* Butterworth-Heinemann, 1999.

Rappaport, A., *Creating Shareholder Value,* The Free Press, 1986.

Stewart, G. Bennett, *The Quest for Value,* HarperBusiness, 1991.

Chapter 13

Copeland, T., and D. Friedman, "The Market Value of Information: Some Experimental Evidence," *The Journal of Business,* April 1992, pp. 241–266.

Cornell, B., and R. Roll, "Strategies for Pairwise Competitions in Markets and Organizations," *Bell Journal of Economics* 12, 1981, 201–213.

Eisinger, J., "Follow the CEO's Money," *Wall Street Journal,* February 16, 2005, page C1.

Index